CW00504890

GLAMORGAN
CRICKETERS

GLAMORGAN CRICKETERS
1889–1920

Andrew Hignell

HALSGROVE

First published in Great Britain in 2019

British Library Cataloguing-in-Publication Data
A CIP record for this title is available from the British Library

ISBN 978 0 85704 341 2

Halsgrove
Halsgrove House,
Ryelands Business Park,
Bagley Road, Wellington, Somerset TA21 9PZ
Tel: 01823 653777   Fax: 01823 216796
email: sales@halsgrove.com

Part of the Halsgrove group of companies
Information on all Halsgrove titles is available at: www.halsgrove.com

Printed and bound in India by Parksons Graphics Pvt Ltd

Contents

Introduction

The first reference to the playing of cricket in South Wales dates from 1771, with a gentleman in Swansea writing a letter to the *General Evening Post*, complaining about young men and boys playing cricket, and swearing, on Sundays. Whilst there was religious disapproval towards such ball games on the Sabbath, by the early nineteenth century, many towns across South Wales could boast cricket clubs. Most were like modern-day golf clubs where members gathered to play amongst themselves, but all of this changed in mid-century following the industrialization of both the valleys and coastal plain.

The influx of people and transport innovations, with the opening of railway lines, were key factors in assisting clubs to stage fixtures, whilst the introduction of newspapers meant it was easier to spread information. The arrival of migrants from England, well-versed in the playing and coaching of cricket, was another important reason behind the nineteenth-century boom in cricketing activity, as was the rise in regional pride and identity, with settlements such as Merthyr Tydfil becoming not just important iron and steel-making centres in South Wales, but having a key role within the national economy.

Besides healthy profits being made from these manufacturing activities, there was money to be made as well by playing and staging cricket By mid-century, there was a number of teams of professional players who travelled from town to town across England, accepting financial challenges for the staging of exhibition games against local teams, whilst the organisers gleefully charged entrance fees as cricket metamorphosed from being a casual recreation into a money-making form of public entertainment.

South Wales was not immune to these trends and during June 1855 the All-England Eleven met a Twenty Two of Neath and South Wales at Court Herbert, with the local team augmented by a number of talented guests from other clubs in the area. Over the course of the next few years, multi-day exhibition games were staged in other towns in South Wales, and in June 1859 a team representing Monmouthshire defeated the All-England Eleven at Newport.

The organizer of this game was George Homfray, a member of an influential family of ironmasters from Glenusk who owned furnaces in Merthyr, Ebbw Vale and Tredegar. His team included players with the flourishing clubs at Newport, Cardiff, Abergavenny, Brecon and Llandovery, and the victory was celebrated with much glee by the local men, with Homfray's team eventually leaving the ground many hours after the visiting professionals had rather shamefacedly departed. Besides being a jolly night, it was also a historic landmark in the development of cricket in Wales as the success of Homfray's team led to the formation in 1859 of the South Wales CC, the first regional team in Wales.

The South Wales CC acted like a quasi-county side, but it was very much a wandering eleven, with the majority of their games held outside Wales, with an annual tour to London lasting for up to ten days, and comprising two- or three-day contests against some of the top gentlemen's teams in the Home Counties including the MCC, I Zingari,

Members of the South Wales Cricket Club seen in 1861. Homfray is sitting in the middle.

Prince's, and Knickerbockers as well as Surrey Club and Ground, plus the Gentlemen of Kent, and their counterparts from Sussex.

By and large, the South Wales CC consisted of gentlemen, educated at public schools in England and Wales, who had the time and money to spend playing cricket outside Wales, augmented by a few talented amateurs from the local area, plus a small number of journeymen professionals who were only too willing to roll up their sleeves for a lengthy bowling spell. The annual visits to London also satisfied the political and social aspirations of these well-heeled young chaps, and there was great merriment within the group in July 1861 after the first Welsh victory at Lord's as Homfray's team defeated the MCC by seven wickets.

Soon afterwards, Homfray's business commitments prompted a move from Newport to Swansea, with the young industrialist duly forming another regional side, fittingly called the Welsh Wanderers, who staged matches against prominent clubs in Pembrokeshire and Carmarthenshire. His team largely comprised amateurs from the Swansea, Neath and Llanelly clubs, plus former pupils from Cheltenham and Clifton College.

Around the same time, leading members of the South Wales CC floated the notion of forming fully constituted county teams and, after a meeting in February 1864 at The Ivy Bush Hotel in Carmarthen, a Carmarthenshire club came into being. Within a few months, over sixty people had enrolled at half a guinea each, but the club remained exclusive as they added a stipulation that "no tradesmen or any of the working class being admitted." Seven fixtures were arranged for 1864 including games against teams assembled by members of the South Wales CC and the Welsh Wanderers "representing" Breconshire, Pembrokeshire and Glamorgan, as well as a match against the crack Clifton club from Bristol.

Another early promotor of so-called county cricket was John Nicholl, a member of Bridgend CC and the son of the Conservative MP for Cardiff. After inheriting his late father's estate at Merthyr Mawr in 1852, the Old Etonian organised a series of fixtures in the grounds of his home involving gentlemen from Glamorgan and further afield, against teams comprising well-heeled chaps from Carmarthenshire and Breconshire. Flushed by the success of these matches, Nicholl also approached the All-England Eleven to see if an exhibition match could be arranged at Merthyr Mawr against a Twenty Two of Glamorgan which would help to raise funds to start a county club. Negotiations however broke down over the financial terms, and no dates were agreed.

The Merthyr Mawr ground, seen whilst hosting a so-called "country house" match which combined healthy recreation with evening entertainment plus plenty of socialising.

Nicholl however was not the only Old Etonian banging the drum for county cricket in Glamorgan because doing the same further west was John Talbot Dillwyn Llewelyn, the son of the Conservative MP for Swansea, and a major figure in the social and political life of the Copperopolis. After graduating in Law and entering the Inner Temple in 1859, JTD opted against a legal career and returned to his family's home at Penllergaer House with his wife, Caroline Hicks-Beach, the daughter of Disraeli's Colonial Secretary, and went into business and politics.

JTD also acted as a kindly benefactor to cricket, and a host of other good causes in the region. He also created the Cadoxton club, near Ynysygerwn, who were strong enough to play the likes of Clifton and the MCC, besides supplying talented amateurs, and some decent professionals, for the South Wales CC. In March 1869 the squire of Penllergaer convened a meeting at The Castle Hotel in Neath at which a Glamorganshire club was inaugurated and the following summer a series of matches took place against the county elevens organized by other members of the South Wales CC.

Mindful of the need to include gentlemen from the east of the county, JTD made contact with some of the influential members of the rapidly expanding Cardiff club to see if the Marquess of Bute, who lived in Cardiff Castle, would allow the new county organization to use the excellent facilities which the Bute Estate had created at the Arms

Park following the diversion of the River Taff away from the western outskirts of the town. With many influential Tories also in the new Glamorganshire set-up, the Marquess readily agreed, and the new county organization used the Arms Park during mid-June 1869 for their inaugural match against a Monmouthshire XI. The two-day contest saw the Glamorganshire side, containing George Homfray and JTD perform with great credit, and with Llewelyn at the helm further fixtures were secured over the course of the next few years.

John Talbot Dillwyn Llewelyn – the father of Glamorgan cricket.

However, the Glamorganshire club folded during the mid-1870s, largely as a result of rising costs in staging matches, with many of the gentlemen preferring to appear instead for their clubs in matches against local rivals. Others were more sceptical of the clubs' rather elitist attitudes, and viewed their activities as little more than a form of social entertainment, and a jolly gathering of Old Boys. The same could also be said about the South Wales CC which had also struggled for funds and did not stage any games between 1866 and 1873. Although they helped to boost club cricket, through the formation of the South Wales Cricket Challenge Cup in 1879, the South Wales CC was still very parochial in its outlook, and 'Old Stager' of the *South Wales Daily News* spoke for many when he wrote in April 1886 "when, oh when, shall we be able to put in the field an eleven sufficiently strong to oppose, with some prospect of success, a really first-class team? Not I fancy until the miserable cliqueism that at present marks the management of some of our leading clubs in swept away, and men are played simply because they know how to play and not because their names are Jones, Brown, Robinson and so on."

His words followed a quite dreadful summer for the South Wales club, as they lost all of their fixtures, and there was an air of resignation when the club's officials met up at The Angel Hotel in Cardiff in December to review the events of the summer. Unanimously, they decided to discontinue the club's activities, with members encouraged to go away and form proper county teams. It was a sea-level change in the outlook of the great and the good in cricketing circles within South Wales, and it was no surprise that within eighteen months Glamorgan County Cricket Club was formed and soon became Wales' leading representative in county cricket.

The two men who were largely responsible for turning the situation around were JTD Llewelyn and John Price Jones, a prominent architect from Cardiff, whose vision and drive – both on and off the field – had helped the town club become established as amongst the premier clubs in Wales. He represented the dynamism and energy of the middle-classes of Victorian Wales, whilst Llewelyn was a symbol of the established order, and the gentry who had first played the game. The love of cricket was the common thread that bonded the pair.

It proved to be a potent combination, with their cause assisted by nationalistic feelings which had swept, like a tidal wave, across the region during the 1880s: an era which saw the National Eisteddfod Society become inaugurated to co-ordinate the cultural and artistic affairs, as well as a University College of South Wales and Monmouthshire, plus the creation of the Welsh Rugby Union, for whom JTD had been one of instigators and acted as President between 1885 and 1906.

Indeed, it had been Jones who, at a meeting in 1886, had proposed dissolving the South Wales CC and forming new county teams which selected the best players within the area, regardless of their social standing or aspirations. He was in the vanguard of change and soon made arrangements for a series of matches during 1887 at Newport, the Arms Park and Llanelly between a Glamorgan side and the Rest of South Wales. Nothing eventually came of the games at either Cardiff or Llanelly, but Jones was able to lead a Glamorgan XI into the field at Newport against an XVIII of South Wales.

John Price Jones, the influential captain of Cardiff CC who helped to convene the meeting in July 1888 at which Glamorgan CCC was formed.

Jones also canvassed the support of other leading club officials and, most importantly, secured the backing of the Swansea Cricket and Football Club. Initially, they were wary of showing too close an allegiance to a scheme that would reinforce Cardiff, and the Arms Park ground, as the cricketing epicentre of the county. Given the excellent facilities which had been created from the mid-1870s at St Helen's, they were keen that Swansea had a slice of the action , and with the full support of the squire of Penllergaer, it did not take Jones too long to persuade William Bryant, the secretary of the Swansea club, that the formation of Glamorgan would be good for both the east and west of the county.

There was also talk amongst Tory circles that Jack Brain, the talented batsman from Gloucestershire and a member of the Oxford University team which had defeated the 1884 Australians, would soon be moving to South Wales to manage his family's brewery in Cardiff. There were strong indications as well that Jack would be happy to throw in his lot with a new county club in South Wales, so in June 1888, JTD Llewelyn wrote as follows to all of the leading clubs in the region:

"I have much pleasure in convening a meeting at the Angel Hotel, Cardiff on Friday, 6th July at six o'clock in the evening to consider the advisability of forming a county cricket club. I need scarcely say that it is essential that the meeting should be thoroughly representative of cricket in the county, and shall be glad therefore if you will do your utmost to attend."

A carde de visite of the Angel Hotel, when the meeting was held at which the Club was founded.

Over thirty representatives attended the meeting at which Glamorgan County Cricket Club came into being. Fittingly, Jones was elected Chairman of the new club, with his team-mate William Yorath, the town's coroner and a leading solicitor, being appointed Secretary. JTD agreed to act as Hon. Treasurer, whilst other leading figures from clubs in the west joined their counterparts from the east on the committee. After an approach from Jones, the Marquess of Bute also agreed to act as the club's President, besides allowing the club to use the Arms Park for their fixtures.

Within a few weeks, a series of trials to be staged on the Arms Park, whilst William Morgan, another influential member of the former South Wales CC and a man whose family had led the wave of industrialization in the Rhondda Valley, organized a practice match in August 1888 for a Glamorgan XI against his cricket club in Llwynypia. Letters were also sent to the officials of a number of English counties, including Herefordshire, Somerset, Worcestershire and Staffordshire, for fixtures in 1889. All said no, but replies in the affirmative came from the MCC, Surrey Club and Ground, and also Warwickshire.

1889 therefore saw Glamorgan CCC play its inaugural matches, with the Club deemed at first to be a third-class county. Through the hard work of Jack Brain, the Club was subsequently admitted into the Minor County Championship for 1897 and through the efforts of the men whose potted biographies appear in the forthcoming pages, the Club was eventually elevated into the County Championship in 1921. Indeed, there were tears in the eyes of JTD Llewelyn, the grand old man of Glamorgan cricket when confirmation of the promotion of the Welsh county into first-class cricket was formally announced in mid-February 1921.

1889

21 June, 1889 was a red letter date in both the Club's history as well as in the annals of Welsh sport as on that day, at Cardiff Arms Park, Glamorgan CCC staged its inaugural inter-county fixture. Warwickshire were the visitors with the fact that the Birmingham-based club had close links with the Ansell family hinting at discussions having involved Jack Brain and others linked with the Cardiff brewery. Even so, Warwickshire only agreed to a fixture if a guarantee of £40 towards match expenses was paid. Fortunately, JP Jones and JTD Llewelyn dipped into their pockets to meet this request.

During the week leading up to the fixture, the Glamorgan committee finalized their squad for the prestigious fixture, but Willie Llewelyn, the talented son of JTD, and William Morgan, a stalwart of the South Wales CC each had niggles and were unable to be considered. On the eve of the game another of the old guard, Lewis Kempthorne, the 35 year-old all-rounder had to belatedly withdraw. The absence of the Neath-born solicitor, as well as Llewelyn and Morgan, was an early blow for the fledgling county, especially as Warwickshire arrived in Cardiff at full strength With several England players in their ranks, the West Midlands side eased to an eight-wicket win on the second afternoon, before batting on for exhibition purposes until shortly before their express train back to Birmingham was scheduled to arrive at Cardiff General.

Despite the best efforts of Secretary William Yorath, no other inter-county matches were arranged that summer, with the rest of the Club's fixture calendar resembling that of the defunct South Wales CC, with a five-day tour to London during the third week of August with games against the MCC plus Surrey Club and Ground, followed the next day by a return contest with the MCC at the Arms Park. The game at Lord's ended in another heavy defeat, by 103 runs, but the Welsh county were victorious at The Oval, winning by six wickets with opening batsman Hastings Watson scoring 58 and William Wilkinson, the Cardiff professional claiming seven wickets. Glamorgan's target in their second innings was only 21 but there were jitters in the camp as four batsmen swiftly returned to the pavilion, before two others from the Cardiff club, Gowan Clark and WH Williams saw them home.

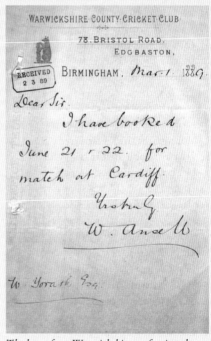

The letter from Warwickshire confirming the Club's first fixture in 1889.

1.
JENKINS, Lewis

Born – Skewen, 8 February 1847
Died – Lonlas, Skewen 16 April 1922
Amateur
Batsman
1st XI: 1871-1889
Clubs: Swansea, South Wales CC, Cadoxton, Briton Ferry Town, Bute Household

Batting and Fielding Record

M	I	NO	RUNS	AV	100	50	CT	ST
1	2	0	7	3.50	-	-	-	-

Career-bests
7 v Warwickshire at Cardiff Arms Park, 1889

There are two reasons why Lewis Jenkins holds a unique place in Glamorgan's history – first, he was the batsman who faced the opening ball in the Club's inaugural fixture against Warwickshire at Cardiff Arms Park in 1889. Secondly, he was the first batsmen to be dismissed as he departed to the second ball of the game, caught off fast bowler John Shilton.

A native of the Neath area, Lewis was a stalwart of the Cadoxton and Briton Ferry Town clubs, as well as the South Wales CC, featuring on a regular basis on their annual tours to London and the Home Counties. His first appearance though at a higher level had come in the Glamorganshire side raised in July 1871 to play Monmouthshire at Usk, but it was the 24 year-old's ability with the ball, rather than with the bat as in later years, which led to his inclusion. Opening the bowling, he claimed six wickets in Monmouthshire's first innings, but his efforts could not prevent a sizeable defeat by eight wickets.

His bowling also led to his selection three years later for the Bute Household XXII against the All-England XI in Cooper's Field in Cardiff. He claimed a couple of wickets against the English professionals but batting at number sixteen, he ended up as top-scorer in the first innings making 17 before being dismissed by James Shaw, the left-arm round-arm fast bowler.

Lewis' batting continued to flourish, as evidenced by his performance at St Helen's in Swansea where he was in the South Wales XVIII which met the 1878 Australians with Lewis top-scoring with 15 in the home team's second innings before being dismissed by another famed fast

Lewis Jenkins – the man who faced the first ball in Glamorgan's history.

bowler, Frederick "The Demon" Spofforth. He made further guest appearances at St Helen's for various Swansea and District teams, including the matches against the United South of England XI in 1876 and the All-England XI in 1877.

His best years were clearly behind him when Lewis made his one and only appearance for Glamorgan against Warwickshire, but given his standing within the South Wales CC, their involvement in sowing the seeds for a county side, and his prolific run-scoring in club cricket, it was fitting that he should open the batting at the Arms Park. Six years later, he also played against the Welsh county for the South Wales CC in a friendly at St Helen's – a game which proved to be his final match of note.

Lewis worked in the tinplate business in Neath, and was also a decent golfer, acting as captain of the Royal Porthcawl Golf Club.

2.
JONES, Daniel Elias ('Danny')

Born – Cardiff, September 1864
Died – Cardiff, 6 July 1908
Amateur
RHB, WK, occ OB
Ed – Cardiff College
1st XI: 1889-1890
Clubs: South Wales CC, Cardiff
Brother of FN, JP and WP Jones

Batting and Fielding Record

M	I	NO	RUNS	AV	100	50	CT	ST
5	9	0	78	8.67	-	-	2	2

Bowling Record

Balls	M	R	W	AV	5wI	10wM
30	0	21	1	21	-	-

Career-bests
25 v Surrey Club and Ground at The Oval, 1889
1/21 v MCC at Lord's, 1889

Danny Jones was an influential figure in both the sporting and economic worlds of Cardiff before his life was prematurely cut short by illness at the age of 44. The fourth son of Alderman Daniel Jones, Danny followed his father and brothers into the construction trade and, after qualifying as an architect, he helped to design several buildings in the Victorian town.

He also inherited his father's love of cricket, with Daniel senior having played for Cardiff against the All-England XI in 1855 and the United All-England XI in 1857. Educated at Cardiff College, Danny first played for Cardiff as a teenager and was also chosen in the club's match against the United England XI in 1882. Three years later, he made his debut for the South Wales CC. As an eager and enthusiastic example of the brave new world of cricket in the region, he was selected to appear for Glamorgan in their inaugural match against Warwickshire in 1889.

In his county appearances, Danny showed great promise as an opening batman and spin bowler, whilst on occasions he also kept wicket. Like many of his contemporaries in Cardiff, Danny also spent the winter months playing rugby for Cardiff, and a measure of both his prowess and popularity can be judged from the fact that for a couple of seasons, he captained their 2nd XV.

The Arms Park was therefore the epicentre of his sporting life, and through rubbing shoulders with many of the other young athletes, he was

Danny Jones

able to secure a series of useful contacts for his family's business. Sadly, Danny never fulfilled his commercial dreams or succeeded his father in the family company, as during the mid-1900s he suffered a series of heart problems. His health never recovered and in July 1908 he died at his home in Colum Road after a long illness.

3.
MORRIS, Alexander William

Born – Cardiff, June 1857
Died – Cardiff, 28 November 1927
Amateur
LHB, LM
Ed – Cowbridge GS
1st XI: 1875, 1889-1897
Captained Glamorgan in 1890
Clubs: South Wales CC, Bute Household CC, Cardiff, MCC

Batting and Fielding Record

M	I	NO	RUNS	AV	100	50	CT	ST
13	23	1	333	15.14	-	1	7	-

Bowling Record

Balls	M	R	W	AV	5wI	10wM
15	0	14	2	7.00	-	-

Career-bests
91 v Monmouthshire at Cardiff Arms Park, 1890
2/14 v Monmouthshire at Cardiff Arms Park, 1890

Born in Cardiff and raised in Penarth, Alex Morris' sporting instincts – like other well-heeled young men at the time – were nurtured at Cowbridge Grammar School. Indeed, it was whilst a teenager at the famous school in the Vale of Glamorgan that he was chosen to

appear for the Bute Household XXII against the All-England XI in 1874, before the following year playing for Glamorganshire against Breconshire in their matches at both the Arms Park and Brecon.

Alex's father, John, was a leading solicitor in mid-Victorian Cardiff with a practice in Angel Street, close to where the Cardiff Arms Hotel was situated. Alex duly completed his legal training and took over the practice, besides playing for the South Wales CC, the MCC and captaining Cardiff CC during 1890 and 1891. His Tory affiliations and membership of the MCC also meant that Alex was a fitting choice as one of Glamorgan's captains in 1890. A dashing left-handed batsman, his finest innings in county colours came that year at the Arms Park as he came within nine runs of posting a century against Monmouthshire.

When his playing days were over Alex maintained his interest in the county's affairs by serving on the Glamorgan committee, whilst his solicitor's practice at 10, Park Place, went from strength to strength. His close contacts with the Bute Estate not only helped his business thrive but, in later life, they also helped both Cardiff CC and Glamorgan

Alec Morris – seen in 1886 in front of the Cardiff pavilion.

CCC as Alex became a valued source of advice as a contingent from the cricket clubs negotiated the regular use of the Arms Park as well as improvements to the ground's facilities.

Alex continued working into his early seventies and the week before his death in late November 1927 he was active in the Glamorgan Assizes with a divorce case.

4.
BANCROFT, William John ('Billy')

Born – Swansea, 2 March 1871
Died – Swansea, 3 March 1959
Professional
RHB, RM, occ WK
Ed – St Helen's School
1st XI: 1889-1914
South Wales 1894-1912, Players of Glamorgan 1899, West of England 1910
Clubs: Swansea, Swansea Tourists
Rugby for Swansea RFC and Wales (33 caps)
Son of William Bancroft (junior) and older brother of Jack Bancroft

Batting and Fielding Record

M	I	NO	RUNS	AV	100	50	CT	ST
230	357	19	8250	24.42	-	-	-	-

Bowling Record

Balls	M	R	W	AV	5wI	10wM
251	12	170	10	17.10	1	-

Career-bests
207 v Berkshire at St Helen's, Swansea, 1903
5/20 v Surrey 2nd XI at St Helen's, Swansea, 1899

Billy Bancroft was one of the leading sportsmen in Wales during the late Victorian and Edwardian era. A cobbler by trade, Bancroft played rugby and cricket for his native Swansea, often alongside his father William (junior), who had been a leading player with the early Glamorganshire club with the family living in a cottage at the St Helen's ground in Swansea which their grandfather William (senior) had secured following his work during the 1870s in helping to create the wicket.

Cricket and rugby were therefore in the Bancroft family's blood and by the late 1880s young Billy was making a mark in both sports. In 1889 he played as a professional in Glamorgan's inaugural county match at the Arms Park, before making his debut for the Swansea rugby 1st XV in October. So impressive was the strong and confident-running full-back that in February 1890 he was drafted into the all-amateur Welsh side – the first of 33 Welsh caps, won in consecutive fashion until the 1901 season.

His prowess at rugby was no surprise given the fact that from boyhood he spent two hours per day kicking, running and catching the ball on the hallowed turf at St Helen's. These were invaluable skills given his slight frame, and his kicking on the run was a highly-prized skill, learnt after years of practice on the outfield at the Swansea ground. However, Wales only won two out of Bancroft's first nine appearances and a few questions were raised about his defensive capabilities. These were swiftly answered in 1893 as Wales, under the captaincy of Arthur Gould – another talented cricketer from Newport – won the Triple Crown for the first-ever time.

The first match of that season saw England visit the Arms Park – a venue where Wales had never previously defeated England – and in the days leading up to the game, there were doubts that the game would go-ahead, before eighteen tons of coal were burned in braziers the night before the game to prevent frost getting at the pitch. It did the trick, and a thrilling game ensued, with England leading Wales 11-9 until a couple of minutes before the final whistle when Wales were awarded a penalty kick, about thirty yards out and just in from the touch-line. Gould called up Bancroft, who insisted on drop kicking the ball rather than opting to place kick. Gould initially disagreed, but Bancroft convinced him that he could slot the ball over the posts to win the game. After a heated exchange, Bancroft duly slotted the ball over the posts to win the game, and after subsequent victories over Scotland and Ireland, Wales lifted the Triple Crown.

Bancroft returned to Swansea as a hero, but despite many fine words on his behalf, plus some magnanimous gestures, he did not derive any financial benefit from Wales' success as rugby was still an amateur sport. In fact, at the time, cricket was Billy's main source of income came from his professional duties with Swansea, topped up by match fees for playing for Glamorgan, plus coaching duties in and around the Swansea area as well as privately for JTD Llewelyn at Penllergaer.

1894 saw Billy enjoy his most successful season to date with the bat for Glamorgan, scoring four half-centuries. By the end of the summer, his stock as an all-round sportsman was in the ascent, and a lucrative offer came his way from Wiltshire to join them on a full-time basis as a professional for the 1895 season. For a couple of weeks, it looked as if Glamorgan's most promising young player would accept the offer which, at the end of the day, would more than provide him with financial security. The reaction however from sporting circles in Swansea was one of complete shock, and public meetings were held in the town to discuss the issue.

A couple of other, highly successful Swansea rugby players had turned professional by playing rugby league for teams based in Lancashire and Yorkshire, but not for the first time, JTD Llewelyn solved a potentially tricky situation by suggesting to Jack Brain, the Glamorgan captain, that the Welsh county themselves should offer Billy decent terms to be their full-time professional. This was in keeping with Jack's thoughts, especially his musing over how the county could become a more professional outfit. On several occasions, amateurs had failed to turn up for matches, and hiring more professional players on a decent retainer was one option, although one with a price for the Welsh county.

However, the committee saw the logic in having a regular professional, especially someone who was locally born and well-known to the sporting public. However, the sticking point was the quite modest sum that the committee originally had in mind, and it may have been no coincidence that around this time, news filtered through about a more lucrative offer to Billy from Wiltshire. Soon after hearing about the details from the Chippenham club, JTD made some more diplomatic noises, as well as dipping into his pocket, allowing more generous terms to be offered to Billy. To the delight of sporting fans in Swansea, he quickly agreed terms with Glamorgan, allowing him to remain with

Swansea RFC.

Billy's fee with Glamorgan was the princely amount of £20 week for twenty weeks, allowing him to continue in the rather paradoxical situation of representing Glamorgan as a professional sportsman during the summer, whilst in the winter, playing as an amateur rugby player for Wales.

His career subsequently blossomed, with Billy subsequently leading Wales on eleven occasions from 1898, including their Triple Crown win in 1900. He also developed a reputation of being one of the game's finest kickers – a richly deserved honour at a time when games were staged using heavy, leather balls. Despite often being saturated with water and mud, Billy developed a skill to almost nonchalantly drop or place kick a ball with unerring accuracy. Another party piece saw Billy catch the ball, before waiting for the opposition to run towards him, but just before they were poised to tackle him, he would jink and quickly dart away, leaving the would-be tackler sprawling on the floor.

As far as Billy's cricket was concerned, he recorded his maiden county century in 1896, with an unbeaten 119 against Monmouthshire, and for the next dozen years he was a stalwart presence in the Glamorgan middle-order in their Minor

Billy Bancroft in cricket mode

County Championship games. In 1899 he enjoyed a fine game against Surrey 2nd XI, scoring 102, and taking a career-best 5/20 with his seam bowling. However, his finest match in Glamorgan ranks came in 1903, fittingly on his home ground in Swansea, as he recorded 207 against Berkshire.

Glamorgan won this match at St Helen's by the commanding margin of an innings and 325 runs, with local newspapers reporting how Billy repeatedly drove with authority, and "gave fewer chances than usual by opting to drill the ball along the ground, rather than chipping it in the air. Overall, it was an innings of authority and power."

In 1905 Berkshire were on the receiving end again, as he made his fourth hundred for Glamorgan with a solid 105. In the course of the next four years, Bancroft added centuries against Northumberland, Devon and Cornwall. In the years leading up to the Great War, Billy succeeded his father as groundsman at St Helen's, and then during the inter-war era, Billy turned his attention to coaching, painstakingly passing on many tips to a host of promising young players in the Swansea area, including Gilbert Parkhouse, who duly went on to play Test cricket for England as well as the pupils of Christ College, Brecon.

In later life, Billy also acted as a match-day steward at the St Helen's ground when Glamorgan were playing their fixtures at the Swansea ground, and for many years, he proudly sat at the foot of the steps leading up to pavilion, opening and closing the gate as batsmen made their way out to bat on the turf which for so many years he and other members of his family had tended.

Billy Bancroft in his Welsh rugby cap.

5.
ROBINSON, Theodore
Born – Beaminster, Dorset, 16 February 1866
Died – West Town, Somerset, 4 October 1959
Amateur
RHB, RM
1st XI: 1889-1891
East of South Wales 1883
Somerset 1884-1894
Clubs: Cardiff, Clifton, South Wales CC, MCC, Flax Bourton, Backwell House.

Batting and Fielding Record

M	I	NO	RUNS	AV	100	50	CT	ST
13	24	1	392	17.04	-	2	8	-

Bowling Record

Balls	M	R	W	AV	5wI	10wM
1820	87	768	52	14.77	5	-

Career-bests
70 v MCC at St Helen's, Swansea, 1890
6/26 v Monmouthshire at Cardiff Arms Park, 1891

Theo Robinson was a wealthy landowner in the Backwell and Flax Bourton area of north-east Somerset who held business interests in Bristol and Cardiff. With few restrictions about who played for the Welsh county, he was able to appear for both Somerset and Glamorgan during the 1880s and 1890s

His experience of playing twice for Somerset in 1884, plus a decent record in club cricket for Cardiff and the South Wales CC, led to the 23 year-old all-rounder being chosen in Glamorgan's line-up for their inaugural match against Warwickshire in 1889. Theo made 34 runs and took a wicket before being invited to play again a few weeks later in the match at Lord's against the MCC.

He duly opened the batting at Lord's and continued in this guise in several of his subsequent appearances, including the game in 1890 against the MCC at Swansea, where he played his finest innings for the Welsh county making a cavalier 70. As an accurate right-arm seam bowler, Theo was, at first, the regular first change in the Glamorgan attack before becoming the opening bowler in 1891 and enjoying his finest hour with the ball at the Arms Park against Monmouthshire where during the second innings, he took a career-best 6/26 as the Welsh county eased to a six-wicket victory.

At the end of the 1891 season, Theo returned to north-east Somerset, where he subsequently established a seed crushing business and took up residence at Backwell House with his sister, brothers and team of servants. He was a generous landowner, providing land for facilities for local residents and funding the construction of tennis courts and bowling greens so that young and old alike could enjoy healthy recreation. Theo re-appeared for Somerset in Championship cricket in June 1892 against Surrey at The Oval, alongside his brother Cres, and duly played in a further seven first-class games for the West Country side in 1893 and 1894. He did not forget his friends in Cardiff and turned out in mid-July 1894 for EM Grace's Gloucestershire XI against Glamorgan in a fund-raising match at the Arms Park. He opened the batting with Grace but only made a single in what proved to be his final appearance in a major game on Welsh soil.

Theo continued to play in club cricket for Clifton and Flax Bourton as well as in country house matches in the grounds of Backwell House where the Robinson family could field their own family eleven against other wandering gentlemen's teams. He also enjoyed other genteel pastimes, including archery at which he represented Great Britain at the 1908 Olympics.

6.
DAVID, Edmund Ussher

Born – St Fagans, 24 April 1860
Died – Nottage, 26 July 1942
Amateur
RHB, RM
Ed – Cheltenham College
1st XI 1889-1900
South Wales CC 1878-1884, Next XVIII v South Wales CC 1878, Cardiff v United
South of England 1880, v Welsh Wanderers 1881, East of South Wales 1883
Clubs: St Fagans, Fairwater, Glamorganshire Hunt
Brother of AE David; Father of RFA David

Batting and Fielding Record

M	I	NO	RUNS	AV	100	50	CT	ST
32	49	3	581	12.63	-	2	19	-

Bowling Record

Balls	M	R	W	AV	5wI	10wM
435	20	268	10	26.80	-	-

Career-bests
85 v Monmouthshire at Rodney Parade, Newport, 1896
4/48 v Monmouthshire at Rodney Parade, Newport, 1896

Edmund David holds a special place in the history of Glamorgan CCC, having led the county in their first-ever match against Warwickshire in June 1889. He struck the first blow in the game by winning the toss and electing to bat, but this was the high point of the match for the Welsh county as David, like his colleagues, struggled against the talented Warwickshire attack.

He made just 0 and 2, as the Welsh county were comfortably defeated, but the former pupil of Cheltenham College subsequently secured a regular place in the county's middle-order as they played a series of friendlies in their quest for higher recognition as a Minor County. Edmund's finest game was against Monmouthshire at Newport in 1896 when he produced career-best performances with both bat and ball, making 85 and returning figures of 4/48 with his nagging off-cutters. Although past his best, David also figured in Glamorgan's side in the Minor County Championship during 1897 and 1898, with his final appearance for the Welsh county coming in 1900 when he appeared, at number nine, in the one-day encounter against WM Brownlee's XI.

Edmund was the son of William David, the influential rector of St Fagans. After leaving Cheltenham College, he became a leading figure with the South Wales CC for whom he played his first major match against the 1878 Australians at Swansea making 8 and 1. He subsequently became a leading figure with both the St Fagans and Fairwater clubs, besides serving on the Glamorgan committee between 1888 and 1907. Edmund served as Land Agent for the Margam Estate, on whose property he helped to oversee the creation of the Margam cricket pitch. He also served on the Port Talbot town council whilst his son Rodney, played for Glamorgan between 1925 and 1929. Edmund was also President of the Land Agents Society in 1931.

Edmund David – Glamorgan's first-ever captain.

Edmund David (extreme right) seen in the mid-1880s with his family and the Reverend William David.

7.
CLARK, *John* <u>Gowan</u>

Born – Aberystwyth, September 1864
Died – Cardiff, 28 November 1937
Amateur
RHB, OB
1st XI: 1889-1903
South Wales v EM Grace's Gloucestershire XI 1894
Clubs: Cardiff
Uncle of NVH Riches

Batting and Fielding Record

M	I	NO	RUNS	AV	100	50	CT	ST
37	58	5	783	14.77	-	3	24	-

Bowling Record

Balls	M	R	W	AV	5wI	10wM
303	8	244	12	20.33	1	-

Career-bests
95 v Monmouthshire at Rodney Parade, Newport, 1891
5/11 v Wiltshire at Cardiff Arms Park, 1892

Gowan Clark played 37 matches for Glamorgan with the accountant having moved to Cardiff during the early 1870s. His family were closely connected with the railway trade with his father serving as an agent for the London and North Western Railway whilst his brother Cresswell also worked in Abergavenny for the Company before emigrating to become General Manager of the South African General Railways.

Gowan also followed in the footsteps of his father and brother by working initially in the audit office of the London and North Western Railway before securing a post in Cardiff with the Rhymney Railway Company for whom he eventually acted as company secretary and accountant until 1918.

A talented batsman and spin bowler, Gowan played for Glamorgan in their inaugural match against Warwickshire in 1889 before becoming a regular in the Welsh county's side during the 1890s and from 1897 in the Minor County Championship. Gowan was a heavy scorer in club cricket for Cardiff and in 1891 at Newport he came within five runs of posting his maiden hundred for the Welsh county as he

Gowan Clark.

made 95 against Monmouthshire – "an innings of freedom and forceful strokes" was one newspapers summary about what proved to be a career-best innings.

Gowan remained a regular in the Glamorgan line-up until 1903, besides acting as captain of the Cradiff club from 1897 until 1902. He subsequently served on the committee of both Glamorgan and Cardiff CC until after the Great War as Glamorgan made their way in first-class cricket, besides acting as auditor for Cardiff Athletic Club.

Gowan was also a prominent member of St Andrew's church in Windsor Place in Cardiff and undertook a lot of work as a layman within the Llandaff Diocese. A bachelor throughout his life, Gowan was also an uncle to Norman Riches and helped to coach the young batsman in his formative years before the Great War.

8.
LINDLEY, James

Born – Sutton-in-Ashfield, 18 July 1844
Died – Mansfield, 15 October 1911
Professional
RHB, RFM
1st XI: 1888-1890
Nottinghamshire 1874
Clubs: South Wales CC, Cardiff, Swansea, St Andrew's, Great Harwood, Sutton-in-Ashfield, Mansfield, Worksop, Wirksworth, Accrington

Batting and Fielding Record

M	I	NO	RUNS	AV	100	50	CT	ST
5	8	1	58	8.28	-	-	2	-

Bowling Record

Balls	M	R	W	AV	5wI	10wM
714	51	256	19 (+8)	13.47	3	-

Career-bests
31* v Surrey Club and Ground at The Oval, 1889
7/45 v MCC at Cardiff Arms Park, 1889

James Lindley.

James Lindley was on the Nottinghamshire staff in 1874 but the right-arm seam bowler never made an appearance for his native county and instead featured as a professional in club cricket for Sutton-in-Ashfield, Mansfield, Worksop and Accrington for whom he played in the Lancashire League between 1872 and 1879.

In 1884 he moved to South Wales to join Swansea and subsequently played as the professional for the South Wales CC, He appeared for the Welsh county in 1888 in their warm-up game against Llywynypia CC before featuring in their inaugural match against Warwickshire in 1889. James appeared in other games during 1889, taking 7/45 against the MCC at the Arms Park with the Western Mail's correspondent noting how "Lindley, right from the beginning, had bowled excellently in the damp conditions, with one delivery splintering the stump of the batsman".

James subsequently became the groundsman at Sutton Town.

9.
LEWIS, *William Edgar*

Born – Lower Newcastle, Bridgend, 26 September 1862
Born – Bridgend, 26 December 1930
Amateur
Batsman
Ed – Charterhouse
1st XI: 1889-1890
Clubs: Bridgend, Penarth, Newport, Cardiff, MCC, South Wales CC, Welsh Wanderers

Batting and Fielding Record

M	I	NO	RUNS	AV	100	50	CT	ST
3	5	1	24	6.00	-	-	-	-

Career-bests
10 v Warwickshire at Cardiff Arms Park, 1889

William Lewis was a prominent member of the South Wales CC with the solicitor appearing in their games, as well as the Welsh Wanderers, besides captaining Bridgend between 1882 and 1888, as well as appearing for Penarth and Cardiff.

Educated at Charterhouse, he was a promising young sportsman, representing the school at both cricket and racquets. His batting skills for the school and the Bridgend club, led to him appearing as a guest for the Newport and District XXII in their three-day match against the United England XI in September 1881. The nineteen year-old was duly caught and bowled by WG Grace in the first innings, but he subsequently went on to play with distinction for the South Wales CC, in addition to making 83 and 50 in the match between East Wales and West Wales which the South Wales CC organized in 1883 at the Arms Park.

William Lewis.

He duly followed his father, Thomas Tamplin Lewis – the registrar of Bridgend and District Court – into the legal profession and qualified as a solicitor in 1887. Two years later he was chosen in the Glamorgan side for their inaugural match, besides appearing in August against the MCC, also at the Arms Park. He played once more for Glamorgan in 1890, again in their contest against the MCC at Swansea.

He was never called up again, largely because of his solicitor's duties and, together with his younger brother Harry – himself a talented cricketer – he played an increasingly active role in his father's practice in Bridgend. Like other well-heeled amateurs, he appeared quite content to play club cricket on Wednesday and Saturday afternoons and, as a member of the MCC, to appear occasionally in their friendlies, besides turning out for the Old Carthusians.

10.
SAMUEL, Astley William

Born – Llandeilo Fawr, Carmarthenshire, March 1861
Died – Newport, 15 December 1937
Amateur
RHB, RM
Ed – Dublin University
1st XI: 1889-1896
Clubs: Swansea, Pontardawe, Morriston, Swansea Tourists

Batting and Fielding Record

M	I	NO	RUNS	AV	100	50	CT	ST
17	26	9	181	10.65	-	-	6	-

Bowling Record

Balls	M	R	W	AV	5wI	10wM
1898	97	985	51	19.31	2	1

Career-bests
46* v Monmouthshire at St Helen's, Swansea, 1892
9/26 v Monmouthshire at Cardiff Arms Park, 1890

Astley Samuel was one of the leading all-rounders in club cricket in South Wales during the 1880s and 1890s. His father, Dr William Samuel was headmaster of the grammar school in Llandeilo Fawr, and like his younger brother Edgar, he initially followed his father into the teaching profession. Whilst Edgar taught at Temple Grove School in East Sheen, Astley trained at Dublin University before teaching in the Uxbridge area.

He returned to his native South Wales during the mid-1880s having accepted a post at the Collegiate School in Pontardawe. He played cricket for the local club, as well as for Morriston before switching his allegiances to the Swansea Cricket and Football club, for whom he was associated for the remainder of his playing career.

Astley also played tennis and hockey for Swansea, but cricket was his number one sport and after some lively bowling spells in club cricket, he was chosen to open the bowling in Glamorgan's team for their inaugural match in 1889. He also made an impression with the bat, scoring an unbeaten 28 and, together with Dan Thissen, defied the visiting

Astley Samuel.

bowlers after they had scythed through the top order. He later claimed 3/56 when Warwickshire batted, and in their second innings, he claimed a further victim in his opening over before the English team secured an eight-wicket victory.

He appeared later in the summer against the MCC at the Arms Park and was an ever-present in the Glamorgan side during 1890, taking 9/26 in the county's opening match of the summer against Monmouthshire at the Arms Park at the end of May. He ended the season as Glamorgan's most successful bowler, claiming 33 wickets at a shade under 15 apiece. It proved to be a happy year in other ways for the youngster as in December he married Lucy Soloman, the sister of his Swansea colleague Herbert Soloman.

The following year, the couple moved to the Clydach area where Astley had secured a post as Master of Tan-yr-Allt School. His academic and domestic commitments saw a reduction in his county appearances, with Astley playing just twice in 1892, once in 1895, and once more in 1896, with his final match being away to the MCC. He claimed five wickets in that game but had to retire hurt in the second innings after scoring a single. Limping off at Lord's was not the most fitting of ends to a county career for the man who had bowled the first-ever ball for Glamorgan.

Astley and Lucy remained for over a dozen years in Clydach before Astley switched careers and moved back to Swansea where he became an auctioneer and estate agent. Once again, it proved to be a very wise move as he subsequently became one of the leading estate agents in the area and literally cashed in on the housing boom in Swansea, Sketty and Mumbles either side of the Great War. After retiring from cricket, Astley became a useful golfer and, together with his good friend and former Swansea and Glamorgan colleague Dr Edgar Reid, became a prominent member of Pennard Golf Club.

11.
THISSEN, Daniel Richard

Born – Morriston, December 1857
Died – Landore, Swansea, 12 November 1928
Amateur
RHB, WK
1st XI: 1889-1900
Clubs: Morriston, Swansea

M	I	NO	RUNS	AV	100	50	CT	ST
21	29	3	316	12.15	-	-	34	14

Career-bests
44* v Wiltshire at Cardiff Arms Park, 1892

Dan Thissen was the first man to keep wicket for Glamorgan, besides being their highest scorer in their inaugural game in 1889.

Born and raised in the Duke Hotel, Morriston, Dan initially played alongside his brothers Frederick and John in the town's cricket team, before changing allegiance to Swansea in 1889. That summer proved to be an important one for the gloveman as he was chosen to appear in all four of Glamorgan's matches. Despite batting at number eleven in the first match, against Warwickshire at the Arms Park, Dan ended up as the top scorer, making 32 and sharing in a jaunty tenth wicket stand of 56 with Swansea club-mate Astley Samuel during which the pair confused their English opponents by calling to each other in Welsh!

Dan Thissen – Glamorgan first regular wicket-keeper.

Dan was Glamorgan's first choice wicket-keeper until 1893 when Sam Brain became available on a regular basis. However, Dan continued to perform with credit for Swansea and appeared for Glamorgan whenever Brain was unavailable, appearing in two Minor County Championship matches – away to Cornwall in 1897 and the game at The Oval against Surrey 2nd XI in 1900.

At around sixteen stone, Dan was a burly yet agile presence behind the stumps and often stood up to the opening bowlers. He also built up a fine relationship with Harry Creber, the talented bowler of left-arm spin and cutters, with Dan letting Harry know what he believed might be an effective delivery with a series of subtle signals.

Towards the end of the 1907 season, Dan indicated to the Swansea officials that, with his fiftieth birthday approaching, he intended to retire. But Creber, Samuel and others persuaded him to continue and Dan duly played a further five seasons. Away from cricket, Dan was a shipping clerk at a tin-plate works besides acting as a deacon at The Old Siloh, Landore. Indeed, it was his duties at the congregational chapel which led him to rarely agree to play cricket on Sundays.

12.
MORGAN, Herbert Edward ('Herbie')

Born – Penarth, 5 October 1870
Died – Lower Penarth Farm, 5 February 1933
Amateur
RHB, RM
Ed – Weston School, Bath
1st XI: 1889-1905
Gentlemen of Glamorgan 1899; South Wales 1894-1907; Combined Glamorgan and
Wiltshire XI 1902
Club: Penarth
Rugby (full-back and centre) for Penarth
Brother of FW Morgan

Batting and Fielding Record

M	I	NO	RUNS	AV	100	50	CT	ST
92	151	6	2831	19.52	4	8	68	-

Bowling Record

Balls	M	R	W	AV	5wI	10wM
206	8	129	7	18.43	-	-

Career-bests
254 v Monmouthshire at Cardiff Arms Park, 1901
3/50 v Wiltshire at Cardiff Arms Park, 1894

Herbie Morgan is another man to hold a very special place in the history of Glamorgan CCC, as he was their first player to score a hundred, and later the first double-centurion as well.

Herbie Morgan – Glamorgan's first centurion.

Born in Cardiff in 1870, the aggressive right-handed batsman was educated at Weston School in Somerset before joining his father, and brother Fred, managing the family's farm at Lower Penarth.

He was only eighteen when he first played for Glamorgan in 1889, yet despite some impressive innings for Penarth CC, the teenager was not initially an automatic selection during the Club's first summer of activity. Everything changed in 1890 after Herbie received a late call-up to play against Monmouthshire at the Arms Park. It proved to be a turning point in his career as, going in at number seven, the youngster single-handedly took apart the visiting bowlers, striking four massive sixes, and fifteen fours as he rattled up 147.

Herbie subsequently became a regular face in the team throughout the next decade as the Welsh side

29

progressed into the Minor County Championship. Even though the standard of bowling was higher, he continued to score freely for Glamorgan, and at the Arms Park in 1901, Herbie struck the first double-hundred for Glamorgan – and at the time the highest ever score in the Minor County Championship – in making 254, with one six and no less than forty fours, as once again, Herbie treated the hapless Monmouthshire bowlers with complete disdain as Glamorgan also made a record total of 538.

By this time, Herbie had become part of the Glamorgan hierarchy, as he served on the county's committee from 1898 until 1909, acting as something of a shop steward and representing the views of the players – both amateurs and professionals. Herbie retired from county cricket at the end of the 1905 season, but he continued to be a prolific run scorer in club cricket. In his youth, Herbie had also been a talented rugby player, appearing for many years for the Penarth club, and after the Great War, he held various civic positions within his beloved home town.

13.
LLEWELYN, William Dillwyn

Born – Ynysygerwn, 1 April 1868
Died – Penllergaer, 24 August 1893
Amateur
RHB, RFM
Ed – Rev. Wilkinson's School, Clifton; Eton College and New College, Oxford
1st XI: 1889-1893
Captained Glamorgan during 1890 and 1891
Oxford University 1890-1891 (Blue each year)
Clubs: Cadoxton, South Wales CC, Bicester, Swansea, MCC, Eton Ramblers, I Zingari
Brother of CLD Llewelyn

Batting and Fielding Record

M	I	NO	RUNS	AV	100	50	CT	ST
14	25	0	418	16.72	-	2	10	-

Bowling Record

Balls	M	R	W	AV	5wI	10wM
295	11	174	6 (+8)	29.00	1	-

Career-bests
99 v Monmouthshire at Cardiff Arms Park, 1893
5 wkts v Devonat St Helen's, Swansea, 1893

Willie Llewelyn might have been one of the greatest batsman in Glamorgan's Minor County days, but, just when on the verge of an illustrious career, Llewelyn took his life in August 1893 by shooting himself in the grounds of Penllergaer House, a few weeks before his marriage to the daughter of Lord Dynevor.

He was the second son of JTD Llewelyn, who had employed William Bancroft (junior) to coach his offspring in private nets laid out in the ground of Penllergaer House. Willie was educated at Eton College, where he won a place in the school's cricket eleven, and also won the Public Schools Racquets competition in both 1886 and 1887. The former year had seen him make his debut in the Eton XI and the following summer he confirmed his rich promise by making 124 against Winchester.

In 1888 Willie went up to Oxford, but failed to make the cricket XI the following summer. Nevertheless, 1889 saw Willie make his Glamorgan debut during their London tour – after making his first appearance in the match against the MCC at Lord's, he was a member of the Welsh county's side which recorded their first-ever victory as they defeated Surrey Club and Ground by six wickets at The Oval.

1890 saw Willie win the first of two Blue's with the young Welshman also making his first-class debut, against the Australians at The Parks. He opened the batting against the tourists and top-scored with 33 in the students first innings, but could not prevent an innings defeat inside two days. A few days later, Willie continued his rich vein of form in Oxford's next match as he struck his maiden – and only – first-class hundred with 116 against the Gentlemen of England.

Later in July, Willie also led Glamorgan for the first time against Somerset at the Arms Park. He played again for the Welsh county during 1891 but after graduating, he took a year out, travelling to Africa and the Far East. He returned to county cricket in 1893 and, besides taking over as the county's Treasurer, he also struck a cavalier 99 against Monmouthshire at the Arms Park.

It seemed that the 25 year-old was poised to play a leading role both on and off the field with Glamorgan, but within weeks of his innings of 99, Willie had tragically taken his life. The contemporary newspapers however described it as a tragic accident, just two days

Willie Llewelyn.

after his brother Charlie's marriage. On that fateful day of 24 August, 1893 he had spent the early morning with his fiancée before travelling to Penllergaer and deciding to walk into the grounds of the House with a fishing rod and his cocking breechloader gun.

According to the newspapers "it is believed that having seen a weasel or some vermin cross the path, he followed it into a copse, dropping his rod and basket as he ran. The hammer of the gun though had probably caught in a branch recoiled and shot the unfortunate gentleman through the heart." His funeral was attended by hundreds of people from the local gentry and sporting world, whilst all of the Glamorgan committee attended as a mark of respect to someone who they had seen as a future captain and administrator of the club.

His obituary in the *Eton College Chronicle* also sums up the measure of the man – "a character in which kindness, simplicity, cheerfulness, uprightness were so combined as to make a peculiarly attractive and delightful personality. He has left innumerable friends, and not a single enemy—nor even any who can say aught but good of him."

14.
MORGAN, William

Born – Llantrisant, September 1862
Died – Porthleven, 22 October 1914
Amateur
All-rounder
Ed – Weston School, Bath and Downing College, Cambridge
1st XI: 1888-1901
Captained Glamorgan in 1889
Welsh Wanderers 1881, Breconshire 1883-1887. WG Grace's XI v XXII of
Herefordshire 1891, West of England 1882-1894.
Clubs: Cardiff, South Wales CC, MCC, I Zingari, Llwynypia, Lansdown

Batting and Fielding Record

M	I	NO	RUNS	AV	100	50	CT	ST
24	37	1	642	17.83	-	2	14	-

Bowling Record

Balls	M	R	W	AV	5wI	10wM
2789	116	1368	77 (+5)	17.77	7	1

Career-bests
91 v MCC at Lord's, 1892
7/79 v MCC at Lord's, 1892

William Morgan, a leading figure in cricket and politics in South Wales, was the first man
to lead out a Glamorgan team at Lord's as he captained the Welsh county
in their inaugural away matches in 1889, against the MCC as well as
Surrey Club and Ground at The Oval.

There were many reasons why this was a very fitting claim to fame.
First, he had been one of the instigators of the meeting at the Angel
Hotel in Cardiff in July 1888 at which the Club came into being,
besides being a founding committee member, and organizing a trial
match against his club Llwynypia during August 1888. Secondly,
his family held a prominent place in the evolving industrial and
political landscape of the Rhondda Valley, with his home, Ty'n-
y-Cymmer House near Pontypridd, being one of the first places

William Morgan.

where coal-mining had taken place in the Rhondda, with his late
father Evan and step-father Josiah Lewis, overseeing industrial activities in the extensive
grounds of the House.

Educated at Weston School and Downing College, he played in the Cambridge
Freshman's Match in 1882 but never subsequently appeared for the Light Blues. However,
the following year he had his first taste of county cricket with Breconshire against
Monmouthshire, and produced a man-of-match performance in the game at Crickhowell,
opening the batting and bowling, besides claiming thirteen wickets to see his side to an

innings victory. Morgan was also the scourge of Monmouthshire again in their match at Newport in 1887, claiming eleven wickets as Breconshire won by ten wickets.

During this time, William also played for Llwynypia – which his father had formed in 1878 – as well as the South Wales CC, the Welsh Wanderers, I Zingari and the MCC, often alongside other young members of the industrial bourgeoise of the area. Not surprisingly he soon became interested in local politics, and in 1889 William became a founder member of the Glamorgan County Council, formed under the Local Government Act of 1888, standing as a Liberal councillor for Treorchy and Treherbert.

The all-rounder's greatest moments on the cricketing field also came at Lord's where, in 1892 for Glamorgan against the MCC side, William opened the batting and the bowling, making 91 and 61, besides claiming thirteen wickets in the match which the Welsh county won by nine wickets. A fortnight later he made his first-class debut in the match between the West of England against the East of England at the United Services ground in Portsmouth, appearing in the West side alongside several of his acquaintances in the Somerset side.

During the late 1890s, William moved from Tynewydd House in Porth to live at number 1 Park Street in Bath where he held several business interests and was a Director of the town's Recreation Ground Company. Despite living in Somerset and playing for the Lansdown club, William continued to play in Minor County Championship games for Glamorgan during 1900 and 1901, with the latter year seeing William play his final game for the Welsh county, against Berkshire at Reading.

He also played a leading role in the West of England for the MCC, helping to assemble a number of teams, including one at Bath in 1901 against a team representing the Netherlands, with William persuading the Brain brothers, Jack and Sam, to turn out against the Dutchmen. Indeed, his final match of note came when, aged 53, William played for the MCC against Monmouthshire at Rodney Parade, Newport in July 1905. Despite having retired from playing, he maintained his interest in cricket by serving on the Somerset committee and helped to oversee the county's matches at the Recreation Ground in Bath.

15.
WILKINSON, William
Born – Kimberley, Notts, 5 July 1859
Died – Nottingham, 6 October 1940
RHB, RFM
Professional
1st XI: 1889
Nottinghamshire 1892-1893
Clubs: Cardiff, Todmorden

Batting Record

M	I	NO	RUNS	AV	100	50	CT	ST
2	3	-	29	9.67	-	-	1	-

Bowling Record

Balls	M	R	W	AV	5wI	10wM
525	40	149	12	12.42	-	-

Career-bests
19 v MCC at Lord's, 1889
4/10 v MCC at Lord's, 1889

William Wilkinson was typical of the journeymen professionals who appeared in club cricket in England and Wales during the late Victorian era. After impressing in his native Nottinghamshire, he moved to South Wales and secured a position as Cardiff's professional in 1888.

The following summer, he was hired by Glamorgan to act as one of their professionals on the London tour, with William making his county debut against the MCC at Lord's, He made a composed 19 and claimed five wickets in the match, before claiming seven in the contest against Surrey Club and Ground, with his 4/39 in Surrey's second innings helping to seal Glamorgan's first-ever victory.

There was no sentiment though the following season from the Glamorgan selectors as they opted to hire other professionals. William duly returned to Nottinghamshire where he subsequently played in four County Championship matches in 1892 and 1893. He was not retained however by the East Midlands county and subsequently found employment in the Lancashire Leagues where he played with some success for Todmorden.

A group of Cardiff cricketers from 1888 with William Wilkinson standing on the extreme left.

16.
YORATH, William Lougher
Born – Cardiff, 2 December 1862
Died – Cardiff, 3 April 1924
Amateur
Batsman
Ed – Bedford School
1st XI: 1889-1890
Clubs: Cardiff, South Wales CC
Rugby for Cardiff

Batting Record

M	I	NO	RUNS	AV	100	50	CT	ST
4	6	0	45	7.50	-	-	3	-

Career-bests
21 v MCC at Lord's, 1889

William Yorath was one of the best-known faces in the legal world of Edwardian Cardiff, besides acting as a Conservative councilor and the City's Coroner for over fifteen years. In his youth, he had also played cricket and rugby for Cardiff, besides playing a key role both on and off the field during the early years of Glamorgan CCC.

The son of a Cardiff brewer, William attended Bedford School where he shone as a young sportsman before subsequently training as a solicitor. William's first major match had been for Cardiff in June 1880 against the United South of England at the Arms Park. In August that summer he also made his debut for the South Wales CC and, in subsequent appearances, played alongside many other leading figures from the legal world. Indeed, it was through his sporting contacts that he was able to set up a successful practice in Cardiff with Fred Jones, another sports-mad young lawyer who also played rugby and cricket to a high standard, with their office just a stone's throw away from the Arms Park.

William Yorath.

By 1886 William was secretary of the Cardiff club, and through a combination of his Conservative links, and friends within the South Wales CC, he became a trusted acquaintance of JTD Llewelyn. In 1888 William agreed to assist his friend in creating Glamorgan CCC, and on the evening of 6 July, he was present at the Angel Hotel in Cardiff as the county club came into being, with William agreeing to act as its first secretary.

In the course of the subsequent weeks, William also helped to organize the trial match against Llwynypia CC, before playing in three games for Glamorgan in 1889. The middle-order batsman made a duck on his debut against the MCC at Lord's but he made 21 in the second innings and retained his place for the subsequent games against Surrey Club and Ground at The Oval and the MCC at the Arms Park in late August. He made one further appearance for Glamorgan in 1890, against the MCC at Swansea, but his legal duties prevented him from making himself available for these two- and three-day games. William subsequently enjoyed a distinguished career in local politics in the Welsh capital, serving as a city councillor, besides acting as deputy mayor in 1905/06 and being President of the Cardiff Law Society.

After retiring from playing cricket and rugby, William enjoyed playing golf and besides being a founding member of Radyr Golf Club, he was a playing member of the Royal Porthcawl Club. He also took great delight in seeing his son Glynne make his way into both the Cardiff 1st XI and 1st XV but Glynne was killed during November 1917 in the Battle of Cambrai. William and his wife never really recovered from the death of his cherished son and he died of heart failure in 1924.

17.
WILLIAMS, *William Henry*

Born – Cardiff, September 1856
Amateur
All-rounder
1st XI: 1888-1893
Colts: 1891
Captained Glamorgan in 1890
Clubs: South Wales CC, Cardiff
Rugby for Cardiff

Batting Record

M	I	NO	RUNS	AV	100	50	CT	ST
9	13	3	108	10.80	-	-	4	-

Bowling Record

Balls	M	R	W	AV	5wI	10wM
135	5	66	1	66.00	-	-

Career-bests
37 v Somerset at Cardiff Arms Park, 1890
1/16 v Surrey Club and Ground at The Oval, 1889

WH Williams, who played nine times for Glamorgan, was a leading member of the South Wales CC during the late 1870s and 1880s, besides rising to a leading administrative position with the Bute Docks Railway Company.

After some good performances with bat and ball in club cricket for Cardiff, his first major matches for the South Wales club came during 1877. Williams played initially against the Gentlemen of Sussex at Hove, before appearing in their games at The Oval and Lord's. He subsequently became a regular face on their London tours, besides playing for

WH Williams.

a Cardiff XXII in their fund-raising games against the United South of England in 1880 and against a United Eleven in 1882.

He was also a talented rugby player besides captaining the Cardiff 1st XI during 1888 and 1889. These two seasons also saw Williams play a role with the embryonic Glamorgan CCC, firstly serving on the Glamorgan committee and helping to advise about the abilities of several young players. He also appeared in the trial match against Llwynypia in 1888 before going on the county club's London tour in 1889, besides leading the Glamorgan side in their match later that summer against the MCC at the Arms Park.

By this time, Williams had risen to the position of Accountant with the Bute Docks Railway Company, and his business commitments meant that he was only able to make one further appearance for Glamorgan in 1890, against Monmouthshire at Cardiff. In 1891 he found time to appear in the matches with Gloucestershire, Monmouthshire and Devon but, at the end of the season, he secured a position with a railway company in the London area and left South Wales.

18.
WATSON, William Hastings

Born – Saltfleet-by-St Peters, Lincolnshire, 15 October 1868
Died – Llandaff, 8 July 1930
Amateur
All-rounder
1st XI: 1889-1893
Clubs: Cardiff, Fairwater

Batting Record

M	I	NO	RUNS	AV	100	50	CT	ST
9	15	1	191	13.64	-	1	1	-

Bowling Record

Balls	M	R	W	AV	5wI	10wM
53	4	27	3	9.00	-	-

Career-bests
58 v Surrey Club and Ground at The Oval, 1889
3/15 v Devon at Exeter, 1893

Hastings Watson was the son of the Rev. William Watson of Louth in Lincolnshire. As a teenager, he had moved to Cardiff where he set up a business importing timber. His business quickly went from strength to strength, with his main customers being the ever-expanding collieries in the South Wales valleys who were seeking pit props, as well as the

Hastings Watson.

plethora of railway companies who were seeking material to use as sleepers.

He was also a talented young sportsman, playing cricket initially for Cardiff, before moving to live in Llandaff and playing for the Fairwater club, where he rubbed shoulders with other well-to-do young gentlemen with business interests in Cardiff Docks.

His success with both bat and ball in club cricket led to his selection for Glamorgan's London tour in 1889, and after a fine innings of 58 against Surrey Club and Ground at The Oval, Hastings played in the closing game of the county's inaugural summer against the MCC at the Arms Park. He appeared again for the next four seasons, and in 1891 played alongside his elder brother Arthur, who was a clerk in holy orders, in the trial match against a Colts XXII at the Arms Park.

Hastings was also a leading member of the Glamorgan Hunt, riding out with hounds on a regular basis and taking part with great success in the point-to-point races which the Hunt held. He met with much success riding his horse Amulet which won the coveted Mackintosh Cup at the Cowbridge Races, besides winning sixteen other races with his other horses, Borodino and Decco. Besides being a decent cricketer and rider, Hastings also excelled at tennis, hockey and rugby, before in later life becoming a fine golfer with the Royal Porthcawl and Radyr clubs.

GLAMORGANSHIRE

COUNTY CRICKET CLUB,

SEASONS 1889-90.

President.
THE MOST NOBLE THE MARQUESS OF BUTE.

Vice-Presidents.

The Right Hon. Lord Aberdare.	J. E. Moore, Esq., J.P.
Sir Hussey Vivian, M.P.	W. Morgan, Esq., J.P.
Sir J. L. E. Spearman, Bart.	Harry Lewis, Esq., J.P.
Sir J. T. D. Llewellyn, Bart.	Fred L. Davis, Esq., J.P.
Colonel E. S. Hill, C.B., M.P.	Thurston Bassett, Esq., M.F.H.
The Hon. H. C. Bruce.	William Rees, Esq., J.P.
His Honour Judge Gwilym Williams.	H. O. Fisher, Esq., J.P.
Chas. C. Williams, Esq., J.P.	Chas. E. Waring, Esq., J.P.
G. C. Williams, Esq., J.P.	Jas. Williams, Esq., J.P.
Colonel Lindsay.	Alderman T. V. Yorath.
J. S. Gibbon, Esq., J.P.	Dr. C. T. Vachell.
O. H. Jones, Esq., J.P.	J. Viriamu Jones, Esq.

Herbert B. Cory, Esq.

Committee.

Mr. W. H. Gwyn, Swansea.	Mr. T. John, Llwynpia.
,, R. J. Letcher ,,	,, Sam. Thomas, Penarth.
,, W. Bryant ,,	,, W. Hemming, Jr., Bridgend.
,, S. Thomas ,,	,, Gomer T. Evans, Pontardawe.
,, J. O. Jones, Cardiff.	,, F. Matthews, Cowbridge.
,, W. H. Williams, Cardiff.	,, L. Kempthorne, Neath.
,, M. S. Foulger ,,	,, L. J. Jenkins, Briton Ferry.
,, A. W. Morris ,,	,, E. W. Davis, Fairwater.

Mr. E. Davies, Aberdare.

Hon. Treasurer.
Sir John T. D. Llewellyn, Penllergare.

Hon. Secretary.
Mr. W. L. Yorath, Westgate Street, Cardiff.

Hon. Auditor.
Mr. T. Farrance, 76, Richmond Road.

An extract from the 1889/90 Annual Report showing the names of the movers and shakers in the fledgling Club.

1890

There was a great mood of optimism within the Glamorgan camp for 1890. The victory at The Oval had seen a decent crowd for the MCC match at the Arms Park, and with £141 taken in gate receipts, a modest profit of £11 was made by the end of the summer. It wasn't much but, at least, it was a start and allowed the Club to arrange identical fixtures for 1890, plus home and away fixtures with both Somerset as well as neighbours Monmouthshire.

Once again, JTD Llewelyn and JP Jones had to help cover some of the guarantees, but with William Morgan having very close links with Somerset, the West Country side were not too demanding in agreeing the fixtures. However, the games at the Arms Park and at Bath – where Morgan lived – each resulted in innings defeats and with four defeats in the other six games, it showed the Glamorgan hierarchy that much needed to be done before they could fly their flag at a higher level.

The summer saw some fresh faces get their first opportunity in county cricket, whilst there was a new venue as well, with Glamorgan – much to the delight of the Swansea contingent – meeting the MCC at St Helen's. There was also a first victory on home soil as in the opening game of the season during May, an innings victory was recorded over Monmouthshire. However, it was the only success of the summer.

There was still a very casual air about the approach of some of the amateurs, such as Astley Samuel who, after a quick net before play against the MCC at Swansea, left the St Helen's ground to make a quick business call and hoping to return in time to bat during the afternoon. His plan however backfired in a rather embarrassing way – his colleagues were bowled out for 57 before lunch, with Astley recorded as 'absent'. After returning and making his apologies, he was chosen again for the London tour, but clearly enjoyed the socializing off the field too much, and after arriving at Bath for the match with Somerset on their way back home, he was reported as being "taken ill and unable to bowl the following day with his customary effect!"

19.
JONES, Ernest William ('Ernie')

Born – Swansea, December 1870
Died – Swansea, 15 September 1941
Amateur
Batsman
Ed – Wycliffe College
1st XI: 1890-1912
South Wales 1905- 1909
Club: Swansea

Batting and Fielding Record

M	I	NO	RUNS	AV	100	50	CT	ST
68	107	5	2507	24.58	2	12	35	-

Bowling Record

Balls	M	R	W	AV	5wI	10wM
75	5	52	0	-	-	-

Career-bests
152 v Berkshire at St Helen's, Swansea, 1903

Ernie Jones was one of the new generation of homegrown players who appeared for Glamorgan during the 1890s and 1900s. In contrast to others with grey whiskers, Ernie was a fresh-faced nineteen year-old when he made his Glamorgan debut against Monmouthshire at the Arms Park in 1890. Indeed, he was still a student at Wycliffe School in Stonehouse, Gloucestershire when he made his debut for Swansea in club cricket during 1886, and a series of highly impressive innings led to his county call-up. He confirmed his rich potential by making 73 in the return match with Monmouthshire at Rodney Parade in 1890.

Two years later, the opening batsman came within four runs of a maiden county hundred as he posted 96 against Devon at the Arms Park, whilst in 1896 he went one run better against Surrey 2nd XI in the inaugural Minor County Championship encounter at The Oval. After a lean summer in 1897, his maiden century duly came during June 1898 on his home soil at St Helen's as he struck 101 against Cornwall.

His work as a chartered shipbroker in his family's business at Swansea Docks prevented him from playing on a regular basis, especially in games away from St Helen's, so it was not until July 1903, once again at Swansea, that he made his second hundred in the Minor County competition, batting at number three, and completing a handsome 152 against Berkshire. By this time, Ernie was very much one of the senior figures in the affairs of Glamorgan Cricket and in 1905 was chosen in the South Wales side in their two-day match against Yorkshire at the Arms Park. Opening the batting with Arthur Silverlock, the prolific batsman from Monmouthshire, Ernest only made 2 in both innings as the White Rose side eased to a 70-run victory.

Four years later, Ernie was given the honour of leading the South Wales team against the 1909 Australians at the Arms Park. By now, he was very much a veteran and lower

Ernie Jones, seen in a team group dated 1905.

in the order but, batting at number six, he made a respectable 17 runs in the three-day match. To the delight of the 10,000 spectators who were shoe-horned into the Cardiff ground, the South Wales batsmen had made a decent start with Arthur Silverlock and Norman Riches adding 74 for the first wicket, and by early-afternoon, the Welsh side had reached 150-3 with Billy Bancroft and Edward Sweet-Escott both scoring freely against the visiting bowlers, before a collapse took place in mid-afternoon, with Ernest being one of the batsman to fall cheaply as the tourists gained the upper hand.

The Welsh batsmen could not repeat their heroics batting for a second time, as the tourists eased to an eight-wicket victory before carrying on batting for exhibition purposes. Despite the reverse, there were many positives for Ernie and the other seniors to smile about, and with the future of Glamorgan Cricket appearing to be in good hands, he was happy to bow out of Minor County cricket.

However, in 1911 with Glamorgan pressing for a place in the knockout finals of the Minor County competition, Ernest was recalled for the match against Buckinghamshire at Aylesbury. Batting at number 4, he made a typically fluent 64 to give Glamorgan a first innings lead, but the weather intervened on the second day and prevented them form securing the victory they needed and a place in the finals. After retiring from cricket, Ernie continued to be a leading figure in the shipbroking world and acted as Chairman of the Swansea Pilotage Authority, serving in this capacity from 1930 until his death in 1941.

20.
LETCHER, Harold *Bertie*

Born – Swansea, 4 June 1871
Died – Bermuda, 15 June 1942
Amateur
All-rounder
Ed – Wycliffe College and London University
1st XI: 1890-1898
Gentlemen of Glamorgan 1899
Clubs: Swansea, Cardiff, Swansea Tourists, Public School Nondescripts.
Rugby for Swansea

Batting and Fielding Record

M	I	NO	RUNS	AV	100	50	CT	ST
108	167	17	2357	15.71	1	10	63	-

Bowling Record

Balls	M	R	W	AV	5wI	10wM
3881	194	2260	102 (+3)	22.16	4	-

Career-bests
156 v South Wales CC at St Helen's, Swansea, 1895
7/66 v Monmouthshire at Cardiff Arms Park, 1891

Bertie Letcher was another homegrown youngster to make his Glamorgan debut in 1890. Like Ernie Jones, he had been schooled at Wycliffe College, but he was not as fortunate on his debut as his contemporary as he made a duck on his first appearance in the match against Monmouthshire at the Arms Park. However, Bertie met with more success opening the bowling and in this capacity, went on to claim over a hundred wickets for Glamorgan, and became a mainstay in the county's attack during the 1890s and 1900s.

His father, Richard, had been a member of the South Wales CC in addition to being a leading figure with Swansea Cricket and Football Club before moving to Cardiff to work for the Glamorganshire Banking Company where he rose to the position of Manager. Bertie inherited his father's love of ball games and flourished at Wycliffe, besides playing with great promise for the Swansea club and London University where he was captain of both the cricket and rugby teams.

After securing a post in Swansea as an insurance broker, Bertie played rugby and cricket for the town club, and regularly made himself available to play for Glamorgan. His brisk seam bowling was a very useful asset to the county side, especially as the Club's finances restricted the number of professional bowlers who could be hired. In July 1891 he took a career-best 7/66 against Monmouthshire at the Arms Park – the first of four five-wicket hauls he claimed during his county career.

Other highlights being 5/42 against Monmouthshire at Swansea in 1894, 5/10 against Herefordshire at Hereford in 1896, 5/45 against Worcestershire at Kidderminster in 1897.

He was also a very handy middle-order batsman and in 1895 he struck 156 against the South Wales CC at Swansea. It was his only hundred for Glamorgan and took full advantage of some gentle bowling by the veterans in a match designed to celebrate the close links between the two organizations. In all, Bertie struck ten half-centuries, including 72 against the MCC at Cardiff in 1896, 73 against Monmouthshire at Newport in 1897 and 75 against Devon at Exeter in 1907.

Bertie led Swansea CC in 1894 and 1895 before three years later moving to Cardiff and joining the town club. With his office based at Cardiff Docks, he also joined the Cardiff Exchange Club, based at the Coal Exchange in Mount Stuart Square and played for their cricket team in their friendlies against local clubs and gentlemen's teams such as the Earl of Plymouth's XI. Whilst based in Swansea, he had been good friends with the Bransby Williams family of Killay House so he frequently appeared for the Public Schools Nondescripts team who played matches in the grounds of the House.

He also joined the Glamorgan committee in 1895, and between 1904 and 1908 acted as assistant secretary to Jack Brain. Bertie moved to Northern Ireland shortly before the Great War having become the manager of an insurance brokerage based in Belfast. He died in 1941 whilst on holiday in Bermuda.

21.
GWYNN, *William Henry*

Born – Swansea, June 1856
Died – Bridgend, 1 April 1897
Amateur
All-rounder
Ed – St John's College, Battersea
1st XI: 1890
Captained Glamorgan in 1890
Clubs: Swansea Workingmen's Club, South Wales CC, Swansea
Rugby for Swansea and Wales (5 caps)
Brother of D Gwynn

Batting and Fielding Record

M	I	NO	RUNS	AV	100	50	CT	ST
2	5	0	72	14.40	-	-	-	-

Bowling Record

Balls	M	R	W	AV	5wI	10wM
165	15	70	3	23.33	-	-

Career-bests
27 v MCC at St Helen's, Swansea, 1890
2/24 v MCC at St Helen's, Swansea, 1890

Bill Gwynn played twice for Glamorgan during 1890 but the talented sportsman met with more fame, albeit very briefly, on the rugby field for Wales, and became the first paid

Secretary of the Welsh Rugby Union before suffering heart and mental problems prior to dying in the Bridgend Asylum at the age of 40.

Born in Swansea and raised in London, the young schoolmaster played cricket, football and rugby in the Home Counties before moving back to his home town during the late 1870s having secured a post at Swansea Parochial School (later National School). Bill duly became a shining light in the sporting activities with Swansea Workingmen's Club which had been created during the 1870s by Pascoe St Leger Grenfell, a prominent businessman and kindly benefactor towards sporting activities who lived in Kilvey.

Bill's batting and cunning off-spin saw the Workingmen's Club secure a series of victories against a number of high-profile and well-established cricket clubs. He switched allegiance to the Swansea club during the early 1880s, with his finest hour in their ranks coming in 1883 as the club won the South Wales Challenge Cup, with Bill's bowling played a key role in the victory over Cardiff.

These were the halcyon years of his sporting career as he captained the Swansea club in 1884/85 and 1885/86. During this time as a half-back, he became known as the first and most able advocates of the passing game. These skills led to five appearances for the Welsh side in the Home Nations Championships during 1884 and 1885 – in the match against Scotland in the former season, he nearly got his name on the scoresheet, but selflessly looked for support rather than touch the ball down having crossed the tryline.

Bill Gwynn, seen wearing his Welsh rugby cap.

In 1890 Bill was appointed captain of Swansea CC so it was quite fitting that his Glamorgan debut should come that summer at St Helen's against the MCC. After a decent score of 27 in the second innings, plus three wickets, he was chosen a month later for the match against Somerset at the Arms Park. He went wicketless against the West Country side, yet despite scores of 24 and 20, was never called up again.

During the early 1890s, he mixed his teaching duties with an administrative role with the Welsh Rugby Union, serving as its first paid secretary from 1892 and also acting as Wales' representative on the International Rugby Football Board. Sadly, he suffered a stroke in 1895 and initially suffered paralysis, preventing him from continuing his teaching duties. Early in 1897, his situation deteriorated as he suffered a mental breakdown. With his mind being deranged, he was taken to the Bridgend Asylum closer to where his brother David, a fellow Welsh rugby international and other family members lived. He died on 1 April with his funeral in Swansea being attended by the great and the good of sport in South Wales.

22.
SHEPHERD, Walter

Born – Swansea, 1863
Died – Swansea, 11 December 1908
Amateur
Batsman and wicket-keeper
1st XI: 1890
Clubs: Swansea, Swansea Tourists

Batting and Fielding Record

M	I	NO	RUNS	AV	100	50	CT	ST
1	2	1	6	6.00	-	-	-	-

Career-bests
6* v MCC at St Helen's, Swansea, 1890

Walter Shepherd, and his brother Edwin, were stalwart members of Swansea CC, with Walter being the club's first choice wicket-keeper from the mid-1880s until the mid-1890s.

With Dan Thissen, the Morriston wicket-keeper, unavailable for the match against the MCC at Swansea in June 1890, Walter was called up for his one and only appearance for Glamorgan. He was a schoolmaster by profession.

23.
MULLINS, Alfred Edward

Born – Chepstow, September 1858
Died – Tidenham, 30 November 1913
Amateur
All-rounder
Ed – Monmouth School
1st XI: 1890
Monmouthshire
Clubs – Chepstow, Tidenham

Batting and Fielding Record

M	I	NO	RUNS	AV	100	50	CT	ST
1	2	0	11	5.50	-	-	1	-

Bowling Record

Balls	M	R	W	AV	5wI	10wM
135	2	64	2	32.50	-	-

Career-bests
8 v MCC at St Helen's, Swansea, 1890
2/44 v MCC at St Helen's, Swansea, 1890

Alfred Mullins was a corn merchant and a very well-known figure in Monmouthshire society who lived at Yewberry House in Tidenham, a village to the east of Chepstow and

Alfred Mullins, in his schooldays.

on the southern flank of the Forest of Dean. A member of both Chepstow CC and Tidenham CC, the all-rounder played in the match at Piercefield Park in 1882 when a XXII of Chepstow and District defeated the United All-England XI, with Mullins gleefully claiming 4/24 as the professional side were dismissed for just 47.

Mullins played for Monmouthshire during the 1880s and made one appearance for Glamorgan in the match against the MCC at Swansea in June 1890. He continued to be a leading all-rounder with the Chepstow during the 1890s and helped them win the Monmouthshire Knockout Cup on several occasions. He was also renowned for always arriving at the club in a pony and trap which he had personally driven from Tidenham.

24.
DONNELLY, Charles William

Born – Basford , Nottinghamshire, December 1865
Died – Flanders, 9th May 1915
Professional
RHB, RFM
1st XI: 1890
Clubs: Hill's Plymouth

Batting and Fielding Record

M	I	NO	RUNS	AV	100	50	CT	ST
1	2	1	0*	-	-	-	-	-

Bowling Record

Balls	M	R	W	AV	5wI	10wM
23	1	13	1	13.00	-	-

Career-bests
0* v MCC at St Helen's, Swansea, 1890
1/13 v MCC at St Helen's, Swansea, 1890

Charles Donnelly played once for Glamorgan in 1890 – he was also amongst hundreds of Allied troops to be fatally poisoned by gas during the Great War on Flanders Fields .

Born in Nottingham in 1865 the seam bowler failed to secure a place on the Trent Bridge groundstaff before accepting a professional appointment with the thriving Hill's Plymouth club during the mid-1880s. These were heady years for the Merthyr-based club as they secured a permanent ground at Pentrebach on land owned by Crawshay Bailey, the owner of the Hill's Plymouth works. Acquiring Charles' services was another bonus, and his lively bowling brought success for the go-ahead club, as well as attracting the interests of the Glamorgan selectors.

Consequently, Charles was chosen for the two-day friendly against the MCC at Swansea, and after getting permission from the Works Manager to play in this prestigious fixture, Charles opened the bowling for the county side. However, he only took one wicket in the first innings and pulled a muscle which prevented him from bowling in the MCC's second innings, as the visitors completed a narrow three-wicket victory.

It proved to be his sole appearance for the Welsh county, but Charles continued to enjoy much success at club level with Hill's Plymouth in the Glamorgan League, created in 1897 for teams in the Taff and Rhondda valleys including Pontypridd, Pentre, Treherbert, Treorchy, Porth, Ynysybwl and Llwynypia. Charles proved to be one of the leading bowlers in the League and played in their representative eleven which met similar teams drawn from other leagues across South Wales.

In 1914 Charles switched from being a clerk at the Hill's Plymouth works to enlisting with the King's Royal Rifle Corps and by the time his battalion were in Flanders he had been promoted to company sergeant-major of the 2nd Battalion. Sadly, Charles lost his life on 9 May, 1915 during a gas attack during the Battle of Frezenberg.

25.
THOMAS, Samuel William

[Played under the nom-de-plume of "E Landers"]
Born – Swansea 1851
Died – Swansea, 7 August 1918
1st XI: 1890
2nd XI: 1892
Colts: 1869
Welsh Wanderers 1879
Clubs: Swansea, South Wales CC, Swansea Tourists CC

Batting and Fielding Record

M	I	NO	RUNS	AV	100	50	CT	ST
1	2	0	7	3.50	-	-	1	-

Career-bests
7 v Warwickshire at Cardiff Arms Park, 1890

Sam Thomas was one of the old guard of South Walian cricket who played for Glamorgan during their early years. In the case of the opening batsman from Swansea CC, Sam made one appearance at county level, against Warwickshire at the Arms Park in 1890.

His first major match had been almost a quarter of a century beforehand as during May 1869, he played at The Gnoll for a Colts XXII against Glamorganshire – the proto-county team which had been formed the year before by JTD Llewelyn following a meeting at The

Castle Hotel in Neath. The match was something of a showcase of the talent in the region, but Sam never won selection for the Glamorganshire team.

However, the batsman did play for the South Wales CC and the Welsh Wanderers, besides appearing for Swansea in their exhibition games against the United South of England at St Helen's in 1876 as well as the game the following year against the All-England Eleven. Sam made a decent 25 against the United South but was dismissed for a duck by WG Grace in the second innings.

Sam continued to be a prolific run-scorer for the Swansea club during the 1880s and his free-scoring efforts the top of the order saw them record several notable victories, especially in the South Wales Challenge Cup in 1883. He was past his best when

Sam Thomas.

he played for Glamorgan in 1890, making 0 and 7, but Sam continued to play a role behind the scenes in assessing emerging talent and in May 1892 led a Colts XXII against Glamorgan at St Helen's. His final match of note came three years later where he opened the batting for the South Wales CC when they met the county side at Swansea.

From the 1880s onwards, Sam played under the non-de-plume of 'E Landers'. Away from cricket he worked as a commercial traveler for an oil company and was a well-known breeder of poultry, who acted as a judge in national competitions.

26.
REID, Dr Edgar

Born – Swansea, 26 June 1865
Died – Swansea, 7 September 1924
Amateur
All-rounder
Ed – Lancaster GS, Swansea GS and Guy's Hospital, London
1st XI: 1890-1900
Club: Swansea
Rugby and hockey for Swansea and Guy's Hospital
Hockey for Wales

Batting and Fielding Record

M	I	NO	RUNS	AV	100	50	CT	ST
6	8	1	74	10.57	-	-	1	-

Bowling Record

Balls	M	R	W	AV	5wI	10wM
250	13	109	7	15.57	1	-

Career-bests
14 v Somerset at Cardiff Arms Park, 1890
5/39 v Warwickshire at Cardiff Arms Park, 1890

Edgar Reid was one of many sporting medics who played cricket for Glamorgan during the late Victorian and early Edwardian era. Born in Swansea, Edgar shone at the many sports staged near his home on the St Helen's Recreation Field, with the young surgeon representing his home town at cricket and hockey besides being a brave and skillful scrum-half for the rugby side.

Whilst training at Guy's Hospital, he won representative honours for cricket and hockey, besides winning a hockey cap for Wales. Cricket though was his favourite recreation and he would regularly pop down from his practice at 161 St Helen's Road to partake in net sessions or to play in matches.

This did however sometimes led to a few issues, such as the match in the South Wales Challenge Cup of 1886 against local rivals Morriston. Swansea had difficulty in raising a side and the game only began at noon after securing the services of three extra players, including Dr Reid. He was not out at lunch and popped back to his practice unaware that the timings for lunch had been reduced from forty-five minutes to thirty. Consequently, when play resumed without the good doctor, the Morriston wicket-keeper removed the bails of the unguarded wicket, and the umpire raised his finger to give Edgar 'timed out'. A furious row duly broke out between the two teams with the match abandoned with Swansea on 48-5.

Fortunately nothing as acrimonious occurred during Edgar's six appearances for Glamorgan, starting with the match against Warwickshire at the Arms Park in 1890 with his accurate seam bowling helping him return career-best figures of 5/39. He was able to play at the Arms Park a fortnight later against Somerset but, after the hiatus in the Challenge Cup match in 1886, he found it difficult to commit to playing on a regular basis in the two-day games. However, in August 1891 Edgar was able to travel to Exeter for the match against Devon, besides playing in the return fixture at St Helen's the following week, whilst in 1894 he secured time-off during late July and played at Lord's against the MCC.

Six years later, and after a decent series of performances for Swansea, Edgar was recalled to the Glamorgan line-up for the match against Northamptonshire at the Arms Park, but the game was ravaged by rain. By this time, golf had become Edgar's sporting passion, and together with several of his friends from the Swansea Cricket and Football Club, he was the founding Secretary of Pennard Golf Club in 1896. A measure of his golfing prowess can be gauged from the fact that two years later, Edgar was the runner-up in the Welsh Amateur Championships at Aberdovey.

His son John also played cricket and rugby for Swansea, but sadly was killed in West Flanders during August 1917 and is commemorated on the memorial plaque at the St Helen's ground. For his part, Edgar spent much of the war away from Swansea and acted as the chief surgeon at the Whitchurch Military Hospital in Cardiff, tending wounded soldiers who had returned by hospital train from the Western Front.

27.
JONES, Frederick Noah ('Freddie')

Born – Cardiff, April 1868
Died – Cardiff, 16 April 1918
Amateur
RHB, WK
1st XI: 1890-1893
Club: Cardiff
Brother of DE, JP and WP Jones

Batting and Fielding Record

M	I	NO	RUNS	AV	100	50	CT	ST
6	11	2	69	7.67	-	-	5	1

Career-bests
28 v Monmouthshire at Rodney Parade, Newport, 1890

Freddie Jones was the youngest son of Alderman Daniel Jones and, like his older brothers, he played cricket for both Cardiff and Glamorgan, besides playing a leading role in the legal life of the Welsh capital.

With first choice wicket-keeper, Dan Thissen unavailable for selection for Glamorgan during July and August 1890, Freddie played in five consecutive matches, starting

Freddie Jones.

with the contest against Somerset at the Arms Park. His neat glovework impressed and he was chosen for the next contest against Monmouthshire at Rodney Parade, plus the away games against Surrey at The Oval and the MCC at Lord's, as well as the match against Somerset at Bath on the journey back home to Wales.

Freddie re-appeared for Glamorgan against Monmouthshire in their away match in July 1893, besides keeping wicket a month later for the Cardiff and District side which met a scratch Glamorgan XI at the Arms Park. Whereas his elder brothers went into the construction trade, Freddie became a solicitor and shared a successful practice close to the Arms Park with William Yorath, his Cardiff and Glamorgan colleague. Freddie also acted as Deputy Coroner for Cardiff.

In his youth, Freddie had also played as a centre three-quarter for Cardiff RFC, whilst later in life he enjoyed lawn tennis and golf. Following a move to live at Bryn Rhos, Romilly Park, he also acted as secretary of Barry Golf Club. His son Kenneth Leslie Jones won the Military Cross whilst serving with the Welch Regiment during the Great War, but Freddie suffered from bouts of ill health during the War before suffering a fatal heart attack in April 1918 whilst working in his Cardiff office with William Yorath.

28.
ROONEY, Edward James ('Teddy')

Born – Shoreditch, October 1868
Died – East Glamorgan, 1945
Amateur
All-rounder
1st XI: 1890
Clubs: Cardiff, St Paul's, Taff Vale, MCC

Batting and Fielding Record

M	I	NO	RUNS	AV	100	50	CT	ST
2	4	0	19	4.75	-	-	1	-

Bowling Record

Balls	M	R	W	AV	5wI	10wM
90	3	44	3	14.67	-	-

Career-bests
11 v Somerset at Bath, 1890
2/23 v Monmouthshire at Rodney Parade, Newport, 1890

Teddy Rooney was the eldest of three brothers who played cricket for Cardiff and Glamorgan during the late Victorian era. Their father Samuel Rooney had been born in Barnet, Hertfordshire in 1841 to a family who had originally hailed from Ireland. Samuel was a surveyor and architect by training, who worked initially in the London area before moving to Cardiff in 1874. The Rooneys initially lived in the suburb of Canton, to the west of the town, before moving to Cathays – another suburb to the north – which had a thriving Irish community.

The rapid expansion of the town and docks of Cardiff meant that there was plenty of work for Samuel Rooney and his sons, with the family's business going from strength to strength. Much of the property development in the Cardiff suburbs was on a leasehold basis, allowing small builders and architects such as the Rooneys to operate on a successful basis, designing and building individual properties on a piecemeal basis. Samuel initially had small offices in the town centre in Queen Street and subsequently St Mary Street, before moving to a larger and more prestigious premises at Cefn Mably Chambers in Quay Street as his son's joined the family business.

The Chambers were a most convenient location for the Rooneys as they lay opposite Cardiff Arms Park where they played cricket in the summer and rugby in the winter. Teddy was a useful rugby player, playing initially for Canton Richmonds before appearing as a three-quarter for Cardiff 1st XV between 1889/90 and 1894/95. However, he met with more success playing for their 2nd XV, whom he captained in 1893/94 and 1894/95. No doubt, his links in the business world, as well as his talents with the oval ball, assisted his elevation to this position. He had many good friends in the rugby world, not least Gwyn Nicholls who married his sister and acted as assistant manager of the Grand Hotel opposite the Arms Park.

Teddy initially played cricket for the Taff Vale Club, who were based in Cathays, near his family's home. The all-rounder subsequently joined Cardiff CC and his prowess with both bat and ball for the town club led to his selection twice for Glamorgan during 1890 in their away matches against Monmouthshire and Somerset. He batted at number five on his debut in the match at Newport, before dropping down the order in the match at Lansdown CC's ground in Bath which resulted in a comfortable innings victory for the Somerset side. Despite decent performances in subsequent years for Cardiff CC, he was not chosen again.

Teddy was married in July 1892 and initially lived in the Cardiff suburbs of Canton and Roath, before moving to live in Hammersmith in London. They subsequently returned to South Wales in 1907 and lived in Rhoose in the Vale of Glamorgan, where Teddy and his wife ran the Kemeys Hotel.

29.
LEWIS, Robert Ajax
Born – Pontypridd, July 1868
Died – Ferryside, Carmarthenshire, 13 December 1913
Amateur
LHB, SLA
Ed – Christ College, Brecon
1st XI: 1890-1892
Clubs: South Wales CC, Cardiff, MCC
Step-brother of William Morgan

Batting and Fielding Record

M	I	NO	RUNS	AV	100	50	CT	ST
9	15	2	172	13.23	-	1	1	-

Bowling Record

Balls	M	R	W	AV	5wI	10wM
195	11	108	6	18.00	-	-

Career-bests
52 v Somersetat Bath, 1890
3/9 v Gloucestershire at Bristol, 1891

Robert Ajax Lewis was another member of the industrial bourgeoisie of the Rhondda Valleys to enjoy a short, but successful, cricketing career with Glamorgan during the 1890s

He was one of nine children born to Josiah Lewis of Ty'n-y-cymmer House in Llantrisant and was educated at Christ College, Brecon where he played in the school's XI between 1883 and 1886, showing great promise as a left-handed batsman and spin bowler. Indeed, it was whilst at school that Robert played in his first major match, albeit as a guest in the Worcestershire side who were playing the South Wales CC at Boughton Park. Having gone along with William Morgan, his step-brother, ostensibly to watch the game and enjoy the socializing, he ended up as a late substitute, and batted at number eleven in each innings.

In 1886 Robert made his debut for the South Wales CC and two years later, played alongside his step brother for Glamorgan in the trial match against Llwynypia. 1890 saw the young lawyer make his county debut, appearing against Monmouthshire at Rodney Parade, before joining William Morgan and the rest of the Glamorgan squad for their short tour to London, with games at Lord's and The Oval before playing Somerset at Coombe Park in Bath where his step-brother was in the process of buying property.

The game against the West Country side saw Robert record his one and only half-century for Glamorgan. He re-appeared for the county in four matches in 1891, including the fixtures at Lord's, Bristol and Exeter, and it was in the game away to Gloucestershire where Robert claimed career-best figures of 3/9 with his left-arm spin. His final game for the Welsh county came during May 1892 when he played against Wiltshire at Swindon, although the following season Robert played for the MCC on their three-match tour to Wales and the Marches, during which he played against Herefordshire and Monmouthshire as well as his former Glamorgan colleagues at Swansea.

Robert initially worked as a lawyer, besides serving on the Glamorgan committee from 1892 until 1895 when he moved to work in the City of London. Indeed, it was whilst living in Paddington that he heard of the tragic death of his brother Dr Ivor Ajax Lewis, who was the Medical Officer for Llantrisant and Porth. Ivor was also a noted fives player besides being a keen golfer and in April 1901 after enjoying a round at the Royal Porthcawl course, he had dined with a friend at the Cardiff and County Club but had a violent and fatal allergic reaction having eaten mussels soup.

A couple of years later, Robert and his wife left London and retired to Carmarthenshire, and they were living at Rock Cottage in Ferryside at the time of his death in December 1913.

30.
THOMAS, William Morgan
Born – Swansea, June 1857
Amateur
RHB, RM
1st XI: 1890
Clubs: Bridgend, Llwynypia, South Wales CC, Welsh Wanderers

Batting Record

M	I	NO	RUNS	AV	100	50	CT	ST
1	2	0	13	6.50	-	-	-	-

Bowling Record

Balls	M	R	W	AV	5wI	10wM
20	0	18	0	-	-	-

Career-bests
9 v Monmouthshire at Rodney Parade, Newport, 1890

A mining engineer by profession, William Thomas had a prolific record as a batsman for both the Llwynypia and Bridgend clubs during the 1880s and 1890s. Had it not been for his professional duties, he would have probably played many more times for Glamorgan with his sole appearance coming in 1890 as a late replacement for the match against Monmouthshire at Rodney Parade.

As a youngster, William had also been a member of the South Wales CC, as well as the Welsh Wanderers, and appeared in several of their games during the 1880s. However, several of his finest innings came later in his career, with one taking place at the age of 51 as William made an unbeaten 140 for Bridgend against the students of Llandovery College.

A view of the original pavilion at the Arms Park, as seen during the match when a combined Glamorgan and Wiltshire side played the 1902 Australians.

1891

Jack Brain, the former Gloucestershire batsman and member of the Cardiff brewing dynasty was appointed Glamorgan captain in 1891. Allied to his skills as a cricketer, he brought both business acumen and a greater element of professionalism to the affairs of the Club. He was also eager to introduce a fresh approach and young talent – this was reflected in the fixture list for his first summer in charge. Gone was the London tour, with August instead seeing home and away fixtures against Devon. There was also a trial match over the Whitsun Bank Holiday against a Colts team containing some of the rising talent in the region.

In addition, Jack used his contacts with Gloucestershire to arrange games at Bristol and the Arms Park against the West Country side, with the latter giving home supporters a chance to watch WG Grace in action against the local stars, and thereby swell the Club's coffers. Indeed, WG batted at number eight and made an unbeaten 34 with *The South Wales Daily News* describing how there was "a huge round of applause at the advent at the wicket of the champion batsman"

With more cash available, some new professionals made their bow, including Tom Burton who was attached to the Bridgend club. His waspish bowling made him a handful for the MCC batsmen at Lord's and with Welsh rugby international Billy Bancroft also making a half-century, Glamorgan recorded their first-ever victory on the hallowed turf at the St John's Wood ground. Several other Welsh rugby internationals appeared that summer, with the Brain brothers – Jack and

Jack Brain, as seen in 1891.

Sam – also persuading some of their talented friends from their student days at Oxford as well as others acquaintances to turn out despite no association with South Wales.

Besides introducing a number of fresh faces, Jack was also instrumental in the creation of a new image for the Club. In their previous games, the Glamorgan players had sported white caps with a red dragon motif, but through his influence this was changed to green caps with a red dragon, plus sweaters with a banding in these more Celtic colours.

31.
WILLIAMS, Jestyn

Born – Miskin Manor 14 April, 1867
Died – Duffryn, Neath 16 June, 1922
Amateur
Batsman
Ed – Charterhouse and Oxford University
1st XI: 1890-1893
Clubs: Fairwater, Miskin Manor

Batting Record

M	I	NO	RUNS	AV	100	50	CT	ST
5	8	-	41	5.17	-	-	1	-

Bowling Record

Balls	M	R	W	AV	5wI	10wM
30	1	15	0	-	-	-

Career-bests
16 v Somerset at Bath, 1890

Playing cricket and other sports with a Corinthian outlook was in the blood of Jestyn Williams, the second son of Judge Gwilym Williams of Miskin Manor who had been the first stipendiary magistrate for Pontypridd and the Rhondda. With his father having been a prominent early member of the South Wales CC and serving on the committee of the Glamorganshire club between 1874 and 1876, it was natural that Jestyn should also wield the willow with good effect..

Educated at Charterhouse and Oxford University, he also showed great prowess at association football, going on to win a Blue as a left-back for Oxford besides winning amateur caps for Wales.

After coming down, Jestyn briefly served with the Third Duke of Wellington's Regiment, before moving back to Miskin Manor and playing cricket for the Fairwater club.

Jestyn made his Glamorgan debut against Monmouthshire at Rodney Parade during August 1890, but bagged a pair. Nevertheless, he was included in the county's squad for the subsequent games in London against Surrey and the MCC, plus the game with Somerset at Bath on the journey home to South Wales.

He was chosen again by the Glamorgan selectors in 1891 for what proved to be a rain-affected contest with Devon at Swansea, whilst Jestyn also featured in 1893 in the trial match involving a Colts XXII as well as later in the season for the game with a Cardiff and District XI. However, he could not translate his form in club cricket for Fairwater or Miskin Manor into a sizeable innings for Glamorgan.

He met though with more success outside cricket, and after marrying the daughter of Joseph Moore-Gwyn, Jestyn became the Land and Mineral agent of Lord Treowen's estate at Llanover. During the early years of the Great War, he served as Quartermaster General with the Monmouthshire Regiment before becoming the Administrator of Works at

Chepstow and Portbury. Jestyn later became the Officer in charge of workshops at the War Pensions Hospital at Chepstow, and together with his wife lived at St Govan's.

32.
BRAIN, Joseph Hugh ('Jack')

Born – Kingswood, Bristol, 11 September 1863
Died – Bonvilston, 26 June 1914
Amateur
RHB, RM, occ WK
Ed – Clifton College and Oriel, Oxford
1st XI: 1891-1908
Captain: 1891-1908: Secretary 1893-1908
Gloucestershire 1883-1889, Oxford University 1884-1887 (Blue all four years), South Wales 1894, Combined Glamorgan and Wiltshire XI 1902.
Chairman of the Minor Counties Cricket Association 1896-1898
Clubs: Clifton, Fairwater, Cardiff, MCC
Brother of WH Brain and uncle of JHP Brain

Batting and Fielding Record

M	I	NO	RUNS	AV	100	50	CT	ST
145	225	17	5236	25.17	5	25	111	50

Bowling Record

Balls	M	R	W	AV	5wI	10wM
514	20	324	20 (+1)	16.20	3	-

Career-bests
144 v MCC at Lord's, 1896
6/62 v VT Hill's XI at Cardiff Arms Park, 1895

Jack Brain was the man who oversaw Glamorgan's elevation from the third-class ranks to a fully-fledged Minor County. During his time in charge of the Welsh county, the influential member of the Cardiff-based brewery drew heavily on his business and sporting contacts across South Wales – as well as further afield – to improve Glamorgan's financial position and their on-field performances, with the side being joint Champions in 1900 and before the Great War one of the strongest sides below first-class level.

It had been all very different back in the late 1880s when Jack first arrived to work in South Wales, with the Welsh county struggling on the field and several cynics wryly suggesting that the new county club would soon go the way of the old Glamorganshire side. Jack moved permanently across the Severn Estuary on a full-time basis during 1890, after completing his studies at Oxford and gaining a little experience in the business world, to oversee the running of the Old Brewery in Cardiff which his uncle, Samuel Arthur, himself an enthusiastic cricketer, had acquired in 1882 through marriage.

Jack had enjoyed a highly successful time at Oxford where, as a Freshman, he was in the XI that defeated the 1884 Australians and later that summer, he hit an attractive 108 for Gloucestershire against the tourists. Many believed Jack would succeed WG Grace as captain of the Gloucestershire side, but it was to Glamorgan that he subsequently devoted his efforts. He began by liaising with officials from top Welsh clubs, so that a Glamorgan Colts side could be raised. He also used his contacts in the west of England to arrange fund-raising games at the Arms Park, besides securing the services of talented amateur batsmen from Gloucestershire and Somerset. On several occasions Jack also dipped into his pockets to hire a couple of professionals, who in addition to playing for the county, could help coach the emerging talent, and work as labourers in the Old Brewery during the winter months.

With a stronger side taking the field, Glamorgan's results improved, with his side winning six of their nine games in 1892, including four successive victories during May and June. The better form also allowed Jack to secure a fixture with the 1894 South Africans – the Welsh county's first game against a touring side – whilst he was instrumental in the hiring of Billy Bancroft as the Club's first professional. The improved results allowed

Glamorgan to hire further paid players as the Club, through Jack's guidance, mounted a campaign to join the Minor County Championship. Jack– who made his maiden century for Glamorgan in 1896 with 114 against the MCC – served as Chairman of the Minor County Cricket Association between 1896 and 1898, and during his time as Chair, the MCC endorsed Glamorgan's application.

To Jack's delight Glamorgan were joint Minor County champions in 1900 – a summer when he was also in the runs with 88 against Surrey 2nd XI at The Oval plus 102 in the return match at the Arms Park. Glamorgan's success mirrored that of Brain's Brewery who in 1882 supplied just 11 pubs in the Cardiff area. By 1900 they either owned or leased 80, as output had increased from around 100 barrels a week to in excess of 1,000, with The Old Brewery becoming the largest in South Wales. In 1899/1900, Samuel Brain was also appointed Lord Mayor of Cardiff.

He also led Glamorgan's application during the autumn of 1904 to host the opening Test of the series against the

Jack Brain, seen in 1891.

58

1905 Australians. The decision went in favour of Trent Bridge by a single vote, but the MCC awarded a fixture to the Arms Park, with the Australians meeting a combined South Wales XI. It was a match, played under warm sunshine, watched by a crowd in excess of 10,000 on the opening day. Many of the visitors enjoyed the Brains ales, and Jack had a broad smile on his face as sales of his family's beer continued to soar.

Jack also met with plenty of success with the bat for Glamorgan. In 1900 he made a sublime 102 against Surrey 2nd XI at the Arms Park, followed the next year with 116 against the Public School Nomads at Swansea. In 1902 at Cardiff he posted 107 against Berkshire, whilst in 1907 at Exeter, he made 117 against Devon. This was a summer when Glamorgan, under Jack's leadership, won the western group in the Minor County Championship in 1907, before losing the final to Lancashire 2nd XI, despite a stubborn 80 from their captain.

Jack Brain, seen in 1902.

It proved to be his swansong as over the winter months, he went into semi-retirement and agreed only to play again in an emergency. This duly happened in 1908 when Glamorgan secured a semi-final tie with Wiltshire, but in the days leading up to the contest, his brother Sam, the Glamorgan wicket-keeper, was injured so Jack donned his brother's gloves and went behind the stumps during the match at Chippenham. Batting down the order, he made 26 in what proved to be his final innings for the Welsh county as they secured a place in the final against Staffordshire at Stoke-on-Trent.

Over the course of the next few years, Jack was delighted to maintain a watching brief as an energetic and influential committee member, as Glamorgan maintained their campaign for first-class recognition. The downswing in the local economy hindered their campaign for a while, but after the Great War, they duly secured a place in the County Championship. Sadly, Jack never lived to see the fruits of his labours, as in June 1914 he was taken gravely ill, and died after a short illness.

A host of tributes were paid to the man who had put Glamorgan cricket on the map, with the *Western Mail* summing up his immense contribution both on and off the field, by saying "his prowess at the wicket won him celebrity; his sportsmanship won him friendship; his generous patronage of the game won him gratitude."

33.
DONOVAN, Michael
Amateur
Batsman
Ed – University College, Cardiff
1st XI: 1891
Colts: 1893
Clubs: Neath, South Wales CC, UC Cardiff

Batting and Fielding Record

M	I	NO	RUNS	AV	100	50	CT	ST
4	8	0	21	3.00	-	-	1	-

Career-bests
17* v Colts XXII at Cardiff Arms Park, 1891

Michael Donovan had a decent record as a young batsman with Neath, and this led to his inclusion for the South Wales CC in their match against Worcestershire in 1885. He subsequently studied at University College Cardiff where he was a mainstay of the student team.

With Glamorgan looking to blood fresh talent, rather than relying on the old stagers, Michael's record for the university and Neath led to his inclusion in the county's side for four matches during 1891. However, he only scored four runs in three matches against county opposition, with his best performance coming during the second innings of the trial match against a Colts side at the Arms Park.

34.
HILDYARD, Rev. Lyonel d'Arcy
Born – Bury, 5 February 1861
Died – Hull, 22 April 1931
Amateur
RHB
Ed – St Edward's School, Birmingham and Magdalene College, Oxford
1st XI: 1891
Oxford University 1884-1886 (Blue); Somerset 1882-83; Lancashire 1884-1885

Batting and Fielding Record

	M	I	NO	RUNS	AV	100	50	CT	ST
Minor	1	2	0	4	2.00	-	-	1	-

Career-bests
4 v Gloucestershire at Cardiff Arms Park, 1891

Lyonel Hildyard was typical of the amateur cricketers with no direct connections with the area who, through the influence of Jack Brain, appeared sporadically for Glamorgan during the 1890s. In the case of the right-handed batsman, he had been a friend of Jack's at Oxford University, yet despite not having any residential qualifications, he played for the Welsh county in their friendly with Gloucestershire at the Arms Park in May 1891.

Lyonel had first played in county cricket for Somerset in 1882 before going up to Oxford and featuring in the university's team which defeated the 1884 Australians. The following summer, he topped the Oxford batting averages, and established a reputation as a first-rate fielder at cover and a safe catcher in the slips.

He was the third son of the Headmaster of Bury Grammar School and, given his links with Lancashire, had appeared for the Red Rose county in eight matches during 1884 and 1885 before graduating and being ordained into Holy Orders. Lyonel had initially been a schoolmaster at St Andrew's College in Chardstock, which led to his appearances for Somerset. Between 1894 and 1908 Lyonel was a minor canon of Windsor before becoming rector of Rowley. He remained here for the rest of his life with an oak portal being erected in the vestry to commemorae his contribution to the local community in East Yorkshire after his death in 1931.

Lyonel Hildyard, seen in 1891 when an undergraduate at Oxford.

35.
KINDERSLEY, Rev. Cyril Edwin
Born – Dorchester, 13 September 1865
Died – Clyffe Knowle, Dorset, 12 January 1938
Amateur
Batsman
Ed – Harrow and Trinity College, Cambridge
1st XI: 1891

Batting and Fielding Record

M	I	NO	RUNS	AV	100	50	CT	ST
1	2	0	0	-	-	-	-	-

Cyril Kindersley was another cricketing cleric, without any links with Glamorgan who played for the Welsh county in their friendly with Gloucestershire at the Arms Park in May 1891..

He had been in the Harrow XI in 1884 before going up to Cambridge where he became good friends with several Welsh sportsmen. After leaving Cambridge, he entered the clergy and served as curate of Rotherham from 1891 until 1893. Despite his duties in Yorkshire he played in the match with Gloucestershire at Cardiff in 1891. He failed to score in each innings and was never called up again.

He subsequently worked at the Harrow Mission from 1893 until 1895, before becoming vicar of Belvedere in Kent. Cyril then moved to Dorset where he served as vicar of Fleet, Sturminster Newton and Wimborne.

36.
BATTY, Rev. Arthur Montague ('Ambo')
Born – Kensington, 11 July 1868
Died – Hove, 26 December 1938
Ed- Haileybury and Oriel College, Oxford
RHB
Amateur
1st XI: 1891

Batting and Fielding Record

M	I	NO	RUNS	AV	100	50	CT	ST
1	2	1	9	9.00	-	-	-	-

Career-bests
Minor County 9* v Gloucestershire at Cardiff Arms Park, 1891

Ambo Batty, a former pupil of Haileybury College, was another vicar who played for Glamorgan against Gloucestershire at Cardiff in 1891, simply because he had been a theology student at Oriel College and was a good friend of Jack Brain.

A sound batsman and useful change bowler, Ambo played with some effect for Oriel, as well as for Walham Grove CC, and in 1889 was chosen in the London and Suburban

Cricket Association XI which played the MCC at Lord's in two one-day matches. In 1891 Glamorgan secured a plum fund-raising friendly with Gloucestershire, so Jack made contact with his old college chum to invite him to play against the West Country side at the Arms Park in what proved to be his sole appearance for the Welsh county.

The following year, Batty entered Holy Orders and subsequently became curate of various parishes in Yorkshire and Durham. Nevertheless, he still found plenty of time to play in local cricket in Northern England, before moving back to the Home Counties in 1911 where he served as rector of West Hackney, and then from 1919 rector of Chingford.

In 1918 and 1919 he played at Lord's for the Clergy against both the Australians and the

Ambo Batty.

Royal Artillery. He subsequently moved to Suffolk in 1924 where he became rector of Redgrave.

37.
MARTYN, Orlando Bridgman

Born – Brompton, Kensington, March 1855
Died – Exmouth, 10 December 1943
Amateur
Batsman
Ed – Cowbridge GS and Merton College, Oxford
1st XI: 1891
Clubs: MCC, Cardiff, South Wales CC, Welsh Etceteras, Wimbledon, Sidmouth, Incogniti
Solicitor
Elder brother of WE Martyn

Batting and Fielding Record

M	I	NO	RUNS	AV	100	50	CT	ST
1	2	0	15	7.50	-	-	-	-

12 v Gloucestershire at Cardiff Arms Park, 1891

Born in the London area, but raised in South Wales, Orlando Martyn was another batsman to play their one and only match for Glamorgan against Gloucestershire at the Arms Park in 1891.

Educated at Cowbridge Grammar School, Orlando had featured in matches for the South Wales CC since 1878 whilst associated with Cardiff CC. He moved to South Devon during the mid-1880s and, as an influential and well-connected member of Sidmouth CC, he oversaw the MCC tour of south-west England in 1888.

He retained his links with friends in South Wales and during 1891 accepted an invitation to play against Gloucestershire in the two-day game at the Arms Park. He proceeded to post an assured 12 in the first innings before being bowled by WG Grace and was one of the few Glamorgan players to appear comfortable in the face of the visiting bowling. The following year, Orlando struck a forthright 67 for the MCC against Glamorgan at the Arms Park, but was never called up again by the Welsh county's selectors.

38.
MIZEN, Charles Arthur
Born – Clifton, Bristol, December 1858
Died – Redland, Bristol, 1 February 1941
Amateur
All-rounder
1st XI: 1891
Club: Cardiff

Batting and Fielding Record

M	I	NO	RUNS	AV	100	50	CT	ST
2	4	0	33	8.25	-	-	-	-

Bowling Record

Balls	M	R	W	AV	5wI	10wM
25	1	15	0	-	-	-

Career-bests
12 v MCC at St Helen's, Swansea, 1891

Charles Mizen played twice in friendlies for Glamorgan during 1891 as the Welsh county's selectors sought out the home-grown talent that could benefit the Club in their ongoing development.

A member of Cardiff CC, the accountant made his debut against Gloucestershire at the Arms Park during May 1891 making 10 and 1, before appearing six weeks later in the game at Swansea against the MCC. He scored 10 and 12, but was not selected again.

39.
SWEET-ESCOTT, William Sidney Rice

Born – Bedford, 10 October 1867
Died – Penarth, 29 October 1926
Amateur
All-rounder
Ed – King Henry VIII, Coventry and Trinity College, Oxford
1st XI: 1891-1899
Club: Cardiff
Rugby for Cardiff
Brother of RB and ER Sweet-Escott

Batting Record

M	I	NO	RUNS	AV	100	50	CT	ST
42	58	12	627	13.63	-	1	20	-

Bowling Record

Balls	M	R	W	AV	5wI	10wM
2882	147	1599	74 (+1)	21.61	4	1

Career-bests
82v Monmouthshire at St Helen's, Swansea, 1894
7/41v Monmouthshire at Rodney Parade, Newport, 1892

Sidney Sweet-Escott was a member of the famous sporting family, closely linked with Penarth and, through marriage, he also became closely associated with the Brain brewing dynasty.

He was one of seventeen children fathered by Reverend William Sweet-Escott, the rector of Brompton Ralph, and his wife Louisa, who was the daughter of Lord Dynevor. Born at Carlton Rectory in Bedford, Sidney grew up in Somerset before the family moved to Penarth. After reading Law at Trinity College Oxford, Sidney entered the legal profession in Cardiff and was articled with Messrs Stephens, David and Co. who were based at the Bute Docks.

Sidney also played rugby and cricket for both the town club and Glamorgan, often alongside his brothers Ralph and Rhys. He duly became one of the mainstays of the Glamorgan side as the Club developed from being a third-class side into a fully-fledged

Sidney Sweet-Escott in his rugby kit.

65

Minor County. His brisk seam bowling proved an asset, most notably on his second appearance for Glamorgan in the trial game in 1891 against a Colts XXII at the Arms Park where his efforts with the ball outshone those of the paid professionals with the young solicitor taking 9/14. "His lively seam bowling proved to be a handful for the youngsters" was the view of one of the correspondents watching from the Press tent.

The following year, he took career-best figures of 7/41 in Monmouthshire's second innings of their match at Rodney Parade. The Uksiders were also on the receiving end of his best batting performance, as in the game at Swansea in 1894 he blasted 82, and all whilst batting at number nine.. It proved to be the one and only occasion when he scored fifty or more at county level, with his innings decorated by some lusty blows.

His final major match came in 1899 when he played for the Gentlemen of Glamorgan against their professional counterparts at the Arms Park. By this time, he had a young family having married, in 1895 Ethel Brain, the niece of his county captain Jack. Like so many of his generation however, Sidney and 'Barbie' were to lose their son, Lieutenant William Arthur who was killed in action in October 1918, just a month before the Armistice.

After retiring from playing cricket, Sidney took up golf and besides having a low handicap, he later acted as Treasurer of the Glamorganshire Club. Sidney had given up his solicitor's practice in 1906 to become a Director of Brain's Brewery. He later became the company's Chairman, holding the post from 1921 until his sudden death in October 1926 having contracted a particularly virulent form of influenza and dying within hours of taking to his bed.

40.
EVANS, *William H*

Amateur
Batsman
1st XI: 1891
Club: St Paul's

Batting and Fielding Record

M	I	NO	RUNS	AV	100	50	CT	ST
2	3	0	7	2.33	-	-	-	-

Career-bests
5 v Colts XX at Cardiff Arms Park, 1891

William Evans played for the St Paul's club in Cardiff and had a decent record as a batsman in local cricket. With Glamorgan seeking fresh, young talent he was included in the county's line-up for two friendlies at the Arms Park during May 1891, first against Gloucestershire and secondly against a Colts XX. William did little of note in either game and was not called up again.

41.
ELDRIDGE, Alfred George
Born – Greenwich, 21 November 1863
Died – Rotherham, 1934
Professional
RHB, RM
1st XI: 1891-1896
South Wales 1894; Wiltshire 1895-1898
Clubs: Swansea, Neath, Trowbridge, Accrington

Batting and Fielding Record

M	I	NO	RUNS	AV	100	50	CT	ST
21	32	8	183	7.63	-	-	3	-

Bowling Record

Balls	M	R	W	AV	5wI	10wM
3155	226	1507	108(+1)	13.95	12	3

Career-bests
32 v Monmouthshire at St Helen's, Swansea, 1894
8/43 v Wiltshire at Swindon, 1894

Alfred Eldridge had a relatively short, but highly successful career with Glamorgan during the 1890s with the seam bowler, who had the priceless knack of making the ball move both ways, taking over 100 wickets for the Welsh county, at a cost of just under 14 runs apiece.

On no less than a dozen occasions Alfred claimed five wickets or more in an innings, but there was nothing hinting this success in his first season with Glamorgan when the professional claimed just one wicket in two friendlies against Gloucestershire during 1891.

His rise into the county side followed a successful time with the Neath club. He switched to Swansea for 1892 before enjoying a stellar summer in 1893 with Glamorgan claiming, in all, 67 wickets. His haul included 15/48 in the trial match against a Colts XXII at the Arms Park, followed by 6/58 against the MCC at Swansea, 6/44 against Devon at Swansea and 7/13 against Monmouthshire at Newport.

1894 saw him top the 50-wicket mark again with five-wicket hauls against Wiltshire at the Arms Park, the MCC at Lord's and against Monmouthshire at both Swansea and Newport. However, his best – and perhaps most influential – return came in the end-of-season game at Swindon where he decimated the Wiltshire batting with returns of 8/43 and 7/48.

Glamorgan may have been the winners of this match by ten wickets, but they were also the losers as a few weeks later, the Trowbridge club offered a very lucrative deal for the seamer, resulting in his departure from South Wales to play for the English county during 1895.

There were uncertainties about his return to Wiltshire for 1896, so Alfred was included in the Glamorgan side for their opening match that summer against Surrey 2nd XI at

The Oval. For once, he went wicketless in the contest but soon afterwards secured a new contract with the Wiltshire club which saw him play for the next three summers in their ranks. July 1896 also saw him clean bowl all ten Monmouthshire batsmen in the second innings of their match at Usk as Alfred returned figures of 10/31 with Wiltshire winning by 96 runs.

His success with Wiltshire duly saw Alfred secure a professional contract with Accrington in the Lancashire Leagues for 1899. But it proved to be his final season as a player before he switched to the world of umpiring, standing in Minor County Championship matches 1900 and 1903. It was only a brief stay in the white coat, as he then moved back to the Home Counties where he became a house decorator and painter.

42.
STORER, George

Born – Bristol, 1873
Professional
Bowler
1st XI: 1891
Club: Cardiff

Batting and Fielding Record

M	I	NO	RUNS	AV	100	50	CT	ST
2	2	0	0	-	-	-	1	-

Bowling Record

O	M	R	W	AV	5wI	10wM
56	18	89	8	11.13	1	-

Career-best
7/25 v Colts XX at Cardiff Arms Park, 1891

George Storer was the professional bowler attached to the Cardiff club in 1891. The Bristolian played against his native county in the opening game of the summer at the Arms Park, but only took a single wicket. He then claimed seven wickets against the Colts XX three weeks later in the trial match at the same ground. However, the mason's labourer was never called up again by the county's selectors as other seam bowlers were given a chance to impress.

43.
LONG, John Peter

Born – Portsmouth, September 1861
Died – Surrey, September 1938
Batsman and spin bowler
1st XI: 1891-1893
Clubs: Swansea, Swansea Tourists CC

Batting and Fielding Record

M	I	NO	RUNS	AV	100	50	CT	ST
6	8	0	57	7.13	-	-	-	-

Bowling Record

Balls	M	R	W	AV	5wI	10wM
45	0	36	0	-	-	-

Career-bests
20 v Devon at Exeter, 1892

John Long had a decent record in club cricket for Swansea, yet his finest performances for Glamorgan ironically came outside Wales. The Swansea-based schoolmaster made his county debut during May 1891 in the friendly against Gloucestershire at the Arms Park, before bagging a pair against the MCC on his home soil at St Helen's.

John put this disappointment behind him and continued to be a steady run scorer in club cricket for Swansea. This lead to his selection in 1892 for the away game with Wiltshire at Swindon and Devon at Exeter, with the latter game seeing John making a composed 20. John re-appeared in 1893 against the MCC at Swansea, making 3 and 2, but this proved to be his final match of note. In contrast, his teaching career blossomed with John later becoming the Principal of Arnold College in Swansea.

44.
BURTON, Thomas

Born – Trowbridge, 1864
Professional
All-rounder
1st XI: 1891
MCC 1889-1890
Club: Bridgend

Batting and Fielding Record

M	I	NO	RUNS	AV	100	50	CT	ST
4	7	3	26	6.50	-	-	2	-

Bowling Record

Balls	M	R	W	AV	5wI	10wM
640	37	24	20	12.30	3	-

13 v MCC at Lord's, 1891
7/25 v Colts XXat Cardiff Arms Park, 1891

Tom was on the MCC groundstaff during 1889 and 1890, before securing a professional appointment with Bridgend for 1891 and 1892. His move to Wales saw the all-rounder appear in four games for Glamorgan during 1891, starting with the two-day friendly against Gloucestershire at the Arms Park during the first week of May. Tom took 5/68 on his debut, before claiming 7/25 in the trial game against a Colts XXII.

Later in August, the opening bowler returned figures of 5/63 in the first innings of the match against the MCC at Lord's before adding two more in the second innings. However, he went wicketless the following week during the match against Gloucestershire at Bristol – this proved to be Tom's final appearance for Glamorgan, and his omission was perhaps more to do with the modest terms offered by the Welsh county rather than a lack of form, as he continued to be a useful bowler for the Bridgend club in subsequent seasons.

45.
WALDRON, Arthur

Born – Llandaff, 7 July 1861
Died – Cardiff, 8 January 1947
Amateur
RHB, WK
Ed – Monkton House School, Cardiff and Magdalen College, Oxford
1st XI: 1891
Clubs: Fairwater, Cardiff, Water Rats.

Batting Record

M	I	NO	RUNS	AV	100	50	CT	ST
1	2	-	13	6.50	-	-	2	1

Career-bests
7 v Colts XX at Cardiff Arms Park, 1891

Arthur Waldron was another prominent figure in the legal world of Cardiff during the late Victorian and early Edwardian era who played county cricket for Glamorgan.

From the mid-1850s, his father Clement had acted as the Probate Registrar and Attorney for the town, working from his solicitors practice based in Church Street and living on Llandaff Green in The White House. It was here that Arthur was born in 1861 and after attending Monkton House School, he studied Law at Magdalene College, Oxford.

Arthur subsequently specialized in property law and, through friendships with Fred Insole of Ely Court and Edward Stock-Hill of Rookwood House, he built up an impressive list of clients. Arthur also became a leading figure in the affairs of Fairwater CC and, through his friendship with Jack Brain, he was invited to keep wicket for Glamorgan in their trial match against a Colts XX at the Arms Park in May 1891.

This proved to be his only appearance at county level, but Arthur continued to play with distinction for Fairwater and Cardiff, besides playing for the Water Rats – a team including many of the rugby-playing young sportsmen of the late Victorian era.

46.
EVANS, Sir David William

Born – Dowlais, 4 November 1866
Died – Cardiff, 17 March 1926
Amateur
Batsman
Ed – Llandovery College and Jesus College, Oxford
1st XI: 1891
Club – Cardiff
Rugby for Cardiff, Oxford University, London Welsh and Wales (5 caps)

Batting and Fielding Record

M	I	NO	RUNS	AV	100	50	CT	ST
2	2	0	8	4.00	-	-	-	-

Career-bests
6 v Colts XX at Cardiff Arms Park, 1891

Sir David Evans was one of the leading solicitors in Cardiff either side of the Great War, and in his youth he represented Wales at rugby, as well as making two appearances for Glamorgan during 1891.

Born in the Merthyr area during November 1866, his father was one of the prosperous merchants in the steel-making town. David attended Llandovery College where he shone both in the classroom as well as on the sports field. His cricketing and rugby-playing skills were subsequently honed at Oxford University where he read Law at Jesus College besides winning rugby Blues in 1887/88 and 1888/89.

He duly returned to South Wales to train as a solicitor, besides playing with distinction as a forward in the Cardiff rugby team. In 1889 David won the first of five Welsh caps, appearing that year against Ireland and Scotland, before being appointed the captain of Cardiff RFC for 1890/91 and 1891/92.

After some decent performances in club cricket for Cardiff, David appeared for Glamorgan against a Colts XX in the trial match at the Arms Park in May 1891. In August he was also chosen for the away match against Devon at Exeter. This proved to be his sole inter-county

David Evans.

71

appearance, with his burgeoning legal duties preventing him from committing to playing in any of the two-day games.

David subsequently acted as legal advisor to Kind Edward VII besides playing a leading role in the fight against tuberculosis. He also served as a member of council for the Cardiff Royal Infirmary and the Prince of Wales Hospital in Merthyr Tydfil. With his father having been a talented musician, David also held an interest in classical music and chaired the Cardiff Music Music Festival between 1902 and 1907.

His tireless efforts led to him being knighted in 1925 "for public service in Wales." However, David developed heart problems during December 1925 and suffered a stroke. He never fully recovered and died the following March.

47.
WATSON, Rev. Arthur Hawtrey

Born – Saltfleet-by-St Peters, Lincolnshire, 18 June 1865
Died – Norwich, 7 July 1952
Amateur
RHB, RM
Ed – Derby GS, Wells Theological College and Keble College, Oxford
1st XI: 1891
Lincolnshire 1889-1892; Suffolk 1904; Gentlemen of Warwickshire 1910-1912
Brother of WH Watson

Batting Record

M	I	NO	RUNS	AV	100	50	CT	ST
1	2	1	7	7.00	-	-	-	-

Bowling Record

Balls	M	R	W	AV	5wI	10wM
50	2	20	1	20.00	-	-

Career-bests
6* v Colts XX at Cardiff Arms Park, 1891
1/20 v Colts XX at Cardiff Arms Park, 1891

Arthur Watson, another cricket-playing cleric, was invited by his brother William to play in the trial match in May 1891 between Glamorgan and a Colts XX at the Arms Park. Even though Arthur had no residential qualification, he turned out for the Welsh county alongside his brother who was establishing a timber importing business in Cardiff. It proved to be Arthur's sole appearance for the Welsh county.

Born in Lincolnshire and educated at Derby Grammar School, Arthur played for Lincolnshire between 1889 and 1892, besides appearing for Suffolk in 1904 and the Gentlemen of Warwickshire between 1910 and 1912. He also represented Somerset at football between 1887 and 1888. Arthur subsequently held curacies in Worcestershire, Warwickshire and Buckinghamshire

48.
INGLEDEW, Hugh Murray

Born – Cardiff, 26 October 1865
Died – Cardiff, 1 February 1937
Amateur
All-rounder
Ed – St Edward's, Oxford and Merton College, Oxford
1st XI: 1891
Breconshire 1884
Club: Cardiff
Rugby for Cardiff, the Barbarians and Wales (3 caps)

Batting and Fielding Record

M	I	NO	RUNS	AV	100	50	CT	ST
5	8	0	114	14.25	-	-	-	-

Bowling Record

Balls	M	R	W	AV	5wI	10wM
105	2	73	2	36.50	-	-

Career-bests
20 v Monmouthshire at Rodney Parade, Newport, 1891
2/37 v Devon at Exeter, 1891

Hugh Ingledew was another prominent member of the legal community in South Wales who played sport to a high level during the late nineteenth and early twentieth centuries. The Cardiff-born solicitor played rugby for Wales and cricket for Glamorgan, besides being a founder member of the Barbarians rugby club, serving on the committee of Glamorgan CCC, acting as Honorary Treasurer of the Welsh county between 1904 and 1912, and then in the early 1920s, playing a leading role in the acquisition of the Arms Park by Cardiff Athletic Cub.

Hugh was born in Charles Street, part of the well-to-do inner suburb of mid-Victorian Cardiff, before growing up in Windsor Place, attending Monkhouse House School and playing his early sport on the Sophia Gardens Recreation Field, often with his solicitor father John Pybus Ingledew gleefully rolling up his sleeves to help the teaching staff with coaching rugby and cricket.

He subsequently went to Oxford, initially to attend St Edward's School, Oxford and then Merton College, where Hugh read Law and whilst

Hugh Ingledew.

in residence he had his first taste of county cricket as he guested for Breconshire in their two-day game against Monmouthshire at Rodney Parade, Newport in 1884.

After coming down, he moved back to Cardiff to continue his training as a solicitor at his father's practice based in the heart of the docklands at Mount Stuart Square, and adjacent to the Coal Exchange. Hugh continued his sporting activities by playing both rugby and cricket for Cardiff, making his debut at fly-half for the Cardiff 1st XV in 1887/88. Two seasons later he was chosen in the Welsh side with the young solicitor making his debut in the infamous match in 1890 away to Ireland – a game noted for the brawl between the two teams at the post-match dinner which saw nine players in court in Dublin the following morning.

Hugh also won caps in the 1891 Home Nations Championship against England and Scotland before later that summer making his debut in county cricket for Glamorgan. The all-rounder's first appearance came against the MCC at Swansea, and his capable batting, accurate spin bowling and agile fielding saw the young solicitor feature in four further games that summer.

1891 proved to be his only summer in Glamorgan's ranks but Hugh remained closely linked with the club, joining the committee in 1892, before taking over as Honorary Treasurer in 1904. He succeeded his father in the family's practice and with a specialism in railway law, Hugh became the solicitor for the Taff Vale Railway Company and was closely involved in many schemes as the company expanded their operations in South Wales.

In 1913 he oversaw the creation of the South Wales and Monmouthshire School of Mines at Treforest – later the Polytechnic of Wales and now the University of South Wales – with Hugh skillfully overseeing the negotiations with the major Welsh coal owners, especially the funding through a levy of one tenth of a penny on each ton of coal which the companies produced.

Together with his wife and children, he lived at Penhill House in Llandaff, overlooking the playing fields at the northern end of Cathedral Road, where the next generation of rugby players and cricketers honed their skills. They were indebted to Hugh for his tireless and diplomatic efforts during 1921 and 1922 in negotiating the acquisition from the Bute Estate of Cardiff Arms Park by Cardiff Athletic Club. His actions helped ensure the playing of county cricket and international rugby in the heart of the Welsh capital city – a fitting tribute for a man who epitomized the Corinthian values of healthy recreation.

49.
JONES, Rev. Owen
Born – Pontllanycharan, Aberystwyth 1860
Died – Llangan, Bridgend, 20 December 1923
Amateur
RHB, RFM
Ed – Llandovery College and Jesus College, Oxford
1st XI: 1891-1897
Breconshire 1884
Clubs: Welsh Wanderers, South Wales CC, Cadoxton, Cowbridge, Bridgend, Gentlemen of Surrey.

Batting and Fielding Record

M	I	NO	RUNS	AV	100	50	CT	ST
17	28	1	418	15.48	-	3	7	-

Bowling Record

Balls	M	R	W	AV	5wI	10wM
1065	43	647	26(+7)	24.88	1	-

Career-bests
79.v Monmouthshire at St Helen's, Swansea, 1892
5/34 v MCC at Lord's, 1894

Owen Jones was reputed to have been the fastest bowler in South Wales during the 1880s and 1890s. The former pupil of Llandovery College was also something of a feisty character and whilst at Jesus College, Oxford, during the late 1870s he was rusticated from the university after causing damage to a railway carriage and travelling in a first-class compartment whilst possessing a third-class ticket!

Owen was a stalwart member of the South Wales CC and played for the gentleman's side on several occasions before getting the call-up to play for the Welsh county in June

Rev. Owen Jones.

1891. His first appearance for Glamorgan saw him appear against the MCC at Swansea. He played again in 1892 in the two matches against Monmouthshire, at Swansea and Newport, posting a career-best 79 in the latter game at Rodney Parade.,

The following year, he made three further appearance for Glamorgan and in the match against Monmouthshire at Swansea Owen posted a combative 52 before returning career-best figures of 5/34 against the MCC at Lord's. Rev. Jones did not play for Glamorgan during 1895 or 1896, but appeared in four further games in 1897 but without any major effect.

He subsequently became a mainstay of the Cowbridge club. He was reputed to have been a man of great physical energy and tact, and frequently restored order in the Vale of Glamorgan town amongst the assorted local ruffians who quaffed in the town's public houses. His own favourite hostelry was The Duke of Wellington, kept by his great friend Arthur Spencer, and in subsequent years it was not unknown for this cricketing cleric to spend a quiet hour there while his team was batting!

Earlier in his career, Owen had taught at Abingdon GS and the Royal Medical College, Epsom before acting as the curate of Llansannor, Cowbridge. He was subsequently appointed to a curacy at Ganarew in Monmouth, allowing him to act as secretary of Monmouth CC.

50.
BOWEN, George Einon
Born – Swansea, June 1863
Died – Porthcawl, 13 January 1919
Amateur
RHB, RFM
1st XI: 1891-1892
Clubs: Morriston, Swansea
Rugby for Morriston, Swansea, Llanelli and Wales (2 caps)

Batting and Fielding Record

M	I	NO	RUNS	AV	100	50	CT	ST
4	6	0	42	7.00	-	-	-	-

Bowling Record

Balls	M	R	W	AV	5wI	10wM
55	2	20	1	20.00	-	-

Career-bests
17 v Monmouthshire at Cardiff Arms Park, 1891
1/0 v Colts XXI at St Helen's, Swansea, 1892

George Bowen was a multi-talented sportsman who, prior to playing county cricket for Glamorgan during the early 1890s, had played rugby with considerable success for Swansea and Wales during the late 1880s.

This was a period of great evolution in the oval-ball game, and George's prowess as a swift-running half-back won him selection in 1887 in the Welsh side that travelled to Edinburgh to play Scotland. The game ended in defeat but he retained his place in the line-up for the match later in the season against Ireland at the neutral venue of Birkenhead. The following season, George won two further caps – against Scotland at Newport, as well against Ireland in Dublin.

Whilst rugby was his stronger suit, George was still a good enough cricketer to win selection for the Glamorgan side. In club cricket, he was a fiery all-rounder, bowling sharp seamers as well as being a batsman who could use the long handle with some effect in the middle-order. However, George had little impact at county level in his four appearances with a sole wicket coming during a ten-ball spell against a Colts XXI at St Helen's.

George Bowen, on his debut for the Welsh rugby team.

After retiring from playing rugby and cricket, George joined the committee of the Welsh Rugby Union. He was also a decent golfer, playing for both the Ashburnham and Royal Porthcawl Clubs. George initially worked at the New Dock chemical works in Llanelli, before moving to a post at the tinplate factory at Morrison. This followed by another move to help manage the Ashburton Tinplate Works in Burry Port. In later life, Bowen was also the Mayor of Kidwelly.

51.
GEOGHEGAN, John Philip Arthur ('Jack')

Born – Colombo, Ceylon 1867
Died – Swansea, 11 April 1916
Professional 1891-1895
Amateur 1896-1901
All-rounder
Ed – St Charles' College and St Thomas' Hospital
1st XI: 1891-1901
Middlesex Colts
Clubs: Notting Hill, Whitehaven, Swansea, Swansea Tourists

Batting and Fielding Record

M	I	NO	RUNS	AV	100	50	CT	ST
13	20	5	236	15.73	-	2	5	-

Bowling Record

Balls	M	R	W	AV	5wI	10wM
170	11	82	6	13.67	-	-

Career-bests
82 v Cornwall at St Helen's, Swansea, 1898
4/57 v Monmouthshire at Rodney Parade, Newport, 1896

Born in Ceylon, and raised in London, Jack Geoghegan had a cosmopolitan background before making Swansea his home from 1889 onwards. During his time in South Wales he played with distinction for the Swansea club and made thirteen appearances for Glamorgan, initially as a professional and subsequently as an amateur.

Jack was educated at St Charles' College and played his first cricket of note for the Notting Hill club in London. His success for them led to his selection as an opening batsman for the Middlesex Colts during 1886 prior to a spell as a professional in Cumbria with Whitehaven. In 1889 he secured a position with the Swansea club and moved to South Wales.

In June 1891 he made his debut, as a professional, for Glamorgan in their match at St Helen's against the MCC. He made 7 and 9* and was not called up again by the Welsh county's selectors until July 1896 by which time he had become an amateur having become the steward of the Colonial Club in Swansea. His return to the Glamorgan side saw him meet with more success as he made 17 and took six wickets in the match against Monmouthshire at Newport.

In June 1898 Jack made a career-best 82 against Cornwall at St Helen's, but the following month saw him involved in an unfortunate spat with officials from the Swansea club, largely over his selection in the Glamorgan squad for their away match with Worcestershire. Having initially been chosen for the match at New Road, the list was subsequently altered which Jack believed was done so that he could play instead for Swansea at Llandovery.

Jack was deeply hurt by this petty-minded meddling by Swansea officials and refused to travel to Llandovery. It also reflected his desire to play at the highest level. Fortunately, matters were patched up with the all-rounder playing for Glamorgan in their subsequent Minor County matches that summer. He continued to play for the Welsh county until 1901, chiefly as a middle-order batsman, with his final appearance coming in a rather light-hearted game against the Public School Nondescripts at St Helen's in which he made an unbeaten 55 against the team raised by the Bransby Williams family of Killay House.

After retiring from playing, Jack became an umpire and stood in a number of games at St Helen's, besides becoming "mine host" of The Duke of Wellington Hotel. On the outbreak of the Great War, he worked with colleagues from the Swansea club in the recruitment of soldiers for the Western Front. Sadly, he had a stroke in 1915 from which he partially recovered, before suffering a second and fatal heart attack during April 1916.

Jack Geoghegan, seen in 1905.

52.
SWEET-ESCOTT, Ralph Bond

Born – Penkridge, 11 January 1869
Died – Germiston, South Africa, 10 November 1907
Amateur
All-rounder and occasional wicket-keeper
Ed – King Henry VIII School, Coventry and Peterhouse, Cambridge
1st XI: 1891-1897
Club: Cardiff
Rugby for Cardiff, Blackheath, Penarth and Wales (3 caps)

Batting and Fielding Record

M	I	NO	RUNS	AV	100	50	CT	ST
25	40	3	574	15.51	-	2	11	-

Bowling Record

Balls	M	R	W	AV	5wI	10wM
95	4	45	0	-	-	-

Career-bests
57 v Monmouthshire at Cardiff Arms Park, 1895

Ralph Sweet-Escott, the third son of the rector of Penarth, followed his brother Sidney into the Glamorgan side during 1891, with his first appearance against Monmouthshire at the Arms Park seeing the two young amateurs play side-by-side for the Welsh county. Like Sidney he also played rugby for Cardiff and won three Welsh caps between 1891 and 1895.

His prowess at half-back stemmed from a fine partnership for the Cardiff club with Hugh Ingledew. The pair were duly chosen in 1891 for the Home Nations match against Scotland, but Wales lost the game by seven tries to zero and it was not until 1894 that Ralph was called up again, this time against Ireland. It was a game which also ended in defeat but his appearance in 1895 against the men from the Emerald Isle saw the half-back finally end up on the winning side.

By this time, Ralph had also enjoyed a successful career with Glamorgan as a forceful batsman and occasional wicket-keeper. After honing his skills at King Henry VIII School in Coventry and Peterhouse, Cambridge, he played on a regular basis for Glamorgan in 1892 and 1893, before posting a maiden half-century against the 1894 South Africans at the Arms Park.

An image of Ralph Sweet-Escott wearing his Cardiff RFC jersey.

The following year he struck another half-century at the Cardiff ground, against Monmouthshire, before focusing his efforts on his career as an architect and surveyor, having been articled to work alongside John Price Jones – the man who had played a leading hand in the creation of Glamorgan CCC in 1888. Whilst working with Jones in Cardiff, Ralph also got married, besides becoming a founder member of the Barbarians RFC and playing lawn tennis to a high standard.

During the early 1900s he emigrated to South Africa and worked initially in East London as a mining engineer, before taking over the running of the Knights Deep Gold Mine in Germiston. Tragically, he contracted enteric fever during late October 1907 and died a fortnight later.

53.
LLEWELYN, Charles Leyshon Dillwyn ('Charlie')
(Later known as Charles Venables-Llewelyn)
Born – Ynysygerwn, 29 June 1870
Died – Newbridge-on-Wye, 24 June 1951
Amateur
Batsman
Ed – Eton College and Christ Church, Oxford
1st XI: 1891-1892
Club: Cadoxton
Son of JTD Llewelyn and brother of WD Llewelyn

Batting and Fielding Record

M	I	NO	RUNS	AV	100	50	CT	ST
2	3	0	4	1.33	-	-	1	-

Career-best
3 v Colts XXI at St Helen's, Swansea, 1892

Charlie Llewelyn, the youngest son of JTD Llewelyn, played twice for Glamorgan during the early 1890s before enjoying a career in politics and public service. Like his elder brother Willie, he was coached by Billy Bancroft in the grounds of his family's home at Penllergaer, before further honing his skills at Eton. Charlie also played for the Cadoxton club, alongside his brother and other leading figures in the political and sporting life of South Wales.

In August 1891 he appeared for the Welsh county against Monmouthshire at Rodney Parade – a game which Glamorgan won by

Charlie Venables Llewelyn – cricketer and politician.

an innings and 169 runs. Charlie's contribution however was a mere single. Nevertheless, he played again in May 1892 for the Glamorgan side against a Colts XXI at St Helen's, scoring 0 and 3, besides taking a catch. The match saw the county side win again, this time by the slender margin of two wickets, giving Charlie the distinction of never having lost whilst playing for the Welsh county.

In 1893 Charlie married the daughter of Richard Venables of Llysdinam, and besides acquiring the extensive estate near Llandrindod Wells, he also became known as Venables-Llewelyn.

Soon after, he entered local politics and subsequently became a Welsh Conservative MP, representing Radnorshire in the House of Commons during 1910. During the Great War, Charlie was an officer in the Royal Welch Fusiliers, before serving as both High Sheriff and Lord Lieutenant of Radnorshire. Between 1940 and 1946 he also acted as Chairman of Radnorshire County Council.

54.
BIGGS, Selwyn Hanam

Born – Cardiff, 2nd Quarter, 1872
Died – Weston-super-Mare, 12 January, 1943
Amateur
All-rounder
Ed – Cardiff College
1st XI: 1891-1900
South Wales 1894
Rugby for Cardiff, London Welsh, Bath, Somerset, Richmond, Barbarians and Wales (9 caps)
Clubs: Cardiff, Water Rats

Batting and Fielding Record

M	I	NO	RUNS	AV	100	50	CT	ST
30	48	12	483	13.41	-	-	22	-

Bowling Record

Balls	M	R	W	AV	5wI	10wM
3706	176	1968	107(+8)	18.39	7	2

Career-bests
47* v MCC at Cardiff Arms Park,1892
8/48 v MCC at Cardiff Arms Park, 1896

Selwyn Biggs was another member of the Cardiff brewing dynasty who played county cricket for Glamorgan and rugby for both Cardiff and Wales.

Whilst in his final year at school in Cardiff, Selwyn followed his elder brother Norman into the town's rugby team, before also winning a place in the Cardiff CC line-up, showing rich promise as a lively opening bowler. In 1891 the talented nineteen year-old made his debut for Glamorgan against the MCC in the august surroundings of Lord's, conceding just 26 runs in sixteen overs during the match.

Selwyn Bigggs in his Cardiff RFC kit and blazer.

For the next nine years, Selwyn played with much success as a bowler on a regular basis for the county side, claiming over a hundred wickets. For example, in 1892 he took 7/92 against Monmouthshire, before claiming ten wickets in the match against the same opponents the following year. His wicket-taking abilities also won him a place in the South Wales side that played EM Grace's Gloucestershire XI in a fund-raising fixture at the Arms Park in 1894.

Selwyn claimed another ten wicket haul in 1896 against the MCC at the Arms Park, including a career-best return of 8/48 from sixteen overs. By this time, he had completed his legal training and his work as a solicitor prevented him from playing regularly in the Minor County Championship from 1897.

However, he found time in the winter months, to train and play for Cardiff RFC and after some impressive performances at fly-half for the town club, he made his debut for Wales in 1895 against England. This was the first of nine caps which Selwyn won, in addition to captaining Cardiff RFC in 1897/98.

He also played rugby for Richmond, London Welsh, Bath, Somerset and the Barbarians, whilst after retiring from cricket, he also proved to be more than adept at golf. His sporting career and legal work though came to an abrupt end as he was badly gassed during the First World War in the Battle of Loos in 1915 and, sadly, Selwyn was an invalid for the rest of his life.

55.
YORATH, Dr Tom Hywel _Bruce_

Born – Cardiff, 9 September 1868
Died – Conwyl Elvet, Carms, 16 October 1943
Amateur
All-rounder
Ed – Guy's Hospital
1st XI: 1891-1895
Clubs: Llanelli, Canton, MCC
Brother of HWF Yorath

Batting Record

M	I	NO	RUNS	AV	100	50	CT	ST
6	10	3	106	15.14	-	-	3	-

Bowling Record

Balls	M	R	W	AV	5wI	10wM
20	0	21	0	-	-	-

Career-bests
29 v Devon at Exeter, 1892

Bruce Yorath was another cricketing medic who briefly appeared for Glamorgan during the early 1890s having enjoyed success with the Canton club.

The son of Thomas Vaughan Yorath, a town councilor, Alderman and chemist, Bruce followed his father into the medical world after training at Guy's Hospital. Whilst an undergraduate, he had his first taste of major cricket as he chosen during August 1889 as a late substitute in the MCC side against Glamorgan at the Arms Park. Bruce made 8 and 7 in the drawn game, but did not appear for the Welsh county for another two years

His decent record as a batsman in the Cardiff and District League eventually led to Bruce's selection for three Glamorgan games during 1891, starting with the match against the MCC at Lord's, followed by the games on their West Country tour against Gloucestershire at Bristol and Devon at Exeter. He visited the later ground again in 1892 on his sole appearance that summer for the Welsh county during which he made a career-best 29.

Bruce's medical duties prevented him from playing on a regular basis, but in 1894 he played again at Lord's in Glamorgan's match against the MCC before making his final county appearance the following year away to Herefordshire.

His father's business in Canton closed shortly afterwards, with Bruce then taking up a post in Abercarn before moving to Conwyl Elvet in Carmarthenshire where he became Medical Officer and Public Vaccinations Officer, based in a surgery in Pontyberem. His move west allowed him to play in club cricket for Llanelli and he lived at The Croft in Conwyl Elvet until his death in 1943.

56.
BRAIN, William Henry ('Sam')

Born – Clifton, 21 July, 1870
Died – Dinas Powis, 20 December 1934
Amateur
RHB, WK
Ed – Clifton College and Oriel, Oxford
1st XI: 1891-1907
Oxford University 1891-1893 (Blue all three years); Gloucestershire 1893, South Wales 1894,
MCC, Combined Glamorgan and Wiltshire XI 1902
Football blue
Father of JHP and MB Brain
Clubs: Cardiff, Fairwater, MCC

Batting and Fielding Record

M	I	NO	RUNS	AV	100	50	CT	ST
105	155	17	2257	16.36	2	4	122	118

Career-bests
113 v Monmouthshire at Rodney Parade, Newport, 1897

'Sam' Brain was Glamorgan's regular wicket-keeper in their early years in the Minor County Championship. He also held a unique record in first-class cricket when playing for Gloucestershire in 1893, by making three stumpings in consecutive deliveries as Charles Townsend completed a hat-trick against Somerset at Cheltenham College.

Like his older brother Jack, Sam was educated at Clifton College, before going up to Oxford and joining the family's brewing business in South Wales in the mid-1890's. Sam's competent wicket-keeping, coupled with his bold and uninhibited strokeplay in the middle order, secured him a regular place in the Glamorgan side from 1896. By the time he retired in 1908, Sam had amassed over 2,000 runs in his career for Glamorgan, plus 240 dismissals. The fact that Sam had almost as many stumpings than catches to his name spoke volumes for his deft glovework and agility as a wicket-keeper.

In June 1897 Sam also struck one of the fastest centuries in Glamorgan's history during the match against Monmouthshire at Newport, with the wicket-keeper reaching three-figures in just 53 minutes. His whirlwind hitting came on the second and final day of the game at the Rodney Parade ground after the home side had avoided following-on in the pre-lunch session. With a first innings lead of 59, the instructions from his brother Jack, the Glamorgan captain, were for quick runs to set up the prospect of a run chase in the final session. By

Sam Brain during his days as a undergraduate at Oxford.

lunch, Glamorgan had slipped to 62-4, and soon after the interval, they lost a fifth wicket. The tempo of the innings then changed with an astonishing stand of 123 in just forty minutes by Sam in partnership with Bertie Letcher. Sam was quickly into his stride with a series of powerful drives as he followed what his elder brother had requested by racing to his fifty with a brace of fours against Foster Stedman, the home side's captain. Sam added three more strongly struck fours in Stedman's next over, whilst at the other end Bertie also swung lustily as the ball disappeared to all parts of the Newport ground.

With Glamorgan now having a quite healthy lead, many felt that Jack Brain would declare, with the correspondent of the *South Wales Daily News* writing "it was thought likely now that every moment would see the visiting captain declare, but runs continued to come with greater freedom than at any period of the match."

Perhaps Jack was enjoying too much his brother's massive blows, one of which went high over the rugby grandstand and into the adjoining road. Stedman then bowled Letcher as he advanced down the wicket, but Owen Jones joined Sam who, soon afterwards, completed his century after a mere 43 minutes at the crease.

Once again, many thought this would prompt the declaration but Sam carried on and hit another trio of lusty fours, before Stedman, who had become quite frustrated by the situation asked Tom Mayes, the Monmouthshire wicket-keeper to take off his pads and come on to bowl. It was meant as a measure of disgust, but it brought about the end of Sam's whirlwind innings as he tamely chipped a ball back to his counterpart, and walked off having struck a six, 19 fours, 3 threes and 7 twos in an explosive 53 minutes at the crease.

Sam Brain seen in natty headgear in 1902.

His efforts failed to see Glamorgan to victory, as after being set a target of 308 in 144 minutes, the Welsh county's bowlers claimed a brace of early victories before, with an hour to go, the heavens opened causing the match to be abandoned as a draw.

Sam also served on the Glamorgan committee from 1901, until his increasing business commitments forced his retirement from the Minor County side. He was subsequently appointed Chairman of Brains Brewery in 1914, but continued to play club cricket for Cardiff and the MCC, and he led the family's business until his death in 1934.

He also took great delight in the way two of his sons – Michael and Pat – both kept wicket in first-class cricket for the Welsh county. Michael made one appearance against Oxford University in 1930, whilst Pat appeared in six matches between 1921 and 1928, and like his father and uncle, was always ready to help out the county whenever they were short of players.

57.
JONES, Rees Gabe (later Rees GABE-JONES)

Born – Vaenor, Breconshire, 7 November 1871
Died – Clydach Vale, 9 November 1927
RHB, RFM
Ed – Llandovery College, Blundell's School and London University
1st XI: 1891-1893
Colts: 1891
Clubs: Cardiff, Clydach Vale, Morriston
Rugby for London Welsh
Father of AR Gabe-Jones

Batting and Fielding Record

M	I	NO	RUNS	AV	100	50	CT	ST
4	5	2	21	7.00	-	-	1	-

Bowling Record

Balls	M	R	W	AV	5wI	10wM
365	29	137	17 (+1)	8.06	1	-

Career-bests
17* v Herefordshire at Hereford, 1893
5/42 v Monmouthshire at Rodney Parade, Newport, 1891

Dr Rees Gabe-Jones was a prominent sportsman and doctor in the Rhondda Valley who played a handful of games for Glamorgan during the early 1890s.

His sporting prowess began at Llandovery College and latterly Blundell's School in Devon, where Rees shone at both cricket and rugby, with the Breconshire-born youngster further honing his sporting and medical skills whilst studying in London. Indeed, his time in the English capital saw him make his rugby debut for London Welsh.

His prowess as a fast-medium bowler, both at school and university, saw him chosen to open the bowling for a Colts XX which met the Glamorgan side in a trial match at the Arms Park in May 1891. He claimed 3/25 from 20 impressive overs, with one of his victims being former Glamorgan captain Edmund David. Further decent performances for the Morriston club saw the young doctor make his debut later in August, against Devon at Exeter, before returning the very impressive figures of 4/5 and 5/42 in the following match against Monmouthshire at Rodney Parade.

A newspaper image of Dr Rees Gabe-Jones.

Rees' medical studies restricted him to just two further appearances in the county side – in May 1892 against Wiltshire at Swindon and in June 1893 away to Herefordshire. In both cases, he performed with credit, and left Jack Brain wishing he was available on a more frequent basis. Rees subsequently joined medical practices in Pentre and Tonypandy, before setting up his own in Clydach Vale. He continued to play, when he was free, for the local cricket team but his sporting activities were curtailed after an accident in November 1902 when he fractured his skull after being thrown from his horse whilst visiting a patient. He lay unconscious in hospital for three days, but recovered from the incident.

He subsequently enjoyed swimming and during June 1910 became a founding member of the Rhondda Golf Club. His son Royston Gabe-Jones played for Glamorgan at the age of fifteen in 1922.

58.
NICHOLL, Louis Dillwyn

Born – Merthyr Mawr, 25 September 1864
Died – Shipston-on-Stour, 5 January 1956
Amateur
All-rounder
Ed – Clifton College and RAC Cirencester
1st XI: 1891-1893
Clubs: Swansea, Bridgend
Brother of JID Nicholl and son of JC Nicholl

Batting and Fielding Record

M	I	NO	RUNS	AV	100	50	CT	ST
6	8	1	217	31.00	-	1	3	-

Bowling Record

Balls	M	R	W	AV	5wI	10wM
5	0	6	1	6.00	-	-

Career-bests
91 v Monmouthshire at Rodney Parade, Newport, 1891
1/6 v MCC at Lord's, 1892

Louis Nicholl was a member of one of the most important sporting and political families in the Vale of Glamorgan. His father John Illtyd Nicholl had been the Conservative MP for Cardiff between 1832 and 1852 besides serving as High Sheriff of Glamorgan in 1884 and lived at the family's home, Merthyr Mawr House, three miles to the south of Bridgend.

Merthyr Mawr was the venue for several of the early county games staged by the Glamorganshire club in which John Illtyd Nicholl was a highly interested party. His son John Cole Nicholl also played in these games during the late 1860s, and with cricket in the family's blood, it was no surprise that his grandsons Louis Dillwyn and John Illtyd Dillwyn should each play for the Glamorgan side during the 1890s.

In all, Louis played six times, and came within nine runs of making a century on debut as he made an excellent 91 against Monmouthshire at Newport in August 1891. Educated at Clifton College and the Royal Agricultural College in Cirencester, his call-up into the county side stemmed from some good performances initially for the Bridgend club, and subsequently for Swansea following his move to live at Hendrefoilan House in Sketty.

He never passed fifty again in his five subsequent matches, although he did make 45 against the MCC at Lord's in 1892. His final appearance for the county came during the visit to Lord's in the following year, and he subsequently acted as a land agent.

59.
BANCROFT, William (junior)
Born – Bury St Edmunds, March 1848
Died – Swansea, 26th April 1906
RHB, RM
Professional
1st XI: 1864-1870, 1891-1892
Clubs: Swansea, Cadoxton, Settle, Dunfermline, and Merchiston Castle
South Wales CC 1874-1886, Radnorshire 1869-1872, Welsh Wanderers 1863-1867,
Breconshire 1872, Players of South Wales 1867-1881, West of South Wales 1883

Batting and Fielding Record

M	I	NO	RUNS	AV	100	50	CT	ST
2	2	-	11	5.50	-	-	-	-

Career-bests
11 v Colts XXII at St Helen's, Swansea, 1892

The son of William Bancroft (senior), he continued the good name of the family in cricketing circles in South Wales. His formative years were spent at the Bryn-y-Mor ground, playing for the Swansea Colts team, and the town's 1st XI, in addition to being coached by his doting father who took great pleasure in passing on tips to his enthusiastic son who showed rich promise – so much so, that he was chosen as a sixteen-year old to play for the Glamorganshire side against Carmarthenshire at Neath in 1864.

Any nerves that William may have had were quelled by the presence of his father in the county side, along with several others from the Swansea club, including JTD Llewelyn, with young Bancroft opening the batting with the Squire of Penllergaer who was to play a major role in his adult life. During his teens, William appeared in several showpiece matches, including Swansea's game against the United All England in 1866 at Brunswick Court, followed two years later by their match at the Bryn-y-Mor ground in the Uplands district against the Australian Aborigines as well guesting, through Llewelyn's influence, for Cadoxton against the United South of England.

1868 also saw William score his first half-century at county level with 51 against Breconshire, whilst the following summer he showed his prowess with the ball by taking 11 wickets against Radnorshire. A bright future was being forecast for the young professional but, with his father still employed by the Swansea club, William accepted lucrative offers to act as a professional in Northern England and Scotland. During the course of the next few years he therefore played for Settle, Dunfermline, and Merchiston Castle, besides appearing for the South Wales CC on their annual visits to London in addition to coaching at Rathway College in Oxford.

In 1875 William returned to Swansea and succeeded his father as the Swansea professional, in addition to acting as private coach to the Llewelyn family at Penllergaer.

The following summer, he played with credit for the Swansea club in their games at St Helen's against the United South of England. The following summer, he performed with credit at the Swansea ground against the All-England Eleven.

Many regard William Bancroft was the finest home-grown all-rounder in South Wales cricket at the time and it was a shame that the winding-up of the Glamorganshire club prevented him from regularly playing at county level during the years when he was at his peak. By the time a new county club had been created in 1888, his skills as a batsman were on the wane.

Nevertheless, he was still a canny bowler and a fine coach, with several of his colleagues

William Bancroft junior – the first leading cricket professional in South Wales and the man responsible for laying out the St Helen's ground at Swansea.

from the Swansea club, including his son Billy and Willie Llewelyn playing for the county side. In 1891, the latter took his life in the grounds of his family's home – he had been due to play the following day for Glamorgan against Devon at Swansea, and with several amateurs unable to play at such short notice, it was William Bancroft who came into the county side as a late replacement alongside Billy. However, the veteran never got onto the field as rain washed out play after just a handful of overs in Glamorgan's 1st innings.

The following year, William and Billy managed to take the field together for Glamorgan at Swansea – and in much more happier circumstances – as the county played a Colts team, several of whom had also benefited from William's wise words in the nets at the St Helen's ground.

60.
DOWNEY, Jenkin ('Shenkin')

Born – Neath, January 1856
Died – Neath, 10 October 1938
Professional
RHB, RM/OB
1st XI: 1891
Clubs: Neath, Llwynypia, Brecon

Batting and Fielding Record

M	I	NO	RUNS	AV	100	50	CT	ST
1	-	-	-	-	-	-	-	-

Shenkin Downey, who enjoyed a long career as a professional in club cricket in the Neath area, had the misfortune never to take to the field on the one occasion when he was chosen by the Glamorgan selectors. His call-up came in late August 1891 but after Glamorgan had opted to bat first against Devon at Swansea, the game was washed out with the county on 44-2 and Shenkin yet to appear.

He had first played for Llwynypia whilst working as a collier, before securing a post at the tin plate works in Neath and playing for the town club. His penchant for hard work was not dimmed by his work in the local factory, with Shenkin often opening the bowling before switching to cutters as the shine wore off.

His final match of note came in June 1920, when at the age of 54, he appeared for the Players of Glamorgan against the Gentlemen of the county, fittingly on his home turf at The Gnoll in Neath. Shenkin also had a brief spell as cricket coach at Christ College, Brecon, besides playing as a professional for the town club.

His son Stanley was killed in the Great War during November 1918, just six days before the Armistice, after being hit by a sniper's bullet whilst serving with The King's Liverpool Regiment.

Shenkin Downey.

Action from a rugby match at St Helens in 1903 with the pavilion , belonging to Swansea Cricket and Football Club, clearly visible in the background.

1892

1892 was Glamorgan's most successful season to date with the Club winning six of their nine fixtures, including home and away victories over Monmouthshire as well as a two-wicket success against a Colts team at St Helen's with the narrow margin of victory at the Swansea ground being testament to the bowling skills of young professional Tom Hordley.

The youngster went on to feature in the 1st XI soon after and returned figures of 15-10-19-4 in the victory against the MCC at the Arms Park. He didn't feature in the victory later in August over the MCC at Lord's, a match which saw veteran all-rounder William Morgan claim thirteen wickets, but his presence in the paid ranks made up for the non-appearance of two others whom the Glamorgan selectors had attempted to hire. Indeed, one of the items at the top of the committee's agenda had been acquiring a professional bowler, with JP Jones offering to assist with the associated costs, providing the successful candidate played for the Cardiff club.

George Porter, the Derbyshire fast-medium bowler was interviewed but he demanded winter employment, preferably in a public house! Despite their close link with Brains Brewery, the Club failed to agree terms with the Peakite. At first, there appeared better news in discussions with Sam Moss, a fiery bowler who was born in Lancashire. He had a decent track record for the Hill's Plymouth club in Merthyr and after taking fifteen wickets at a cost of just ten runs against the Colts team, a position was agreed with Cardiff. But his success alerted his native county and Sam duly returned north in the hope of joining the Lancashire staff.

61.
GAGE, Henry Frederick ('Harry')

Born – Abbots Leigh, Bristol 1861
Died – Radyr, Cardiff, 12 October 1906
Amateur
All-rounder
1st XI: 1892-1893
Somerset Colts 1882
Clubs: Long Ashton, Swansea, Penarth, Pontypridd

Batting and Fielding Record

M	I	NO	RUNS	AV	100	50	CT	ST
3	4	1	52	17.33	-	-	1	-

Bowling Record

Balls	M	R	W	AV	5wI	10wM
115	4	59	10	5.90	1	-

Career-bests
32 v Monmouthshire at St Helen's, Swansea, 1892
5/23 v Colts XXI at St Helen's, Swansea, 1892

Harry Gage was another member of the mercantile elite of South Wales – with no birthplace or family association with the region – who found time to mix business with pleasure by playing county cricket for Glamorgan.

Born into a farming family in South Bristol, the all-rounder first made a name for himself playing for the Long Ashton club and winning a place in the Somerset Colts team of 1882. Harry plus his wife and young family moved to Swansea in 1889 where, together with his younger brother Frank, they set up a tobacconist's business.

Harry joined the Swansea Cricket and Football Club, and after some decent performances, he was chosen in May 1892 to play at the St Helen's ground for Glamorgan in their trial match against a Colts XXI. Batting at number four, he scored 17 and 9, besides returning figures of 10-2-23-5 in the Colts first innings. He added three more

wickets with his seamers in their second innings and in July played at St Helen's once again for Glamorgan in the two-day game against Monmouthshire. He made a steady 32 in the first innings and claimed a couple of wickets during a nine-over spell.

His business commitments meant that he only made one further appearance at county level, in 1893 in the match at Exeter against Devon. Harry and his family subsequently moved to live in Stanwell Road in Penarth having opened a new tobacconists shop and cigar dealership in the well-to-do resort. The success of the business saw them later move to Radyr, another bijou suburb, besides opening a new branch of the business in Pontypridd, for whom Harry also played cricket.

Harry Gage.

He was also a useful golfer and was a member of Radyr Golf Cub. However, in 1905 his wife Margaret suddenly died and the following year, he also passed away. having contracted pneumonia, with many of his close friends saying that he had never really recovered from the loss of his beloved wife.

62.
MOSS, Samuel

Born – Salford, 1867
Died – Featherstone, 7 August 1923
Professional
RHB, RFM
1st XI: 1892
Staffordshire 1897-1900, Lancashire 2nd XI 1894
Clubs: Newcastle-upon-Tyne, Cardiff, Hill's Plymouth, Bacup, Padiham, Haslingden,
Barnsley, Batley, Burslem, Walsall
Father of SE Moss

Batting and Fielding Record

M	I	NO	RUNS	AV	100	50	CT	ST
1	1	0	2	2.00	-	-	-	-

Bowling Record

Balls	M	R	W	AV	5wI	10wM
92	10	10	15	0.67	1	1

Career-bests
2 v Colts XXI at St Helen's, Swansea, 1892
11/8 v Colts XXI at St Helen's, Swansea, 1892

Sam Moss was typical of the journeymen professionals who enjoyed a brief career with Glamorgan in the Club's early years, but whereas many played for the Welsh county late in their career, it was Sam's youthful and energetic performances in South Wales which first brought him to the public's attention.

Born in Salford, and raised in the Manchester area, he secured a position with the Hill's Plymouth club in Merthyr for 1890 and during the next two years, he proved to be amongst the fastest bowlers in the club cricket. His success resulted in his selection in 1892 for Glamorgan against a Colts XXI at Swansea. He took 11/8 in their first innings and 4/2 a second time around, with his success soon coming to the attention of the Lancashire officials.

The following year saw Sam play for the Bury and Enfield clubs, besides appearances in the Lancashire Club and Ground side, plus the 2nd XI team run by Lancashire. However, there were a few who questioned his action and in the match in 1894 against Surrey 2nd XI he was called for throwing. With doubts over his action, Lancashire did not offer him terms and he subsequently secured professional appointments with Newcastle-upon-Tyne in 1895, Haslingden in 1896, and Bacup between 1897 and 1900,

He also played for Staffordshire between 1897 amd 1900, but in the latter season was called again for throwing in a match for Bacup in 1900. Despite the stigma attached to being called, Sam subsequently secured positions from the early 1900s onwards at Barnsley, Batley, Burslem, and Walsall, before playing his final years with the Padiham club. He retired from playing after the Great War and retained a keen interest in cricket. Tragically, in 1923 Sam was killed whilst walking along a railway line in the Featherstone area to watch a game.

63.
DONOVAN, John ("Johnny")
Born – Cardiff, December 1859
Died – Penarth, 20 April 1921
Professional
RHB, OB
1st XI: 1892-1895
South Wales 1894
Clubs: Cardiff, Taff Vale, Tynant, Garth

Batting and Fielding Record

M	I	NO	RUNS	AV	100	50	CT	ST
9	15	2	236	18.15	-	1	2	-

Bowling Record

Balls	M	R	W	AV	5wI	10wM
15	0	17	0	-	-	-

Career-bests
98* v Monmouthshire at Rodney Parade, Newport, 1892

Johnny Donovan was the popular professional with Cardiff CC between 1883 and 1895 who played in nine matches for Glamorgan between 1892 and 1895.

His first major matches came in 1883 after some decent performances for the Cardiff club. The 24 year-old right-handed batsman and spin bowler was chosen in the South Wales CC's team for their matches against the MCC and the Bryn-y-Neuadd club in North Wales. The following year Johnny was the South Wales club's professional for their London tour, whilst in 1885 he represented the Club against the MCC at the Arms Park.

Johnny's somewhat belated call-up to the Glamorgan side came in 1892 and, as if to prove a point, he struck an unbeaten 98 in his second appearance during the game against Monmouthshire at Newport. He was only chosen

Johnny Donovan, who in addition to playing for Glamorgan, assisted a number of clubs in the Cardiff area as well as the Taff Valley.

once in 1893, before being chosen as an opening batsman in Glamorgan's game against the South Africans at the Arms Park in June 1894. He again showed his talents as a batsman, making a composed 33 in the first innings. In July he also featured in a South Wales XI which met EM Grace's Gloucestershire's XI in a fund-raising game at the Arms Park in aid of the Albion Colliery Disaster Fund.

His infrequent appearances at county level and his fine record for Cardiff, hints at the fact that the financial terms offered by Glamorgan were insufficient to secure his regular services. Donovan also coached the Tynant club at Radyr, north of Cardiff, in 1894 and 1895.

64.
HORDLEY, Edward Thomas ('Tom')

Born – Cannock Chase, 24 April 1875
Died – Foleshill, Coventry, September 1929
Professional
All-rounder
1st XI: 1892-1894
Colts: 1892-1893
Clubs; Hill's Plymouth, Bridgend

Batting and Fielding Record

M	I	NO	RUNS	AV	100	50	CT	ST
10	12	3	25	2.78	-	-	3	-

Bowling Record

Balls	M	R	W	AV	5wI	10wM
882	53	399	26	15.35	-	-

Career-bests
8 v Monmouthshire at St Helen's, Swansea, 1892
4/19 v MCC at Cardiff Arms Park, 1892

Tom Hordley was another journeyman professional who played for Glamorgan during the early 1890s. A blacksmith by profession, he had been born in Staffordshire but was brought up in the Dowlais area of Merthyr Tydfil with his cricket-playing skills soon winning him a place in the Hill's Plymouth side.

The burly fast bowler made his Glamorgan debut in May 1892 against Wiltshire at Swindon, before winning selection for the remaining games of the season, during which he claimed 4/19 against the MCC at the Arms Park. The correspondent of the *South Wales Daily News* wrote how "Hordley, having struck with his first ball, then sent down four maidens in succession and stifled the batsmen with his accuracy." Once again, Glamorgan's funds at the time were insufficient to secure his regular employment.

Tom Hordley.

65.
DAVIES, David Edward
Born – Cwmavon, Merthyr Tydfil 1Q/1862
Amateur
Batsman
1st XI: 1892
Club: Cardiff

Batting and Fielding Record

M	I	NO	RUNS	AV	100	50	CT	ST
1	1	0	6	6.00	-	-	-	-

Career-bests
6 v MCC at Cardiff Arms Park, 1892

David Davies was a solicitor in Cardiff who made one appearance – as a late substitute – for the Welsh county against the MCC at the Arms Park in 1892.

66.
FARR, Charles Frederick
Born – Brecon, March 1860
Died – Holywell, Flintshire, 1 January 1914
Amateur
Batsman
1st XI: 1892
Clubs: Swansea, Swansea Tourists

Batting and Fielding Record

M	I	NO	RUNS	AV	100	50	CT	ST
1	1	0	2	9200	-	-	-	-

Career-bests
2 v Monmouthshire at St Helen's, Swansea, 1892

Charles Farr, a member of the Swansea club, was another to make one appearance for Glamorgan, as a late replacement in their side which met Monmouthshire in 1892 at St Helen's..

The chartered accountant made 2 in his sole innings, and despite never being chosen again for county level, he remained a consistent performer in club cricketl for the Swansea club.

Charles Farr.

67.
YOUNG, George Avery

Born – Tynemouth, June 1866
Died – Penarth, 21 January 1900
Amateur
Batsman
Ed – Malvern School
1st XI: 1892-1893
Clubs: Garth, Bridgend
Rugby for Cardiff and Wales (2 caps)

Batting Record

Career-bests
61 v MCC at Lord's, 1892

Welsh rugby international George Young was one of a number of sporting gentlemen who represented Glamorgan during the 1890s, not because of outstanding abilities with bat or ball but because of their fleet footedness and athletic prowess in the field, in contrast to some of the more immobile and portly amateurs.

His father Charles Young had played for the Glamorganshire club in 1871 before becoming a well-known shipbroker in Cardiff Docks. He was also a leading light with the Garth club in Morganstown following a move during the 1860s from his native north-east England. Educated at Malvern College, George also played for the Garth club before becoming one of the stars of Frank Hancock's Cardiff rugby team.

George Young, as seen wearing his Welsh rugby cap and jersey.

Initially, a forward, George moved into the three-quarters and enjoyed a fine season with the club during 1885/86 and went on to win Welsh caps in the 1886 Home Internationals against England and Scotland. Wales lost both games and George never won further honours, although he led the Cardiff club with distinction during 1887/88 and 1888/89.

George had been a decent schoolboy cricketer, and his flowing strokeplay and nimble fielding for the Cardiff and Bridgend clubs, attracted the attention of the county selectors. All three of his appearances for Glamorgan came outside Wales – in 1892 he appeared in the away matches against Devon at Exeter and the MCC at Lord's, with George making a handsome 61 in the latter match. He was chosen again the following year for the visit to Exeter, but with increasing commitments in his father's business, this was the final time he was able to appear for the Welsh county.

Having moved to live in Plymouth Road in Penarth, George suffered from ill health during 1899 and he died the following January.

1893

After bad luck had dogged Glamorgan in 1892, it was tragedy which accompanied the Club's affairs during 1893 with the death of Willie Llewelyn – the son of JTD and a man tipped to be a future leader of the county side.

A sketch of the ill-fated Willie Llewelyn.

Everything though appeared satisfactory as Glamorgan won five of their opening eight games and once again recorded home and away victories over Monmouthshire, besides doing the double over Devon at Swansea and Exeter. Willie Llewelyn had scored an attractive 50 against Devon at St Helen's, whilst in late July he had also led the Welsh county to an innings victory against Monmouthshire at Newport.

Willie had also scored a superb 113* for the Eton Ramblers against the Old Wykehamists at Winchester, so all seemed very rosy in the cricketing world of Willie Llewelyn. But barely a month afterwards, he was found dead in the grounds of Penllergaer House.

The Club's officials were still in sombre mood when they met a few weeks later to discuss the financial situation. Gate money for the summer had fallen to just £73 and despite the second summer of decent form, there was an apparent ambivalence by the general pubic who seemed more interested in the faster moving game of rugby.

68.
NICHOLL, John Illtyd Dillwyn

Born – Merthyr Mawr, 1 May 1861
Died – Merthyr Mawr, 20 September 1935
Amateur
All-rounder
Ed – Eton and Christ Church, Oxford
1st XI: 1893-1895
Clubs: Bridgend, MCC, Wimbledon
Brother of LD Nicholl and son of JC Nicholl

John Nicholl.

Batting and Fielding Record

M	I	NO	RUNS	AV	100	50	CT	ST
2	3	0	38	12.67	-	-	-	-

Bowling Record

Balls	M	R	W	AV	5wI	10wM
120	4	56	6	9.33	1	-

Career-bests
18 v Colts XXII at Cardiff Arms Park , 1893
6/56 v Colts XXII at Cardiff Arms Park, 1893

John Nicholl was the eldest son of John Cole Nicholl of Merthyr Mawr. Like his younger brother Louis, John made two appearances for Glamorgan, though neither were against county opposition, reflecting his lesser abilities as a cricketer. Nevertheless, the Old Etonian was a handy spin bowler and on his county debut, during May 1893 against a Colts XXII at the Arms Park, he took 6/56 in the youngster's second innings.

By this time, John had qualified as a barrister in Bridgend having read Law at Christ Church, Oxford who he also represented at cricket. In March 1894 he succeeded his late father as the resident of Merthyr Mawr House, and later that year also joined the Glamorgan committee. His standing within local society saw him selected by his colleagues on the club's selection panel for the friendly in June 1895 against the veteran members of the South Wales CC. The game at Swansea saw John rub shoulders with many other leading figures from the legal world as well as former acquaintances of his late father.

In August 1886 John played for the MCC against the South Wales club in their final game at Swansea. At the time, the young lawyer was training in South London and was also affiliated to the Wimbledon club. John continued to play for the MCC during the 1890s and appeared on their Wales and the Marches tour in games against Monmouthshire, Herefordshire and Glamorgan between 1895 and 1897.

In 1910 John became vice-chairman of the Glamorgan Quarter Sessions, besides rising to the rank of Colonel in the Glamorgan Yeomanry and during the Great War acting as their chief recruiting officer in the Bridgend area.

69.
SAULEZ, Edmund Harrison
Born – Sea Point, Dublin, 21 February 1867
Died – Havant, 19 November 1948
Amateur
Batsman
Ed – Harrow
1st XI: 1893
Europeans 1894/1895
Clubs: Cardiff, Fairwater

Batting and Fielding Record

M	I	NO	RUNS	AV	100	50	CT	ST
8	14	2	250	20.83	-	-	5	-

Career-bests
45 v Monmouthshire at Rodney Parade, Newport, 1893

Edmund Saulez, an Army officer, played eight times for Glamorgan during 1893 whilst based at Maindy Barracks. Born in Eire, raised in Hampshire and educated at Harrow, his family had links with South Wales through his uncle Vincent who had served as rector of St John's church in Canton. He was quite an influential figure in the development of the Cardiff suburb as Rev. Saulez encouraged his parishoners to form a cricket team, and the rise of both the Canton cricket club, and Alexandra Park as a sporting venue, were the result of his encouragement of healthy recreation.

Edmund had initially served with the Royal Dublin Fusiliers and the Suffolk Regiment, before moving to South Wales. During his time in Cardiff , Edmund played for both the Cardiff and Fairwater clubs. This led to a friendship with Jack Brain, with Edmund making his Glamorgan debut in May 1893 against the Colts XXII at the Arms Park. Having made 39 against the youngsters, Edmund then appeared against Herefordshire at Hereford, scoring 30 and 43, before playing in a further six matches that summer, with his final appearance coming at Lord's in the game with the MCC.

Edmund then enjoyed a distinguished military career in the Indian Army, during which time he also appeared in domestic cricket for the Europeans during the 1894/95 season. He served in the North-west frontier and oversaw transport operations. Having risen to the rank of Major, he was later based in Calcutta before returning to the U.K. after the Great War and lived in Bedfordshire and Hampshire. His wife Anna was the daughter of Alex Dumbleton, a talented amateur cricketer who played for the Royal Engineers, and whose brother Horatio also played for Hampshire, besides appearing in inter-services cricket.

70.
SCHOFIELD, Thomas David

Born – Bridgend, September 1864
Died – Bridgend, 2 January 1928
Amateur
RHB, WK
1st XI: 1893-1896
Colts: 1891
Clubs: Bridgend

Batting and Fielding Record

M	I	NO	RUNS	AV	100	50	CT	ST
6	8	0	26	3.25	-	-	6	4

Career-bests
Minor 16 v Cardiff and District XI at Cardiff Arms Park, 1893

Tom Schofield was one of the best amateur wicket-keepers in South Wales during the late Victorian and early Edwardian era. Given his success in club cricket with Bridgend, he would have made more than eight appearances for Glamorgan had the county not been able to call upon Sam Brain on a regular basis.

Having first played cricket in his youth for Bridgend, Tom gained further experience by appearing in a decent standard of cricket in both Northern England and North America before returning to live and work in his native town. His first appearance for Glamorgan came at the Arms Park during May 1893 against a Colts XXII before featuring in the line-up away to Herefordshire as well as in the friendly against a Cardiff and District XI. He subsequently made a single appearance in 1894, 1895 and 1896.

An advertising and bill-posting agent by trade, Tom joined the county committee in 1903 and helped the Club promote its Minor County fixtures, as well as helping to plan the campaign for first-class status. He was still assisting the committee in 1920 when the campaign achieved its goal, and Schofield was a very proud Club Chairman during their inaugural summer in the County Championship.

Tom Schofield.

Tom also acted as secretary of Bridgend RFC, having first played for the town club whilst at school. From 1894 until the early 1920s, he was a well-known rugby referee, officiating in club, county and – from 1907 – international matches, besides being a national selector after the Great War. He also founded the Bridgend and District League, and advised the Welsh Rugby Union on a number of issues, including making the scrum less violent and much safer for its participants.

The compassionate side of Tom's character was also to the fore during the Great War as he served with the Glamorgan Motor Volunteers driving ambulances with injured troops to various military hospitals and rest homes throughout South Wales.

71.
MORRIS, Frank Hall (later FH BYNG-MORRIS)
Born – Laleston, Bridgend, 16 July 1869
Died – Tonbridge, 21 October 1954
Amateur
RHB, WK
Ed – Malvern
1st XI: 1893-1896
Clubs: Swansea, Monmouth

Batting and Fielding Record

M	I	NO	RUNS	AV	100	50	CT	ST
3	6	1	51	10.25	-	-	2	1

Career-bests
16 v Monmouthshire at Cardiff Arms Park, 1893

Frank Morris was a member of the coal and copper mining family who created the Morriston suburb of Swansea. Frank was the sixth of youngest child born to George Byng Morris of Danygraig, and later Laleston House near Bridgend, who served as both High Sherrif and Deputy Lieutenant of Glamorgan.

Educated at Malvern, George became an engineer, specializing in mining operations, and whilst in his twenties, he played three times for Glamorgan, twice in games at the Arms Park, and once at Swansea against the MCC. Indeed, he was a prominent member of the Swansea club, even whilst still at school, and showed great dexterity as a wicket-keeper besides learning several tricks of the trade from Dan Thissen whose livelihood in Morriston was intertwined with Frank's family.

Had Sam Brain not been Glamorgan's first-choice gloveman, Frank would have played more often at county level. He was first selected in 1893, starting with the game against Monmouthshire at Cardiff in June 1893 and his brief career in county cricket ended in the corresponding fixture at the same venue in August 1896. Other members of his family showed great talent in sporting pursuits, with his elder brother George playing rugby for Swansea and winning five caps for Wales, whilst his sister Fanny was also well-known in lawn tennis circles, representing Somerset.

During the late 1890s Frank moved to Cheltenham before moving to the Kensington area of London during the 1930s. By this time, he had changed his surname to Byng-Morris, having been granted by deed poll this alteration in 1927.

72.
REES, Edward Lennox ('Eddie')

Born – Southampton, March 1868
Died – St Mellon's, 13 October 1911
Amateur
RHB, RFM
1st XI: 1893-1896
Clubs: Cardiff, St Paul's

Batting and Fielding Record

M	I	NO	RUNS	AV	100	50	CT	ST
9	15	5	47	4.70	-	-	6	-

Bowling Record

	Balls	M	R	W	AV	5wI	10wM
Minor	868	42	360	20 (+5)	18.00	1	-

Career-bests
17 v MCC at Lord's, 1896
6/42 v Herefordshire at Hereford, 1895

Eddie Rees was reputed to be the fastest amateur bowler in South Wales during the 1890s. The fast round-arm bowler had shot to prominence with some wicket-laden performances for the St Paul's club in the Cardiff and District League. He subsequently joined the Cardiff club, and went on to play in nine matches for Glamorgan between 1893 and 1896.

His debut, against Monmouthshire at the Arms Park in June 1893, saw him go wicketless besides bagging a pair, but he met with more success in his next appearance, at Exeter in late July as he claimed 4/44 in the contest against Devon. After a solitary appearance during 1894, he played in three matches the following year, After a seven-wicket match haul against Monmouthshire in July at Usk, he returned his best-ever figures in the county's ranks the following month, taking 6/42 in Herefordshire's first innings.

Eddie made three further appearances during 1896 but his bowling prowess, appeared to be on the wane as he took just five wickets in 41.4 overs. Despite not playing again for Glamorgan, he continued to appear for Cardiff and in August 1904 he was a member of the Gentleman's team which met the Players of Glamorgan in a fund-raising contest at the Arms Park.

73.
SANT, Stuart _Arthur_

Born – Llandaff, 10 June 1870
Died – Chertsey, Surrey, 1 March 1958
Amateur
Ed – Cardiff Proprietry School and Cardiff College
1st XI: 1893
Clubs: St Paul's, Cardiff, St Mary's, Coleford

Batting and Fielding Record

M	I	NO	RUNS	AV	100	50	CT	ST
1	2	0	21	10.50	-	-	-	-

Career-bests
21 v Herefordshire at Hereford, 1893

Arthur Sant was another member of the sporting community of Cardiff during the 1890s to appear once for Glamorgan. The son of William Sant, the well-to-do owner of Pwllcoch Farm in Llandaff, attended Cardiff Proprietry School where he rubbed shoulders as a young sportsman with the likes of the Biggs brothers and the Ingledews. He continued this friendship into adult life and besides playing rugby for Cardiff 2nd XV, he became one of the leading cricketers in the Cardiff and District League.

Following some decent batting performances for the St Paul's club, Arthur was chosen in the Colts squad to meet Glamorgan at Swansea in May 1892. He was however unable to travel and as a result the Colts played one man short. This may have been the reason why he did not feature again for Glamorgan until June the following year in the away match against Herefordshire. By this time, he was playing with good effect for the St Mary's club and, batting at number five, he made a steady 21 in the second innings of the match on Widemarsh Common.

It proved to be his only appearance at county level as he began a peripatetic career in the hotel trade. Having moved initially to work in London, he got married in June 1895, before moving with his wife Frances to work in the Forest of Dean, where he played for the Coleford club. They then moved back to the Home Counties where he worked in Battersea, Kensington and Kent, before retiring to live in Chertsey where he became a noted breeder of St Bernard dogs.

74.
CULLEN, *John Stewart*
Born – Cardiff, 9 August 1868
Amateur
Batsman
1st XI: 1893
Colts: 1893
Clubs: St Paul's, Cardiff

Batting and Fielding Record

M	I	NO	RUNS	AV	100	50	CT	ST
1	2	0	21	10.50	-	-	-	-

Career-bests
14 v Herefordshire at Hereford, 1893

Like Arthur Sant, John Cullen's solitary appearance also came at Widemarsh Common in 1893 when Glamorgan travelled to Herefordshire with a side including several young players who had impressed in junior leagues.

In the case of the Cardiff-born accountant, he had also impressed playing for the St Paul's club and continued the good name of his family in cricketing circles.

His father Tom was well-known to senior figures in the Glamorgan camp, having been a member of the South Wales CC and in 1868 had played for East Glamorgan in the match the Club organized against an eleven representing the west of the county at Merthyr Mawr.

Tom Cullen was also an accountant and John followed in his footsteps working for amongst others, both Hancock's and Brain's, no doubt as a result of his sporting links. John also played in May 1893 for the Glamorgan Colts side which was assembled to meet the county side in a trial match at Cardiff Arms Park. He made 0 in his only innings, but three weeks later was in the squad for the county's match at Hereford.

75.
DAVIES, William *Arthur*

Born – Llandovery, June 1870
Died – Margam, 1 March 1960
Amateur
All-rounder
Ed – Queen's College, Taunton
1st XI: 1893
Colts: 1893
Clubs: Taibach, Aberavon

Batting and Fielding Record

M	I	NO	RUNS	AV	100	50	CT	ST
2	3	0	0	-	-	-	3	-

Bowling Record

Balls	M	R	W	AV	5wI	10wM
100	6	49	7	7.00	1	-

Career-bests
6/11 v Herefordshire at Hereford, 1893

Arthur Davies was another young cricketer to be bloodied by Glamorgan in their away match at Hereford during 1893. In the case of the former pupil of Queen's College, Taunton he impressed with the ball, taking 6/11 in the Herefordshire 2nd innings and won selection for the next game, against Devon at St Helen's. However, he went wicketless in the match and, like his two innings in Hereford, he failed to score.

Born in Llandovery, he had a decent playing record for the Taibach and Aberavon clubs, besides playing rugby for Aberavon and serving on their selection committee. In May 1893 Arthur was also chosen to play for the Colts XXII in their trial match at the Arms Park. He took 4/34 in the Glamorgan first innings, and impressed with the bat in his two innings. Nevertheless, when it came to playing for the 1st XI, Arthur was dismissed three times for nought!

However, Arthur did open his batting account later in August when called up as a substitute for

Arthur Davies.

Tom Hordley in the Cardiff and District side which met Glamorgan at the Arms Park. After scoring a single, Arthur took 3/44 as his team beat the scratch county XI.

Arthur later became a successful coal exporter with the Cwm Duffryn Colliery, where he rose to the position of Director. He also became a well-known figure in local politics and was mayor of Port Talbot. Arthur remained a loyal supporter of Glamorgan CCC and served on the county's committee between 1924 and 1926.

76.
HUGHES, Francis Edward

Born – Maidstone, 19 December 1860
Died – Maidstone, 4 June 1914
Amateur
Batsman
Ed – Tonbridge School, St John's College, and New Hall, Oxford
1st XI: 1893
Clubs: Cardiff, Fairwater, The Mote

Batting and Fielding Record

M	I	NO	RUNS	AV	100	50	CT	ST
1	1	0	0	-	-	-	-	-

In July 1893 Frank Hughes received what all young cricketers in South Wales must have dreamt about – a late call-up to play in the Welsh county's side. The match in question was against Herefordshire at the Arms Park with the message coming via his good friend and business partner Sidney Sweet-Escott with whom he shared a solicitors practice near to the Cardiff ground. Sweet-Escott was a member of the Glamorgan side who found themselves one man short, but the call to his chum did not lead to a glittering debut as Frank was dismissed for nought in what proved to his only innings in county cricket.

The son of a solicitor based in Maidstone, Frank had been educated at Tonbridge School, before reading Law at Oxford University, and continuing his training in South Wales. He had been a decent schoolboy cricket, appearing for the Mote Club on several occasions in their major matches against the MCC and the Royal Engineers. He was limited to college cricket at Oxford, before joining the Cardiff and Fairwater clubs following his move to South Wales, allowing the trainee solicitor to mix and mingle with the great and good of local society.

He later bought a property in Penarth and made a few appearances for the seaside town's club, but by the time the 1901 Census was taken, Frank had returned to Kent to run his family's solicitors' practice.

77.
ROONEY, Robert Alexander
Born – Stoke Newington, 2 September 1872
Died – Brentford, 1940
Amateur
All-rounder
1st XI: 1893-1901
Colts: 1893
Club and Ground: 1913-1923
Clubs: Cardiff, St Paul's, St Fagans

Batting and Fielding Record

M	I	NO	RUNS	AV	100	50	CT	ST
13	17	3	274	19.57	-	1	5	-

Bowling Record

Balls	M	R	W	AV	5wI	10wM
24	0	19	0	-	-	-

Career-bests
54* v MCC at Cardiff Arms Park, 1900

Robert Rooney was the younger brother of Teddy Rooney and followed him into the family's thriving construction business in Cardiff during the late Victorian and Edwardian era. With an office near the Arms Park, and good links with the Bute Estate – the major landowners in the Welsh capital – the Rooney's were a well-connected family.

Robert Rooney, as seen in 1912.

Like his brothers, Robert played cricket and rugby for the Cardiff club, although he was a better cricketer than a rugby player, appearing initially at the age of 20 in 1893 for a Colts side in a trial match against a Glamorgan XI at the Arms Park. It was not the first time he had played against the county's team as in 1889 he, along with other young members of the Cardiff club had been called into the MCC side to play against the Welsh county at the Arms Park.

In 1893 Robert played in the rain-ravaged game at the Arms Park against Herefordshire, before appearances in 1894 against Monmouthshire at Rodney Parade in Newport and Wiltshire at the County Ground in Swindon. Pressure of work meant that he was unavailable to play for Glamorgan again until 1899 during which season he played against Monmouthshire as well as travelling to Reading for the game with Berkshire.

1900 was easily his most successful summer in Glamorgan's ranks, with a half-century against the MCC at the Arms Park, plus several other decent innings. His final match for the Welsh county came in 1901 away to Wiltshire, but he continued to play with success for the Cardiff club, and on several occasions appeared in the Gentlemen's team with met the Players of Glamorgan.

Robert lived initially in Womanby Street, where the family also had an office, before marrying Clara Nicholls, the sister of Welsh rugby legend Gwyn Nicholls who was the manager of the nearby Grand Hotel in Westgate Street, and opposite the Arms Park. Robert subsequently moved from his digs in the nearby street to live in the Hotel, before he and his wife lived in the thriving suburb of Canton. He subsequently built a more substantial property in Whitchurch, called Treoda Villa, where he and Clara lived until the 1920s.

His final match of note came in May 1923 when he featured in a Glamorgan Club and Ground XI which played a Cardiff XI at the Arms Park. After retiring from playing for Cardiff, Robert became associated with the St Fagans club, for whom he acted as umpire.

78.
ROONEY, Samuel

Born – Llandaff, December 1874
Amateur
All-rounder
1st XI: 1893-1894
Colts: 1892-1893
Clubs: Penarth, St Paul's, St Andrew's
Brother of EJ Rooney and RA Rooney

Batting and Fielding Record

M	I	NO	RUNS	AV	100	50	CT	ST
4	8	0	63	7.86	-	-	2	-

Bowling Record

Balls	M	R	W	AV	5wI	10wM
129	3	73	2	36.50	-	-

Career-bests
23 v Cardiff and District XI at Cardiff Arms Park, 1893
2/61 v Cardiff and District XI at Cardiff Arms Park, 1893

Sam Rooney junior was the youngest of Robert Rooney's sons – each shared their father's love of cricket and played cricket for Cardiff, with Sam making four appearances during the 1890s. The least talented of the Rooney clan, Sam had the distinction to make his Glamorgan debut on their visit to Lord's in August 1893 and his call-up into the side to play the MCC stemmed from some decent performances in the Cardiff and District League for St Paul's and St Andrew's, as well as for the Penarth club.

A fortnight later he appeared as well in the scratch county XI which played a Cardiff and District XI at the Arms Park, whilst the following summer he also played for Glamorgan against Monmouthshire at Swansea, making 2 and 14 in what proved to be his final game for the Welsh county.

Sam continued to feature in local club cricket, besides playing a leading role in the family's architect's business.

79.
SWAIN, George William

Born – Stepney, Middlesex, April 1872
Died – Sheffield, March 1951
Amateur
Batsman and wicket-keeper
1st XI: 1893-1894
Colts: 1891-1893
Clubs: Mackintosh, Cardiff

Batting and Fielding Record

M	I	NO	RUNS	AV	100	50	CT	ST
2	3	0	55	18.33	-	-	1	-

Career-bests
24 v Cardiff and District XI at Cardiff Arms Park, 1893

George Swain was a leading light with the Mackintosh club, created during 1890 in the suburb of Roath in Cardiff. Based at the former Plasnewydd House, the creation of the club followed a decision by the owner, the Mackintosh of Mackintosh, to meet the leisure and recreational needs of those living in the rapidly expanding residential area.

Like hundreds of others living in Roath, George worked in Cardiff Docks and the Middlesex-born civil servant, rapidly became one of the stars of the Mackintosh club, with his batting and wicket-keeping impressing several good judges. His success led to selection in the Colts Trial in May 1891, but he bagged a pair in the match at the Arms Park and did not feature in the corresponding feature the following year.

However, a good run of scores in 1892, and early in 1893 saw George chosen as the wicket-keeper in the Colts trial in 1893, besides an appearance for the scratch county XI against a Cardiff and District side during August. This was more of a social jamboree than a series game of cricket but he was able to show his credentials, opening the batting with scores of 24 and 19.

His name had clearly gone down in various notebooks as he joined the Cardiff club for the following summer, and after further impressive innings George made his Glamorgan debut in August 1894 against Wiltshire at Swindon, making 12 in what proved to be his only innings at county level. George subsequently rose to the rank of superintendent in the Mercantile Marine Department at Cardiff Docks.

80.
COPE, Sir William (later Lord Cope of St Mellons)
Born – Roath, Cardiff, 18 August 1870
Died – St Mellons, 15 July 1946
Amateur
All-rounder
Ed – Repton School and Clare College, Cambridge
1st XI: 1893
Clubs: Cardiff, Fairwater
Rugby for Cardiff, Cambridge University, Blackheath and Wales (1 cap)
Football Blue

Batting and Fielding Record

M	I	NO	RUNS	AV	100	50	CT	ST
1	2	0	18	9.00	-	-	-	-

Bowling Record

Balls	M	R	W	AV	5wI	10wM
30	1	13	1	13.00	-	-

Career-bests
16 v Cardiff and District XI at Cardiff Arms Park, 1893
1/13 v Cardiff and District XI at Cardiff Arms Park, 1893

William Cope made his sole appearance for Glamorgan in their scratch XI for the two-day friendly against a Cardiff and District XI at the Arms Park in August 1893. The son of Matthew Cope, a colliery and quarry owner from St Mellons, he learnt his cricket and rugby at Repton and Clare College, Cambridge where he read Law, besides winning a football Blue, but bizarrely not a rugby Blue!

The young barrister then returned to South Wales where he played cricket for Cardiff and Fairwater, besides winning a place in the Cardiff 1st XV. Some sturdy performances as a forward for Cardiff and Blackheath led to his selection in the Welsh side for the Home Nations Championship game against Scotland in 1896. Although Wales won the game, it proved to be his sole cap. By this time, he had been called to the Bar and practiced in London, before returning to South Wales and entering local politics, besides serving as a Director of the Albion Colliery and an electric power station.

William Cope in his Cardiff RFC jersey.

After serving as a Major in the Glamorgan Yeomanry during World War One, he became Conservative MP for Llandaff and Barry between 1918 and 1929, during which time he was also Comptroller of the Royal Household, and a Junior Lord of the Treasury. He was made a Baronet in 1928 and was subsequently elevated to the peerage in 1946. In his youth, he had been a keen huntsman and rode his horses in local point-to-points.

81.
ROFFEY, Sir George Walter
Born – Brentford, 21 May 1870
Died – Templecombe, 13 March 1940
Professionl
All-rounder
Ed – Harrow
1st XI: 1893
Clubs: Cardiff, MCC, Incogniti

Batting and Fielding Record

M	I	NO	RUNS	AV	100	50	CT	ST
1	2	1	0	-	-	-	-	-

Bowling Record

Balls	M	R	W	AV	5wI	10wM
182	8	90	4	22.50	-	-

Career-bests
2/39 v Cardiff and District XI at Cardiff Arms Park, 1893

Walter Roffey also appeared in the scratch Glamorgan XI against Cardiff and District at the Arms Park in August 1893. At the time, the county hierarchy were assessing his credentials and prospects – despite his private schooling – as a potential professional having impressed as an all-rounder on Surrey's junior staff, with Walter having made a forthright 54 for Surrey 2nd XI against Hertfordshire at The Oval in July 1889. The cancellation of the Minor County fixture with Wiltshire in August 1893, and the arrangements for a game involving prominent members of Cardiff CC gave the Glamorgan selectors an opportunity to give Walter and others a trial.

He subsequently played with success – as an amateur – for the MCC and Incogniti, before running a highly successful grain merchants and becoming Chairman of the Home Cereals committee. During the Great War, he also served as Minister of Food during 1917 and 1918, and with the support of David Lloyd George, he suggested some radical solutions to overcome the fuel and manpower shortages which the nation faced. These included reducing the output at many breweries – something that met with opposition – but, thankfully, the position eased and Walter's radical plans never saw fruition.

The husband of Lady Constance Roffey, he was knighted in 1918 and lived at Batans Hall, Wingfield in Surrey.

82.
BIGGS, Norman Witchell

Born – Cardiff, 3 November 1870
Died – Sakaba, Nigeria, 27 February 1908
Ed – Cardiff College and Trinity Hall, Cambridge
Amateur
Batsman
1st XI: 1893
Clubs: Cardiff, St Andrew's, Water Rats
Rugby for Cardiff and Wales (8 caps)

Batting and Fielding Record

M	I	NO	RUNS	AV	100	50	CT	ST
1	2	0	11	5.50	-	-	-	-

Career-bests
6 v Cardiff and District XI at Cardiff Arms Park,1893

Norman Biggs was the oldest of three sports-mad brothers who all represented Glamorgan CCC and Cardiff RFC, whilst in Norman's case he also won eight Welsh rugby caps in the late 1880s and early 1890s.

Hs father, John Biggs, was a master brewer from Somerset who lived in the affluent inner suburb of Park Place in Cardiff, and owned several premises in the Welsh capital as well as in Bath which were both subsidiaries of Hancock's. Norman showed rich promise as a schoolboy sportsman, and during the late 1880s the student at Cardiff College won a place at Cambridge University. Indeed, in December 1888 he became the youngest player to be capped by Wales as he took the field at St Helen's, Swansea aged just 18 years and one month against New Zealand. Broken ribs whilst playing at Cambridge prevented Norman from adding a rugby Blue to his impressive sporting c.v.

After coming down, Norman took up a post in the South Wales Constabulary, but he still found plenty of time to play rugby for Cardiff and cricket for the St Andrews club. His fine play on the wing for the town club won him further international honours and during January 1893 Norman dazzled on the wing for Wales and scored a fine try in a dramatic 12-11 victory over England at the Arms Park.

During the spring of 1893, Norman was drafted into the scratch XI for the match at the Arms Park against a Cardiff and District XI. He made 6 and 5, but despite the odd

Norman Biggs.

appearance for the Water Rats in fund-raising matches, this was the nearest Norman came to a place in the county's eleven. Norman led the Cardiff rugby XV in 1893/94, and continued to play on the right wing for Wales before leaving South Wales to work in both London and Bath. During this time, Norman played rugby for London Welsh, Richmond and Somerset, besides captaining Bath in 1899/1900.

He served as a private in the Glamorgan Yeomanry during the Boer War, but in 1901 was invalided home after being struck by a sniper's bullet which entered one of his legs below the knee and exited through the thigh. Norman duly recovered and returned to the Cape before securing a position as Superintendent in the Nigerian Police. However, in February 1908, he met a decidedly sticky fate as he was struck by a poisoned arrow during a native ambush in the Sakaba district near a village called Chinuka. Norman survived for a further five days but succumbed to secondary bleeding from the wound.

83.
CASEBOURNE, Frederick
Born – West Hartlepool, September 1870
Died – Grimsby, 5 January 1963
Professional
Seam bowler
1st XI: 1893
Durham Colts 1891
Buckinghamshire 1892

Batting and Fielding Record

M	I	NO	RUNS	AV	100	50	CT	ST
1	2	0	3	1.50	-	-	1	-

Bowling Record

Balls	M	R	W	AV	5wI	10wM
115	11	44	3	14.67	-	-

Career-bests
3 v Cardiff and District XI at Cardiff Arms Park, 1893
3/44 v Cardiff and District XI at Cardiff Arms Park, 1893

Fred Casebourne was a journeyman professional who was given a trial by the Welsh county during their match during August 1893 at the Arms Park against a Cardiff and District XI. However, he did little to impress and was not called up again.

Born in West Hartlepool, Fred had played for the Durham Colts in 1891, before moving south and playing Minor County cricket for Buckinghamshire the following year.

84.
WILLIAMS, Llewellyn J
Amateur
Batsman
1st XI: 1893
Club: Cardiff

Batting and Fielding Record

M	I	NO	RUNS	AV	100	50	CT	ST
1	2	-	3	1.50	-	-	-	-

Career-bests
2 v Cardiff and District XI at Cardiff Arms Park, 1893

Llewellyn Williams, a member of Cardiff CC, also appeared in the scratch county XI which met the Cardiff and District XI. He did little of note in the contest.

85.
COURTIS, Sir John Wesley
Born – Williamstown, Melbourne, Australia, 19 February 1859
Died – Llandaff, 19 December 1939
Amateur
Batsman
Ed – Monkton House School and Melbourne University
1st XI: 1893
Club: Cardiff

Batting and Fielding Record

M	I	NO	RUNS	AV	100	50	CT	ST
1	1	0	12	12.00	-	-	-	-

Career-bests
12 v Cardiff and District XI at Cardiff Arms Park, 1893

Sir John Wesley Courtis – another man to play for the scratch Glamorgan XI in 1893 against Cardiff and District – was a prominent figure in the public life of Cardiff during the late Victorian and Edwardian era, serving as a magistrate for 45 years and acting as the city's Lord Mayor in 1911/12. During his term of office, John had the pleasure of welcoming King George and Queen Mary to the city to lay the foundation stone for the National Museum of Wales in Cathays Park

His father – an Australian entrepreneur – had arrived in Cardiff with his wife and family 1868. Soon after, he purchased a brickworks in the Whitchurch area, largely as a speculative venture. It proved to be a most lucrative move as in the course of the next decade, a wave of housebuilding took place in the northern suburbs, with John's father gleefully supplying the material to the plethora of builders who were looking to literally cash in on the growth of the coal metropolis.

Flushed with the profits from his thriving business, he was able to send John to Monkton House School. John subsequently completed his studies in Australia, before returning to Cardiff and setting up a stockbroking business. Besides playing cricket for the Cardiff club, John enjoyed a meteoric rise in local society and in 1886 married Marian, the daughter of John Osborne Riches, who was the business partner of David Davies of Ocean Collieries and one of the leading coal magnates and railway contractors in the region.

John subsequently enjoyed a career in local politics, and in 1898 was elected to the city council. He was a loyal supporter of Sir Herbert Cory, the Conservative MP for Cardiff from 1915-1923, besides acting as Chairman of the management committees for both Glan Ely Hospital and Cardiff Infirmary. Knighted in 1911, he also acted as High Sheriff of Glamorgan in 1916.

John and his family lived initially at Fairwater Croft, from which he remained a loyal supporter, and benefactor, of Glamorgan CCC generously dipping into his pockets on several occasions to boost the Club's coffers. He subsequently moved to London to become a member of the Stock Exchange and after retiring and handing over the business to his son Walter, he and his wife moved back to live in Llandaff at Llwynderw House.

John Courtis.

86.
BIRCHAM, *Humphrey Francis William*

Born – Brecon, June 1875
Died – Pozieres, France, 23 July 1916
Amateur
Batsman
Ed – Eton College and RMC Sandhurst
1st XI: 1893
Monmouthshire 1892; Royal Marines; United Services
Clubs: Cardiff, Newport, MCC, I Zingari, Greenjackets

Batting and Fielding Record

M	I	NO	RUNS	AV	100	50	CT	ST
1	2	0	19	9.50	-	-	-	-

Career-bests
17 v Cardiff and District XI at Cardiff Arms Park, 1893

Humphrey Bircham, who died on the Somme in 1916 was typical of the gentlemen cricketers who appeared in both Minor County and country house matches during Glamorgan's first two decades. Having played for Monmouthshire during 1892, he was also chosen for his one and only appearance for Glamorgan in the match against Cardiff and District the following summer.

Born in Brecon during 1875, he was the son of Francis Bircham, who had served in the Royal Horse Artillery, besides playing for both Breconshire and Monmouthshire. Humphrey was something of a schoolboy prodigy at Eton College, playing for the 1st XI before his 17th birthday, and holding a place in his final year at the College in 1893.

Later that summer, he accepted a place at Sandhurst and began his military career. Nevertheless, he still found time to play in club cricket for Cardiff and Newport, as well as for I Zingari, the MCC, the Royal Marines, Greenjackets and the United Services. After leaving Sandhurst, he joined the King's Royal Rifle Corps in February 1896, and rose to the rank of captain in 1901, besides being twice mentioned in dispatches during the Boer War, during which he was wounded at Brakenlaatge in October 1901.

Humphrey was elevated to the rank of Major in February 1914 and commanded the 2nd Battalion of the Kings Royal Rifles during their time on the Western Front, during which they took part in the Battle of Ypres. Yet again, Humphrey was mentioned several times in dispatches and his gallant actions in leading his men earned him the DSO.

In July 1916 Humphrey also took part in the Battle of the Somme, but his bravery was to cost him his life. His unit were deployed on the evening of July 23rd to mount an attack north of Mametz Wood on a newly dug "switch" line to the north-east of the village of Pozieres. The Rifles were supported to the left by the Royal Sussex Regiment and to the right by the 10th Battalion of the Gloucester Regiment. Prior to their attack, there was an intense artillery barrage for around seven minutes, but this lit up the skyline and alerted the German troops to the presence of the Rifles poised to attack their trenches. To make matters worse the attacks to the left and right-hand flanks failed and the Germans counter-attacked on both flanks with hand grenades and shells. During this skirmish, Humphrey was struck by a shell and fatally wounded.

87.
LEWIN, H.
Professional
1st XI: 1893

Batting and Fielding Record

M	I	NO	RUNS	AV	100	50	CT	ST
1	2	1	3	3.00	-	-	-	-

Bowling Record

Balls	M	R	W	AV	5wI	10wM
155	13	42	4	10.50	-	-

Career-bests
3* v Cardiff and District XI at Cardiff Arms Park, 1893
2/12 v Cardiff and District XI at Cardiff Arms Park, 1893

Lewin was one of the professionals who was given a trial by the Glamorgan selectors in the friendly against a Cardiff and District XI.

1894

In an attempt to arouse some interest in Glamorgan's affairs and boost gate receipts, Jack Brain used his contacts within the MCC to secure a game for June 1894 against the South Africans at the Arms Park – it was the Welsh county's inaugural contest against an international side, and resulted in a ten wicket defeat. The summer also witnessed Glamorgan's players combine with those from neighbouring Monmouthshire to meet an eleven chosen by EM Grace in a two-day game at the Arms Park to raise funds for the Albion Colliery Disaster which, on 23 June, had seen the death in Cilfynydd, north of Pontypridd, of 290 men and boys, plus 123 pit horses in what was the second-worst disaster in the history of the South Wales Coalfield.

Grace's XI were dismissed for 45 with the wickets shared by rugby international Selwyn Biggs and Sam Lowe, a fast bowler with links with Nottinghamshire who was being courted by Glamorgan. The South Wales side duly won by 55 runs, and as well as helping the relief effort for the stricken community, the discussions with Lowe eventually reached a successful outcome.

For much of the summer however, Glamorgan had to rely once again on the professional services of Alfred Eldridge. He rounded off another decent summer with Glamorgan by taking fifteen wickets in the ten-wicket victory against Wiltshire. But his efforts at Swindon led to the 31 year-old seamer being offered a lucrative contract for 1895 by the Trowbridge club. With the prospect of appearances for Wiltshire, Eldridge duly left South Wales.

His departure was a turning point however in the history of Glamorgan CCC as Jack Brain and his fellow committee members realized that the hiring of a homegrown professional would boost public interest and give the Club a much sharper Welsh identity. Their choice was Billy Bancroft, who had played for more modest sums in previous season. His reward was a retainer of £2 a week for 20 weeks, plus match bonuses and an opportunity to coach some of the emerging talent.

The view from the pavilion seating at the Arms Park.

88.
MARLEY, Kenneth Ramsden

Born – Thornfield House, Darlington, 11 February 1865
Died – Brentford, 18 December 1915
Amateur
RHB, RFM
Ed – Marlborough
1st XI: 1894
Clubs: Cardiff, Water Rats

Batting and Fielding Record

M	I	NO	RUNS	AV	100	50	CT	ST
1	2	0	82	41.00	-	-	-	-

Career-bests
49 v Wiltshire at Cardiff Arms Park, 1894

Kenneth Marley was a talented cricketer who also won honours at lawn tennis, being the men's champion at Penarth Lawn Tennis Club in twelve successive seasons between 1889 and 1900, besides being runner-up in the Welsh Lawn Tennis Championships of 1892, which coincidently was held on his home turf in Penarth.

1892 proved to be a hectic summer for the amateur sportsman as during August he also accepted an invitation to open the batting for the Gentlemen of Durham against the Fettesian Lorettonians at the schools' annual cricket festival.

The son of a well-to-do mining engineer in Darlington, Kenneth was educated at Marlborough where he shone as a hard-hitting batsman and a lively right-arm seam bowler. He subsequently moved to South Wales to set up his own coal exporting business and, using his father's contacts, he soon had a thriving business.

Kenneth also joined Cardiff and, after some useful performance, was called up by the county selectors in 1894 for the match against Wiltshire at the Arms Park. He impressed with scores of 33 and 49, but his commitments at Cardiff Docks, meant that it proved to be his sole appearance at county level

89.
BARLOW, Thomas Marriott

Born – Pendleton, Salford, December 1864
Died – Chester, 27 January 1942
Batsman
Amateur
Ed – Heversham School
1st XI: 1894-1897
Clubs: Cardiff, South Wales CC, Garth
Glamorgan Treasurer 1891-1903
Rugby for Cardiff and Wales (1 cap)

Batting and Fielding Record

M	I	NO	RUNS	AV	100	50	CT	ST
11	18	0	233	12.94	-	2	7	-

Bowling Record

Balls	M	R	W	AV	5wI	10wM
20	2	9	0	-	-	-

Career-bests
75 v Herefordshire at Hereford, 1895

Tom Barlow was a prominent solicitor and amateur sportsman in South Wales during the years leading up to the Great War. Born and educated in Lancashire, he moved to Cardiff in 1881 to train as a solicitor, under JL Wheatley the town clerk. He joined the town's cricket and rugby clubs, with his first major match for Cardiff coming in 1882 when he appeared in their exhibition match against the United England Eleven.

Having played a series of decent innings for Cardiff, and built up some useful contacts in the legal world, he was chosen by the South Wales CC in 1883 to play against both North Wales and the Bryn-y-Neuadd club in the country house matches at Llanfairfechan.

Tom injured his knee during the mid-1880s but, despite this, his athletic fielding more than made up for some of the shortcomings of his older, and less mobile, colleagues in the South Wales side. His stylish batting also drew favourable comment, and no less a judge than WG Grace invited Tom to move to the Bristol area and to qualify for Gloucestershire. With a decent job in the Welsh capital, and some influential friends in the legal world of South Wales, the young solicitor politely declined the offer and remained in Cardiff.

After a series of decent performances at full-back for the Cardiff 1st XV, Tom was also chosen for Wales in April 1884 for their international against Ireland at the Arms Park. He enjoyed a decent debut, and many thought he would be chosen again, but a bad injury, precipitated by a series of heavy tackles, swiftly ended his rugby-playing career.

By the time Glamorgan were formed in 1888, cricket and golf had become the principle recreations for the go-ahead solicitor, who subsequently became a founder member of the Glamorganshire Golf Club in Penarth in 1890 as well as the Royal Porthcawl club the following year. His burgeoning career as a solicitor restricted his involvement in cricket, but through his business contacts in Cardiff, Tom was persuaded to join the Glamorgan committee in 1891. Two years later he accepted the post of Treasurer – a position he held until 1903, before accepting a similar post with the Welsh Golfing Union in 1923.

In 1894 his work commitments allowed Tom to make himself available to the county selectors, and that summer he made his county debut, fittingly in the match against the MCC at the Arms Park. The following year, Tom showed what might have been had he been available more often, by scoring an attractive 75 in the away match against Herefordshire.

Tom played regularly in 1896 as Glamorgan pressed for elevation into the Minor Championship and he opened the batting with his good friend Jack Brain in the showcase encounter at the Arms Park against Worcestershire – against whom he had also played for the South Wales club back in 1885. Tom made a composed 21 and 19, but he was one of only a few Glamorgan batsmen to emerge with any credit from the encounter as Worcestershire recorded a comfortable nine wicket victory.

Despite the reverse, Glamorgan were elevated to the Minor County Championship in 1897, and in their inaugural season, the Welsh county were pressing for top spot in the table. The wear and tear of two-day games against decent opposition had prevented Tom from appearing in the Welsh county's line-up, but the talented batsman was drafted into the side for the vital match against Wiltshire at Swindon. However, he only made 3, before rain interrupted the contest and washed away Glamorgan's hopes of a first title.

Tom Barlow, seen at the Glamorganshire Golf Club in 1892.

With his knee increasingly causing him pain when running quick singles, the match with Wiltshire in 1897 proved to be Tom's final appearance on the field for the county club. Although he continued to serve on the Glamorgan committee until 1908, Tom enjoyed the less painful demands of playing golf, being beaten on the final green in the first Welsh Championships at Aberdovey in 1895 before winning the Welsh Amateur Championships at Porthcawl in 1900. He was runner-up again at Rhos-on-Sea in 1903, and either side of World War One, Tom was one of the leading amateur golfers in South Wales, and served as Honorary Treasurer of the Welsh Golfing Union between 1900 and 1924, before retiring from his solicitors' practice and serving as Secretary from 1925 until his death in 1942.

His brother Harry, was a master at Clifton College.

90.
HICKLEY, Victor Allen

Born – Ashcott, Bridgwater, 6 December 1873
Died – Bishop's Hull, Taunton, 5 January 1956
Amateur
Batsman
Ed – Radley College
1st XI: 1894-1898
Club: Cardiff

Batting and Fielding Record

M	I	NO	RUNS	AV	100	50	CT	ST
8	14	1	254	19.54	-	2	4	-

Career-bests
62 v Monmouthshire at Rodney Parade, Newport, 1897

Born in Somerset and educated at Radley College in Berkshire, Victor Hickley learnt his trade with Brain's Brewery and through a friendship with Sam Brain, the talented young batsman also played for Glamorgan during the 1890s.

Having opted not to follow his father, Rear Admiral VG Hickley into a naval career, he moved to South Wales to commence his training with Brain's and during 1894, after some decent innings for Cardiff, he made his Glamorgan debut, aged just 20, against the MCC at Cardiff Arms Park. His made a single appearance again in 1895 against Monmouthshire at Usk, before playing on a regular basis during 1897, during which he struck half-centuries against Monmouthshire at Rodney Parade and Surrey 2nd XI at the Arms Park.

Having completed his training he then served in the 4th Battalion of the British Army during the Boer War, and after returning to the UK, Victor worked in Tipperary and Staffordshire, before sunning a brewery in Leeds in South Yorkshire.

91.
THOMAS, Henry Trevellyan ('Harry')

Born – Swansea 1876
Ed – Gonville and Caius College, Cambridge
Amateur
Batsman
1st XI: 1894-1898
Club: Swansea
Hockey for Swansea and Wales (2 caps)

M	I	NO	RUNS	AV	100	50	CT	ST
5	9	1	66	8.25	-	-	-	-

Career-bests
24 v MCC at St Helen's, Swansea, 1898

Harry Thomas was a talented all-round sportsman playing both hockey and cricket for his home town of Swansea, besides winning international hockey honours for Wales, as well as being chosen five times to play county cricket for Glamorgan during the mid-1890s.

The son of Dr Jabez Thomas a surgeon and JP in Swansea, Harry made his debut for Glamorgan against Monmouthshire on his home turf at St Helen's when aged just eighteen. He made 18 and 4 and, as expected, impressed with his nimble fielding. It was not though until 1898 that Harry played again at county level and, in the intervening years, he had graduated from Cambridge University, besides winning a couple of hockey caps for Wales.

He played four further times for the Welsh county during 1898, including making another appearance at Swansea, this time in the contest with the MCC, during which he made his career-best score of 24. Harry subsequently pursued a career in the chemical industry besides playing hockey and cricket for Swansea. However, in 1910 he emigrated to Japan and became Managing Director of Lever Brothers factory in Kobe.

A photo of Harry Thomas as a twenty-year old.

92.
HOLMES, Thomas Edward
Born – Leicester 1875
Amateur
Batsman
Ed – Oakham School, University College, Cardiff and the University of London
1st XI: 1894

Batting and Fielding Record

M	I	NO	RUNS	AV	100	50	CT	ST
1	2	0	4	2.00	-	-	-	-

Career-bests
4 v Monmouthshire at Rodney Parade, Newport, 1894

Thomas Holmes, a young medical student, played in one match for Glamorgan, as a late substitute, away to Monmouthshire in 1894, scoring 4 and 0.

Educated at Oakham School, Thomas played initially in club cricket for Melton Mowbray before impressing for the Cardiff University side whilst starting his medical studies at university in South Wales. He completed his training in London before returning to the East Midlands to run a medical practice in Leicester.

93.
HILL, Percy Montgomery Tickell

Born – Llandaff, 28 September 1877
Died – Clifton, 27 April 1944
Amateur
Batsman
Ed – Epsom College
1st XI: 1894-1898
Clubs: Fairwater, St Fagans, South Wales Hunts.
Brother of VT Hill

Batting and Fielding Record

M	I	NO	RUNS	AV	100	50	CT	ST
2	3	0	14	4.67	-	-	-	-

Bowling Record

Balls	M	R	W	AV	5wI	10wM
6	0	8	0	-	-	-

Career-bests
13 v Cornwall at Penzance, 1898

Percy Hill was the youngest son of Sir Edward Stock Hill of Rookwood House in Llandaff and, like his elder siblings, he mixed his business career with a sporting one, playing county cricket for Glamorgan, and playing with success for Fairwater, St Fagans and the South Wales Hunts.

Born at Rookwood and educated at Epsom College, he was the least talented, from a cricketing point of view, of Sir Edward's sons, yet in 1897 when only sixteen, he played as a late replacement in the match against Wiltshire at Swindon. The withdrawl of David Mullens of Cardiff saw the schoolboy being drafted in – early editions of local newspapers however still referred to Mullens as batting at number 7 and making nought, but this was rectified the following morning. Percy though didn't get a chance to bat again in the match as Glamorgan eased to a ten wicket victory.

The following year he played for his brother Vernon's team which met Glamorgan in a two-day game at the Arms Park in early August. It was a star-studded eleven with CB Fry and Sammy Wood also appearing – the teenage Hill batted at number nine and made 4, besides a single wicket as first change bowler, as the light-hearted contest ended in a jolly draw.

Percy Hill, seen on his wedding day.

Some decent performances in club cricket saw Percy play again for Glamorgan during August 1898 in their match with Cornwall at Penzance. He met with greater success with the bat, making 13 and 1 in what proved to be his final county game. Like his brothers, Percy spent time living in north-east

Somerset, playing for Lansdown and the Somerset Stragglers.

During the closing years of the Great War, Percy also joined the Royal Flying Corps before living at the Manor House in St Nicholas from which he ran the successful garage business known as the Queens and Royal in Westgate Street in Cardiff, opposite the Arms Park, and serving guests staying at the Queens and Royal Hotel, besides another garage in Cathedral Road.

94.
BINCH, David

Born – Calverton, December 1869
Died – Basford, December 1951
Professional
Bowler
1st XI: 1894-1900
Players of Glamorgan 1894
Clubs: Lancaster, Calverton, Penarth

Batting and Fielding Record

M	I	NO	RUNS	AV	100	50	CT	ST
3	3	0	16	5.33	-	-	1	-

Bowling Record

Balls	M	R	W	AV	5wI	10wM
100	2	77	2	38.50	-	-

Career-bests
16 v Herefordshire at Hereford, 1895
1/9 v Northamptonshire at Northampton, 1900

David Binch, who made three appearances for Glamorgan, spanning six seasons, was a member of a cricketing family in Basford, Nottinghamshire with his elder brother Frank securing a post on the staff of the East Midlands county before playing for Berkhamsted in the Home Counties and Whalley in Lancashire.

Like his brother, David was a medium-fast bowler and held professional engagements with Lancaster and Calverton before moving to South Wales to take up a similar post with the Penarth club. In 1894 he was chosen by the Welsh county for the away match against Wiltshire at Swindon, but David was taken ill on the morning of the game and was recorded as being "absent" in the scorebook.

Fortunately, he met with better health following year when he appeared against Herefordshire at Widemarsh Common, and claimed his maiden wicket at county level, besides making 16. Despite his success with bat and ball for Penarth, David did not play again for the Welsh county until 1900 when he was in their line-up for the match against Northamptonshire at Northampton. He continued to play with decent success in club cricket and in 1904 was chosen in the Players side that met the Gentlemen of Glamorgan at the Arms Park.

1895

Billy Bancroft's first season as Glamorgan's full-time professional was a modest one with the Welsh county drawing six of their seven games. Their sole victory came in the opening match of the summer as the Club, rather than looking ahead by playing a team of Colts, met an eleven raised by the stalwart members of the South Wales CC. The match at Swansea was a clear sign to all and sundry that the days of the old gentlemen's club had come to an end and after a fine 156 by Bertie Letcher, Glamorgan eased to a nine-wicket victory.

In another way of severing links with the past, as well as saving money, no game took place in 1895 against the MCC at Lord's with the gap in the Club's calendar being filled by a fund-raising contest at the Arms Park against an All-England XI raised by Llandaff-born Vernon Hill, who was playing for Somerset and had been up at Oxford with Jack Brain.

There was still a minority on the committee who questioned whether the county should continue its activities and the *South Wales Daily News* summed up the feelings of the majority as it previewed the game with the following words of support – "Cricketers in Glamorgan have to thank JH Brain more than anyone else for the continuation of the county club. It was a

Gowan Clark (left) and a young Norman Riches walking out to the middle at the Arms Park in the late 1890s.

happy idea of the popular captain to invite the co-operation of Vernon Hill in bringing a representative eleven with a view to popularize the game locally."

Hill's team included several of his Somerset colleagues plus the legendary CB Fry with the Sussex amateur top-scoring with an elegant 71 and showing why the England selectors had included him for their winter tour. But international acclaim was far from the minds of the plucky cricketers who turned out of the cash-strapped Glamorgan side during 1895.

95.
SCOTT, Joseph Moreland

Born – Tynemouth, 5 April 1862
Died – Plymouth (at sea), 15 April 1896
Amateur
Batsman
Ed – Rugby School
1st XI: 1895
Northumberland 1878-1891
Clubs: Priory Gate, Tynemouth, Cardiff, Bridgend, Swansea, Llanishen

Batting and Fielding Record

M	I	NO	RUNS	AV	100	50	CT	ST
2	3	1	26	8.67	-	-	-	-

Career-bests
12 v South Wales CC at St Helen's, Swansea, 1895

Joseph Scott had a decent record in club cricket in north-east England, before his business interests brought him to South Wales. He played twice for Glamorgan during 1895, and might have played more but tragically, during the following April, he died whilst travelling aboard the SS *Sir Charles Tennant* which was sailing from Newcastle-upon-Tyne to Genoa.

His cricketing career began with Northumberland in 1878 when he was still a pupil at Rugby School. He was a member of the school's XI in 1879 and 1880 before playing for the Priory Gate and Tynemouth clubs. His father was a leading shipowner, based initially in Newcastle-upon-Tyne, before opening a branch of the business in Middlesbrough and subsequently Cardiff.

Joseph duly moved to South Wales to look after the new operation, and played at first for Cardiff before appearing for Bridgend in 1894 and then Swansea in 1895 – a summer which also saw him play for Glamorgan in June against the South Wales CC at St Helen's, as well as against Herefordshire in early August. Joseph lived in the well-to-do suburb of Llanishen and also joined their Athletic Club, but during the spring of 1895 he suffered from a bout of poor health, and arranged a holiday in Italy, believing that the Mediterranean air would improve his condition.

He secured passage on a vessel from Newcastle-upon-Tyne but was taken ill soon after sailing and died several hours later as the ship was entering the English Channel. It duly landed at Plymouth where Joseph's body was transferred for travel back to the family's home in the north-east.

96.
EDWARDS, JP
Amateur
Spin bowler
Ed – Llandovery College
1st XI: 1895
Club: Bridgend

Batting and Fielding Record

M	I	NO	RUNS	AV	100	50	CT	ST
3	2	0	5	2.50	-	-	2	-

Bowling Record

Balls	M	R	W	AV	5wI	10wM
250	11	142	5	28.40	-	-

Career-bests
4 v South Wales CC at St Helen's, Swansea, 1895
2/35 v South Wales CC at St Helen's, Swansea,1895

Edwards was a talented spin bowler with Bridgend who played three times for Glamorgan during 1895. After making his debut against the South Wales CC at Swansea, he played in successive games in July against Herefordshire at the Arms Park and Monmouthshire at Usk.

97.
WOLFE, Arthur
Born – Oystermouth, Swansea, January, 1867
Died – Eccleshall Bierlow, 1 March 1934,
Amateur
Batsman
1st XI: 1895
Club: Swansea
Association football for Swansea

Batting Record

M	I	NO	RUNS	AV	100	50	CT	ST
1	1	-	9	9.00	-	-	-	-

Career-bests
9 v South Wales CC at St Helen's, Swansea, 1895

Arthur Wolfe was a leading member of the Swansea association football team, besides playing once for Glamorgan against the veterans of the South Wales CC at St Helen's in 1895, with his appearance in the light-hearted match being more to do with his availability than any rich vein of form for the Swansea 1st XI.

A talented centre-half, Arthur led Swansea AFC for several seasons during the 1890s and was the manager of a tinplate works in Morriston.

98.
LOWE, Samuel
Born – Kirkby-in-Ashfield, 19 July 1867
Died – Nottingham, March 1947
Professional
RHB, RFM
1st XI: 1895-1902
Nottinghamshire 1894, South Wales 1894
Club: Cardiff
Brother of R Lowe

Batting and Fielding Record

M	I	NO	RUNS	AV	100	50	CT	ST
76	99	29	650	9.29	-	-	43	-

Bowling Record

Balls	M	R	W	AV	5wI	10wM
10880	555	5157	336 (+5)	15.35	25	9

Career-bests
36* v Surrey 2nd XI at Cardiff Arms Park, 1898
8/37 v Wiltshire at Cardiff Arms Park, 1901

Sam Lowe was the first English-born professional to consistently perform with credit for Glamorgan in Minor County cricket, besides being the first bowler for the Welsh county to perform a hat-trick in the competition.

The fast-medium seam bowler first came to the attention of the Welsh county whilst playing for Nottinghamshire Colts, and during July 1894 he had been invited to play in the South Wales side against an XI chosen by EM Grace of Gloucestershire to raise funds for the relief effort associated with the explosions at Albion Colliery. The 26 year-old claimed 5/22 and whilst in South Wales was sounded out about a professional position with Cardiff and, *inter alia*, the Glamorgan club for 1895.

Aware of this offer, he was chosen by Nottinghamshire the following month for their County Championship fixture against Lancashire at Old Trafford. Sam went wicketless in this match – which proved to be his sole first-class appearance – and after playing for Nottinghamshire Colts against the Yorkshire Colts at Bramall Lane, Sheffield in May 1895, and no likelihood of a 1st XI place, he moved to South Wales and played for Glamorgan in their friendlies that summer against the South Wales CC, the MCC and Vernon Hill's XI.

He impressed in these games, as well as for Cardiff, and duly secured a full-time position with both club and county for 1896. His first full summer in South Wales saw Sam claim a total of 35 wickets, including 8/96 against Surrey 2nd XI, but it was the following summer – Glamorgan's first as a Minor County – when he hit the headlines against Cornwall at Swansea as he claimed the Club's first hat-trick and guided them to their first win in the new competition.

Sam could generate pace from most surfaces, even on the slow St Helen's wicket: the venue for his hat-trick against Cornwall in 1897. His feat was described as follows by the *South Wales Daily News* – "Hosking, who had laboured for twenty minutes for just one was caught in the slips off Lowe, who had had downright bad luck to date. But with his next ball, the Cardiff bowler knocked over the middle stump of Colville-Smith, the Cornwall captain, and with his next, he bowled Trevarthen, so performing the hat-trick and gaining unstinted applause from the small band of spectators who had gathered at the St Helen's ground."

Glamorgan had batted disappointingly in their first innings, but Sam's efforts secured an 11-run lead. However, the Welsh county fared much better in their

Sam Lowe.

second innings with Billy Bancroft and Bertie Letcher each making attractive fifties before Cornwall were left with a target of 259 in the three hours and twenty minutes that remained. It seemed a reasonable target, but they collapsed in dramatic fashion within the space of just three-quarters of an hour, and were bowled out for a paltry 25. Sam took five further wickets, as did William Lambert, and the Nottinghamshire man then led the Glamorgan side off the field to a standing ovation from the Swansea faithful as the Welsh county secured their first win in the Minor County Championship.

Sam's most successful season with Glamorgan came during 1901 when he claimed 80 wickets at 11 runs apiece and claimed nine five-wicket hauls during a fine summer with the ball. After a twelve-wicket haul against Monmouthshire at Cardiff in July, plus eleven wickets in the game at the same ground with Wiltshire, Sam took a career-best 8/37 at the Arms Park against Wiltshire during the first week of August before three weeks later at the same ground taking 7/77 against the South Africans.

The following year, Sam claimed 42 wickets and played his final game for the Welsh county against Devon at Exeter in the August of a summer which had seen the seam bowler also turn down a lucrative contract with a club in South Africa. He remained in South Wales acting as groundsman-professional to the Cardiff club until 1906.

99.
PULLEN, William Wade Fitzherbert

Born – Itchington, Gloucestershire, 24 June 1866
Died – Southampton, 9 August 1937
Amateur
RHB, occ WK
Ed – Long Ashton School, Bristol University and London University
1st XI: 1895
Somerset 1881, Gloucestershire 1882-1892
Clubs: South Wales CC, Cardiff, Clifton, Thornbury, Grasshoppers

Batting and Fielding Record

M	I	NO	RUNS	AV	100	50	CT	ST
6	7	0	190	27.14	-	-	2	-

Career-bests
77 v Herefordshire at Hereford, 1895

William Pullen was something of a child prodigy, playing for Somerset in a friendly against Hampshire in 1881 when only fifteen years and two months old. He subsequently played for his native Gloucestershire before enjoying a distinguished academic career, chiefly at Cardiff University, which saw the gifted batsman play for Glamorgan.

His father, Sam, had been a leading member of Clifton CC, who also played for the South Wales club, so it was no surprise that young William inherited his father's love of cricket. He made his first appearance for Gloucestershire aged sixteen and made a composed 71 against Yorkshire at the Cheltenham Festival, an innings described in '*Cricket – A Weekly Record of the Game*' as "a display of extraordinary merit for a cricketer of such inexperience."

The College Ground proved to be a hunting ground for the young batsman as two years later, it was the venue for his career-best 161 against Middlesex. By this time, he had commenced his training as an engineer under the tutelage of Tom Hurry Riches, the superintendent of the locomotive department of the Taff Vale Railway, based in Cardiff and himself an enthusiastic cricketer who in 1880 played for Cardiff against the United South of England.

Whilst based in Cardiff, he also played for the town club as well as the South Wales CC before taking a sabbatical from county cricket in 1886 having secured a Whitworth Scholarship and becoming a student at the Royal College of Science in London. In 1887 William returned to the West County to commence a doctorate at Bristol University, and for the next few years mixed his studies with playing for Gloucestershire and the Thornbury club. In one game for the latter he and EM Grace added 311 for the first wicket.

In 1892 William became a junior lecturer at Cardiff University – a decision which brought to an end his first-class career with Gloucestershire, but the resumption of his association with the Cardiff club plus a brief return to county cricket in 1895 as he appeared in all four of Glamorgan's inter-county games, plus the matches against the MCC and Vernon Hill's XI.

It proved to be William's only summer with the Welsh county following his appointment as Head of the Mechanical Engineering department at the South Western Polytechnic, Chelsea. Professional Pullen then moved to Lancashire following his promotion to Senior Inspector of the county's Technological Branch of the Board of Education.

During these years, he also co-authored several books on engineering, besides being an examiner at the City and Guilds of London Institute. In 1926 William retired from teaching and examining and moved to live in Southampton, coincidentally the town where his county cricket career had begun as a teenager back in 1881.

William Pullen.

100.
McKAY, John Frederick
Born – Swansea, June 1860
Died – Cardiff, September 1936
Amateur
All-rounder
1st XI: 1895
Clubs: Cardiff, Newport

Batting and Fielding Record

M	I	NO	RUNS	AV	100	50	CT	ST
1	1	0	2	2.00	-	-	1	-

Bowling Record

Balls	M	R	W	AV	5wI	10wM
50	3	16	1	16.00	-	-

Career-bests
2 v Monmouthshire at Usk, 1895
1/8 v Monmouthshire at Usk, 1895

A tailor by trade, John McKay played once for Glamorgan in 1895, against Monmouthshire at Usk. The game in July clashed with the General Election and local newspapers commented how "a majority of the first choice players were unable to get away."

He had a decent recent in club cricket for Cardiff, before opening a new business in Newport and switching his allegiance to Monmouthshire for whom he played between 1900 and 1902.

101.
DUNFORD, William Benson
Born – Radstock, March 1869
Died – Pontypridd, September 1936
Amateur
Batsman
1st XI: 1895
Clubs: Cardiff, Cardiff Commercials

Batting and Fielding Record

M	I	NO	RUNS	AV	100	50	CT	ST
1	1	1	0	-	-	-	-	-

Career-bests
0* v Herefordshire at Hereford, 1895

William Dunford enjoyed a decent career in club cricket with Cardiff Commercials, and subsequently the town club, and during August 1895 he made his solitary appearance for Glamorgan in their away match with Herefordshire.

Born in Somerset, William was brought up in Merthyr Tydfil before training as a carpenter and working as a carriagemaker with the Taff Vale Railway.

102.
YORATH, Herbert William Friend
Born – Canton, Cardiff, March 1875
Died – Cardiff, 1 June 1954
Amateur
Batsman
1st XI: 1895
Clubs: Canton, Cardiff
Brother of THB Yorath

Batting and Fielding Record

M	I	NO	RUNS	AV	100	50	CT	ST
1	1	0	10	10	-	-	1	-

Career-bests
10 v Monmouthshire at Usk, 1895

Herbert Yorath, was the younger brother of Bruce Yorath and also played cricket for the Canton and Cardiff clubs, besides appearing once for Glamorgan during 1895.

His one game at county level came during mid-July 1895 when Herbert was called up to play against Monmouthshire at Usk. He made 10, but the clerk to a colliery company at Cardiff Docks, was never chosen again.

1896

Since his arrival in South Wales, Jack Brain had meticulously overseen the expansion of his family's brewery in Cardiff plus the opening of a host of new public houses selling their ales and lagers. Besides having a keen business acumen, Jack knew the value of perseverance, and holding firm goals at times of worry. These were just two of the qualities he brought to Glamorgan Cricket and, through his actions, the 1890s saw the Club transformed from a moderate and ragbag eleven to a fully-fledged Minor County side.

1896 was a pivotal season in this transformation with the Club building on the progress made during the previous summers by arranging additional friendlies that summer against Worcestershire and Surrey 2nd XI. Each were a useful yardstick against which the Welsh county could assess their talent, although the games against Surrey saw a draw at The Oval and an innings defeat at the Arms Park.

The contest with Worcestershire also ended in a nine-wicket defeat but Brain held true to his principles that the Club's form and finances would only improve if they played regularly at a higher level. His belief in speculating to accumulate was boosted by innings victories over Herefordshire and the MCC, plus a thrilling two-wicket success against Monmouthshire at Rodney Parade.

The victory epitomized the new spirit within the Glamorgan side, as well as showcasing the batting abilities of Billy Bancroft. After being set a target of 211, and losing five quick wickets, the professional

Billy Bancroft – Glamorgan's first homegrown professional cricketer – seen in his Swansea RFC kit.

led a counter-attack and struck a superb 119 to see the Welsh county to victory. It was the dawn of a new era as plans began for an application to join the Minor County Championship in 1897 and during the second half of the summer a number of players were given opportunities to display their wares ahead of the new challenges.

103.
CARRINGTON, William George

Born – Herne Hill, 16 May 1880
Died – Flanders, Belgium, 28 April 1918
Professional
Batsman
1st XI: 1896
South London Schools, Surrey Colts, Surrey Club and Ground

Batting and Fielding Record

M	I	NO	RUNS	AV	100	50	CT	ST
1	1	0	10	10.00	-	-	1	-

Career-bests
10 v Surrey 2nd XI at The Oval, 1896

Nine days after his sixteenth birthday, William Carrington made his debut for Glamorgan in their match against Surrey Club and Ground at The Oval in late May 1896. He had no attachment whatsoever with the Welsh county as at the time, he was a junior professional on the Surrey staff. His selection followed Sam Brain being taken ill the night before the game at The Oval. A telegram was hastily sent that evening to Tom Barlow enquiring if he could catch an early morning train up to London, but with the answer being in the negative, the Surrey teenager was drafted in by Glamorgan as a very late replacement.

He duly scored 10 batting at number nine in the order, besides taking a catch, but the drawn game proved to be his only cricket match of note, Despite having represented London Schools, he did not play any further representative cricket and instead appeared in club cricket in the East End.

William was residing in Tottenham when the Great War broke out in 1914. He duly joined the 1st Battalion of the Leicestershire Regiment, and underwent basic training in Cambridge before crossing the Channel on 10 September, 1914. William and his battalion duly became veterans of various actions on the Western Front, including the action at Hooge in 1915, the Battles of Flers-Courcelette and Le Transloy in 1916, as well as the Battle of Hill 70 in 1917.

They subsequently were involved in The Hundred Days Offensive, but sadly on 28 April, 1918 William lost his life during a skirmish in Flanders as the British Army attempted to make further inroads into German-held territory.

104.
MANN, *Arthur Henry*

Born – Warwick, 7 July 1876
Died – Folkestone, 23 July 1972
Amateur
Batsman
Ed – Warwick School
1st XI: 1896
Warwickshire Club and Ground 1893
Club: Cardiff

Batting and Fielding Record

M	I	NO	RUNS	AV	100	50	CT	ST
4	7	0	116	16.57	-	1	2	-

Career-bests
58 v Herefordshire at Hereford, 1896

Arthur Mann was a talented young cricketer who played four times for Glamorgan in 1896 before enjoying a distinguished career as a journalist acting as editor of the *Evening Standard* and the *Yorkshire Post*, besides being a Governor of the BBC.

Educated at Warwick School, his prowess with the bat won him a place in the school's XI as well as several appearances for the Warwickshire Club and Ground team. Rather than become a professional cricketer, Arthur moved to South Wales to commence his training as a journalist and joined the staff of the *Western Mail* newspaper whose offices were in St Mary Street, Cardiff, just a six hit away from the Arms Park.

Arthur also joined Cardiff CC, and after some decent innings, he was chosen as a reserve for Glamorgan's away match with Herefordshire in June 1896. When Sidney Sweet-Escott dropped out, Arthur duly made his debut and impressed with a composed innings of 58. His efforts saw him chosen in the starting line-up for the return game at the Arms Park, as well as the visit to Lord's to play the MCC plus the match with Monmouthshire at Cardiff. However, only made 58 more runs in six innings and was not called up again.

As one door closed, another opened as the young journalist and his wife returned to the West Midlands where Henry became sub-editor of the *Birmingham Daily Mail*. In 1905 he was appointed editor of the *Birmingham Daily Dispatch*, before moving to London in 1912 following his appointment as London editor of the *Manchester Daily Dispatch*. His star was clearly in the ascent as three years later he became editor of the *Evening Standard*, before being appointed editor of the *Yorkshire Post* in 1919.

Arthur remained with the *Yorkshire Post* until 1939, during which time he won acclaim for his independence of thought, besides making the headlines himself in 1936 during Edward VIII's abdication. In particular, he broke the Press silence over the King's action in wishing to marry American divorcee Wallis Simpson, as he published criticism which the Bishop of Bradford had voiced. A couple of years later Arthur also opposed Neville

Chamberlain's policy of appeasement with Nazi Germany, before becoming embroiled in a series of arguments with the owners of the *Yorkshire Post* following their decision to merge with the *Leeds Mercury*. The run-ins led to Arthur's resignation, but he remained in the Media, serving as a Governor of the BBC between 1941 and 1946. In later life, Arthur was a decent golfer and apparently twice declined a knighthood during the 1920s, believing that it would interfere with his journalism.

105.
JOHNSON, Richard Hargrave Townley

Born – Islington, July 1874
Amateur
All-rounder
1st XI: 1896-1908
Club: Penarth
Rugby for Penarth

Batting and Fielding Record

M	I	NO	RUNS	AV	100	50	CT	ST
10	17	3	170	12.14	-	-	4	-

Bowling Record

Balls	M	R	W	AV	5wI	10wM
163	8	159	2	79.50	-	-

Career-bests
31* v Herefordshire at Hereford, 1896
1/42 v Monmouthshire at Rodney Parade, Newport, 1896

Richard Johnson was one of the enthusiastic young men, with a professional background, who played rugby and cricket for Penarth during the 1890s. His success on the cricket field led to ten appearances for Glamorgan before the well-to-do accountant emigrated to South Africa.

The son of Townley Johnson, a well-known accountant in Penarth, who had attended Cowbridge GS before moving to work initially in the London area. Richard was born in Islington before the family moved back to South Wales, with Richard following in his father's footsteps by securing a post with one of the thriving railway companies who served the Docks at Penarth and Cardiff.

Success for Penarth, and a friendship with Herbie Morgan, led to his selection for Glamorgan in June 1896 for the away match with Herefordshire, He made an unbeaten 31 and appeared in four further matches that summer before moving to London where he worked

An image of Richard Johnson as a sixteen year-old, playing for Penarth CC.

138

for the next four years, before moving back to South Wales and joining the Swansea club.

He re-appeared for Glamorgan in 1902 against Monmouthshire at St Helen's but his work commitments meant that he was not seen again in the Welsh county's ranks until 1905 when he appeared in three further Minor County Championship matches, as well as the contest at Neath against the Gentlemen of Carmarthenshire.

The Gnoll was also the venue in 1908 for his last match of note as he played in the Minor County Championship contest against Carmarthenshire. At some stage during the subsequent months, Richard decided to emigrate to South Africa, and was married in Cape Town during 1911.

106.
MULLENS, David

Born – Chippenham, Wiltshire, July 1861
1st XI: 1896-1900
Amateur
Seam bowler
Clubs: Cardiff, Canton, Taff Vale

Batting and Fielding Record

M	I	NO	RUNS	AV	100	50	CT	ST
2	4	1	11	3.67	-	-	1	-

Bowling Record

Balls	M	R	W	AV	5wI	10wM
99	1	77	3	25.67	-	-

Career-bests
6 v Berkshire at Cardiff Arms Park, 1900
2/55 v Worcestershire 2nd XI at Cardiff Arms Park, 1896

David Mullens had a decent record as a bowler in the Cardiff and District League and played with success for Canton and the Taff Vale clubs, before joining Cardiff. His move to the premier club and his continued success led to a couple of appearances at county level – against Worcestershire 2nd XI in 1896 and Berkshire in 1900.

Both were at the Arms Park, with the plumber unable to commit to travelling to away matches owing to pressure of work. Indeed, David had been chosen in 1894 to play in the match at Swindon against Wiltshire, but had to cry off the night before the game.

David Mullens.

107.
MENDELSON, Wallingford ('Wally')
Born – Temuka, New Zealand, 29 December 1872
Died – Durban, South Africa, 19 August 1902
Amateur
RHB, occ WK
Ed – Christ College, Christchurch, Otago University and Jesus College, Cambridge
1st XI: 1896
Canterbury 1894
Clubs: Cardiff, MCC
Rugby for Otago and Cambridge University

Batting and Fielding Record

M	I	NO	RUNS	AV	100	50	CT	ST
2	4	0	33	8.25	-	-	1	-

Career-bests
19 v Herefordshire at Cardiff Arms Park, 1896

Wally Mendelson was another example of the players with no residential qualifications who appeared for Glamorgan during the Club's early years. In fact, Wally's roots could not have been further away from South Wales, as the son of a Polish Jew was brought up in Christchurch, New Zealand and played for Glamorgan whilst staying with relatives in Cardiff whilst a student at Jesus College, Cambridge.

The young Kiwi was an outstanding schoolboy sportsman excelling at athletics, rugby and cricket for Christ's College, Christchurch, before reading Law at Otago University from 1891. Whilst at Otago Wally won a place in the university's rugby and cricket side, and after some impressive performances in the XI he was chosen in the Canterbury side for the inter-provincial match against Hawkes Bay in April 1894. Wally made 7 in his only innings. A few months later he travelled to the UK to commence his studies at Cambridge. Wally duly enjoyed an excellent first term at Jesus College, winning a place at full-back for the Varsity Match. Soon afterwards, he aggravated an old knee injury and had to give up rugby. However, Wally continued to excel at athletics, winning a long jump Blue in 1895 and in the process beat CB Fry, the well-known England cricketer. Wally also won a half-blue at billiards, and appeared for his college at cricket, but never made the Cambridge XI.

However, Wally had a taste of county cricket during 1896 when spending the summer vacation with relatives in South Wales. Each summer he joined the Cardiff club and in July 1896 Wally impressed whilst opening the batting against Weston-super-Mare. The *Western Mail* newspaper commented how the student "hit in splendid style, all round the wicket and repeatedly found the boundary. Everybody expected to see him make the coveted century, but when he was 97 he was bowled by a slower ball." His efforts helped Cardiff to a 103-run victory whilst his name went down in their official's notebook as someone on which to keep an eye.

The following week Wally made his Glamorgan debut as the Welsh county found themselves short after their captain Jack Brain failed to recover from a leg injury sustained the night before the match at the Arms Park against Surrey 2nd XI when he collided with a stone wall whilst out riding his bicycle near Fonmon Castle. After arriving at the ground with a gammy leg, Jack got a message to Wally's relatives and the student hastily made his way to the Arms Park. It did not prove to be a fairytale start as Wally was bowled first ball by Walter Lees for a duck.

Wally made 4 in the second innings, and during mid-August was chosen again for Glamorgan, this time on merit, for the match against Herefordshire at the Arms Park having played some decent innings opening the batting in club cricket with Jack Brain who was now restored to full fitness. Opening the batting with Bertie Letcher he made 19 and 10 as the Welsh county won by six wickets.

In 1897 Wally completed his legal training in the London area, and played several times for the MCC, before returning to New Zealand the following year and setting up a practice in Timaru. In 1902 he was on the move again as he travelled to South Africa to seek new opportunities, but within a couple of months of being in Durban, Wally was found dead at a boarding house.

108.
LOWE, Richard ('Dick')

Born – Kirkby-in-Ashfield, 18 June 1869
Died – Kirkby-in-Ashfield 3 July 1946
Professional
RHB, LM
1st XI: 1896-1901
Nottinghamshire 1891; Lord Sheffield's XI 1891; Sussex 1893-1894
Clubs: Kirkby Portland, Rishton, Church, Cardiff
Brother of S Lowe

Batting and Fielding Record

M	I	NO	RUNS	AV	100	50	CT	ST
59	84	7	1493	19.39	-	7	56	-

Bowling Record

Balls	M	R	W	AV	5wI	10wM
2610	137	1250	86	14.53	5	1

Career-bests:
87 v Wiltshire at Swindon, 1897
8/54 v MCC at St Helen's, Swansea, 1898

Dick Lowe followed his elder brother Sam to South Wales after brief spells in county cricket with his native Nottinghamshire and Sussex, as well as spending time in the Lancashire League with Rishton and Church. Indeed, it was whilst playing for Church in July 1896 that Dick had a trial with Glamorgan and appeared for the Welsh county against the MCC at the Arms Park. Dick had a decent game scoring 41 and taking 5/58 in the MCC's first innings. Terms were duly agreed with both the Cardiff club and in 1897 he made his first appearance in the Minor County Championship. Glamorgan for 1897. Dick duly spent the next five years in the Welsh county's colours, though not without an element of controversy over his bowling action.

The all-rounder enjoyed a decent first summer in Glamorgan's ranks making 487 runs, including scores of 78 against Monmouthshire, plus 86 and 87 in the two games with Wiltshire, besides claiming 22 wickets with his left-arm seam. Dick began 1898 in good form with the ball, claiming 6/41 against Surrey at The Oval, 6/25 against Worcestershire at the Arms Park and then took fourteen wickets in the friendly against the MCC at St Helen's.

Richard Lowe.

It was during these games that a few mur-murings occurred about his action. Dick had suffered from a shoulder strain during the winter and had slightly altered his action. Several of the Worcestershire batsmen questioned the legitimacy of Dick's action at Cardiff, but neither of the local umpires took action.

Two neutral umpires – Val Titchmarsh and Jim Phillips – were appointed for the return game at New Road, and on the opening day, Dick was called for throwing by square-leg umpire Titch-marsh. This was the first time this had happened to any bowler in the Minor County Championship and there was plenty of comment in the Press the following morning. On being quizzed by the local hacks about the reason for the call, Titchmarsh stated "when Dick fully raises his left arm above his head, he throws the ball."

With Glamorgan dismissed for 31 and 86, there was not a second chance for Dick to bowl at New Road, and with two local men officiating the next match against Monmouthshire at the Arms Park, the scrutiny of Dick's action came from the Glamorgan hierarchy assembled in the pavilion. Dick only bowled fourteen overs against Monmouthshire, plus one more in the next game against Wiltshire, and the fact that he played solely as a batsman for the rest of 1898 indicates that there were some concerns amongst the Welsh county's ranks.

These worries continued in 1899 when Dick was ever-present in the Glamorgan line-up but again primarily as a batsman, and only bowling a couple of overs all season. The concerns may have also preyed on Dick's mind as in 1899 he only passed fifty once in sixteen innings, and with his batting powers seemingly on the wane, he re-modelled his action once again. His new action passed muster in the games during mid-summer against Surrey 2nd XI and the MCC, but although he claimed eight wickets in the match with Berkshire, his bowling was not as effective as before.

1901 duly proved to be his last year of county cricket, and although he was still effective with the bat for Cardiff, Dick failed to pass fifty all summer for Glamorgan and ended with a tally of 163 runs from fifteen innings. His final match of note duly came in mid-August as he appeared against the South Africans, scoring 7 and 0. It was an inglorious end to a career at county level which had offered much, but had been embroiled in controversy.

109.
LLEWELLYN, John Griffith
Born – Penarth, March 1867
Amateur
Batsman
1st XI: 1896
Club: Penarth

Batting and Fielding Record

M	I	NO	RUNS	AV	100	50	CT	ST
1	2	1	5	5.00	-	-	-	-

Career-bests
3* v Monmouthshire at Rodney Parade, Newport, 1896

John Llewellyn was another amateur who played once for Glamorgan, and like the others, his appearance came at short notice having agreed to travel to Newport to watch and support his colleagues Richard Johnson and the Morgan brothers from the Penarth club. He was duly called into the side when another amateur dropped out on the morning of the game.

It proved to be quite a memorable game for John as having made 2 in the first innings batting at number 9, he was in the middle in the second innings when the winning runs were struck as Glamorgan narrowly defeated their neighbours by two wickets.

John was a rate collector by trade and besides playing cricket for Penarth, he acted as Treasurer of the town's rugby club from 1891 until 1898.

110.
MORGAN, Frederick Walter
Born – Penarth, September 1866
Died – Penarth, 2 February 1932
Amateur
Seam bowler
1st XI – 1896
Brother of HE Morgan
Rugby for Penarth
Clubs – Penarth, South Wales CC

Batting and Fielding Record

M	I	NO	RUNS	AV	100	50	CT	ST
1	1	0	3	3.00	-	-	-	-

Bowling Record

Balls	M	R	W	AV	5wI	10wM
60	3	33	1	33.00	-	-

Career-bests
3 v Monmouthshire, at Rodney Parade, Newport, 1896
1/33 v Monmouthshire at Rodney Parade, Newport 1896

Fred Morgan was the elder brother of Glamorgan's first centurion, Herbie Morgan but whereas young Herbie shone with the bat, Fred was more of a bowler.

The farmer's son from Lower Penarth had a fine record in the Cardiff and District League, taking 8/8 for Penarth against Barry Dock in 1888, before the following year claiming 8/10 against St Mary's. He was also a member of the South Wales CC and his first match of note came in 1886 when he played for the Next XVIII against the Club's 1st XI at Newport in June 1886 as they showcased some of the rising talent in the area.

Ten years later Fred made his Glamorgan debut but, aged 30, he was past his best when he made his one and only county appearance against Monmouthshire at Rodney Parade. His belated appearance saw him play, not only alongside Herbie, but several others from the Penarth club. At the time, Fred was also Chairman of Penarth RFC, holding office between 1894 and 1898.

With Herbie running the family's farm, Fred opted for a career in local business, and became managing owner of the Canton Sawmills in Cardiff. After retiring from cricket, Fred took up bowls and became captain of the Windsor Bowling Club, situated in the resort town on land owned by the Earl of Plymouth.

Like his brother, Fred had also been a useful rugby player in his youth, and took great pride in representing Penarth. This was also the case in later life as he spent over twenty years as a member of Penarth Urban District Council before , before serving as the town's mayor. He died during February 1932 having suffered a fatal heart attack whilst erecting stalls at St Augustine's ahead of a bazaar at the well-known Penarth church.

111.
REES, Rev. Richard Morgan
Born – Pontypridd, 22 April 1875
Died – Porthcawl, 28 June 1932
Amateur
RHB, RM, occ WK
Ed – St John's School, Leatherhead and Magdalene College, Oxford
1st XI: 1896-1904
Clubs: Cardiff, Treherbert

Batting and Fielding Record

M	I	NO	RUNS	AV	100	50	CT	ST
5	9	0	75	8.33	-	-	5	-

Bowling Record

Balls	M	R	W	AV	5wI	10wM
5	0	8	0	-	-	-

Career-bests
25 v Wiltshire at Swindon, 1897

The Reverend Richard Rees was another cricketing cleric who played for Glamorgan during their days as a Minor County.

His father was also a man of the cloth, based at Treherbert Parsonage. Young Richard showed great promise as a sound batsman and a capable batsman whilst at St John's School in Leatherhead, and duly featured in the school's XI between 1891 and 1893 before going up to Oxford to read History at Magdalene College.

During his summer vacations Richard played cricket for both Treherbert and Cardiff, and in late August 1896, he made his debut for Glamorgan against Monmouthshire at the Arms Park. He made a further three appearances the following August, each in games outside Wales, as he featured in the contests with Wiltshire at Swindon, Worcestershire at Kidderminster and against Cornwall at Penzance. Given the costs in covering the professionals expenses, his availability for all three matches must have been welcomed by the Welsh county's Treasurer.

Richard then opted to follow his father into the clergy, and after being a junior chaplain at Bordesley, he secured a curacy at St John's in Cardiff. His return to South Wales allowed him to play again in local cricket, as well as making a further appearance for Glamorgan in 1904, once again in an away fixture, against Devon at Exeter.

After leaving St John's, Richard subsequently became Chaplain of Christ Church, Oxford before serving as rector of Semley in Wiltshire.

1897

1897 was a seminal year in the history of Glamorgan CCC and followed a decision the previous September for the Club to raise their sights even further and enter the newly created Minor County Championship. The proposer of this motion was none other than Jack Brain, and with promises of financial help from various patrons, plus the creation of the Glamorgan Cricket League for 1897, it didn't take long for the Club's officers to support his suggestion.

The requirements laid down by the MCC for playing in the newly-created competition were a minimum of eight fixtures with other minor county sides. Agreements were immediately secured with Worcestershire, Cornwall, Wiltshire, and after a few weeks, a draft programme of games was prepared. It helped greatly that Jack was a leading figure on the Minor Counties committee and few arms needed twisting as the mandarins at Lord's admitted the Welsh county into the competition for 1897.

After a draw with Surrey 2nd XI at The Oval, Glamorgan staged their first fixture on Welsh soil in the new competition, meeting Monmouthshire at Rodney Parade. Whilst being a landmark in Welsh sporting history, it was also a personal milestone for the Brain family as Sam made one of the fastest centuries ever recorded by a Glamorgan batsman, and all from the unlikely position of number 7, as he raced to 113 in just 53 minutes.

Glamorgan's celebrations were cut short in the next match as they lost by an innings to Worcestershire at the Arms Park. But in the following game at Swansea, they recorded their first success in the competition as they defeated Cornwall by 233 runs. Their comprehensive victory was set up by some outstanding bowling from the professionals Sam Lowe – who claimed the first-ever hat trick for the Welsh county – plus William Lambert, the former Middlesex seamer who had joined Glamorgan at the start of the season. The pair were to the fore again as Glamorgan recorded a ten-wicket victory over Wiltshire and when they visited Penzance at the end of August, the Welsh county did the 'double' over Cornwall by winning by 144 runs.

The Glamorgan team which played Cornwall in 1897.

112.
PRUEN, Frederick Hamilton

Born – Didbrook, Gloucestershire, 21st April 1872
Died – Brighton, 13 September 1948
Amateur
Batsman
Ed – Llandaff Cathedral School, Repton School and Durham University
1st XI: 1897
Colts: 1893
Clubs: Cardiff, Newport, St George's, Benwell.

Batting and Fielding Record

M	I	NO	RUNS	AV	100	50	CT	ST
1	1	0	21	21.00	-	-	-	-

Career-bests
21 v Surrey 2nd XI at The Oval, 1897

Frederick Pruen was a talented schoolboy cricketer, both at Llandaff Cathedral School and Repton College in Derbyshire. After graduating from Durham University, he worked as an Assistant Registrar at University College, Cardiff, and after some decent innings for the Cardiff club, he was chosen in the Glamorgan side during June 1897 for their match against Surrey 2nd XI at The Oval.

He scored 21 in what proved to be his one and only innings at county level. Four years before, Frederick had also played for the Colts XXII against the county side in their trial match at the Arms Park, but did little to stake a claim for a place in the county side as he made just 1 and 6.

He was the youngest son of Rev. Hudson Boyce Pruen, the vicar of Didbrook and Twyning. Frederick, however, did not follow his father into the ecclesiastical world and after serving as Assistant Registrar at University College, Cardiff, he was appointed Secretary of Armstrong College, Durham in 1899. The College specialised in medicine and physical science, with Frederick remaining in post until after the Great War, besides acting as secretary of the Durham University Secondary Schools committee.

Frederick continued to play a good standard of club cricket whilst in the north-east, appearing for the St George's and Benwell club, whilst in 1905 he helped the latter win the Tyneside Senior League. He remained in contact with his cricketing friends in South Wales, and during early September 1903 whilst on holiday with his wife in South Wales, Frederick played for George Robey's XI against The Earl of Plymouth's XI at St Fagans.

Frederick Pruen.

147

113.
LAMBERT, William ('Bill')

Born – Hatfield, Middlesex, 19 April 1843
Died – St Fagans, 4 March 1927
Professional
RHB, RM
1st XI: 1897-1898
Middlesex 1874-1877, Hertfordshire 1875-1887, Northumberland
Clubs: MCC, Bury, Nelson, Bridgend

Batting and Fielding Record

M	I	NO	RUNS	AV	100	50	CT	ST
12	19	9	38	3.80	-	-	5	-

Bowling Record

Balls	M	R	W	AV	5wI	10wM
1560	63	845	60	14.08	5	3

Career-bests
7* v Cornwall at St Helen's, Swansea, 1898
9/86 v Wiltshire at Swindon, 1897

Bill Lambert was one of the journeymen professionals who appeared for Glamorgan during their early years in the Minor County Championship. By the time, however, of his ‚first appearance against Monmouthshire at the Arms Park in 1897, Bill was very much in the veteran stage of his career and, at 54 years and 81 days, he is the oldest debutant in the Club's history.

His first match of note had come in July 1865 when he played for the Middlesex Club and Ground side against the South Wales CC at Islington. After a spell on the Lord's groundstaff, Bill had a brief first-class career with Middlesex between 1874 and 1877, before playing for Hertfordshire and the MCC. He then plied his trade as a brisk round-arm bowler in the Lancashire League with Bury and Nelson, before venturing further north and playing for Northumberland. In 1896 he agreed terms with Bridgend and this led to his appearance in the Glamorgan attack for the next two seasons.

By now, Bill was bowling off-cutters with the wicket-keeper standing up rather than back as in his early days when he generated quite a bit of pace from his slingy action. He enjoyed a decent first season with the Welsh county taking, in all, 57 wickets at a shade over 12 runs apiece. Bill claimed eleven wickets in the match during July against Cornwall at Swansea, plus nine in the return game in August at Penzance, besides taking ten wickets in the contest with Wiltshire at the Arms Park in late July.

However, his finest hour in Glamorgan's ranks – and the last hurrah of a distinguished career – came during the return game at Swindon in mid-August as he took 9/86 in 26.1 overs and scythed through the Wiltshire batting in a match which the Welsh county needed to win to maintain their bid for the Minor County Championship title. He bowled unchanged during the Wiltshire innings, aided by several breaks because of rain, which also helped to spice up the surface as the home side were dismissed for 151 and forced to follow on. But the weather came to Wiltshire's assistance the following day as the game ended in a watery draw with Wiltshire on 63/6 and Lambert having bagged a dozen wickets.

Despite his bowling success, he was something of a liability in the field, and this became increasingly apparent the following summer. Having claimed a solitary wicket against both Surrey 2nd XI at The Oval and Cornwall at St Helen's during June, he was omitted for most of the remaining matches, although perhaps out of sentiment he appeared against the MCC at Swansea, with the veteran taking his final wicket for the Welsh county.

An approach by the Earl of Plymouth saw Bill switch his allegiance to St Fagans the following summer where he largely acted as the club's groundsman besides helping to coach the Earl's aspiring three sons – Other, Ivor and Archer. Bill also advised the Earl as a new wicket was laid for the St Fagans club a mile or so to the south of the village at Court Farm, with the Earl spending £2,880 on the new surface and later creating a large glass-fronted pavilion. Bill was active again in 1907 as the club moved again to Penhefyd Farm, much closer to the village, off Croft-y-Gennau Road.

During these years, Bill worked closely at the new cricket ground and bowls club with Hugh Pettigrew, the Head Gardener on the Earl's estate, who also acted as Honorary Secretary to the St Fagans cricket club. Bill remained living in St Fagans for the rest of his life with his daughter and son-in-law running The Plymouth Arms in the village. It was in the upstairs lodgings in the famous hostelry that Bill died during April 1927.

His brother George was a noted real tennis player, acting as the professional at Hatfield House – the home of the 2nd Marquess of Salisbury – in Hertfordshire, and was world champion between 1871 and 1885.

114.
RUSSELL, *William*

Born – Robertsbridge, Sussex 1870
Died – Cowbridge, 8 March 1908
All-rounder
Professional
1st XI: 1897-1906
Middlesex 2nd XI 1894-95, Combined Glamorgan and Wiltshire XI 1902
Clubs: Cowbridge, Glamorgan Gypsies

Batting and Fielding Record

M	I	NO	RUNS	AV	100	50	CT	ST
102	153	13	2665	19.04	1	10	73	-

Bowling Record

Balls	M	R	W	AV	5wI	10wM
11658	787	3816	270(+4)	14.13	14	5

Career-bests
143 v Berkshire at Cardiff Arms Park, 1899
7/43 v Devon at Exeter, 1903

William Russell was a canny spin bowler and forceful batsman who played over a hundred times for Glamorgan between 1897 and 1906 having moved to South Wales from the Middlesex groundstaff.

William had spent a couple of years at Lord's so without the immediate prospect of playing 1st XI cricket he welcomed an offer in 1896 from Harry Ebsworth, the owner of Llandough Castle, to act as groundsman-professional at Cowbridge. He had also received an offer to join his native Sussex, but it was only for a year. By moving instead to South Wales to work for such an influential figure as Ebsworth, there were also likely to be opportunities to play for Glamorgan.

Ebsworth had already invested considerable sums in acquiring the five and a half acre field, known as Cae Wyndham, at the western end of the market town, and had employed Kent's Alex Hearne in laying a wicket and creating practice facilities. The presence of the former Middlesex all-rounder in the area was good news for the Glamorgan hierarchy who duly included William in their squad in early June for their away match with Surrey 2nd XI.

However, the terms offered to the Cowbridge club for his release to travel and play in the two-day contest at The Oval were quite modest. With plenty or work to be done at Cae Wyndham, Ebsworth refused to release him, and several attempts were made by the Glamorgan officials to get Ebsworth to change his mind. But the financial terms remained largely the same and the well-to-do businessman stood firm. In fact, Harry Ebsworth

William Russell, seen in 1905.

was not the sort of man to be trifled with as his lavish home contained tokens of his skill with the rifle, including an enormous stuffed brown bear which he had, apparently, shot at close range whilst on a business trip to Russia.

Russell's unavailability for Glamorgan's first game in the Minor County Championship was a blow to Jack Brain, and it came as no surprise that Ebsworth was pilloried in the Press for what was portrayed as selfish actions rather thinking of the good his release would create. The *Western Mail*'s correspondent summed up the situation by saying "Russell's inclusion would help the side to win a match in which the victory would do the Welsh county no end of good, for the winning or losing of this game may have much to do with the future of Glamorgan cricket."

The game ended in a draw, but an olive branch came from Ebsworth a month later as he released Russell for the match against the MCC at the Arms Park. The all-rounder however went wicketless, besides scoring just 9 and 14, and in the eyes of the Glamorgan Treasurer did not really justify the sum demanded for his release. Consequently, the Welsh county looked elsewhere for their professional talent for the remainder of the 1897 season.

With caustic comments still being made in the Press, the general consensus was that the dispute with Ebsworth was not doing anybody any favours, especially as the businessman's motives were simply to raise the standard of cricket in Cowbridge by having a county cricketer in their ranks, and someone who could help attract better players and decent fixtures.

In a bid to settle things, Ebsworth agreed during June 1898 to release Russell for the match against Cornwall at Swansea. Once again, the all-rounder did little in the game, making a duck and taking a sole wicket as Glamorgan won by ten wickets. Nevertheless, it was a start, and a deal, agreeable to both parties, was duly reached the following month. With the ink barely dry on the paperwork, the all-rounder took ten wickets and struck a vibrant half-century against Wiltshire at the Arms Park, before a month later taking eleven wickets in the visit to Penzance for the away game with Cornwall.

He also impressed greatly as a fielder at cover point, and proof that his star was in ascent came during 1899 as William struck 143 against Berkshire at the Arms Park, besides sharing a stand of 148 for the third wicket with Herbie Morgan. Their efforts saw the Welsh county amass 428 – at the time, the Club's highest innings total – and the following day, Berkshire were forced to follow-on before succumbing to the Welsh bowlers for a second time as Glamorgan secured an innings victory.

Although he failed to reach three figures in 1900, William's spin bowling was to the fore again, with a ten-wicket haul against Wiltshire at Swansea, plus nine against both Surrey 2nd XI at The Oval and Berkshire at Reading, with his efforts in the latter game helping Glamorgan to share the Minor County title. The next two summers saw him make, in all, just over 500 runs whilst a tally of just 60 wickets suggested his bowling prowess was on the wane. There were rumours of heavy drinking and during 1903 some Glamorgan officials considered whether or not to terminate his contract after some erratic behavior both on and off the field. But during the final match of the season William bounced back to form, claiming a ten-wicket match haul against Devon at Exeter, besides taking career-best figures of 7/43.

But William only took seven wickets the following summer for Glamorgan besides averaging a modest nine with the bat. In his defense, William had picked up a few niggling injuries and to his great delight, he was back to form in 1905 with 456 runs as well as 30 wickets. It was not though the start of the renaissance to his career he had hoped, as he made only 105 runs at an average of a mere six in 1906, and despite taking 6/8 against Durham at the Arms Park, his loss of form and further tales of heavy drinking led the Glamorgan committee to opt against using his services

It was a sad ending to his county career after all of the discussions with Harry Ebsworth and the mud which had been slung in his direction by the Press. But worse was to follow for William as the loss of the Glamorgan contract hit him hard. His health deteriorated during 1907 with some believing his off-field excesses had finally caught up with him. Nevertheless, he had been a very popular and well-liked professional at Cowbridge and, following his death in March 1908, there was a massive turn out from the local community at his funeral.

115.
CADOGAN, John Philip

Born – Neath, March 1866
Died – Cardiff, 29 June 1918
Amateur
Batsman
1st XI: 1897-1906
Clubs: Maesteg, Merthyr, Cathays Wesleyans, Cardiff, St John's

Batting and Fielding Record

	M	I	NO	RUNS	AV	100	50	CT	ST
Minor	3	4	2	95	47.50	-	-	2	-

Career-bests
Minor County 39 v Monmouthshire at Cardiff Arms Park, 1900

John Cadogan, a leading figure in the coal and shipping trades at Cardiff Docks, played three times for Glamorgan over the period of ten years.

The eldest of seven children, his father had initially worked in the coal and ironworks in the Llynfi Valley before moving to work in the USA. John spent his childhood in the States before returning to work initially in Maesteg. He soon showed rich promise for the town's cricket club and was coached by Joseph Lovering, the well-known professional with the South Wales CC and early Glamorganshire club.

John then entered the coal importing trade in Merthyr after securing an appointment with Crawshay Brothers of Cyfarthfa. John was on the move again in 1890 as he became a coal and pitwood merchant for the French-based company of A. Capelle and Sons, with John managing the operations of their branch at Cardiff Docks. Together with Job Morgan, his father-in-law, John subsequently became a partner in a shipping company called Morgan and Cadogan, based in Mount Stuart Square, where, literally in the shadow of the Cardiff Coal Exchange, the company built up excellent trading links with Spain and France.

His cricketing career also went from strength to strength following his move to Cardiff. After some decent batting performances for St John's and Cathays Wesleyans – two of the leading junior sides in the area – he joined the town club and with further impressive innings under his belt, the Glamorgan selectors called him up during August 1897 for the away game with Wiltshire at Swindon.

John marked his debut with a composed innings of 21, but it was not until August 1900 that he was available again, this time for the home match at the Arms Park against Monmouthshire, where he again made decent scores of 39 and 18*, leaving the county's hierarchy wishing that John's business commitments at Cardiff Docks would allow him to play on a more regular basis.

However, John joined the Glamorgan committee in 1901 and served until it was disbanded at the outbreak of the Great War during August 1914. During this time, John helped the Club plan their fund-raising campaign for higher honours, besides featuring in the trial match at the Arms Park in August 1906 against a Colts XVIII as, after an unbeaten innings of 17, he helped to run his eye over the young emerging talent. By this time, John was also involved with many good causes in Cardiff, acting as vice-chairman and honorary treasurer of the Prince of Wales Hospital and other good causes designed to improve the life of seamen in the docks area.

Like so many other shipowners at Cardiff Dock, John lost several vessels during the war with Nailsea Court and Boynton each being torpedoed and sunk by German U-boats. Their loss and the potential impact on the business, weighed heavy on his mind. Soon after, his health had deteriorated and John suffered a heart attack. He recovered but suffered a second, and fatal, attack during the summer of 1918 and never saw Glamorgan scale the heights of first-class status.

John Cadogan, seen in front of the pavilion at Cardiff Arms Park in 1903.

116.
PHILLIPS, Martin Mostyn
Born – Cardiff, January 1869
Died – Cardiff, June 1922
Amateur
RHB, RFM
1st XI: 1897
Clubs: Cardiff, Cathays, St Mary's

Batting and Fielding Record

M	I	NO	RUNS	AV	100	50	CT	ST
3	4	1	5	1.67	-	-	1	-

Bowling Record

Balls	M	R	W	AV	5wI	10wM
85	7	39	2	19.50	-	-

Career-bests
3 v Worcestershire at Kidderminster, 1897
1/15 v Wiltshire at Swindon, 1897

Martin Phillips had a good record as a fast-medium bowler in the Cardiff and District League, and following some decent performances for the St Mary's and Cathays clubs, the tailor was recruited by Cardiff where he continued to impress with some lively seam bowling.

Eager to blood new talent, the Glamorgan selectors called upon his services for three away during August 1897. Martin's debut came against Wiltshire at Swindon, before appearances in the back-to-back matches against Worcestershire at Kidderminster and Cornwall at Penzance. However, he did little of note at county level and although not called again by Glamorgan, Martin remained a handy seam bowler in club cricket for Cardiff

1898

1898 saw Glamorgan win four of their ten Minor County fixtures as well as defeating the MCC by four wickets at Swansea. The victory at St Helen's stemmed from a fine bowling performance by Richard Lowe, who claimed fourteen wickets and, after yet another victory over the MCC, it must have been a surprise for Jack Brain and others within the Glamorgan hierarchy to read the words of playwright Edward Verrall Lucas. In a book called *Willow and Leather*, he wrote "on a fine day when the match is not important enough to crowd the ring, when for instance the MCC are playing Glamorganshire, the Pavilion cat has the pleasant habit of sunning itself on the turf!"

1898 also saw the debut for Glamorgan of Harry Creber, a spinner whose feats were to subsequently see the Welsh county onto first-class status. His acquisition complemented the efforts of the Lowe brothers, plus Bill Lambert and William Russell as Glamorgan were able to take to the field with a decent bowling attack. On the batting front, Jack Brain was still to the fore with some high-class innings, whilst Ernie Jones, a stalwart from the Club's early years, also made 101 against Cornwall at Swansea as the Welsh county showed that they could be a real force in the Minor County competition.

The summer also saw some quite colourful amateurs make their first appearance in the county's team, including Dr Richard Moynan who had starred as a batsman with Cowbridge CC, besides being a well-known jockey in local point-to-points. The irascible doctor enjoyed putting bat to ball in club cricket, but frequently opted not to field and instead made excuses that he had to leave to see a patient who apparently had just taken a turn for the worse. Remarkably, his client always made a swift enough recovery to allow Richard to join his team-mates in a local tavern in Cowbridge where they heartily celebrated a victory or drowned their sorrows after a defeat.

William Russell, as seen in 1902.

117.
ALEXANDER, Hubert Griffiths

Born – Pontypridd, 9 September 1873
Died – Gileston Manor, St Athan, 20 December 1954
Amateur
Batsman
Ed – Tavistock GS
1st XI: 1898
Clubs: Cardiff, Penarth, Dinas Powis, Water Rats.
Rugby for Penarth, Newport, Glamorgan and the Barbarians

Batting and Fielding Record

M	I	NO	RUNS	AV	100	50	CT	ST
4	7	2	42	8.40	-	-	2	-

Career-bests
14* v Wiltshire at Cardiff Arms Park, 1898

Hubert Alexander was a member of the well-known Cardiff family of auctioneers. Their roots lay in Newmarket, the racing town in Suffolk, with Hubert's great-grandfather having moved to South Wales to become stable manager at Fonmon Castle, the castellated home of the Jones family to the south of Cowbridge whose later owner, Oliver Henry Jones had played cricket for the Glamorganshire club.

The Alexanders, through marriage, subsequently ran the grocery business in the village of Penmark, and with the business thriving, Hubert's father was able to be educated at Cowbridge Grammar School. Born in 1841, David Alexander had trained as a surveyor before setting up business in Pontypridd in conjunction with William Prichard Stephenson, a Yorkshire-born auctioneer. In 1877 the pair moved to Cardiff as Stephenson and Alexander of 5/6 High Street came into being.

Their business went from strength to strength, with David's staunch support of the Liberal cause helping to secure for the practice a role as advisors to the Town Council. The 1875 Cardiff Improvement Act had also given the town's Corporation the power to provide public pleasure grounds, so David was able to help the council on their negotiations with local landowners including the Marquess of Bute and Lord Tredegar.

Hubert joined the family business during the 1890s, Educated at Tavistock Grammar School and Sherborne, he was a talented all-round sportsman, playing rugby for Newport, Penarth and the Barbarians, besides playing cricket for, amongst others, Cardiff, Penarth, Dinas Powys and Glamorgan.

Hubert made four appearances for Glamorgan during 1898, starting with the match against Surrey 2nd XI at The Oval during early June. He played against Worcestershire at New Road, and twice at the Arms Park, against Monmouthshire and Wiltshire, but made little impact as a batsman, and despite some useful scores in club cricket, Hubert did not re-appear for Glamorgan in subsequent years.

Like his father and grandfather, Hubert was very well-connected and held an interest in many country sports, besides acting as a senior steward for the Bath and West Agricultural Society. His wife, Edith, was the daughter of newspaper magnate John Duncan, with the pair subsequently living at Gileston Manor in the Vale of Glamorgan, with Hubert adding golf to his recreational interests.

Later in life, he also served on the governing body of the Church in Wales, and was Chairman of the Prince of Wales' Orthopaedic Hospital. Hubert had become a partner in the family's business shortly before the Great War and during the late 1920s, he helped Glamorgan secure office space at 6 High Street, adjacent to the auctioneer's main office. It was here that Maurice Turnbull and Johnnie Clay planned their fund-raising campaign which kept the Club afloat during the 1930s, whilst in 1948, it was to the High Street office that telegrams of congratulations were sent to Wilf Wooller and his Championship-winning squad.

Hubert continued as a partner in his family's business until his sudden death shortly before Christmas 1954.

Hubert Alexander.

118.
CREBER, Harry

Born – Birkenhead, 30 April 1872
Died – Uplands, Swansea, 27 March 1939
Professional
RHB, LM / SLA
1st XI: 1898-1922
Cap: 1921
Combined Glamorgan and Wiltshire XI 1902, South Wales 1912
Clubs: Orton, Liverpool, Swansea.

Batting and Fielding Record

	M	I	NO	RUNS	AV	100	50	CT	ST
Minor	192	240	80	1665	10.41	-	1	62	-
F-c	33	58	28	155	5.16	-	-	6	-

Bowling Record

	Balls	M	R	W	AV	5wI	10wM
Minor	6671.2	1597	17617	1207(+24)	14.60	123	38
F-c	5457	177	2550	95	26.84	5	1

Career-bests
Minor –   53 v Monmouthshire at Rodney Parade, Newport, 1900
               9/56 v Carmarthenshire at Stradey Park, Llanelli, 1908
First-class – 13* v Sussex at St Helen's, Swansea, 1922
               7/47 v Hampshire at St Helen's, Swansea, 1922

Harry Creber was the first great spin bowler to play for Glamorgan with the left-arm twirler claiming, in all, 1326 wickets for the Welsh county in a career spanning twenty seasons. In 1905 he also became the first Glamorgan bowler to take over a hundred wickets in a season; a feat he repeated the following year with a career-best tally of 133 victims.

Besides his bowling prowess, he also won notoriety for the fact that he was ambidextrous, and could bat equally effectively either left- or right-handed. Indeed, there are tales of him spinning a coin in the changing rooms or on the pavilion balcony in order to decide before going out which way he was going to bat.

As befitted a crafty and wily bowler, he often swopped stances mid-innings in a bid to put off the opposition bowler. The most famous example of his switching stances came in 1908 during the Minor County Championship play-off final between Glamorgan and Staffordshire at Stoke-on-Trent. Glamorgan had been dismissed on a rain-affected wicket for 60, before dismissing Staffordshire for 134 with Harry claiming four wickets. Shortly before the close of play, he was pressed into service as night-watchman as the Welsh county ended the opening day on 9/1.

Having previously locked horns with Sydney Barnes, Harry decided the following morning to have a bit of fun with the master bowler and, during the course of the opening overs, he changed stance on three occasions, each time causing a delay to play as the sightscreens were trundled back and fore into position.

Irritated by Harry's whimsical actions, Sydney ran in and, rather than bowling over-arm, lobbed the ball under-arm towards the batsman. The delivery struck Harry on the pads in front of the stumps and the umpire having decided that Sydney's change of bowling style was no worse than the batsman's change of stance, duly raised his finger as he departed l.b.w. for an eventful 9. It was the prelude to the further clatter of wickets as eight more tumbled soon afterwards with Staffordshire clinching the Minor County title shortly before lunch.

Born in Birkenhead in 1872, Harry had played between 1890 and 1894 as a left-arm seamer for Liverpool CC before joining the Orton club His continued success as both a seamer and a spin bowler led to the offer of a contract with Swansea in 1898 and a chance to play Minor County cricket for Glamorgan. He duly moved to South Wales, and made his debut for the Welsh county in their match with Surrey 2nd XI at The Oval in 1898. It was a hugely successful move for the man who could start bowling left-arm

Harry Creber.

seam before switching to left-arm spin and Harry remained closely associated with the Swansea club until his death shortly before the Second World War.

After taking a relatively modest haul of 31 wickets in 1898, Harry claimed 97 wickets in 1899 and displayed his prowess as a slow bowler by taking 7/57 against Monmouthshire at the Arms Park, 6/29 against the MCC at Cardiff and 8/81 against Berkshire at Reading – a trio of performances which showed the Glamorgan hierarchy that they now had a clever and match-winning spinner in their ranks.

However, he did not meet with as much success as expected during the early 1900s, before enjoying a stellar season in 1905 as Harry became the Club's first bowler to take in excess of 100 wickets in a season. During the summer, his wickets cost just 15 runs apiece, with returns of 13/82 against Wiltshire at Chippenham, 11/148 in the match with the MCC at Cardiff Arms Park, plus a ten-wicket haul in the match against Surrey 2nd XI at The Oval.

During his wicket-laden season, approaches came from Lancashire to return to the north-west, but Swansea Cricket and Football Club offered improved terms to Harry. He repaid their faith in his abilities by taking 133 victims at 12 runs apiece for the Welsh county during 1906, with 15 five-wicket returns and 7 ten-wicket hauls including 12/88 against Durham at Sunderland, 11/110 against Northumberland, plus 13/85 against Wiltshire at the Arms Park.

Harry only claimed 73 wickets during 1907 but the following year he bounced back to form with 98 scalps and in the contest with Carmarthenshire at Stradey Park in 1908, he came close to becoming the first Glamorgan player to take all ten wickets in an innings. In the end, Harry finished with career-best figures of 9/56 in the home team's first innings and completely baffled the inexperienced Carmarthenshire batsmen.

Another wicket-laden summer in 1911 saw Harry claim 82 wickets at just 14 runs apiece, with 7 five-wicket hauls. 1912 saw the spinner claim 15/73 in the overwhelming innings defeat of Monmouthshire at the Arms Park, followed in 1913 by an eleven-wicket haul against Kent 2nd XI at Swansea, plus 12 wickets against Norfolk at Lakenham in September 1913 as he became the first-ever Glamorgan bowler to claim 1,000 wickets for the Club.

1914 saw Harry claimed 41 wickets with a solitary five-wicket haul, before the spinner carefully tended the St Helen's wicket as the Swansea ground was taken over by the military for the next four years. When cricket resumed in 1919, Harry decided to call time on his playing career with Glamorgan and focused his efforts on tending the Swansea wicket, besides turning out for the Swansea club.

However, after the Welsh county secured first-class status for 1921, Harry gleefully returned to action, making his Championship debut at the age of 49 and claiming 45 wickets in the Welsh county's inaugural season at the highest level. This was followed by 50 the following year before, at the age of fifty, Harry forever hung up his bowling boots with the commendable total of 1326 wickets at an average of 15 runs apiece.

In the subsequent summers, Harry mixed tending the St Helen's wicket with bird fancying, and he won many prizes at shows for his Yorkshire canaries. He also stood as an umpire in Glamorgan's Championship match at Swansea against Nottinghamshire in August 1925 when Harold Chidgey, the appointed official, was taken ill.

Harry died during March 1939 with the *South Wales Evening Post* paying him the following tribute – "not only will he be remembered as a cricketer, but as an endearing personality whose life and interests were centred upon St Helen's. In the summer he was rarely out of shirt and flannels, plus a straw hat, and in winter only the bitterest weather made him wear an overcoat." Maurice Turnbull, the Glamorgan captain, also paid a glowing tribute at Harry's funeral – "the grandest character I have known in Welsh cricket." His sons Arthur and Harry junior were also useful cricketers with the former appearing for the Welsh county and Scotland, whilst the latter played for many years for the Swansea club.

119.
ARKELL, Thomas <u>Norman</u>
Born – Boxted, Essex, January 1864
Died – West Parley, Dorset, 6 March 1951
Amateur
Batsman and wicket-keeper
Ed – Shrewsbury School and Magdalene College, Oxford
1st XI: 1898
Clubs: North Oxford, Cardiff

Batting and Fielding Record

M	I	NO	RUNS	AV	100	50	CT	ST
2	3	0	15	5.00	-	-	-	-

Career-bests
8 v Cornwall at Penzance, 1898

Norman Arkell, a Cardiff-based solicitor, played twice for Glamorgan in their Minor County Championship matches in 1898.

Educated at Shrewsbury School and Oxford University, he was the son of Rev. John Arkell, the rector of St Ebbe's in Oxford. Both of his appearances came in away matches during August 1898, starting with the match at Penzance against Cornwall and followed by the contest with Monmouthshire at Rodney Parade.

Norman subsequently ran a solicitors practice in Thornbury with William Davis Canning. It was later dissolved by mutual consent during December 1913 before Norman moved to work in Oxfordshire and subsequently Dorset.

120.
SMITH, Douglas James
Born – Batley, 29 May 1873
Died – Grahamstown, South Africa, 16 August 1949
Professional
RHB, OB occ WK
1st XI: 1898-1910
Somerset 1896-1898, Worcestershire 1901-1904
Clubs: Bridgwater, Yeovil, St Fagans, Fairwater
Son of J Smith (Yorks and Lancs) and brother of W Smith (Somerset and Wilts)

Batting and Fielding Record

M	I	NO	RUNS	AV	100	50	CT	ST
16	25	2	365	15.87	-	1	5	1

Bowling Record

Balls	M	R	W	AV	5wI	10wM
186	10	91	4	22.75	-	-

Career-bests
69 v Dorset at Cardiff Arms Park, 1907
2/15 v Northumberland at Newcastle-upon-Tyne, 1905

Like his father John – a fast round-arm bowler with Yorkshire – Douglas Smith led a peripatetic existence as a professional cricketer, playing county cricket for Somerset, Worcestershire and Glamorgan before emigrating to South Africa where he became an umpire of note and stood in the Fifth Test of the 1913/14 series between South Africa and England.

Born in Yorkshire, Douglas first secured a place on the staff of Worcestershire where he was a junior professional between 1889 and 1893. At the time, his father was the groundsman at New Road, but Douglas never made the 1st XI. He subsequently moved to the West Country, playing initially for Bridgwater and also helping to coach at Queen's College, Taunton.

Douglas made his first-class debut for Somerset against Gloucestershire at Bristol in April 1896, following some run-laden seasons in club cricket with Yeovil. Despite his success at club level, Douglas lost his place in the West Country side during 1897, and aware that he was not being retained the following year, he approached Glamorgan's officials during 1898 about the prospect of playing for the Welsh county.

He duly made his Glamorgan debut against Monmouthshire during the last week of August 1898 in the end-of-season match

Douglas Smith, seen in a St Fagans' team photo in 1906.

at Rodney Parade. It proved to be an inauspicious first appearance as Douglas was bowled second ball by Arthur Silverlock and did not get another chance to open his account for the Welsh county as rain washed out the second day of the game. No terms were agreed for 1899 so Douglas headed off to South Africa to coach and play.

During the winter months Douglas became the first English professional to score a century in club cricket in Durban before playing for Perthshire in Scotland. He then returned to the West Midlands and was chosen during May 1901 by Worcestershire for their back-to-back Championship matches against Lancashire at Old Trafford and

Yorkshire at Dewsbury. Thirteen months later, Douglas made three further appearances for the West Midlands side, before adding four more during 1904.

By this time though, he was resident in South Wales having been hired by the Earl of Plymouth in 1903 to act as one of the professionals attached to the St Fagans club, with his duties including looking after the wicket at their ground in Court Field, besides assisting Bill Lambert with the coaching duties. Given the fact that the Earl also owned property at Hewell Grange, near Redditch, it is likely that Douglas was first approached by the Earl about the work at St Fagans and the possibility of playing for Glamorgan when he was playing for Worcestershire.

Douglas made his debut for the Welsh county in June 1905 during their north-east tour, which included games against Northumberland at Newcastle-upon-Tyne and at Hartlepool against Durham. He only scored 7 runs besides taking four wickets with his off-spin, so it was not until July 1906, after some decent performances for the St Fagans club, that he played again for Glamorgan appearing in four matches during July. He then appeared in eight out of Glamorgan's ten games during 1907, and came within two runs of a maiden fifty for the Welsh county at Blandford Forum against Dorset, before making 69 against the same opponents at the Arms Park.

1907 was a successful summer for the Welsh county as they defeated Surrey 2nd XI in the semi-final of the Minor County competition before meeting Lancashire 2nd XI in the final at the Arms Park. Douglas was a member of the victorious side which defeated Surrey, but he was left out of the side for the final in favour of Sam Brain. His omission was not too upsetting as by this time Douglas had secured a post in South Africa – the country which was now playing an increasingly large part in his life, ironically having played for South Wales against their touring team at the Arms Park during his last season as a Glamorgan player.

Douglas had initially playing and coached in East London during the winter months, besides playing for the South African Zingari, before securing a post in September 1907 as cricket coach at St Andrew's College in Grahamstown. He spent 45 years at the College and became something of a local legend. As one newspaper wrote, "Modest and unassuming, Douglas was always willing and ready to do a good turn and give advice."

He also became a leading umpire in South Africa, standing in Currie Cup matches between 1908/09 to 1927/28, besides officiating in February 1914 in the Test Match at Port Elizabeth where England beat South Africa by ten wickets. A confirmed bachelor, Douglas also amassed sufficient wealth to leave a generous bequest to his adopted home at the College in Grahamstown, and the Douglas Smith Scholarship, offering one student each year from St Andrew's a scholarship to Cambridge University, remains in place today.

His brother William also played for Somerset during the late 1890s before enjoying a hugely successful career in Minor County cricket with Wiltshire between 1899 and 1913. During this time, William also played for the combined Glamorgan and Wiltshire side which met the 1902 Australians at the Arms Park.

121.
MOYNAN, Dr Richard Michael
Born – Tellamon, King's County, Ireland, 1859
Died – Cowbridge, 23 April 1921
Amateur
Batsman
Ed – Dublin University and the Irish Royal College of Physicians
1st XI: 1898
Clubs: Cowbridge, Glamorgan Gypsies, Penarth, Barry

Batting and Fielding Record

M	I	NO	RUNS	AV	100	50	CT	ST
1	1	0	4	4.00	-	-	-	-

Career-bests
4 v Monmouthshire at Rodney Parade, Newport 1898

Richard Moynan was one of the great characters of club cricket in the years leading up to the Great War, with the master surgeon playing for several teams, most notably Cowbridge, in the Vale of Glamorgan. He also played once for Glamorgan during 1898.

Born in Ireland and educated at Dublin University and the Irish Royal College of Physicians, Richard moved to South Wales shortly after graduating in the early 1890s and initially worked at a practice in Pontypridd. In 1883 he married Emma Davies, the daughter of one of his colleagues, before spending a short period of time in Newport. By the 1891 Census he was living in Cowbridge and it was in the market town in the Vale of Glamorgan that he spent the next thirty years, tending the sick and poorly, besides acting as Cowbridge's surgeon.

Given his upbringing in Southern Ireland, he had a love of hunting and other equine sports, and besides owning several racehorses, Dr Moynan was also a member of the Glamorganshire Hunt and was a regular rider at local point-to-points. He also took a liking to cricket, especially batting, and after some decent innings for the Cowbridge club, he made his Glamorgan debut in 1898 in their end of season clash with Monmouthshire at Rodney Parade.

Although never called upon again by the county selectors, Richard continue to mix his medical duties with playing for the Cowbridge club. In 1898/99 Richard was appointed Mayor of Cowbridge, before being appointed Medical Health Officer for Cowbridge Borough in 1901. Soon afterwards, he became surgeon-lieutenant to the Glamorgan Yeomanry and acted as a medical advisor as events unfolded leading up to the start of the Great War.

Tragically in July 1917 Harold, one of his twin boys, was killed during the Third Battle of Ypres whilst serving with the South Wales Borderers. The loss of a treasured son was something which the popular and happy-go-lucky doctor never fully recovered and in 1921 he died of septic pneumonia.

1899

1899 saw Glamorgan record six victories, with home and away wins over both Wiltshire and Berkshire. Herbie Morgan, the hard-hitting batsman from Penarth, also struck a maiden championship hundred in the opening game of the season at The Oval, before making 105 against Berkshire at the Arms Park – a match which also saw William Russell weigh in with a career-best 143.

On the bowling front, Harry Creber, the left-arm spinner, claimed 97 wickets and enjoyed a real purple patch during early August, by taking 26 wickets in the space of four days as Glamorgan defeated Wiltshire at the Arms Park and Berkshire at Reading. Throughout the summer, Harry received useful support from Sam Lowe as for the first time in Glamorgan's short history as a Minor County, the Welsh county possessed a potent spin attack to exploit the worn surfaces in these multi-day matches.

However, the standout performance of the season came in late June during the match with Surrey 2nd XI at Swansea, as Billy Bancroft, on his home ground, hit 102 and then took a hat-trick as the visitors were beaten by 53 runs. Jack Brain was delighted by this and the other victories, but there were a few financial worries as the season drew to a close. The increased travelling costs and expenditure on professionals meant that over £200 was owed to the bank, and in a clever bid to garner reduced travel costs, the selection panel on several occasions chose Horace Beesley, a talented young batsman with the Penarth club, whose father just happened to be the General Manager of the Taff Vale Railway!

In their Annual Report, the Glamorgan committee expressed their deep regret at "the unsatisfactory balance sheet and called upon members to do all they can to improve the finances by introducing new members or procuring further donations." Fortunately, events of 1900 meant that there was no shortage of support.

Harry Creber, wearing a large sunhat in a team photograph from 1902.

122.
PRICHARD, Hubert Cecil Collins (later known as COLLINS-PRICHARD)

Born – Stapleton, Bristol, 6 February 1865
Died – Pwll-y-Wrach, Cowbridge, 12 November 1942
Amateur
RHB
Ed – Clifton College, Magdalene College, Cambridge and RMC Sandhurst
1st XI: 1899
Gloucestershire 1896
Clubs: Bridgend, St Fagans, MCC

Batting and Fielding Record

M	I	NO	RUNS	AV	100	50	CT	ST
4	7	1	106	17.67	-	1	1	-

Career-bests
50 v MCC at Cardiff Arms Park, 1899

A member of the Prichard family of Pwll-y-Wrach Manor in the Vale of Glamorgan, Hubert was a well-known figure in South Wales – and beyond – mixing a military and sporting career with good effect before becoming, through the marriage of his son, a member of the family of well-known novelist Agatha Christie.

The eldest son of landowner Charles John Collins Prichard, Hubert was born in Bristol and educated at Clifton College, Cambridge University and Sandhurst, Hubert opted, at first, for a career in the services. Shortly after graduating, he was commissioned as a captain in the East Yorkshire Regiment for whom he served until 1897. In his closing years with the military, Hubert appeared twice for his native Gloucestershire in May 1896, against Somerset and Yorkshire in matches at Bristol. In his youth he had been a lively seam bowler but, by the time of his county debut, he was more of a batsman and a most agile fielder, especially in the slips.

After leaving the Army, Hubert moved back to the family home at Pwll-y-Wrach where he ran the estate, besides playing cricket for Bridgend and winning a place for three matches during 1899 in the Glamorgan side. The first came in mid-June against Surrey 2nd XI at The Oval and, having made 0 and 18, Hubert played later in the season at the Arms Park against both Monmouthshire and the MCC, striking a career-best 50 against the latter.

In August 1899 Hubert also played for the Gentlemen of Glamorgan against the Players at the Arms Park, before playing again the following May at the same ground in the friendly against WM Brownlee's XI. Despite not playing again at county level, Hubert continued to play with good effect in club cricket for the MCC and St Fagans, besides organizing matches in the grounds of Pwll-y-Wrach.

He maintained his military connections through service with the Glamorgan Yeomanry. During the Great War he was also Commandant of several German POW camps in Scotland, for which he was awarded the CBE in 1919. Married in 1905, his son

Hubert de Burr Prichard married Rosalind Hicks, the daughter of Agatha Christie, before being killed during the Second World War in August 1944.

123.
ROWNTREE, Riston Ernest

Born – Sunderland, January 1876
Died – Tynemouth, 9 August 1919
Amateur
All-rounder
1st XI: 1899
Clubs: Cardiff, Fairwater

Batting and Fielding Record

M	I	NO	RUNS	AV	100	50	CT	ST
2	3	0	8	2.67	-	-	3	-

Bowling Record

Balls	M	R	W	AV	5wI	10wM
185	6	128	4	32.00	-	-

Career-bests
7 v Surrey 2nd XI at St Helen's, Swansea, 1899
2/40 v Surrey 2nd XI at St Helen's, Swansea, 1899

Riston Rowntree was a talented cricketer, born in the north-east of England, who had a brief taste of Minor County cricket whilst stationed at Maindy Barracks in Cardiff and serving with the Welch Regiment.

Corporal Rowntree played for Glamorgan during late June 1899 against Surrey 2nd XI at Swansea and Monmouthshire at the Arms Park, but without the effect with either bat or ball he had enjoyed in club cricket. He subsequently returned to Yorkshire after securing a post at St Peter's School, York. He continued to be a decent performer at club level, but did not play any more representative cricket.

124.
BEASLEY, Sir Horace Owen Compton, CBE

Born – Brentford, 2 July, 1877
Died – Putsey, 1 January, 1960
Amateur
Batsman
Ed – Westminster School and Jesus College, Cambridge
1st XI: 1899
Clubs: Penarth

Batting and Fielding Record

M	I	NO	RUNS	AV	100	50	CT	ST
3	6	1	26	5.20	-	-	3	-

Career-bests
10 v Cornwall at Truro, 1899

Horace Beasley was the son of the General Manager of the Taff Vale Railway. The Beasleys had previously lived in the Chiswick area, with young Horace attending Westminster School where he showed promise as a cricketer and footballer. He subsequently went up to Cambridge to read Law, and whilst in residence at Jesus College, won football Blues between 1896 and 1899, and led the Cambridge XI in his final two years. On coming down, he opted not to follow his father into the railway world, and trained instead to be a barrister.

Horace subsequently became a leading figure in Conservative politics in South Wales, and this – together with his close allegiance to the Taff Vale company – soon won him many friends within Glamorgan's hierarchy. It was these contacts, and the possibility of securing discounts on tickets for travel to away matches, as much as his prowess on the cricket field, that prompted his selection for three of the county's fixtures in 1899, including the away matches in the Minor County Championship against Cornwall at Truro and Wiltshire at Trowbridge.

Beasley made little impact in these matches and soon after, he concentrated his efforts on his legal career. He initially worked in South Wales, before moving to Burma after the Great War where he became a High Court Judge. In 1929 he moved to India in 1929 where he served as Honorable Chief Justice of Madras until 1937. He was knighted in 1930, before returning to the UK in the late 1930s, and subsequently being awarded a CBE after acting as President of the Pensions Appeal Tribunals Board between 1943 and 1958.

1900

1900 began with dark clouds still looming over the Club's finances, but to Jack Brain's delight, these were dispelled during the summer as Glamorgan shared top spot place in the Minor County Championship, with Durham and Northamptonshire.

During the Club's most successful summer to date, Surrey 2nd XI were defeated both at home and away, with Jack Brain leading by example with a century at the Arms Park plus an imperious 88 at The Oval. Billy Bancroft also chipped in with two half centuries, whilst Harry Creber ended the season with 60 wickets.

New signing Jack Nash showed promise as an off-spinner, but it was the all-round form of William Russell which was the cornerstone of Glamorgan's success during 1900. He scored 283 runs, including a fiercely struck 93 against Monmouthshire, besides taking 42 wickets at around 10 apiece to give the Glamorgan attack an even sharper edge. Russell's haul included 10/57 as Wiltshire were defeated by eight wickets, 9/86 in the innings victory over Surrey and 9/68 as Berkshire were beaten at Reading by seven wickets.

By the end of the season, Glamorgan's overdraft had been reduced to £150, and in their Annual Report the committee were able to make some positive noises about the future, but Jack Brain still noted that there was still plenty of work to be done, especially in attracting decent crowds to home matches at the Arms Park and St Helen's.

In a bid to raise funds, some stars from the rugby world were chosen by the Glamorgan officials who also selected Arthur Silverlock, the prolific professional from Newport and Monmouthshire to play in a friendly at the Arms Park, chiefly in the hope that he might switch allegiance and play for Glamorgan. This never came about, but 1900 did see Norman Riches, a gifted young batsman from Cardiff, make his county bow. He duly became one of the leading players for the next three decades

	Played	Won	Lost	Drawn	Points	Percentage.
Glamorgan	8	5	0	3	5	100.00
Durham	8	4	0	4	4	100.00
Northamptonshire	14	3	0	11	3	100.00
Buckinghamshire	8	3	1	4	2	50.00
Northumberland	10	3	1	6	2	50.00
Oxfordshire	8	2	2	4	0	—
Wiltshire	10	2	2	6	0	—
Bedfordshire	8	3	4	1	—1	—14.28
Surrey Second Eleven	9	2	3	4	—1	—20.00
Berkshire	10	2	5	3	—3	—42.85
Norfolk	8	0	2	6	—2	—100.00
Hertfordshire	10	0	3	7	—3	—100.00
Cambridgeshire	8	0	4	4	—1	—100.00
Staffordshire	8	0	4	4	—4	—100.00

GLAMORGAN.

Hon. Secretary : MR. J. H. BRAIN, Cardiff.

Glamorgan enjoyed a most successful season in 1900, going through their competition fixtures without suffering a single reverse. They took part in eight matches, of which five were won, and the remaining three drawn, and together with Durham and Northamptonshire, Glamorgan headed the Second-Class Counties Champion-

An extract from the 1901 Wisden, showing Glamorgan on top of the table.

169

125.
SILVERLOCK, Arthur John

Born – South Hackney, December 1867
Died – Ardleigh, Colchester, 4 June 1949
Professional
RHB, RM/LBG
Ed – Crouch End School, South Hackney
1st XI: 1900
Monmouthshire 1892-1914, South Wales 1894, Minor Counties 1901, Combined
Glamorgan and Wiltshire XI 1902.
Clubs: London Ivanhoe, South West Ham, Newport, Dedham

Batting and Fielding Record

M	I	NO	RUNS	AV	100	50	CT	ST
1	1	0	0	-	-	-	-	-

Bowling Record

Balls	M	R	W	AV	5wI	10wM
54	0	42	0	-	-	-

"One of the very best cricketers who has ever appeared in South Wales" – the opinion of the cricket correspondent of the *Evening Express* newspaper in 1899 after Arthur Silverlock, the professional, attached to the Newport club hit an unbeaten 211 and took 7/21 during the match against Penarth in 1899.

In all, 'Silver' scored over 25,000 runs and claimed nigh on 2,000 wickets for Newport during an association which ran from 1892 until 1914. Few professionals throughout South Wales have come close to matching his superlative efforts with bat and ball, yet bizarrely Glamorgan's supporters never saw the Hackney-born professional score a single run for them as he was dismissed for a second ball duck by Gloucestershire's Gilbert Jessop whilst appearing for the Welsh county in their friendly against WM Brownlee's XI at the Arms Park in 1900.

Born in the East End of London, 'Silver' played his earliest cricket for the Ivanhoe and South West Ham clubs, before being invited to bat and bowl in the nets at Lord's. What appeared to be an audition for the MCC groundstaff turned into a contract with the Newport club as he was spotted by Horace Devey, the former Middlesex bowler who acted as Newport's professional during

Arthur Silverlock, seen in 1905.

170

the early 1890s. 'Silver' duly travelled to Rodney Parade for a net and so began in 1892 his prolific batting and wicket-laden career in South Wales.

After a decent first season with Newport and Monmouthshire, Glamorgan's officials invited 'Silver' to play in 1893 for the Cardiff and District XI against the scratch county XI at the Arms Park. His selection may have been part of an attempt to lure him to Cardiff and a place in the Welsh county's line-up, but nothing came of the approaches, apart from innings of 44 and 49 against the Glamorgan XI.

His subsequent feats with bat and ball for Monmouthshire and Newport were nothing short of outstanding. In 1895 he scored 120 and took sixteen wickets against Herefordshire, besides making an unbeaten 187 against Glamorgan. In 1902 he made 170 for Newport against Swansea, besides appearing in 1902 for the combined Glamorgan and Wiltshire XI against the Australians at the Arms Park.

'Silver' was also an automatic selection for the South Wales teams between 1905 and 1909 which saw the cream of the talent in Glamorgan and Monmouthshire unite forces in games against international touring sides and English counties. Indeed, in 1905 he opened the batting against both Yorkshire and the Australians, before making scores of 61 and 64 against the 1908 Philadelphians, besides taking 6/61 with his spin bowling against Yorkshire in 1906.

In 1905 he posted 206* for Monmouthshire against Berkshire, and 'Silver' continued each summer to decorate his appearances in Minor County cricket with sizeable scores. However, shortly after making 142* against Carmarthenshire in 1908, he had a disagreement with Newport's officials and announced at the end of the season that he would be returning to London to help his brother who ran a thriving restaurant business.

Not everything however went according to plan on the catering side, as 'Silver' returned to Newport as an amateur mid-way through 1909, and scored an unbeaten 246 against

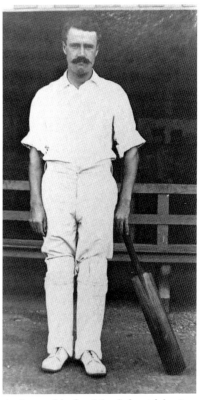

An image of Arthur Silverlock, with bat in hand, taken in 1898.

Carmarthenshire. He was duly restored as Newport's professional for 1910 and remained in South Wales until the end of the Great War. He subsequently played for the Dedham club in East Essex and ran a smallholding, supplying his brother's business with fresh garden vegetables.

126.
CAMERON, Dr Alexander William Cumming

Born – Kilmore and Kilbride, Argyll, 3 March 1866
Died – Swansea, 14 March 1957
Amateur
All-rounder
Ed – George Watson's College and Edinburgh University
1st XI: 1900-1913
Gentlemen of Glamorgan 1899-1914
Club: Swansea
Rugby for Scotland 1887-1894 (3 caps)

Batting and Fielding Record

M	I	NO	RUNS	AV	100	50	CT	ST
18	25	3	284	12.91	-	-	11	-

Bowling Record

Balls	M	R	W	AV	5wI	10wM
791	14	451	24	18.79	2	-

Career-bests
39 v Wiltshire at Swindon, 1901
6/89 v Surrey 2nd XI at Cardiff Arms Park, 1900

Born and raised in Scotland, Dr Alex Cameron became the first – and so far only – person to play rugby for his native country and cricket for Glamorgan, the county where he subsequently worked and lived for sixty years.

The eldest son of Rev. Patrick Cameron he overcame the death of his father when he was just eight years old, and shone at both rugby and cricket whilst a pupil at George Watson's College. He continued in this vein whilst a student at Edinburgh University before playing both sports for the Watsonians club.

He met with much success on the cricket field, taking 10/21 with his medium pace bowling in a game against Hawick, whilst his prowess at full-back in the oval ball game saw him win a place in the Edinburgh and then the Glasgow rugby teams before winning the first of three Scottish caps in 1887, ironically against Wales at Edinburgh.

Through his rugby-playing Alex became friends with Welsh international Dr Teddy Morgan and in 1897 he moved to Swansea to share a practice with his chum. He duly joined the Swansea club and following some decent performances and warm recommendations by the Swansea contingent in the Glamorgan side, he made his debut for the Welsh county during June 1900 at St Helen's against Wiltshire, He made an assured 33 in his maiden innings and went wicketless, but on his second appearance, against Surrey 2nd XI at the Arms Park he took 6/89. By this time, he had switched to bowling off-cutters and off-spin, with his high, slow action deceiving many batsmen in both club and county cricket.

His medical commitments meant that he could not play on a regular basis, but 1901 saw him appear in five matches and he added another five-for to his tally as he claimed 5/35 against Devon, appropriately on his home turf at St Helen's. By this time, he had risen to the captaincy of the Swansea club, whom he led in 1900 and 1901.

Dr Cameron made sporadic appearances again in 1902, and later 1905, before making three appearances in 1910, plus one more in 1911, 1912 and 1913, with each of these being at matches at St Helen's. His final game for Glamorgan in 1913 was against Wiltshire at Swansea – a game in which he batted at number nine, scoring 27 and 1, and didn't bowl.

Besides his on-field role during these years with the Welsh county, Alex also served on the Glamorgan committee between 1905 and 1920, overseeing the rise of the Club as a Minor County, prior to their elevation into first-class cricket. In particular, he was on the match-day committee which oversaw the smooth running of Glamorgan matches at the Swansea ground, besides the catering operations with his wife lending a hand to ensure that everything ran smoothly in the kitchens.

Alex Cameron in his rugby kit.

127.
BUSH, Percy Frank

Born – Cardiff, 23 June 1879
Died – Cardiff, 19 May 1955
Amateur
RHB
Ed – St Mary's Hall, Penarth Collegiate School and University College, Cardiff
1st XI: 1900-1903
Club: Cardiff
Rugby for Cardiff, London Welsh and Wales (8 caps). Great Britain to New Zealand and Australia 1904

Batting and Fielding Record

M	I	NO	RUNS	AV	100	50	CT	ST
4	6	0	12	2.00	-	-	2	-

Bowling Record

Balls	M	R	W	AV	5wI	10wM
18	0	16	1	16.00	-	-

5 v Wiltshire at St Helen's, Swansea, 1900
v Surrey 2nd XI at The Oval, 1903
1/16 v Monmouthshire at Rodney Parade, Newport, 1900

Percy Bush was the golden boy of Welsh rugby in the 1900s with his maverick talents with the oval ball winning him many plaudits. Whilst his swift and unpredictable running skills and deft handling won him fame on the rugby field, he also had prowess with bat and ball in hand and during the early 1900s Percy also made four appearances for Glamorgan.

Percy was born into a well-known family in Cardiff, with his father James being one of the town's leading sportsmen during the 1860s and 1870s, and was closely involved with both the Cardiff cricket club, as well as the Tredegarville rugby club who were amongst the pioneers of the oval-ball game in Wales. Percy began with rugby career – and probably his cricket career too – with junior Canton teams, including St Vincent's and Cardiff Romilly. In 1896, he attended University College Cardiff where he quickly established himself as captain of rugby, besides winning a place in their cricket eleven, where his swift fielding drew favourable comments.

Rugby was his first love and whilst playing one afternoon for the University at the Arms Park, he was spotted by an official of Penygraig RFC who invited both Percy, and his brother Fred, to play for the Rhondda club. They each accepted the offer, and Percy went on to both play and lead the Penygraig club in the highly competitive and combative Glamorgan League. In 1899 he switched to Cardiff RFC – a move which also saw him play regularly for the town's cricket club, and after some useful all-round performances led to his selection for Glamorgan against Wiltshire at Swansea in 1900, followed by the friendly with Monmouthshire at Newport.

Percy made little impact in these games, but his agile fielding won many fine comments. His mere presence also helped to swell the gate receipts and it was perhaps because of these reasons that he was chosen again in 1902 for the match with Berkshire at the Arms Park, and again the following year when Surrey 2nd XI visited Cardiff. Yet again, Percy had modest success with the bat in these games, and despite shining in the field, the Glamorgan selectors did not call upon his services again.

Percy Bush wearing his Welsh rugby jersey in 1903.

Cricket's loss was rugby's gain as Percy's career in the oval ball game took off. In 1904 he was selected for the British Lions tour to Australia and New Zealand, despite having not won a Welsh cap. Nevertheless, he was the Lions' outside half in all four Tests and became the star of the tour, dubbed "Will O the Wisp" by the Australian press. In all, he scored 104 points, with twelve tries, eight dropped goals, four penalty kicks, and twelve conversions. His ability to elude tacklers at will, whether by side stepping off either foot, dodging or swerving was widely admired, as was his knack of stopping dead as opponents swept past. Added to this were his kicking skills, both out of hand, and from place kicks.

Percy duly made his Welsh rugby debut in 1905 in the historic victory over New Zealand at the Arms Park. Despite being a debutant in the Welsh jersey, the All Blacks were worried by Bush's presence, and it was because of their preoccupation with his running skills at fly-half that the only try of the famous match was scored. Following Percy's decoy run to the right, Wales then moved the ball to the left, allowing Dr Teddy Morgan – another legendary Welsh sportsman and Glamorgan cricketer – to cross the line.

Despite this virtuoso performance, Bush only went on to win a further seven caps, explained by rugby historians by his inability to develop a successful understanding with established scrum-half Dickie Owen. Both men liked to control events behind the scrum and were therefore not compatible at half back. There was probably some truth in this, as Percy's best match in a Welsh jersey was when he was partnered by his Cardiff team-mate, Dicky David and in what became known as "Bush's Match", he helped create all six tries and dropped a goal in the stunning 29-0 victory over Ireland in 1907.

Percy also captained the Cardiff club for three seasons, including 1905/06 when just one fixture was lost at the hands of New Zealand, when a foolhardy error by Percy, who fatally delayed touching the ball down in goal, cost Cardiff the game. However, he made amends the following season by captaining the club to victory over the South Africans by 17-0.

After graduating from Cardiff University, Percy had been teaching at Wood Street School, but in 1910 he tendered his resignation and took up a business post in Nantes. He continued to play when in France, captaining the Stade Nantais club and famously scoring all 54 points in one match against Le Havre. After the Great War, he was appointed vice consul in Nantes, and awarded the Palm d'Honeur. He retired in 1937 and returned home to Cardiff where he was celebrated as one of the most brilliant if mercurial sportsmen from the Welsh capital.

Percy Bush walking out to field at the Arms Park in 1906 with wicket-keeper Ted Fletcher behind him.

128.
BARRY, Ian

Born – Cape Town, South Africa, 16 September, 1875
Died – On active service, 29 October, 1918
Amateur
Batsman
Ed – Dulwich College
1st XI: 1900
Club: Cardiff

Batting and Fielding Record

M	I	NO	RUNS	AV	100	50	CT	ST
1	1	1	24	-	-	-	1	-

Career-bests
24* v Wiltshire at St Helen's, Swansea, 1900

Born in South Africa and educated at Dulwich College in London, Ian Barry was typical of the transient amateurs with cosmopolitan backgrounds who played for Glamorgan during their days as a Minor County.

During the late 1890s, the civil engineer secured a position in the thriving Docks at Cardiff and, after some impressive performances in club cricket for Cardiff, including an innings of 97 against Llanelli in late May, he was drafted into the Glamorgan team for the Minor County Championship match against Wiltshire at Swansea during the first week of June 1900.

He had opened the batting whilst at Dulwich so it was no surprise that Ian made an unbeaten 24 in what proved to be his one and only innings for the Welsh county. Local newspapers reported that Ian "knocked the bowling all over the field to the evident delight of the large crowd."

He moved away from South Wales shortly afterwards, and later served with the Royal Marines. Ian died in October 1918 whilst on active service.

129.
HOWELL, Percival T.

Born – Cardiff, June 1877
Died – Neath, June 1953
Amateur
Batsman
1st XI: 1900
Club: Cardiff

Batting and Fielding Record

M	I	NO	RUNS	AV	100	50	CT	ST
1	2	0	6	3.00	-	-	-	-

6 v Monmouthshire at Rodney Parade, Newport, 1900

Percy Howell was another amateur who played once for Glamorgan during their Minor County days, with the accountant with Cardiff Corporation appearing against Monmouthshire at Newport in 1900. He was a good friend of several Cardiff cricketers and this probably explains his call-up at short notice when another player dropped out of the morning of the game at Rodney Parade.

He was a good athlete and was a member of Cardiff Harriers. Percy also served on the committee of Cardiff CC during the early 1900s.

130.
GIBSON, Arthur
Born – Danby, Yorkshire, June 1874
Amateur
Batsman and occasional spin bowler
1st XI: 1900-1909
Club and Ground: 1922
Captain: 1908-1909
Clubs: West Hartlepool, Cardiff
Brother of WD Gibson

Batting and Fielding Record

M	I	NO	RUNS	AV	100	50	CT	ST
57	85	9	1140	15.00	-	4	32	-

Bowling Record

Balls	M	R	W	AV	5wI	10wM
198	11	130	4	32.50	-	-

Career-bests
66 v MCC at Cardiff Arms Park, 1900
1/6 v Berkshire at Reading, 1905

Arthur Gibson was a Yorkshire-born gentleman who captained Glamorgan during 1908 in the wake of Jack Brain's retirement, before serving on the county committee and acting as the Club's Secretary during their early years in Championship cricket

Born in Yorkshire during the summer of 1874, he learnt his cricket whilst living in the White Rose county, before briefly moving to work in Croydon, South London. In his early twenties he moved to north-east England where he set up a timber importing business, besides playing with distinction for West Hartlepool CC.

The autumn of 1899 saw Arthur on the move again as he began operations in South Wales, with his company importing pit props from the Baltic through Cardiff Docks. He joined the town club and the following summer made his debut for Glamorgan, scoring 66 against the MCC at the Arms Park. This remained his career-best score, but the Yorkshireman proved to be a steady batsman and an astute captain in subsequent years, leading both Cardiff and Glamorgan. Fortunately, his business commitments allowed him to play on a regular basis, and having acted as a wise lieutenant to Jack Brain during 1906 and 1907, Arthur took to the reins in 1908. The previous summer had seen Glamorgan reach the final of the Minor County competition, only to lose at the Arms Park against Lancashire 2nd XI.

Under Arthur's shrewd captaincy, Glamorgan reached the final again in 1908, but only after an additional match was arranged between Glamorgan and Monmouthshire, who were level at the top of the Western Division to decide which of the two teams should progress to the semi-final against Wiltshire at Chippenham. Unfortunately, heavy rain limited play to just two and a half hours on the first day, with Glamorgan making 138. No play was possible on the second day with the MCC ruling, quite perversely, that Glamorgan should go through to the semi-final because they had topped the group the previous year.

In the hope that Glamorgan would lift the Minor County title outright, Jack Brain had come out of retirement for the play-off against Monmouthshire, and with Arthur being unavailable for the semi-final against Wiltshire, the veteran batsman remained in command as Glamorgan routed Wiltshire for just 41 with Harry Creber taking 8/18. Arthur was back at the helm for the final with Staffordshire at Stoke in early September, but Sydney Barnes took a fifteen-wicket match haul to see his side to a nine-wicket victory.

Glamorgan reached the final again in 1909 – a season when Arthur shared the captaincy duties with Tom Whittington – with the Welsh county defeating Nottinghamshire 2nd XI in the semi-final at the Arms Park. Their victory though was based on first innings scores, with Glamorgan making 136 compared to the East Midlands county who made 92 in their first innings. Rain then interrupted the contest, but events were not without controversy as Harvey Staunton, the Nottinghamshire captain, subsequently wrote to the Secretaries of both the MCC and the Minor Counties Cricket

Arthur Gibson, as seen in 1908.

Association pointing out that some of his players had seen the Cardiff groundsman sweeping and tampering with the wicket early on the third day in contravention of the rules of the competition.

Whether this was sour grapes or not is unclear, but Glamorgan secured a place in the final, against Wiltshire at the Arms Park. Arthur lost the toss and saw the visitors secure a vital lead on first innings. With both Creber and Riches carrying injuries, Arthur saw the Wiltshire side amass a decent lead before dismissing Glamorgan for 159. He himself had filled the vacancy at the top of the order but he was one of six victims for Audley Miller as Wiltshire won by 164 runs.

With his business thriving, Arthur informed the committee over the winter months that he would be standing down from playing, with the game against Wiltshire being his last major match for the Welsh county. Arthur continued however to serve on the Club's committee until 1932. He also spent time during 1922 and 1923 acting as Hon. Secretary – a period which saw the Club's officials trying to raise funds to ensure the long-term visibility of Glamorgan as a first-class county. Unfortunately, one of these schemes in 1923 subsequently backfired with Arthur appearing in court in Cardiff after a members' sweepstake was deemed an illegal lottery.

The outcome of the hearing was that the Club were issued with a fine, but with shaky resources this was the last thing they wanted at a time when every penny was treasured, and Arthur duly spent the next eighteen months overseeing, with a combination of Yorkshire grit and nous, a series of other, low-key activities which helped the Club stay afloat.

131.
NASH, Albert ('Jack')

Born – Blean, Kent, 18 September 1873
Died – Battersea, 6 December 1956
Professional
RHB, RM/OB
1st XI: 1900-1922
Club and Ground: 1920-1923
Cap: 1921
Clubs: Cardiff, Haslingden, Enfield, Uddingston, Neath.
First-class umpire 1926-1930

Batting and Fielding Record

	M	I	NO	RUNS	AV	100	50	CT	ST
Minor	123	158	35	985	8.01	-	-	104	-
F-c	36	65	9	315	5.62	-	-	6	-

Bowling Record

	Balls	M	R	W	AV	5wI	10wM
Minor	22629	1230	8962	633 (+6)	14.04	58	15
F-c	7270	364	2901	133	21.81	11	2

Career-bests
Minor –   44 v Monmouthshire at Cardiff Arms Park, 1908
             9/33 v Oxford Harlequins at Cardiff Arms Park, 1908
First-class –   28 v Derbyshire at Queen's Park, Chesterfield, 1921
             9/93 v Sussex at St Helen's, Swansea, 1922

May 1921 'Jack' Nash, a stalwart member of Glamorgan's Minor County side, became – at 47 years and 271 days – the oldest person to make their debut in the County Championship.

The following year the veteran off-cutter also came so close to taking all ten in an innings as he took 9/93 against Sussex at St Helen's and, for the second time in his county career was deprived by his spin partner, Harry Creber, of claiming all ten as the left-armer removed Harold Gilligan. Back in 1908, Creber had also seen one of the Oxford Harlequins batsmen caught on the boundary's edge at the Arms Park in 1908 with the off-cutter claiming the other nine wickets for just 33 runs in a career-best performance.

Jack's feat at Swansea in 1922 could not conjure up a Glamorgan victory as Sussex recorded an innings victory. It also came in his final season of county cricket as he announced his retirement at the end of what was, by his own high standards, a disappointing summer with just 42 wickets at 28 runs apiece, compared with 91 at an average of 18 during the county's maiden Championship season, more than twice as many taken by his colleagues. Amongst his returns that summer were figures of 6/37 against Leicestershire at Cardiff, 6/66 against Worcestershire at Kidderminster, plus 7/34 and 8/82 in the return game at Swansea.

Throughout his outstanding career Jack had cheerfully shouldered the brunt of the bowling with Harry Creber, delivering seam-up with the new ball before switching to slower cutters. Their subtle wiles were one of the factors behind Glamorgan's success as a Minor County and their elevation to the first-class ranks. Jack had few pretensions as a batsman and was a tail-ender for most of his county career. He did though once make a hundred, albeit in a light-hearted game in 1908 for Cardiff Thistles against Penarth Wednesdays.

Jack had learnt his cricket in Kent before joining Cardiff CC in 1900, with his duties as the club's professional, including tending the wicket at the Arms Park and assisting with the training programme undertaken by the Cardiff rugby players. Changes to the qualification regulations for inter-county games meant that Jack at first could only appear in friendlies with him playing for Glamorgan against the MCC at Cardiff in 1900 and 1901, as well as the South Africans in the latter summer.

Jack Nash, wearing his Cardiff cap in 1902.

Jack made his Minor County Championship debut in the match with Wiltshire, again at the Arms Park, in 1902. He opened the bowling with Sam Lowe and marked his debut with five-wicket haul, before claiming 6/56 and 6/42 against Surrey 2nd XI in the games at The Oval and Swansea.

He returned some outstanding match figures during 1903 at the Arms Park, including 10/94 against the MCC and 12/77 against Berkshire in the same year. Jack also featured in the South Wales teams which met the 1905 Australians, the 1906 West Indians and the 1909 Australians at Cardiff, with the proud groundsman spending many long hours in preparing a pristine surface for these showcase games.

His most prolific summer though was 1910 when he claimed, in all games, 93 wickets with 11 five-for's and 4 ten-wicket hauls, with his finest performance of the summer again coming on his home turf as he took 7/74 and 9/56 against Somerset at the Arms Park. Once again, it was not sufficient to see Glamorgan to victory over the West Country side, and Jack was prevented by the Sweet-Escott brothers from taking all ten, as Henry caught Ernie Robson off Rhys' off-spin.

After his wicket-laden summer, it came something of a blow both for the Cardiff club and Glamorgan when Jack accepted a lucrative offer in 1911 to move to Haslingden in the Lancashire Leagues. The background to his decision to leave the Arms Park was linked to the county's modest financial position. With the Earl of Plymouth heading a fund-raising campaign, Glamorgan were unable to guarantee a decent match fee for Jack, despite his success with the ball in 1910. With a good offer on the table from the Lancashire club, and an uncertain future for the Welsh county, Jack decided to accept Haslingden's offer.

An image of Jack Nash from 1908.

It proved though to be only a brief spell with Haslingden as a disagreement took place during their match with Accrington in June. It was a windy day, causing the umpires to dispense with the bails. But Jack disagreed with their decision and refused to bowl, believing the laws of cricket had been compromised. A heated row took place after the match, resulting in Jack leaving their employment and returning to Wales with Neath CC.

However, Jack was back in the Lancashire Leagues the following summer as he played for Enfield, before being on the move again, as he joined the Uddingston club in Glasgow, where he stayed until 1919. With Glamorgan poised to become a first-class side, noises were made to Jack about returning to South Wales. Through a friendship with Tom Whittington, the off-cutter once again joined Neath for 1920 before re-joining Cardiff for 1921 and achieving his long held ambition of playing first-class cricket. At the end of the season, he further developed his groundsmanship skills by being seconded to the Treorchy club and overseeing the renovation of their wicket at Ystradfechan Park.

Jack played a further season of first-class cricket in 1922, and after retiring at the end of the summer from county cricket, he continued to play for Cardiff besides tending the Arms Park wicket. However, in 1926 he joined the first-class umpires list and stood in 104 games before finally departing the first-class scene in 1930.

132.
CORDING, George Ernest

Born – Tredegar, 1 January 1878
Died – St Mellons, 2 February 1946
Amsteur
RHB, occ WK
Ed – St Paul's College, Cheltenham and University College, Cardiff
1st XI: 1900-1923
Cap: 1921
Clubs: Cardiff, Welsh Cygnets

Batting and Fielding Record

	M	I	NO	RUNS	AV	100	50	CT	ST
Minor	19	27	1	314	12.08	-	1	13	7
F-c	19	34	4	498	16.60	1	1	16	2

Career-bests
Minor –   58   v Berkshire at Cardiff Arms Park, 1900
First-class –   101   v Worcestershire at St Helen's, Swansea, 1921

George Cording was Glamorgan's wicket-keeper in their inaugural County Championship match in 1921 and, later in that summer, the 43 year-old made 101 against Worcestershire at Swansea, thereby becoming the Club's oldest player to hit a maiden Championship century.

The right-handed batsman first played for the county against Berkshire in 1900, and soon showed promise, hitting 28 and 58 on his debut. However, during the years leading up to the Great War, George's teaching commitments at Howard Gardens Secondary School in Cardiff restricted his appearances for the county.

He became available on a more regular basis after the Great War, and epitomised the spirit amongst the band of amateur players who loyally devoted their spare time to Glamorgan Cricket during the 1920's as the club strove for recognition in the first-class game. George was also ready to step in behind the stumps, and indeed, the 43 year-old Cording was Glamorgan's wicket-keeper in their inaugural Championship match in 1921 against Sussex at the Arms Park. Despite his grey hairs, the veteran only conceded a handful of byes, and he also showed good form with the bat.

At the time, George was also captain of the Cardiff club – a position he also held in 1922 – and often invited schoolboys to bowl at him in the outdoor nets at the Arms Park. Before taking guard he would place a penny on each of the stumps, and would generously hand over the coins if one of the pupils dismissed him.

After retiring from club cricket, George continued to promote the game amongst the schoolboys of South Wales, and helped to ensure that there was a steady stream of young talent for the club to draw upon. Indeed, George served as founding Chairman of the Welsh Secondary Schools Cricket Association in 1926 besides being heavily involved with the National Playing Fields Association

George also served on the Glamorgan committee and gave a helping hand to the Club during the Second World War as their officials attempted to maintain interest in cricket. A number of fixtures were therefore arranged during 1944 and 1945 as a means of keeping up the morale of the public, and to also raise funds for the War Effort. At the time, George was working with the National Fire Service and amongst the fixtures organized were games against the firemen. Despite being well into his sixties, Cording acted as a tireless Match Secretary, making sure that the cricket-starved public of South Wales got a number of chances to take their minds off the horrors of War.

An image of George Cording taken in 1933.

133.
RICHES, Norman Vaughan Hurry

Born – Tredegarville, Cardiff, 9 June 1883
Died – Whitchurch, Cardiff, 6 November 1975
Amateur
RHB, RM , occ WK
Ed – Monkton House School, Abingdon School, Chard Grammar School, University College, Cardiff and Guy's Hospital
1st XI: 1900-1934
2nd XI: 1935
Club and Ground: 1920-1929
Cap: 1921
Captain: 1913-1914, 1921, 1929
Minor Counties, MCC
Club: Cardiff
Father of JDH Riches

Batting and Fielding Record

	M	I	NO	RUNS	AV	100	50	CT	ST
Minor	136	212	28	7228	39.28	16	36	129	27
F-c	82	138	8	4419	33.99	6	28	39	6

Bowling Record

	Balls	M	R	W	AV	5wI	10wM
Minor	227	9	143	3	47.67	-	-
F-c	129	1	79	0	-	-	-

Career-bests

Minor –   217* v Dorset at Blandford Forum, 1907
              1/1 v Berkshire at Cardiff Arms Park, 1902
First-class – 177* v Leicestershire at Aylestone Road, Leicester, 1921

Norman Riches was Glamorgan's finest batsman during their Minor County days as well as during their first decade of Championship cricket. In 1921 Norman also led the Welsh county in their inaugural season of Championship cricket, and proudly captained them to their first win against Sussex at the Arms Park.

In 1911 Norman also became the first-ever batsman in the history of the Minor County competition to score over 1,000 runs in the season, confirming the view that he was the best batsman outside the first-class game, and when available, he was regularly chosen for the Minor Counties in their representative games against touring teams and other first-class sides.

Following his stellar summer in 1911, the MCC authorities considered him for a winter tour to the West Indies, with noises being made to other Glamorgan officials about Norman's availability. At the time, he was working alongside his father at their thriving dental practice in Dumfries Place in Cardiff. "I'm not sure that he would get time off for the winter," was the response by Tom Whittington, the county's Hon. Secretary and Norman's opening partner. It was a throwaway comment, but the MCC officials took it as a matter of fact and Norman was not invited. He was rightly annoyed when subsequently hearing about the initial enquiry, especially as his father would have been only too happy to release his talented son over the winter, and Norman's relationship with his fellow batsman was never the same afterwards.

Norman had been born into one of the most well-known cricketing families in the Cardiff area with his father Hugh being a stalwart member of the South Wales CC, besides having represented the town club in their exhibition game against the United South of England Eleven. His uncles, Tom and Charles were also leading figures with both Cardiff CC and the Taff Vale Railway, with the latter being the engineer and locomotive superintendent with the railway company. His cousin Gowan Clark had also been a leading batsman with Cardiff and Glamorgan, and coached him from an early age in the nets at the Arms Park.

He made his debut for the Cardiff 2nd XI aged 14, before making his 1st XI debut in July 1899. By this time, he had also attended Chard Grammar School where he had

Norman Riches, seen at Hove in 1924.

been coached by several of the Somerset professionals. As a patriotic and proud Cardiffian, there was no question of the schoolboy representing the West Country side with Norman making his debut for Glamorgan in their final match of the 1900 season at home to Monmouthshire. He was dismissed for nought but a few weeks later he showed his rich potential playing for the Gentlemen of South Wales against the Players of Glamorgan at the Arms Park where the schoolboy made 13 against the professional attack.

His next innings for Glamorgan in 1901 – against Wiltshire at Swindon – saw him fail to score, but the youngster made a composed 34 in the end of season contest against Devon at Exeter. A maiden fifty then followed in August 1902 against Monmouthshire at Swansea, and being based at Cardiff University he was a regular in the Glamorgan line-up during 1903 and the following June, he struck 183 against Monmouthshire at Swansea before continuing his medical studies in London. There were fanciful rumours that Norman might be chosen by WG Grace to play for London County, but nothing came of these suggestions, with his next couple of hundreds at county level coming against Northumberland with Norman making 109 at Swansea in 1905 and an unbeaten 178 at the Arms Park the following summer.

All of these centuries were testament to his rock-solid technique, honed from his early years in the nets at the Arms Park as well as games in the back garden of his parent's house in the prosperous suburb of Tredegarville, besides schoolboy games when a pupil at Monkton House School who used Sophia Gardens for their recreational activities. Norman possessed a wide range of strokes, especially off his legs, and he relished toying with opposition fielders, with his party piece consisting of a series of singles pushed around so that the fielding captain was forced into readjusting the field, before gleefully smashing a boundary through the gap which he had craftily created.

In his youth, Norman had bowled medium pace on an occasional basis, claiming the first of three wickets for Glamorgan against Berkshire

Norman Riches in the nets at the Arms Park during the late 1930s.

in 1902. He also represented University College, Cardiff at football, whilst from 1904 he also kept wicket for Glamorgan. Norman's tally of 27 stumpings in Minor County cricket, plus six first-class games, confirmed his prowess behind the timbers.

However, it was in front of the stumps, standing with bat in hand, that Norman made his name and during July 1907 the opening batsman struck a purple patch of form as he made 171 against Devon at Exeter, followed next match by a maiden double-hundred with 217* against Dorset at Blandford Forum. However, it was 1911 which was Norman's finest in the Minor County competition, ironically having missed the second part of the previous year having contracted enteric fever. His scores opening the batting during his record-breaking summer of 1911 included 90 against Wiltshire at Trowbridge, 159 against Monmouthshire at Swansea, 65 and 150 in the contests with Carmarthenshire at St Helen's and Llanelli, an unbeaten 167 against Monmouthshire at Newport, plus a majestic 194 during the closing match of the summer with Buckinghamshire at Neath.

The following year he made his debut for the Minor County's representative team, whilst in 1913 and again in 1914 he led the Glamorgan side as they strove to regain the sort of success on the field which had seen the start of a campaign for their elevation into first-class cricket. The outbreak of the Great War, plus a spell of military service in the Army Medical Corps put paid to these lofty thoughts. But with more than a half an eye on the future, Norman was tasked by the committee to oversee the Club's administration until life returned to normal. He duly oversaw the arrangement of several fund-raising games, before appearing in eight of the Welsh county's matches arranged for 1920.

Having played such a high-profile role within the Club over a dozen years or more, Norman was delighted to be sounded out by the Glamorgan hierarchy about his availability to lead the side again during 1921 should their application to the MCC for first-class status prove successful. Norman had two reasons to smile soon afterwards – first, his father agreed to hire a locum in their practice and secondly, the MCC endorsed Glamorgan's application.

It proved to be a fairytale start for Glamorgan in the first-class world as, under Norman's captaincy, they beat a full-strength Sussex side by 24 runs in their inaugural County Championship match at the Arms Park in May 1921. Many of the crowd at the Cardiff ground surged onto the field at the fall of the final Sussex wicket in order to personally congratulate Norman and his team. All of the players then gathered on the first-floor balcony of the Cardiff pavilion with both captains making impromptu speeches. Arthur Gilligan, the Sussex leader was most gracious in his praise of Norman's captaincy before congratulating the Welsh side, saying "they gave us a magnificent game, and we do not mind being beaten in the slightest. We have been down until today, but today we might have won. We did not – Glamorgan did, and I congratulate them very much."

Later that summer, Norman struck the first of his six Championship hundreds, making an unbeaten 177 against Leicestershire at the Aylestone Road ground. But having achieved his long-held dream of leading Glamorgan in first-class cricket, Norman duly stood down from the captaincy at the end of 1921, and returned to his father's practice. He also spent time with other prominent sportsmen in the city helping to establish Cardiff Athletic Club and securing favourable terms from the Marquess of Bute over the lease of his beloved Arms Park.

Like so many others, the ground held a special place in Norman's heart and given his family's long association with the Arms Park, and doubts over the future of the ground as a sporting venue, Norman became the flag bearer of the campaign to preserve it in the heart of the Welsh capital. As a result, he disagreed with some of his fellow committee members who organized for Championship matches to take place outside Cardiff. Their motives were solely based on saving money, rather than sentiment, with the Cardiff club asking for a decent fee to use the pristine facilities. But with gate receipts falling, expenditure of professionals rising and other clubs offering cheaper alternatives, the mid and late 1920s saw fewer county matches at the Arms Park

Norman also devoted a lot of his spare time promoting the creation of a Welsh national team, including players from other parts of the Principality, in annual games against the MCC, Scotland and Ireland, besides fixtures against touring teams. His actions on behalf of the Welsh Cricket Union met with criticism from some within Glamorgan CCC who believed that that the dentist should be devoting his energies towards the county and making himself available on a more regular basis, thereby strengthening the Glamorgan batting and halting the run of defeats.

He silenced some of the doubters with scores of 170 against Derbyshire at Swansea in 1924, and 136 in the game with Derbyshire at Pontypridd in 1926, but his finest Championship innings came in 1928 when, aged 45, he hit a masterful 140 against a powerful Lancashire attack. Norman played his final Championship match in June 1934 aged 51, against Worcestershire at the Arms Park. He also led the side and batted at number 3 in what proved to be a draw. The following summer he also played in Glamorgan 2nd XI's Minor County match against Berkshire at Reading, and opening the batting, he made 115 – his final hundred for the county in representative games.

He continued to play in club cricket for Cardiff until 1939. He subsequently became a Trustee and Patron of Glamorgan CCC, besides acting as Chairman and President of Cardiff CC. In September 1948, after the Welsh county had secured their first Championship title, Norman was one of the umpires, along with Jack Hobbs, at one of the commemorative matches held in South Wales to celebrate the achievements of Wilf Wooller and his team. However, during the 1950s he was at loggerheads with the Glamorgan captain as he opposed attempts for the Club to move from the Arms Park and create a base instead at Sophia Gardens.

A caricature of Norman Riches, showing his ramrod straight bat and forward defensive.

Norman gained the support of civic leaders but when the plans for redeveloping the Arms Park into a National Stadium resurfaced during the 1960s, the days of county cricket at the Arms Park were numbered. The summer of 1966 duly saw the final batch of Glamorgan fixtures before the move to Sophia Gardens, whilst during September he donned the white coat again and was one of the umpires during Cardiff's last match at the Arms Park – the ground where six decades before he had first played for the club.

1901

Cheered by their success in 1900, Glamorgan's officials took steps the following summer both on and off the field to build on their progress. Off the field, the Welsh county, thanks to a link with the *Western Mail*, introduced the availability of up-to-date scorecards at their matches at the Arms Park with a printing press loaned by the newspaper situated in a tent near the entrance from Westgate Street.

At Swansea, new seating and raised terraces were installed, thanks to the financial support of JTD Llewelyn, whilst the fixture list was enhanced by a plum fixture with the 1901 South Africans. The Springboks however proved far too strong for the Welsh county and ran out victors by 132 runs, but a decent crowd was attracted to the Arms Park, allowing the small debt from the previous summer to be erased.

The highlight on the field was a record breaking batting performance against Monmouthshire at the Arms Park as Glamorgan made 538 and Herbie Morgan, in his first county innings of the summer, scored a career-best 254. The batsman from Penarth struck one six and forty fours, but the Monmouthshire bowlers did have one thing in their defence, as they had spent much of the morning session with just seven men on the field, as four of their team had been delayed by a train crash whilst travelling from Newport, with Glamorgan only offering a solitary substitute.

The 1901 season also saw home and away victories against both Monmouthshire and Devon, with Arthur Osborne – another talented young batsman from the Penarth club – scoring 110 against Monmouthshire at the Arms Park and laying the foundations for a victory by an innings and 215 runs. Osborne also made 109 at Reading in the match against Berkshire and his emergence alongside fellow young batsmen Norman Riches and Tom Whittington, gave the Glamorgan selectors great hope for the future.

The Glamorgan team which met Devon at Exeter in 1901.

134.
COLLEY, Robert Henry
Born – Clifton, Bristol, June 1867
Died – Cardiff, 3 June 1949
Amateur
All-rounder
1st XI: 1899
Colts: 1893
Club: Cardiff

Batting and Fielding Record

M	I	NO	RUNS	AV	100	50	CT	ST
1	1	0	0	-	-	-	-	-

Bowling Record

Balls	M	R	W	AV	5wI	10wM
80	9	30	0	-	-	-

Robert Colley is one of a handful of players to have the dubious distinction of failing to score in their only innings for Glamorgan. In his case, Robert also went wicketless when he was given a chance to bowl.

The Bristol-born builder was chosen in the Glamorgan squad for the match against Surrey 2nd XI at The Oval in 1899. The all-rounder though failed to take a wicket, or score a run, despite a good record in club cricket for Cardiff. Six years before, he had also featured in the trial match in 1893 at the Arms Park, when he was chosen for the Colts XXII which met the county side, scoring 10 and 6, but not taking a wicket.

135.
OSBORNE, Arthur James
Born – Westoe, South Shields, 14 December 1876
Died – Barry, 10 January 1961
Amateur
LHB, LM
Ed – Modern School, South Shields
1st XI: 1901-1911
Durham Colts – 1895
Clubs: South Shields, Penarth, Barry

Batting and Fielding Record

M	I	NO	RUNS	AV	100	50	CT	ST
47	69	6	965	15.32	2	-	22	-

Bowling Record

Balls	M	R	W	AV	5wI	10wM
1987	84	1019	63 (+1)	16.17	4	-

Career-bests
110 v Monmouthshire at Cardiff Arms Park, 1901
6/40 v Philadelphians at Cardiff Arms Park, 1903

Born and raised in north-east England, Arthur Osborne moved to South Wales during the late 1890s to continue the family's work as master coppersmiths. After six successful seasons with the Penarth club, he duly became a stalwart of Barry Athletic Club, and during the 1900s he also played county cricket for Glamorgan.

The talented all-rounder also had the distinction of scoring two centuries for his adopted county during his debut season with Glamorgan. Both came during 1901 with Arthur opening the batting and making 110 against Monmouthshire at the Arms Park in July during a stand of 250 for the first wicket with Herbie Morgan, his colleague from the Penarth club. The following month, he scored 109 against Berkshire at Reading, but this time his good friend Herbie only made a single, so after the clatter of other wickets, it was during a stand with Sam Brian that Arthur eventually reached three figures.

Remarkably, the left-hander never passed fifty in his other 67 innings for Glamorgan, with his next highest score being 41 against Surrey 2nd XI at The Oval in 1905. It was his left-arm cutters which led to his inclusion in the Welsh county's ranks in subsequent seasons, with Arthur – also now batting lower in the order – taking 5/21 against Devon at Exeter in 1902, 6/40 against the Philadelphians at the Arms Park in 1903 and 5/9 against Monmouthshire at Swansea in 1904.

He continued to play regularly for Glamorgan until 1905 – a summer which had earlier seen him switch allegiance to Barry – but his work commitments only allowed a couple of appearance in 1906, and his final appearance for Glamorgan came five years later in the rain-affected contest with Carmarthenshire at Llanelli. He continued to meet with great success with his bowling, taking 8/13 against Whitchurch in 1907.

Arthur Osborne, seen in 1902.

Born and raised in South Shields, his exploits for the local cricket club had brought him an appearance for the Durham Colts in 1895. However, it was his father Herbert's decision to move to Barry Docks which led to his son playing at county level.

136.
THACKERAY, Alec Guy

Born – Cardiff, January 1882
Died – Cardiff, 25 July 1909
Amateur
Batsman
Ed – Uppingham
1st XI: 1901-1906
Clubs: Cardiff, Fairwater

M	I	NO	RUNS	AV	100	50	CT	ST
11	16	1	330	22.00	-	2	6	-

Bowling Record

Balls	M	R	W	AV	5wI	10wM
144	4	94	1	94.00	-	-

Career-bests
78 v Northumberland at Newcastle, 1906
1/17 v Wiltshire at Chippenham, 1904

Guy Thackeray of Glan Ely House was the son of Alexander Thackeray, a leading stockbroker in Cardiff who had played for the Glamorganshire club between 1871 and 1874. Guy was a decent cricketer himself, having played for Uppingham prior to making his debut for Glamorgan in 1901. He then followed a brief military career with the Monmouthshire Militia, before returning to South Wales four years later and taking over as the captain of Cardiff CC.

With Jack Brain announcing that he was happy to stand down as Glamorgan captain at the end of 1906, Guy was announced as his successor. But later that winter the Army Lieutenant was posted to the United States. He returned eighteen months later and after successfully resuming his cricketing career with Cardiff, noises were also made about his return to the county side in 1909, and if successful, a leadership role with the Club.

Guy appeared regularly in 1905 and 1906, making 53 against Wiltshire at Chippenham and 78 against Northumberland at Newcastle. Given his military and social contacts, he was clearly seen as the right sort of chap to be the county's captain. Sadly, this was not to be the case as in July 1909 he was taken

Guy Thackeray (left) takes to the field at the Arms Park in 1906 during the match against the West Indians, with Foster Stedman to his left and Norman Riches in front.

seriously ill with acute pneumonia at the Angel Hotel in Cardiff and after being admitted to hospital, he died shortly afterwards at the premature age of 27.

137.
WILLIAMS, Dyson Bransby
(changed name by deed poll to Dyson Brock)

Born – Sketty, 13 October 1877
Died – London, 18 April 1922
Amateur
RHB
Ed – Malvern College and Trinity College, Oxford
1st XI: 1901-1921
Club and Ground: 1912-1920
Clubs: Swansea, Public School Nondescripts

Batting and Fielding Record

	M	I	NO	RUNS	AV	100	50	CT	ST
Minor	16	26	2	351	14.63	-	-	11	-
F-c	1	2	0	14	7.00	-	-	-	-

Career-bests
Minor –   43 v Kent at Bromley, 1913
First-class –   9 v Hampshire at Cardiff Arms Park, 1921

Dyson Bransby Williams was one of thousands of souls who were broken either physically or mentally – or both – by the horrors of War with the cricketer who had mixed duties from 1901 as a player and the Club's Treasurer, taking his life in 1922.

Born in October 1877, he was the third son of civil engineer Morgan Bransby Williams of Killay House situated in spacious grounds west of Swansea. Cricket was in the Bransby Williams' blood with country house matches taking place in the grounds of his home, whilst his eldest son George created during the late 1880s a team called the Public School Nondescripts as the Bransby Williams boys, together with their well-heeled friends from other well-to-do families in the area played matches against the leading club sides and other scratch elevens.

Dyson attended Malvern College where he represented the school at both cricket and association football before going up to Trinity College, Oxford where he read History. After graduating in 1900 he dabbled in various occupations before training to be a solicitor and qualified in 1911. By this time, he was well known in the cricketing world of South Wales having graduated from club cricket for Killay in the Swansea and District League plus country house games in the grounds of his home to the Glamorgan side which played in the Minor County Championship.

He made his debut for the county in June 1901 playing against Monmouthshire at Rodney Parade, and duly became the first player from the Swansea and District League to win honours at county level. However, Dyson did not re-appear for Glamorgan for eleven years as his legal training and establishing his practice in Swansea took priority.

1912 was a red letter year for Dyson as he captained Swansea and returned to the Glamorgan side, finishing in fourth place in their batting averages and posting a career-best unbeaten 43 against Kent 2nd XI. In May 1912 Dyson also changed his middle name by deed poll to Brock. Through his friendship with Tom Whittington, the Neath-born solicitor who was Glamorgan's captain, Dyson also agreed to succeed Hugh Ingledew, the Welsh rugby international, as Glamorgan's Treasurer as the decision-making powerhouse of the Club shifted west.

Whilst very proud of his achievements in securing a place in the Glamorgan side, Dyson was happiest though playing in the more relaxed and convivial world of cricket at Killay House, especially playing for the Public School Nondescripts. As historian Jack Morgan later recalled, "Dyson Williams, with his panama covering his baldness, was a familiar figure on the cricket field in those days We were engaged in amateur theatricals together and this led to many invitations to play cricket at Killay House, and there is no better way of enjoying the game. Something went out of cricket when those house parties became a diminishing feature in the sporting life of south Wales."

He was also well known locally as an amateur singer, and poet, and briefly after the War, appeared as Florian in a production of *Princess Ida* at Swansea's Grand Theatre. As the *South Wales Daily Post* later noted, Dyson participated in these theatricals as wholeheartedly as he did his cricket – "His was a particularly ambitious mind, never content with the ordinary accomplishments in sport or in art. His chief characteristic was his amiability. He was a man of generous instincts, and when he gave his services, he gave them fully and enthusiastically."

Given these traits of character, Dyson became a fine soldier and a popular officer. He also took part in the recruitment, and training at the St Helen's ground of the 14th (Swansea) Battalion of the Welch Regiment, and to Dyson went much of the credit for its initial formation under Colonel Benson on 16 September, 1914, with Dyson himself acting as captain and adjutant.

It was no surprise either that Dyson swiftly rose to the rank of Lieutenant Colonel and was second-in-command of the battalion. 1916 saw Dyson and the Swansea Battalion travel to France where they were thrown into the attack on Mametz Wood in which so many Welshmen lost their lives. Dyson, himself, was severely wounded advancing up the slope leading to the wood and it was feared that he would die in the ambulance train. For a long period "he lay between life and death", and his actions won him the Military Cross, but this was of little comfort as so many of his comrades and friends lost their lives.

He returned to the battalion in 1917, and subsequently showed outstanding leadership at Ypres, with his regiment going over the top at Pilkem Ridge and routing the crack Prussian "Cockchafers". It was an action which deservedly earned Dyson the DSO. In the same year his "Swansea's" also won high honours in an attack on the salient known as Caesar's Nose, and subsequently figured in the Ancre crossing and the engagements at Auveley Wood.

During the peace negotiations in 1918 Lieutenant Colonel Williams was also chosen to act as a guide to Prime Minister Lloyd George over the Somme battlefield. It was no surprise therefore that in December he succeeded Colonel Brooke to the command of the

Swansea Battalion. But the War had taken its toll, and if truth were known, Dyson never fully recovered from the bloody horrors with the man who marched through Swansea at the head of his battalion in June 1919 to present the colours to the Mayor being a very different fellow to the happy and jolly man who had marched off to war five years before.

In July 1919 Dyson was invalided out of the Army, largely as a result of the injury to a lung sustained whilst on the Somme and he returned to live with his mother and brothers at Killay House. He did not, however, return to the legal profession, and in the following year had his name removed from the rolls to engage in a stock and share business. This failed, as did the Welsh Aviation Company in which Dyson had speculated. He continued to play a bit of cricket and continued to serve as Glamorgan's Treasurer, although his heart was not really in the Club's affairs and he only agreed to carry on to help out his old friend Tom Whittington who was now actively seeking assurances and support from English counties to support Glamorgan's campaign for first-class status

Dyson Williams, seen at Swansea in 1909.

Whittington was fortunate enough in the autumn of 1920 to secure the minimum of eight home and away fixtures with existing first-class counties, and there was great celebration when the MCC endorsed Glamorgan's application to join the County Championship in 1921. By this time, Dyson's best years were behind him but he still managed to make an appearance in first-class cricket, at the ripe old age of 44, as he appeared in the last match of Glamorgan's first County Championship season of 1921, against Hampshire at Cardiff. He duly made 5 and 9 as Glamorgan, dismissed for 37 and 114, lost by an innings inside two days.

But Dyson's mind lay elsewhere – his great friend Tom Whittington described how his friend's character had been completely shattered by his wartime experiences – and in 1921 he left Swansea to try his luck in London and elsewhere. In particular, he went to live with an old Army comrade, Major Arnold Wilson, who had become a boxing promoter, at his house at Maidenhead. Williams duly became a close friend of the world light-heavyweight champion, Georges Carpentier, with whom he wrote a song with the music penned by Dyson under the pseudonym Florian Brock, to the words by Carpentier himself, called

"Vagabond Philosophy" It was sub-titled "I'll be all right", and it poignantly included the following lines:

"And so in life you'll get a regular knockout blow.
Don't lie and grouse, but try to smile.
And have the pluck to cry.
The mud and dust will soon rub off.
I'll be all right, by and by."

But Dyson's optimism proved to be misplaced, and shortly before the publication of "Vagabond Philosophy" he was declared bankrupt. He vanished for a while after the bankruptcy hearings, with his brother Morgan finding him "in a rather down and out state and took him to his home in Maidenhead where he stayed for a while. Whilst with his brother, Dyson spoke about his financial problems, attributing the situation to an inadequate Army pay, coupled with the cost of maintaining his law firm during the War. In truth his betting and gambling, in addition to taking out loans at a heavy interest, had had a crippling effect on his personal situation and these were the real reasons for his predicament.

In late February his world fell in as his mother died. A confirmed bachelor, Dyson told a friend he felt "desolate", and soon afterwards went to Belgium to play the casinos. His behaviour relapsed again as cheques started to bounce, whilst Dyson also deceived the owner of a bar into giving him the sum of £200 for a cheque, which then bounced. His debts to Wilson also mounted, but he was able to write to Wilson saying: 'I have at last struck a bit of luck, just when apparently things were hopeless. I shall be able to pay you back what you have let me have.' Wilson had that letter on 19 April. Tragically, the day before, the charlady had gone to clean Wilson's offices in St Martin's Court in London. She found the room full of gas, with Dyson slumped to the floor. The gas stove had two taps fully turned on. The 45-year-old solicitor-cum-soldier and cricketer had become yet another, if belated victim of the War, with the coroner duly recording a verdict of "suicide while of unsound mind".

138.
REES, Edward *Stanley* Cook
Born – Swansea, 9 May 1881
Died – South Africa
Amateur
Batsman and spin bowler
1st XI: 1901-1914
Club: Swansea

Batting and Fielding Record

M	I	NO	RUNS	AV	100	50	CT	ST
36	60	1	750	12.71	-	3	21	-

Bowling Record

Balls	M	R	W	AV	5wI	10wM
18	0	24	0	-	-	-

Career-bests
82 v Carmarthenshire at Stradey Park, Llanelli, 1910

Stanley Rees was brought up in Gorse Lane, alongside the St Helen's cricket and football ground, so it was no surprise that he went on to play cricket for Swansea, besides making 36 appearances for Glamorgan before emigrating after the Great War to South Africa.

Stanley made his debut as a 20 year-old in Glamorgan's match against Monmouthshire at the Arms Park in July 1901. His agile fielding at point was the highlight for the youngster as he was dismissed for a single in his maiden innings, whilst his three overs of spin were dispatched for 24.

He featured in four inter-county matches the following year, again doing little of note with the bat.

In July 1903 Stanley made an assured 41 against Berkshire on his home turf at St Helen's, before posting his maiden fifty against the same bowlers the following year at Reading. His work commitments however meant however that Stanley did not play for Glamorgan again until the last week of June, 1909, when he appeared on their West Country

Stanley Rees seen in a photograph taken in 1902.

tour to meet Devon at Exeter and Cornwall at Penzance.

The following year, Stanley enjoyed his most productive summer in Glamorgan's ranks, making 82 against Carmarthenshire at Llanelli during May 1910, before scoring 55 against Monmouthshire at The Gnoll, Neath in mid-July. Four years later, he appeared in a further six games for the Welsh county but he failed to transfer his good form opening the batting for Swansea into runs for Glamorgan, amassing just 165 runs in his dozen innings.

His father David was a superintendent on the nearby Mumbles Railway, and Stanley followed him into working as initially a clerk on the Great Western Railway. He subsequently rose to a managerial position before moving to live and work with a company in the Transvaal after World War One.

139.
WHITTINGTON, Thomas Aubrey Leyson

Born – Neath, 29 July 1881
Died – St Pancras, London, 19 July 1944
Amateur
RHB
Ed – Weymouth School, Merchiston College and Corpus Christi, Oxford
1st XI: 1901-1923
Club and Ground: 1914-1923
Cap: 1921
West of England 1910, Minor Counties, MCC
Captain 1908-1912, 1919-1920, 1922-1923, Secretary 1909-1922
Clubs: Neath, Cardiff

Batting and Fielding Record

	M	I	NO	RUNS	AV	100	50	CT	ST
Minor	88	133	5	3361	26.27	4	11	31	1
F-c	47	85	6	1152	14.58	-	4	10	-

Bowling Record

	Balls	M	R	W	AV	5wI	10wM
Minor	81	3	54	3	18.00	-	-
F-c	5	0	12	0	-	-	-

Career-bests
Minor –   188 v Carmarthenshire at Stradey Park, Llanelli, 1908
                3/26 v Surrey 2nd XI at The Oval, 1904
First-class –   60 v Hampshire at Southampton, 1922

Tom Whittington, a solicitor in Neath, was the man whose efforts off the field ensured Glamorgan secured first-class status for 1921.

The Neath-born batsman had been a most influential figure in Glamorgan's affairs either side of the Great War, and having served as the Club's Honorary Secretary since 1909 he was tasked in 1920 with securing sufficient promises of fixtures for the following summer to meet the MCC requirements for elevation to first-class status. Thanks to financial assistance from a third party, he successfully achieved this task and in recognition of his outstanding efforts he became the first-ever Life Member of Glamorgan CCC.

Born in 1881, Tom's father had been a Scottish rugby international in 1873, who also played for the early Glamorganshire club in 1869 after moving to South Wales to become Medical Officer to Neath Rural District Council. Tom subsequently read Law at Oxford and the right-handed batsman made his Glamorgan debut in 1901. After making an impressive 78 against the Public School Nondescripts at St Helen's, Tom appeared Devon at Swansea and Surrey 2nd XI at the Arms Park. A handful of appearances followed in 1902 and 1903 as he completed his legal studies, with Tom also spending the latter summer playing for Cardiff having been articled to a practice in the town as part of his training.

He subsequently became a regular from 1904 in the county side and formed a productive opening partnership with Norman Riches, besides proving himself to be an astute leader of Neath CC in club cricket. With Riches still heavily involved with his father's dental practice, and other candidates falling ill, Tom was invited to take over the Glamorgan captaincy for 1908. He subsequently remained in the role until 1912 and during this time also struck four centuries – all against Carmarthenshire – with scores of 188 at Llanelli in 1908, 133 at Swansea plus 107 at Llanelli in 1910 , followed by 176 at Swansea, in 1911. June 1910 also saw him make his first-class debut as he appeared in the West of England

A cigarette card of Tom Whittington.

side, led by Gilbert Jessop, which met the East of England in a fund-raising three-day contest at the Arms Park.

During the autumn of 1910 he was also sounded out by the MCC about his availability for their tour to the West Indies. He answered in the affirmative and duly visited the Caribbean with the MCC party led by Arthur Somerset of Sussex. Tom proved to be the mainstay of the tourists' batting, making 86 and 154 in the game against British Guiana – a match which also saw him add 230 for the first wicket with Bernard Holloway, another amateur attached to Sussex. Their efforts at the time were a Caribbean record and underpinned an MCC victory by 235 runs. Tom also made 115 against All Jamaica at Kingston and ended the tour with a handsome aggregate of 685.

Norman Riches, his opening partner with Glamorgan, also held ambitions to tour with the MCC and in 1912/13 both men were considered. Tom readily said yes, but there were doubts about Norman's availability. Had he been asked directly, Norman would have agreed to tour but a throwaway comment by Tom had been misconstrued and the relationship between the two batsmen was never the same afterwards, as evidenced by the fact that Tom only played once for the Wales team which Norman did so much to create through the Welsh Cricket Union.

Tom, as you would expect with someone with a legal background, had a meticulous outlook to his role of Honorary Secretary and during the winter of 1909/10 had spent many long hours with the Club's President, the Earl of Plymouth, and other committee members, co-ordinating a fund-raising campaign which would hopefully see Glamorgan elevated into the first-class game. He also persuaded Sussex, Worcestershire and Somerset to accept fixtures with the Welsh minor county, as well as arranging the West-East game at the Arms Park, in which he had made his first-class debut. But his tireless efforts fell flat and with a trade slump soon afterwards, the campaign did not raise sufficient funds to consider an application to the MCC.

When life got back to normal after the Great War, the campaign for elevation was back at the top of the Club's agenda, and with Tom still holding his post, he was tasked during 1920 in meeting the MCC's requirement of fixtures with at least eight existing first-class counties, besides drumming up the relevant financial support. Aware of the importance of the task, and how much work it had taken to just get three back in 1910, Tom took a semi-sabbatical from his practice and was delighted when Sir Sidney Byass, the owner of the Margam Steelworks, agreed to give Glamorgan a £1,000 loan over a ten-year period from 1920 in order to seed-fund their campaign and, in particular, to meet the guarantees requested by English counties for fixtures in 1921.

Tom Whittington (left) and Norman Riches walking out to bat – they formed the first great opening partnership for Glamorgan.

With his nest egg safely stowed in the Club's coffers, Tom started to contact the English counties. Somerset quickly agreed, followed by Gloucestershire, Worcestershire, Derbyshire, Leicestershire, Northamptonshire and Sussex although, in a couple of cases where sizeable concerns existed about the viability of a fixture with the Welsh county, Tom was forced to agree to an additional guarantee of £200 towards the games. The enthusiastic Secretary duly reported back to the Club's committee in November 1920 that he had secured home and away fixtures with seven first-class counties. Jubilant at the news, the committee told him to "obtain the eighth at any cost whatsoever", but as it turned out strong persuasion was not needed, as both Lancashire and Hampshire readily agreed to Tom's approach, and during the spring of 1921 the MCC endorsed Glamorgan's application and formally elevated them to first-class status.

Although he was almost 40, Tom played in eleven of the matches in 1921, besides acting as vice-captain. He only scored 303 runs at an average of a shade under 16, besides hitting just one half-century. With Norman Riches standing down at the end of the season, Tom agreed to take over as the Club's leader and drew a line under his work as a solicitor. It meant so much to him that Glamorgan made a decent fist of things as a first-class county, but his dream turned into something of a nightmare. His team lurched from one defeat to another, and with just two fifties to his name, he ended the year with only 469 runs and an average of 13.

The Club's deficit also rose to £2,800 by the end of the summer, and it would have been much higher had a number of money-saving measures not been implemented during the second half of the season, with Tom asking his fellow amateurs to cover the costs of hosting their opposite numbers in hotels or pubs adjacent to the Cardiff or Swansea ground, whilst their wives, daughters and mothers were cajoled into helping to prepare the sandwiches and bake the cakes for the lunch and tea taken by the professionals rather than spending money on professional caterers. Indeed, it was said about one gentleman that he owed his place in the Glamorgan side more to the prowess of his wife in the kitchen than his own abilities with either bat or ball!

With ever-rising debts, there was a decrease in both the number and quality of professionals whose services Tom could call upon. The standard of accommodation booked by Tom for away matches also showed a marked decline. In several cases, bedrooms were taken in public houses rather than in the more expensive and luxurious hotels. There were though few dissenting voices, especially as some of the more thirsty professionals felt that staying in a tavern was something of a perk!

The situation was sufficiently grim during the autumn of 1922 for Tom and the rest of the Club's officials to seriously consider returning to the Minor County ranks, but after all of his efforts – plus the support of so many leading figures in the sporting and business world – Tom was determined to press on. The others agreed, but things went from bad to worse, with just one victory during the eighteen Championship matches between May and July. The only success had come during the first week of June when Northamptonshire were beaten at Swansea, and with the Club's finances showing no turnaround, and his own form not improving, with just one fifty in 28 innings, Tom Whittington resigned the captaincy and handed over the reins to Johnnie Clay.

In recognition of his efforts, the committee awarded him Life Membership, but at the end of the season, Tom left South Wales having accepted a teaching post in Sussex believing that all of his hard work had been in vain and that Glamorgan's existence as a first-class county was over. Fortunately, he was wrong in the latter, with the injection of fresh, young talent helping the Welsh county perform better. During his summer holidays, Tom was delighted to head back to Neath to see friends and family, and to catch up with his beloved Glamorgan and to watch their new rising stars live the dream which he had helped to create.

140.
SOLOMAN, Herbert George ('Herbie')
Born – Swansea, June 1871
Died – Swansea, 1 December 1925
Amateur
Batsman
Ed – St Andrew's College
1st XI: 1901
Clubs: Swansea, Swansea Tourists

Batting and Fielding Record

M	I	NO	RUNS	AV	100	50	CT	ST
1	1	0	38	38.00	-	-	-	-

Career-bests
38 v Public School Nondescripts at St Helen's, Swansea, 1901

Herbie Soloman was a stalwart of the Swansea
Cricket and Football Club who appeared
once for Glamorgan in their light-hearted
friendly against the Public School
Nondescripts at St Helen's in July
1901.

He was also a talented swim-
mer and in later life served as
President of the Welsh Amateur
Swimming Association.

An insurance broker by
trade, Herbie lived at Hill
House, Bishopston and was a
leading light with many good
causes linked to improving life
for the residents of Swansea.
He was also Chairman of the
Glamorgan County Asylum,
Hon. Seceretary of the Swansea
Lifeboat Fund and a Harbour
Trustee. His sister married Swansea
team-mate Astley Samuel.

Herbie Soloman.

202

141.
HOARE, Walter Robertson

Born – Marlow Bucking, Hampshire, 27 October 1867
Died – Lychpit, Dorset, 1 July 1941
Amateur
Batsman
Ed – Eton and Trinity College, Cambridge
1st XI: 1901
Norfolk
Clubs: MCC, Free Foresters, Eton Ramblers
Brother-in-law of VT Hill

Batting and Fielding Record

	M	I	NO	RUNS	AV	100	50	CT	ST
Minor	1	2	0	14	7.00	-	-	-	-

Career-bests
14 v South Africans at Cardiff Arms Park, 1901

The son of Rev. Walter Hoare, Walter junior followed in his father's footsteps by attending Eton, where he made the XI in 1886, besides playing for their football team, and showing prowess at fives and athletics. He then went up to Cambridge and despite appearing in the 1889 Seniors Match he remained a fringe player with the Cambridge XI.

After coming down he went into the brewing business and became involved with the Red Lion Brewery in East Smithfield, but he maintained an interest in cricket by playing for Norfolk, the MCC, Free Foresters, and the Eton Ramblers. Indeed, in 1891 he struck a hundred for the Old Etonians against the Old Harrovians.

His appearance for Glamorgan in 1901 against the South Africans stemmed from his presence in South Wales after a romance with Constance Hill, the sister of Vernon Hill and the daughter of Sir Edward Stock-Hill of Rookwood. The pair got married in 1897, with Walter subsequently joining Cardiff and continuing his training as a brewer. After some decent performances for the town club, he was drafted into the county side for the match against the South Africans.

Walter Hoare.

He also acted as a Director of the Union Assurance Company besides overseeing the creation of Ingram House, a sizeable property in Stockwell which provided accommodation for up to 200 bachelors. Walter later lived with Constance at Daneshill House in Basingstoke which was designed by award-winning architect Sir Edwin Lutyens.

He also diversified his business interests into the operation of a nearby brickworks which provided the building blocks for the suburban expansion of Basingstoke either side of the Great War. During the hostilities, Walter served as a Captain in the 4th Battalion of the Hampshire Regiment.

1902

1902 saw the first-ever visit to Cardiff by an Australian touring team. It followed the MCC agreeing to a request led by Jack Brain for a match to take place in the Welsh capital against a combined Glamorgan and Wiltshire XI. The two-day contest attracted an enormous crowd, with around 12,000 people in attendance, far surpassing the previous ground record, with trains packed with excited cricket supporters travelling to Cardiff from as far away as Milford Haven in the west and Swindon in the east.

The combined side batted first, and made 121, albeit in 52 overs after some doughty resistance from the Minor County batsmen, especially Sam Brain who made a dogged 32* and defied the Australian attack for over two hours. William Overton, the Wiltshire slow bowler, and Glamorgan's Harry Creber were soon amongst the wickets with the Swansea spinner dismissing the first three Australian batsmen as the tourists also struggled in the face of some spirited bowling.

Both Overton and Creber claimed four wickets apiece, before Ernie Jones and Bert Hopkins staged a late fightback to guide the Australians to a 27-run lead on first innings. Herbie Morgan then unfurled some aggressive strokes and to the delight of the local supporters made a fine fifty, whilst Walter Medlicott, Wiltshire's Oxford Blue also made an unbeaten half-century as the combined side set the tourists a target of 155. Second time around however, the Australians found runs easier to come by before easing to a six-wicket victory.

Tom Barlow, the Glamorgan Treasurer, was delighted to report gate receipts in excess of £1,300 as the Club enjoyed their most lucrative season to date. But on the field, the Welsh county rose just one place to finish fourth. Glamorgan did the double once again at the Arms Park and Exeter against Devon, but only three other victories were recorded with successes at the Arms Park by seven wickets and an innings against Wiltshire and Berkshire, plus a thrilling one-wicket win over Monmouthshire at Swansea.

The score card for the match against the 1902 Australians.

142.
GIBBS, Reginald Arthur

Born – Cardiff, April 1882
Died – Penylan, Cardiff, 28 November 1938
Ed – Queen's College, Taunton
Amateur
Batsman
1st XI: 1902-1914
Clubs: Cardiff, Penarth
Rugby for Cardiff, Penarth, Barbarians and Wales (16 caps). Great Britain to Australia
and New Zealand 1908

Batting and Fielding Record

M	I	NO	RUNS	AV	100	50	CT	ST
33	54	6	957	19.94	-	4	12	-

Career-bests
95 v Monmouthshire at Rodney Parade, Newport, 1913

Reggie Gibbs was a talented rugby player who won sixteen caps on the wing for the Welsh rugby side, besides playing in 33 matches for Glamorgan between 1902 and 1914, as well as acting as one of the Club's advisors as they prepared for first-class cricket during the spring of 1921.

Educated at Queen's College, Taunton, Reggie made his debut for Glamorgan against Wiltshire at Trowbridge in 1902. It proved to be his only appearance of the summer for the son of a Cardiff shipowner, but during the course of the next dozen summers, Reggie proved himself to be a capable batsmen when called upon by the county's selectors, besides winning honours on the rugby field and in 1905 scoring a try in the historic Welsh victory over the New Zealanders at the Arms Park

Reggie also scored a try for Cardiff against the 1907 South Africans and during 1908 he scored six tries in four matches whilst wearing the red shirt of Wales. His swift running, and avoidance of the tackle, made him a popular figure with the supporters and it came as no surprise that during 1908 he was the top scorer for the Anglo-Welsh team in New Zealand with 28 points in ten appearances.

As far as his cricket-playing was concerned, Reggie played three times for Glamorgan during 1906 before being taken ill with appendicitis in the match against Wiltshire at Trowbridge. He duly recovered and posted a pair of forties against Dorset at the Arms Park later that summer.

Reggie appeared on a regular basis for Glamorgan during 1910, making 80 against Carmarthenshire at Swansea, plus an unbeaten 53 against Monmouthshire at Neath. A resident of Penarth, he had previously led the town's rugby club in 1903/04 before being elevated to the captaincy of Cardiff RFC during 1910/11. It was a summer which also saw Reggie make his final appearance for the Welsh rugby team during the following spring with his record of seventeen tries remaining as a Welsh record until surpassed by legendary scrum-half Gareth Edwards during 1976. 1913 saw Reggie play his finest innings for Glamorgan, as he posted a career-best 95 against Monmouthshire at Rodney Parade, before in 1914 making an unbeaten 59 against Wiltshire at the Arms Park. By this time, his rugby days were well and truly over, over having toured Australia and New Zealand with the Anglo-Welsh team in 1908. His devotion to cricket saw Reggie serve on the Glamorgan committee between 1910 and 1926, whilst in the spring of 1921 Reggie, together with Sam Brain and JTD Llewelyn formed a sub-group to advise Tom Whittington as he made arrangements for the Club's first-class fixtures, as well as the suitability of various professionals

Reggie Gibbs.

His daughter Shelagh was a Welsh international golfer whilst his son Patrick was a decorated pilot with the RAF and was noted for specialised torpedo attacks against Nazi shipping during the Second World War.

143.
PREECE, Trevor

Born – Cowbridge, 13 October 1882
Died – Whitchurch, 21 September 1965
Professional
RHB, OB
1st XI: 1902-1923
Club and Ground: 1915-1929
Clubs: Cardiff, Barry and St Fagans
Hockey for Cardiff, Barry and St Fagans
Father of HWT Preece

Batting and Fielding Record

	M	I	NO	RUNS	AV	100	50	CT	ST
Minor	13	21	2	326	17.16	-	2	3	-
F-c	1	2	0	8	4.00	-	-	1	-

Bowling Record

	Balls	M	R	W	AV	5wI	10wM
Minor	60	1	36	2	18.00	-	-

Career-bests

Minor –   73 v Carmarthenshire at Stradey Park, Llanelli, 1908
             2/21 v Devon at Plymouth, 1920
First-class –   4 v Lancashire at Cardiff Arms Park, 1923

Trevor Preece made his Glamorgan debut against Monmouthshire at Swansea in August 1902 but it would be another twenty-one years before the right-handed batsman and off-break bowler would make his one and only first-class appearance against Lancashire at the Arms Park.

Born in Cowbridge, Trevor played hockey and club cricket for Cardiff, Barry and St Fagans during the years prior to the Great War. Having first played county cricket for Glamorgan against Monmouthshire at Swansea in 1902, he made another appearance against Berkshire at Reading in 1903 before playing in six further games during 1908 during which Trevor struck 73 against Carmarthenshire at Llanelli as well as an unbeaten 34 against Cornwall at the Arms Park.

He remained a heavy run scorer in club cricket either side of the Great War and during 1920 made 52 for Glamorgan against Devon at Plymouth. In 1925 he succeeded Jack Nash as groundsman at the Arms Park – a position he held until 1939. In August 1932 he was involved in a rather unsavoury incident during Glamorgan's County Championship match against Nottinghamshire. The game in question saw the visiting bowlers – Harold Larwood and Bill Voce

Trevor Preece, seen in 1933 with scythe in hand, tending the Arms Park wicket.

– experiment with Bodyline bowling ahead of England's winter tour to Australia in what subsequently became known as 'Bodyline' tactics. With the prospect of an enthralling contest, a massive crowd turned up at the Cardiff ground expecting fireworks from the visiting bowlers, but instead Maurice Turnbull and Dai Davies proceeded to share a record partnership of 220 for the third wicket during a memorable three and a quarter hour's play as the Welsh county amassed 502 – at the time, their highest-ever total in first-class cricket.

Having made a superb century, Turnbull left to a standing ovation whereas the Nottinghamshire bowlers departed somewhat shamefaced, with several muttering about the feather-bed wicket. Their complaints continued into the night, as the hotel bars and pubs adjoining the Cardiff ground were full of talk about the remarkable happenings. The visitors were soundly of the opinion that the wicket was to blame, so after airing their views about its docile nature, a group of players headed back to the Arms Park and expressed their contempt by urinating on the wicket, much to the disgust of Trevor who rang Maurice to alert him to the situation.

The Glamorgan captain had been dining, as usual, in the Grand Hotel with the Nottinghamshire captain, and after settling the bill, Maurice hastily made his way back to the ground. By this time, news of the prank had spread like wildfire around the city centre watering holes, and a couple of local pressmen had wandered into the Arms Park to view the damp and rust-coloured patches on the wicket. One of these was Harry Ditton – alias 'Nomad' of the *Western Mail* – and aware of his fantastic scoop, Harry quickly filed his copy for the morning edition.

But the story never saw the light of day as Maurice persuaded the Editor to dispose of Ditton's story. "Think of the embarrassment it will cause to English cricket and to Glamorgan Cricket in particular," was his heartfelt argument which, much to his relief, won the day. The following morning, a posse of reporters assembled at the Arms Park from soon after breakfast time as Trevor and his colleagues began their preparatory work with the wicket still under cover.

But unbeknown to them, Trevor had already removed the urine-damaged turf and, when the covers were rolled away shortly before the start of the day's play, there was nothing to see. Maurice duly continued his innings and ended up making 205, before he was caught at fine-leg attempting another boundary.

1903

1903 saw the appearance of another touring team in a game at the Arms Park, as the Philadelphians met Glamorgan. Despite being strengthened by the presence of Vernon Hill, the Somerset amateur, the Welsh county proved little match for the tourists, as they were dismissed for 92 and 88 inside two days with the Americans agreeing to a second contest until their booked express after day three arrived at Cardiff General railway station.

As far as the Minor County competition was concerned, Glamorgan again finished in 4th place in the table, and registered just four victories, including an innings win over Berkshire. at Swansea, where Billy Bancroft recorded a career best 207. Later in the season, they recorded the double at Reading, but this time in nail- biting conditions. Glamorgan were set the seemingly modest task of chasing 39 runs to win, but a hatful of wickets fell, and the Welsh county's innings was held together by William Russell, who was the only batsman to get into double figures. His five colleagues had all recorded ducks, and there was a collective sigh of relief as the professional struck the winning runs with just one wicket in hand.

Off the field, there were growing concerns about the modest size of the Arms Park pavilion, whose original design in 1867 had been along the lines of an Alpine chalet. It was hardly the sort of structure required if Glamorgan were going to stage more matches against international teams, and move into first-class cricket.

More grandiose premises were needed so during 1903 Jack Brain launched a fund-raising campaign for a new pavilion. £1,460 was raised at a special bazaar, held in the Park Hotel in Cardiff and organized by the town club, whilst a couple of rugby matches were also staged during the autumn with designs for the new structure being submitted to also cater for the oval-ball game.

Jack Brain (second right) leads out members of the Glamorgan team from the original pavilion at Cardiff for a match in 1902. Sam Brain is second left and Norman Riches third right.

144.
LEWIS, Wyndham L.

Amateur
Batsman
1st XI: 1903
Club: Cardiff

Batting and Fielding Record

M	I	NO	RUNS	AV	100	50	CT	ST
1	-	-	-	-	-	-	-	-

He was a batsman with Cardiff who was drafted in as a late replacement into the Glamorgan side for the match at the Arms Park in June 1903 against Monmouthshire. However, he cut a rather anonymous figure as he did not bat, bowl or take a catch in the rain-affected draw.

145.
PEATFIELD, Albert Edward

Born – Retford, June 1874
Died – Retford, 12 December 1953
Amateur
Batsman
1st XI: 1903
Clubs: Hill's Plymouth, Lancashire Nomads, Rhuddlan

Batting and Fielding Record

M	I	NO	RUNS	AV	100	50	CT	ST
5	9	0	120	13.33	-	-	4	-

Career-bests
44 v Philadelphians at Cardiff Arms Park, 1903

Schoolmaster Bert Peatfield moved from his native Nottinghamshire to South Wales during the early 1900s and took up a post at Merthyr County School. He also joined the Hill's Plymouth club and following some decent innings, was drafted into the Glamorgan side in July 1903 for their match against Devon at the Arms Park.

Although he failed to repeat his run-scoring abilities on his county debut, Bert made an assured 44 against the Philadelphians a fortnight later, besides playing with confidence in their Minor County matches with Wiltshire and Berkshire.

But soon afterwards, Bert was on the move again having secured a post in North Wales at Rhuddlan Grammar School before gaining a teaching post in Lancashire. The latter saw him appear for an England XI against the West Indians at Blackpool in 1906, allowing him to lay claim as being the first Glamorgan cricketer to play for England. He served as a mechanic with the Royal Flying Corps during the Great War.

146.
HILL, Vernon Tickell

Born – Llandaff, 30 January 1871
Died – Woodspring Priory, Weston-super-Mare, 29 September 1932
Amateur
LHB, RM
Ed – Rev. Cornish's School, Clevedon, Winchester College and Oriel College, Oxford
1st XI: 1903-1905
Clubs: Cardiff, Oxford Harlequins, MCC, Free Foresters, Somerset Stragglers
Oxford University 1892 -1893 (Blue both years) and 21 matches for Somerset 1891-1892
Brother of PMT Hill and father of ML Hill (Somerset, Cambridge Univ. and
Glamorgan) and EVL Hill (Somerset)

Batting and Fielding Record

M	I	NO	RUNS	AV	100	50	CT	ST
5	9	0	46	5.11	-	-	4	-

Bowling Record

Balls	M	R	W	AV	5wI	10wM
108	4	43	0	-	-	-

Career-bests
17 v Philadelphians at Cardiff Arms Park, 1903

Vernon Hill, the son of Edward Stock Hill of Rookwood House at Llandaff, won cricket Blues at Oxford during 1892 and 1893. Besides earning fame as a bold striker of the ball after a fine innings of 114 in the 1892 Varsity Match, he also played county cricket for Somerset, making and famed for his fearless approach, he would often place wagers with local bookmakers on how many runs he might score.

Vernon Hill, as seen in a photograph taken in 1903.

His cavalier and never-say-die approach to batting in 1898 saw Vernon to 116 during what proved to be a record-breaking seventh-wicket stand with Sammy Woods against Kent at Taunton, with the pair adding 240 in even time. Although the contest ended in a draw, Vernon's batting had attracted the attention of many notable people, and it was no surprise that he was included in Pelham Warner's touring team to the USA the following winter having visited the States with Frank Mitchell's XI three years before.

He took over the captaincy of Cardiff CC during 1903 and 1904, and subsequently played a highly important role off the field, helping his good friend Jack Brain in staging a number of

fund-raising fixtures at Cardiff which helped to boost the county's finances as they attempted to swell the coffers for a bid for first-class status. He was influential in persuading several well-known amateurs to turn out in these exhibition games, and it was Vernon's idea that the county should stage an annual Gents-Players match as part of a weekly festival of cricket at the Arms Park.

Vernon also played in a handful of games for Glamorgan, albeit with little success. The first in 1903 saw him appear against the Philadelphians at the Arms Park, before making three further appearances in Minor County Championship matches during 1905. With his best years well behind him, Vernon's contributions against Monmouthshire, Devon and Wiltshire were all quite modest.

Having trained as a barrister, he subsequently moved with his wife Gwynedd – the daughter of Lieutenant-Colonel Evan Llewelyn of Langford Court – to Woodspring Priory near Weston-super-Mare where his family owned a dairy farm. He took over its operations, as well as the Mendip Lodge Estate, and besides running its horticultural

Vernon Hill, seen in the nets during the late 1890s.

business, he oversaw the farm's supply of milk for trains on the Great Western Railway.

Noted for his autocratic air, Vernon became aware that one of his staff was helping himself to milk destined for the GWR. He lined up his employees, loaded a gun, and shot five bottles on a nearby gate, before informing his staff that if the pilfering continued, the culprit would suffer a similar fate to the glass bottle! Fortunately, little persuasion was needed for the culprit to own up and passengers on the local expresses were able to enjoy what was provided from the Hill's farm.

During the Great War, he served initially as a Captain in the 12th King's Royal Rifle Corps where, no doubt, his shooting abilities stood him in good stead once again, before subsequently taking a position at the Staff College in Camberley. Although his roots were in South Wales, Vernon served as President of Somerset CCC in 1930.

147.
POOLE, Thomas Goodman

Born – Hardingstone, Northants, December 1869
Died – Cardiff, 16 November 1913
Professional
RHB, RM
1st XI: 1903
Leicestershire Colts
Clubs: Hugglescote, Dalkeith, Paisley, Cardiff , Lowerhouse, Belfast

Batting and Fielding Record

M	I	NO	RUNS	AV	100	50	CT	ST
1	2	1	2	2.00	-	-	-	-

Bowling Record

Balls	M	R	W	AV	5wI	10wM
60	3	23	0	-	-	-

Career-bests
2 v Philadelphians at Cardiff Arms Park, 1903

Tom Poole.

Tom Poole was the professional with the Cardiff club during 1903 and 1904. During his association with South Wales, he was also called up by the Glamorgan selectors to play against the Philadelphians in 1903 at the Arms Park. He did little of note though in what proved to be his sole county appearance.

Tom had been on the Leicestershire staff during 1895 and 1896 before securing professional posts in Scotland with Dalkeith and Paisley. He moved to Northern Ireland in 1901, to play for Belfast, before switching to the Lancashire Leagues with Lowerhouse in 1902.

His success in the Lancashire Leagues helped Tom gain a position with Cardiff for 1903 and 1904. Whilst an effective bowler at club level, he never secured further opportunities to play at county level.

148.
MOORE-GWYN, Howell Gwyn ('Croppy')

Born – Duffryn Clydach, Neath, 7 July 1886
Died – Midhurst, Eastbourne, 31 July 1956
Amateur
RHB, occ WK
Ed – Winchester College and RMA Sandhurst
1st XI: 1903-1912
Army 1923
Punjab Governor's XI 1929/30
Clubs: Neath, MCC, I Zingari, Old Wykehamists and Greenjackets
Son of JE Moore-Gwyn and brother of JG Moore-Gwyn

Batting and Fielding Record

M	I	NO	RUNS	AV	100	50	CT	ST
8	16	1	229	15.27	-	1	5	1

Career-bests
63 v Devon at Devonport, 1906

Howell Moore-Gwyn followed in the footsteps of his father, Joseph, by playing county cricket. Both father and son attended Winchester College, with Moore-Gwyn senior appearing for the Glamorganshire club between 1870 and 1874 before Moore-Gwyn junior played eight times for Glamorgan from 1903 until 1912, before having a most distinguished military career.

Howell's debut at county level, against Berkshire at Reading, came as a seventeen year-old wicket-keeper batsman following some decent performances in school cricket, as well as for Neath. He had just left Winchester when he next appeared in August 1905, against Monmouthshire at Newport, and by the time of four further appearances in August 1906 Howell had become a cadet at Sandhurst. The summer also saw his finest innings in Glamorgan's colours, with a composed innings of 63 during the end of season match against Devon at the Devonport Services ground in Plymouth.

He subsequently became a Second Lieutenant in the 4th Battalion of the Rifle Brigade and for the next few years mixed his military duties in Malta with visits back home, allowing him to make occasional appearances for Glamorgan in the Minor County Championship, plus the all-amateur Gentlemen of Glamorgan side, as well as club cricket for Neath, the MCC and other military teams. His final appearance in a Minor County game took place in 1912 at Swansea, where he kept wicket against Staffordshire.

The following year the gentleman from Duffryn House in Bryncoch near Clydach became an Adjutant in the 4th Battalion and in August 1914 he travelled across the English Channel with the British Expeditionary Force where he duly fought in France and Belgium. After being promoted to the rank of Major, Howell won the Military Cross in June 1915 following his brave actions in the skirmishes at St Eloi and Hooge. He then served with the Battalion in Salonika and briefly acted as commander, besides winning the Croix de Guerre in May 1917. Around this time, he was briefly transferred to the War

Office in London before spending time with the Mediterranean Expedition Force between July 1917 and May 1918, before returning to the Continent for the final throws of the Great War. He remained on French soil until August 1919, during which time he had added the DSO to his decorations.

Known to his military friends as 'Croppy', he subsequently served in Dublin between 1919 and 1921 before becoming a Staff Officer at Sandhurst. He then spent time with the King's African Rifles from 1924 to 1928, yet despite his many duties, he still found time to play plenty of cricket, appearing for the MCC, the Army and I Zingari. During this period, he also won the Army racquets doubles championship on eight occasions.

In 1928 'Croppy' joined the 1st Battalion of the Rifle Brigade in India, and the following year appeared for the Free Foresters on their tour of India in 1929/30 where he played in a first-class game against the Punjab Governors XI at Lahore. In 1931 Howell was in charge of the Battalion during the Kashmir disturbances, with his prompt and outstanding actions helping to avoid a critical situation and earning a personal congratulatory message from the Viceroy.

In 1934 he was promoted again to the rank of Lieutenant-Colonel whilst serving in Sudan before becoming a Colonel in May 1940. 'Croppy' retired in October 1942 but retained a keen interest in the sporting activities of servicemen by acting as Hon. Secretary of the Green Jackets club – a position he held until his death in July 1956. Howell's brother John also played county cricket for Glamorgan. Their grandfather Howel Gwyn had been Conservative MP for Penrhyn, Falmouth and Brecon between 1847 and 1868, before playing a leading role in the public life of Neath and encouraging the playing of cricket at The Gnoll. Howell's wife Winifred Gilbertson also came from a prominent family in sport, industry and politics in Neath.

Howell Moore-Gwyn.

149.
LEWIS, Henry Leveson Tamplin ('Harry')
Born – Lower Newcastle, Bridgend, 1867
Died – Bridgend, 6 July 1912
Amateur
RHB, RM
1st XI: 1903
Colts: 1892-1893
Clubs: Bridgend, Llwynypia

Batting and Fielding Record

M	I	NO	RUNS	AV	100	50	CT	ST
1	2	0	20	10.00	-	-	-	-

Bowling Record

Balls	M	R	W	AV	5wI	10wM
18	0	16	0	-	-	-

Career-bests
12 v Devon at Exeter, 1903

Like his elder brother William Edgar, Harry Lewis was a talented cricketer and mixed his sporting activities with work in his family's legal practice in Bridgend.

Harry was a prominent member of the Bridgend club and, like his brother, the MCC. In fact, his first major match was for the MCC against the South Wales Cricket Club at Swansea in a two-day game in August 1886. The nineteen year-old did little of note in the game, but it was a measure of both his standing and promise that he was chosen to play alongside the cream of amateur talent in the region at that time.

He subsequently appeared for the MCC in their game against Monmouthshire at Rodney Parade in Newport in 1891. Harry also appeared twice in Glamorgan's pre-season matches during the early 1890s, on both occasions playing for the county's colts team, first at Swansea in May 1892, and secondly at the Arms Park in 1893.

It was to be a decade though before Harry appeared in Minor County cricket. In the intervening years, the well-travelled gentleman had begun business interests in South Africa where he also acquired property in Transvaal, before returning to the UK in the early 1900s and continuing his playing career as a right-handed batsman and seam bowler with Bridgend and the MCC.

After some decent performances in club cricket during 1903, Harry was drafted into the Glamorgan side for the end of season match away to Devon. It was his solitary appearance.

150.
MORGAN, Dr Edward ('Teddy')

Born – Abernant, 22 May 1880
Died – North Walsham, 1 September 1949
Amateur
All-rounder
Ed – Christ College, Brecon and Guy's Hospital
1st XI: 1903-1913
Clubs: Cardiff, Sketty
Rugby for Cardiff, London Welsh, Newport, Sketty, Surrey, Kent and Wales (16 caps)
Uncle of EN and WG Morgan

Batting and Fielding Record

M	I	NO	RUNS	AV	100	50	CT	ST
3	6	1	10	2.00	-	-	2	-

Bowling Record

Balls	M	R	W	AV	5wI	10wM
36	2	18	3	6.00	-	-

Career-bests
5 v Devon at Exeter, 1903
3/18 v Devon at Exeter, 1903

Dr Teddy Morgan, who played three times for Glamorgan, holds a special place in Welsh sporting history as the man who not only scored the winning try for Wales in their first-ever victory over New Zealand in 1905, but was the person responsible for the singing of national anthems ahead of sporting events, having responded to the All Blacks 'haka' at the Arms Park by leading his team and the crowd in a rendition of 'Mae Hen Wlad Fy'n Hadau'.

Teddy Morgan, seen in his Welsh rugby jersey in 1905.

This tour in 1905 by the New Zealand rugby players to Europe and North America has gone down in sporting history as legendary. The Kiwis scored no less than 976 points and conceded just 59. They won 34 out of their 35 matches with their sole defeat coming in front of 47,000 jubilant Welsh supporters at the Arms Park.

After the All Blacks had run onto the ground to much applause, they performed their legendary "haka" in front of a silent crowd before the home supporters, led by Dr

Teddy, the Welsh winger and medic from Swansea, sang the Welsh national anthem in an attempt to reduce the perceived psychological advantage of the Maori war-dance. It was the first time a national anthem had been sung before a sporting fixture and has become standard fare at any international sporting contest.

As far as the match was concerned, Dr Teddy was soon in the action, sprinting some 25 yards down the wing to score a try at the Westgate Street End. Up in the air went hats, handkerchiefs and newspapers, whilst the roar of emotion and cheers of delight were so loud that a cart-horse bolted down Westgate Street and galloped off towards Cardiff General railway station! Wales duly went into half-time with a 3-0 advantage but the tourists were far from happy, believing that the refereeing of John Dallas was poor, especially in the scrums.

Besides not keeping up with play, the Scot had also blown his whistle too early for the break. Throughout the interval further Welsh hymns and anthems were sung as the crowd did their bit to maintain Welsh ascendancy. The second half proved to be tough and uncompromisingly physical as, fuelled by anger, a wave of All Black attacks took place, before with ten minutes remaining, Bob Deans almost reached the Welsh try-line before being tackled just short by Morgan and Rhys Gabe, though for years New Zealanders have claimed Deans placed the ball over the try-line. After some heroic defense by the Welsh side during the closing minutes, the final whistle to signal a totemic victory for the men in red jerseys.

Educated at Christ College, Brecon, Teddy mixed his medical studies at Guy's Hospital with sporting endeavors, playing cricket for Glamorgan and rugby for the London Welsh club. Indeed, it was whilst attached to the latter that Teddy won the first of sixteen Welsh rugby caps against England in 1902.

His outstanding cricketing record at the Brecon school, plus decent performances for the Hospital's team saw Teddy win a place in the Glamorgan side for their visit to Exeter for the match with Devon in August 1903. The allrounder had more success with the ball than the bat, claiming 3/18. It was a full ten years before he appeared twice more for Glamorgan, each time during August 1913 in matches at St Helen's, against Kent and Wiltshire. By this time, Dr Teddy had a practice in Sketty, and had played with much success for Swansea CC. However, he met with little success in these games for Glamorgan, scoring just four runs in as many innings.

After the Great War Teddy became a noted golfer with the Pennard club and played in the Glamorgan Amateur Championships. He subsequently moved in 1927 to a practice in east Anglia and lost the sight in his right eye during an accident at a partridge shoot in October 1938. His son Guy was a playwright, besides being a film critic for the *Daily Express* during the 1930s.

1904

Work had begun at the Arms Park during the autumn of 1903 on the creation of the new pavilion. By the New Year, the shell of the building was complete with its elaborate design for the new matching the grandiose dreams of Glamorgan, and its urbane supporters, with two turrets as well as other castellated effects, flanking a raised balcony plus a seating area below. Also incorporated was a spacious gymnasium – frequented presumably by the burly rugby players rather than the gentlemen cricketers – whilst at the rear, there was a stable area for the groundsman's horse.

On match days, access to the new pavilion was confined to Glamorgan members, but the Club's officials also introduced a new category of membership aimed at junior members. Known as Holiday Tickets, this ten shilling package allowed under eighteens from midsummer to join older gentlemen within the pavilion as well as using the practice nets.

On the field, Glamorgan were handicapped by an injury to Jack Brain, but Norman Riches was available for most of the season having completed his dental studies. He celebrated by hitting 183 against Monmouthshire at Swansea as Glamorgan inflicted a heavy innings defeat against their neighbours.

A postcard of the new pavilion created at the Arms Park in 1903/04 as Glamorgan made a bid to host Test cricket in Cardiff.

Three other games were won, with Berkshire defeated at the Arms Park by four wickets, plus home and away successes over Devon, with Jack Nash taking 6/53 in the first innings at St Helen's, and Harry Creber 6/77 in the second as the visitors fell to a five-wicket defeat. Morale was therefore high in the Glamorgan camp, especially with a stream of favourable comments about the impressive new facilities.

151.
GIBSON, William Henry

Born – Islington, 17 July 1854
Died – Swansea 9 May 1930
Amateur
Batsman
1st XI: 1904
Club: Swansea

Batting and Fielding Record

M	I	NO	RUNS	AV	100	50	CT	ST
1	1	1	7	-	-	-	-	-

Bowling Record

Balls	M	R	W	AV	5wI	10wM
30	0	34	0	-	-	-

Career-bests
7* v Devon at St Helen's, Swansea, 1904

William Gibson was a schoolmaster by profession who made one appearance for Glamorgan, as a late substitute in their match against Devon at Swansea in July 1904.

Born and raised in London, he subsequently taught in Barnsley in Yorkshire, as well as briefly in Lancashire before moving to Swansea during the mid-1890s to take up a post at the local Grammar School.

An enthusiastic cricketer, he played for Swansea, and through his friendship with the Bancrofts, oversaw coaching by the Glamorgan professionals at the Grammar School and at St Helen's.

152.
ELLIS, Henry Augustus

Born – Cambridge, 20 June 1872
Died – Bishopston, Swansea, 30 October 1966
Amateur
All-rounder
Ed – The Perse School and Trinity Hall, Cambridge
1st XI: 1904-1906
Clubs: Cardiff, Swansea, Mumbles

Batting and Fielding Record

M	I	NO	RUNS	AV	100	50	CT	ST
4	6	1	112	22.40	-	-	2	-

Bowling Record

Balls	M	R	W	AV	5wI	10wM
18	0	10	0	-	-	-

Career-bests
41 v Berkshire at Reading, 1904

The St Helen's ground overlooking Swansea Bay has witnessed some memorable feats of big-hitting, most notably in 1968 by Nottinghamshire's Sir Gary Sobers. In the years before the Great War, it was local batsman Henry Ellis who time and again gleefully struck the ball out into, and over, the Mumbles Road.

An architect by profession, he had been born and educated in Cambridge. He began his professional career in the university town before moving briefly to Cardiff and then heading further west to Swansea in 1898 to join the practice of Alfred Bucknell which had been established since 1870 and had seen the creation by the Gloucestershire-born architect of the Calvinstic Methodist Church in St Helen's Road plus the Board School in Waunarlwydd. Henry subsequently took over the eminent practice and remained in the area for the rest of his life. His son Colin joined his father in the practice in 1935, before selling it to the Gammon Partnership in 1980.

Henry had been a talented batsman at The Perse School and Trinity Hall, Cambridge with his big-hitting feats for Swansea drew the attention of the Glamorgan selectors. He duly made his debut against Berkshire at Reading in 1904 and struck a lusty 41. Pressure of work meant that he did not re-appear at county level until June and July 1906 when Henry was chosen for the home and away fixtures with Monmouthshire, at Swansea and Newport respectively, plus the contest with Northumberland at the Arms Park.

Henry made 30 on his home turf at St Helen's, plus 37 at the Arms Park, yet despite impressing many good judges, his business commitments prevented him from playing again in the Minor County Championship. He was appointed captain of Swansea in 1909 and, during July 1914, Henry found time to appear at St Helen's for the Gentlemen of Glamorgan against their counterparts from Carmarthenshire. By this time he was also playing cricket for the Mumbles club.

153.
WAITE, Arthur Edgar

Born – Farley, Somerset, 19 May 1878
Died – Hove, December, 1946
Professional
All-rounder
1st XI: 1904
Club: St Fagans

Batting Record

M	I	NO	RUNS	AV	100	50	CT	ST
1	2	1	34	34.00	-	-	-	-

Bowling Record

Balls	M	R	W	AV	5wI	10wM
72	4	30	1	30.00	-	-

Career-bests
30* v Berkshire at Reading, 1904
1/21 v Berkshire at Reading, 1904

Arthur Waite was one of the junior professionals employed by the Earl of Plymouth, with his duties including assisting Douglas Smith, Bill Towse and the other senior professionals in

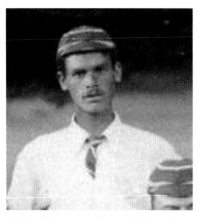

tending the wicket used by the St Fagans club, as well as working as a gardener on the Earl's Estate. After the Great War, Arthur assisted Trevor Preece who had become Head Groundsman at the club's ground in Crofft-y-Genau Road.

With a decent record as a bowling all-rounder for the St Fagans club, Arthur was released by the Earl to play for Glamorgan on their visit to Reading to play Berkshire in 1904. He claimed one wicket with his medium-pace bowling as well as making an unbeaten 30 batting at number nine in the Welsh county's first innings. Local newspapers commented how "he hit strongly with Nash for the last wicket."

Arthur Waite, in a photograph from a St Fagans team photograph in 1904.

154.
SWEET-ESCOTT, Edward _Rhys_

Born – Brompton Ralph, Somerset, 27 July 1879
Died – Penarth, 1 July 1956
Amateur
RHB, OB
1st XI: 1902-1921
Clubs: Penarth, Cardiff

Batting and Fielding Record

	M	I	NO	RUNS	AV	100	50	CT	ST
Minor	63	104	13	2013	22.12	2	8	34	-
F-c	1	2	0	13	6.50	-	-	-	-

Bowling Record

	Balls	M	R	W	AV	5wI	10wM
Minor	209	3	142	6	23.67	-	-

Career-bests

Minor –   129 v Carmarthenshire at Stradey Park, Llanelli, 1909
             2/12 v Dorset at Cardiff Arms Park, 1907
First-class –   13 v Worcestershire at Kidderminster, 1921

Rhys Sweet-Escott was the youngest member of the famous sporting family from Penarth. An architect and surveyor by profession, he was through marriage, also related to Frank Hancock, with his wife being the sister of the great rugby player for Cardiff and Wales, and member of the famous brewing family who, like Rhys, also hailed from Somerset.

He had grown up in Penarth, for whom he played rugby, but cricket and hockey were his sporting passions. A sound right-handed batsman and occasional off-spinner for Penarth, Rhys followed his elder brothers Ralph and Sidney into county cricket by making his Glamorgan debut in the rain-affected draw with Monmouthshire in June 1902. His training as an architect meant that Rhys did not re-appear in the county's side until August 1904, playing against Surrey 2nd XI at the Arms Park, and Devon at Exeter.

Rhys duly became a regular member of the Glamorgan side for the next six seasons, making an unbeaten 97 against Berkshire at the Arms Park in 1905, largely with the help of the lower order, and had he had received support from Jack Nash, the Cardiff professional, the young Penarth amateur might have made a deserved and chanceless maiden hundred. As the correspondent of the *Evening Express* wrote "it was the anxious hope of everyone on the ground that the three runs for his century would be forthcoming. It was entirely a question of whether Nash would keep his end long enough. Instead of playing steadily, the professional went in for slogging, with the result he was bowled."

The following summer Rhys was also chosen in the South Wales team which met Yorkshire at the Arms Park, whilst in 1907 he enjoyed a highly productive time on the county's West of England tour which involved consecutive matches at Penzance, Exeter and Blandford Forum. Having made 93 against Devon during a productive stand with

Norman Riches, the pair had a field day against Dorset sharing an unbroken stand of 244 for the fifth wicket, with Riches making a double-century and Rhys his maiden hundred for Glamorgan. At the close of play on the first day of the contest, he proudly walked off unbeaten on 104 and the next day saw the Glamorgan bowlers complete an innings victory. His selection duly followed for the South Wales team which met the South Africans at the Arms Park.

He also enjoyed a good start to the 1909 season and, following some elegant innings for Cardiff, he struck an unbeaten 83 against Monmouthshire at Rodney Parade. In the next match Rhys made a career-best 129 against Carmarthenshire at Llanelli with his innings full of flowing drives on both sides of the wicket, plus delicate late cuts. Amongst his colleagues in the Glamorgan side was his young nephew Henry Sweet-Escott.

A fortnight later Rhys was in the runs again on the West Country tour, making 61 against Cornwall at Penzance and he was duly chosen in the South Wales team which met the 1909 Australians. He enjoyed a lean time in 1910, failing to pass fifty in seventeen innings, but did serve on the county committee as the Club began their first attempt at securing first-class status. It was more his lack of form with the bat, than the failure of the fund-raising scheme that led Rhys to take a brief sabbatical from cricket, during which he won two Welsh hockey caps during 1912.

Suitably refreshed, Rhys returned to the Glamorgan side in 1913 and made a typically attractive 87 against Surrey 2nd XI at the Arms Park. Further appearances followed during 1914 before Rhys served in an

Rhys Sweet-Escott, as seen in 1905.

administrative capacity for the Army during the Great War. He returned to cricket with Cardiff in 1919 and duly made a couple of appearances for Glamorgan the following summer. Although past his best, Rhys also turned out for the Club in 1921 in their County Championship fixture against Worcestershire at Kidderminster in what proved to be his one and only first-class appearance.

1905

During the autumn of 1904, Glamorgan's officials came so very close to a quite audacious coup in bringing Test cricket to Cardiff. It followed an application to the MCC to stage the first Test of the 1905 series against Australia, with Jack Brain and others making a series of presentations to MCC officials. Nottinghamshire also approached Lord's and after listening to their talk, the MCC committee voted on whether the game should be allocated to Trent Bridge or the Arms Park. An equal number of votes were cast in favour of each venue and it was only after the Chairman's casting vote that Nottingham won the day.

But they had been highly impressed by Glamorgan's words, and the MCC officials awarded a three-day match between South Wales and the Australians to the Arms Park. It drew a crowd in excess of 10,000 people to the Arms Park, with many locals hoping that the cream of talent from Glamorgan and Monmouthshire could hold their own. Indeed, the correspondent of *The South Wales Daily News* wrote "cricket in South Wales needs the fillip a first-class exhibition will give and if so, it will help Glamorgan take in the near future her rightful place in the cricket world."

The reality was that the Australian bowlers proved far too strong with only Billy Bancroft offering any lengthy resistance. The Australian batsmen then put the Welsh bowling to the sword, as Charlie McLeod struck a vibrant century to give his side a lead of 229 runs. He then claimed some early wickets as South Wales slipped to 80-3. Another defeat looked likely but a heavy storm washed out much of the final day.

Glamorgan may have held dreams of achieving first-class status but their results in 1905 proved to be far from distinguished. Bancroft was the only batsman in form and ended the season with an average of 51 – a feat which brought him a 20-guinea cheque from Sir John Llewelyn. The only crumb of comfort on the bowling front came from the perseverance (and perspiration) of Harry Creber who took 100 wickets in all games. His success masking the club's very slender bowling resources, with Creber delivering a total of 542.3 overs, often bowling unchanged throughout the game.

The Welsh county slipped back to ninth place in the table, with the summer's lowest point coming at Chippenham when Wiltshire's two professional bowlers dismissed the Welsh team for just 20 – the lowest total by any Glamorgan team. Despite the brash hyperbole in the local newspapers, it showed that much work was still needed if Glamorgan were going to play in the County Championship.

The view from the pavilion at the Arms Park, during the game between South Wales and the 1905 Australians.

155.
SEYMOUR, The Honourable Reginald <u>Guy</u>

Born – Alcester, Warwickshire, 15 January 1880
Died – Woodstock, Oxford, 4 January 1965
Amateur
Batsman
1st XI: 1905
Clubs: St Fagans, Glamorgan Gypsies, Somerset Strugglers, United Hunts

Batting and Fielding Record

M	I	NO	RUNS	AV	100	50	CT	ST
2	4	0	14	3.50	-	-	1	-

Career-bests
8 v Durham at Hartlepool, 1905

The grandson of the Fifth Marquess of Hertford and Lady Emily Murray, Guy Seymour was brought up in Warwickshire before following his father, Major Ernest Seymour into a military career

He initially served with the Royal North Devon Yeomanry in the Boer War, and soon rose from the rank of Lieutenant to Captain of the 27th Squadron. However, in 1901 during

Guy Seymour.

skirmishes near Rustenburg, Guy was wounded and forced home. He duly recovered and began training as a land agent with the Earl of Plymouth in South Wales.

Guy's move to South Wales saw him play for St Fagans and the Glamorgan Gypsies. Some decent innings in club cricket led to him being chosen in the Glamorgan squad for their northeast tour in 1905. Guy played at Newcastle-upon-Tyne against Northumberland and at Hartlepool

against Durham, but made 3, 1, 8 and 2 and was never called up again by the Glamorgan selectors.

In 1915 Guy enlisted again in the Royal North Devon Yeomanry and served as an Adjutant, firstly in Gallipoli before moving to Palestine in 1917 where he was injured again during fighting near Tel el Sheria. He was evacuated to a military hospital and subsequently was stationed in Marseilles in Southern France until the end of hostilities. After the War, Guy acted as Land Agent for Lord Wharton of Halswell, and lived at Goathurst in Somerset. During this time, he also played cricket for the Somerset Strugglers and the United Hunts.

156.
HORSPOOL, James

Born – Burton-on-Trent, 6 August 1874
Died – Cardiff, 10 September 1960
Amateur
RHB, WK
1st XI: 1905-1913
Clubs: Hill's Plymouth, Swansea, Cardiff

Batting and Fielding Record

M	I	NO	RUNS	AV	100	50	CT	ST
6	7	2	44	8.80	-	-	5	4

Career-bests
11* v Surrey 2nd XI, at The Oval, 1905

James Horspool kept wicket for both Cardiff and Swansea, besides making five appearances for Glamorgan prior to the Great War. From 1924 he also served as secretary of the Cardiff club and, together with his wife, ensured that the off-field arrangements ran smoothly, especially the catering when the Welsh county played at the Arms Park..

The son of a brewery foreman in Burton-on-Trent, James left school at fourteen and initially worked under his father as a telephonic clerk. He subsequently left Staffordshire and moved to South Wales to work at first in a brewery in Merthyr Tydfil. He played for a summer for the Hill's Plymouth team before securing a sales position with a brewery in Swansea. James duly joined the Swansea, and further developed his wicket-keeping skills under the tuition of Dan Thissen.

His neat glovework soon attracted the attention of the Glamorgan selectors and when Sam Brain was unable to keep during the middle of the 1905 season, James made five appearances for the Welsh county, with his debut taking place at the St Helen's ground against Northumberland. Through his links with both Sam and Jack Brain, James secured a sales position with the Cardiff brewery, switched his allegiance to the city club, and remained in the Welsh capital until his death during 1960.

James was appointed captain of Cardiff in 1913 and during July returned to the county side for the match against Monmouthshire at the Arms Park. After serving in the defence unit at Cardiff Docks during the Great War, James led the Cardiff club again in 1919 and also joined the Glamorgan committee.

His prime role with the county club, was to oversee arrangements as they moved into the first-class world, whilst his wife Gladys also played a role behind the scenes,

James Horspool, seen in 1912.

especially with the catering. In her youth, Gladys had been captain of the Cardiff Ladies water polo team, and by the 1920s she was now a leading light with the tennis section of Cardiff Athletic Club, whose courts ran alongside the boundary at the Westgate Street end of the Arms Park ground. However, during county matches, Mrs Horspool's chief role was overseeing the work of the wives and girlfriends of the other amateurs in ensuring that the players were adequately fed and watered during the lunch and tea intervals, often at no cost to the cash-strapped county club.

James served as secretary of Cardiff until 1945, and in the words of the *South Wales Echo*, proved to be "one of the most loyal, efficient and popular officials connected with any sports organization in South Wales."

157.
RATTENBURY, Gilbert Leach

Born – Cardiff, 28 February 1878
Died – Penarth, 14 August 1958
Amateur
RHB, RFM
1st XI: 1905-1912
Club and Ground: 1930
Gloucestershire 1902-1909
Warwickshire 2nd XI 1911
Clubs: Schoolmasters (Bristol), Cardiff, Moseley, Northern

Batting and Fielding Record

M	I	NO	RUNS	AV	100	50	CT	ST
25	35	6	412	14.21	-	1	12	-

Bowling Record

Balls	M	R	W	AV	5wI	10wM
2394	85	1119	50	22.38	3	-

Career-bests
55 v Durham at Cardiff Arms Park, 1906
7/37 v Berkshire at Cardiff Arms Park, 1905

The son of a Devon-born draper, Gilbert Rattenbury was born and raised in Cardiff before his parents moved back across the Severn Estuary to open new premises in Bristol. After completing his studies, Gilbert became an insurance broker besides showing great promise as a fast bowler and free-hitting batsman for the Schoolmasters club in Bristol.

As a result, July 1899 saw him play for Gloucestershire 2nd XI against Monmouthshire at Bristol but he bagged a pair and failed to take a wicket. Nevertheless, he continued to impress for the Schoolmasters and during June 1902 Gilbert made his County Championship debut for Gloucestershire against Worcestershire at the Ashley Down ground. Once again, he failed to claim a wicket, and after a first innings duck, he got off the mark with the bat scoring 7 in the second innings.

Gilbert was not called upon again for seven years by Gloucestershire and during this time, he mixed playing in club cricket in Bristol and Cardiff, with a series of appearances for Glamorgan in the Minor County Championship. He marked his debut for the county of his birth by taking 7/37 in Berkshire's second innings of their game at the Cardiff Arms Park in July 1905. The following month Gilbert took six second innings wickets in the return game at Reading having also picked up a 'six-for' against Durham at the Arms Park.

Gilbert subsequently became a regular face in the Welsh county's line-up during the next couple of seasons, and against Durham at the Arms Park during July 1906, he displayed his batting talents with a muscular half-century. Despite his success in club cricket in Bristol, Gilbert was only able to play on an occasional basis for Glamorgan

Gilbert Rattenbury, seen at Reading in 1905.

during 1907 and 1908, with Gloucestershire showing a renewed interest in the lively seam bowler, with the county's selectors recalling him in mid-July 1909 for the match against the Australian tourists at Bristol. The game duly saw him take his maiden wicket as he bowled Victor Trumper, but he bagged a pair again and was not called up again to play for the West Country side.

A fortnight later, Gilbert returned to Minor County action with Glamorgan, before making a further six appearances in 1910. But the following year he was promoted to the role of manager in an insurance business in King's Norton, a suburb of Birmingham. He duly joined Moseley and played during 1911 for Warwickshire 2nd XI, claiming four wickets and top-scoring with 46 in the away match against Leicestershire 2nd XI at Aylestone Road.

With Glamorgan pressing for honours in the 1912 Minor County Championship, Gilbert made three further appearances for the Welsh county, in their home and away fixtures with Staffordshire, as well as the contest with Surrey 2nd XI. However, he went wicketless in each game and did little of note with the bat in what proved to be his final appearances in inter-county matches.

Two years later, Gilbert was on the move again as he was promoted to a branch in Liverpool. However, the outbreak of the Great War brought a temporary halt to his cricketing activities as he served as a Lance-Corporal in the 5th Regiment of the King's Liverpool Regiment. He survived the horrors of the War and was back playing again for the Northern Club for whom Gilbert was a regular in 1921 in their 1st XI in the Liverpool and District Competition. His heart though still lay in South Wales, and in 1923 Gilbert secured a transfer back to Cardiff where he continued to play for the city club as well as for the Glamorgan Club and Ground XI until 1930.

158.
SPILLER, William ('Billy')

Born – St Fagans, Cardiff, 8 July 1886
Died – Cardiff, 9 June 1970
Amateur
RHB
Ed – Lansdowne School
1st XI: 1905-1923
Cap: 1921
Clubs: Cardiff, Barry
Rugby for Cardiff RFC and Wales (10 caps), Bowls for Glamorgan

Batting and Fielding Record

	M	I	NO	RUNS	AV	100	50	CT	ST
Minor	4	6	1	46	9.20	-	-	1	-
F-c	13	22	0	411	18.68	1	1	7	-

Bowling Record

	Balls	M	R	W	AV	5wI	10wM
F-c	24	0	31	0	-	-	-

Career-bests

Minor –   24* v Surrey at St Helen's, Swansea, 1905
First-class –   104 v Northamptonshire at Northampton, 1921

"Excuse me officer – aren't you the man who scored Glamorgan's first Championship hundred?" Anyone arrested by P.C. Billy Spiller of the South Wales Constabulary would have been entitled to say this after the policeman's exploits with the bat in 1921. But being a supporter of Glamorgan was – and still is – no defence in a court of law, so if the county's supporter ended up being fined or serving a custodial sentence, it may have been a small crumb of comfort to know that the arresting officer was none other than the batsman who holds a unique place in the Club's history.

Billy's landmark century came during July 1921 against Northamptonshire at the County Ground in Northampton, and occurred during an extended two-month break that the 35 year-old – regarded by many as the finest batsman in club cricket in South Wales – had been able to secure in an attempt to assist the Welsh county during their inaugural season as a first-class team.

At the start of the season, Billy had informed Norman Riches, his Cardiff colleague and county captain, that he would do his best to get eight weeks of leave during July and August, and he did not let his good friend down. Billy began his sabbatical by travelling to Kidderminster for the match with Worcestershire before heading to Northampton for the next game, where on July 26th 1921 he reached three figures with an all-run four on the legside after batting for a shade under three hours. His efforts though were in a losing cause ass Glamorgan were beaten by 244 runs. It had been sixteen long years earlier that the St Fagans-born cricketer had first appeared for the county in the Minor

County Championship. However, his work commitments restricted Billy to just two games in 1905, plus one each in 1906 and 1908 – the latter being the final of the Minor County Championship as the Welsh county travelled to Stoke to play Staffordshire. His presence bolstered the middle order but could not prevent the home team from securing a comfortable nine-wicket victory.

It was easier for Billy to take half-days in order to play rugby, and from 1903/04 he featured in the Cardiff 1st XV as well as in the Glamorgan Police team. His strong running in the centre and deft handling skills saw Billy win the first of ten Welsh caps against Scotland at the Arms Park in February 1910 . Three seasons later, he was appointed captain of the Cardiff side and he celebrated his elevation by scoring the only try of their match against the touring Springboks at the Arms Park, touching the ball down barely a six hit away from the cricket square where he had shone during the summer months.

After his exploits during 1921 for Glamorgan, the county hierarchy were hoping that Billy might be able to secure enough leave to play cricket on a more regular basis. Although he still enjoyed the game, the unrelenting day-to-day grind of the county circuit and late night travelling had affected his play, with Billy only making one other half-century. Consequently, he only made one Championship appearance in each of the next two seasons, playing against Yorkshire at Headingley in July 1922 followed by the game during June 1923 against Gloucestershire at the Victoria ground in Cheltenham

By this time, his cricketing allegiance were with Barry Athletic for whom he remained a mainstay of their batting for many years. In later life, he also represented Glamorgan at bowls and eventually retired from the Glamorgan Police Force with the rank of Inspector.

Billy Spiller, first centurion in County Championship cricket.

1906

1906 saw fixtures once again with Northumberland and Durham, and during June and July Glamorgan recorded home and away victories against their north-eastern opponents. Norman Riches struck 178* against Northumberland at the Arms Park whilst Harry Creber claimed 23 wickets in the wins over Durham at Sunderland and Cardiff. Both were shoo-ins for the South Wales side in their next high-profile match against the West Indians, but unlike the game the previous year, the weather could not save the Welsh side from a heavy defeat as the men from the Caribbean romped to a 278-run victory.

Several of Glamorgan's senior players struggled as the summer unfolded. Sam Lowe had retired when the season got underway and by the end of August William Russell and Herbie Morgan had both followed suit. As a result 1906 saw a number of new faces, including Percy Morris, the Swansea cricketer who subsequently was one of Glamorgan's opening bowlers in their inaugural Championship encounter in 1921.

In an attempt to find fresh talent, Jack Brain also resurrected the fixture against a Colts XXII, but few of the youngsters looked up to playing in the higher standard. The correspondent of the *Western Mail*, who twelve months before had been poised to herald Glamorgan's elevation to the first-class ranks, now adopted a more gloomier tone in his report on this game, writing "any talented youngsters were conspicuous by their absence."

At the age of 43, *anno domini* was also catching up with Jack Brain, so after discussions with other Club officials, he agreed to stand down as captain and hand over the reins to a younger man for 1907. At the end of the season, Guy Thackeray, the 24 year-old batsman from Cardiff, was announced as Glamorgan's new captain, with the Club hoping that the Army Lieutenant would mould a new and more successful team. However, a few weeks after the announcement, Thackeray was posted to the United States, and plans for a new captain were shelved.

The Glamorgan team which met Berkshire at Reading in 1905.

159.
FLETCHER, Edwin Valentine Archer ('Ted')

Born – Gloucester, January 1877
Died – Cardiff, 11 June 1922
Amateur
RHB, WK
1st XI: 1906
Clubs: Cardiff, Cardiff YMCA

Batting and Fielding Record

M	I	NO	RUNS	AV	100	50	CT	ST
1	2	0	5	2.50	-	-	-	1

Career-bests
5 v Wiltshire at Trowbridge, 1906

Ted Fletcher, a wicket-keeper with Cardiff was another man to play once for the Welsh county, having been chosen for the visit to Trowbridge to play Wiltshire.

The 29 year-old was a draughtsman by profession and he completed a stumping off the bowling of Harry Creber shortly before the home side cruised to a ten-wicket victory. Having made 5 and 0, it was Ted's sole contribution to their win.

Ted Fletcher.

160.
MORRIS, William <u>Percy</u>

Born – Swansea, 19 June 1881
Died – Swansea, 30 July 1975
Amateur
RHB, RM
1st XI: 1906-1925
2nd XI: 1935
Cap: 1922
South Wales 1912
Clubs: Swansea, Swansea Tourists

Batting and Fielding Record

	M	I	NO	RUNS	AV	100	50	CT	ST
Minor	46	75	3	1084	15.06	-	3	28	-
F-c	8	16	1	157	10.46	-	-	6	-

Bowling Record

	Balls	M	R	W	AV	5wI	10wM
Minor	732	25	434	27	16.15	1	-
F-c	204	9	99	2	49.50	-	-

Career-bests

Minor –   56 v Wiltshire at Cardiff Arms Park, 1911
           9/28 v MCC at St Helen's, Swansea, 1920
First-class – 30 v Essex at St Helen's, Swansea 1925
           1/11 v Leicestershire at Aylestone Road, Leicester, 1922

Percy Morris was a Swansea man through and through, so it was fitting that the all-rounder's best-ever bowling figures for Glamorgan, plus his highest score in the County Championship, should come at the St Helen's ground.

It was at the ground overlooking Swansea Bay where the son of Major Bertie Morris of Ael-y-Bryn House in the Mumbles had been coached from a young age by various members of the Bancroft family. Percy's father had trained at RMC Woolwich before serving with the Royal Artillery, but with a growing family back home in the Mumbles, he resigned his commission and became a metal merchant .

In January 1900 Major Morris died prematurely of pneumonia, aged just 39 and, after completing his studies, it was young Percy who took over the running of what became a highly successful brokerage. The young businessman also secured a place in the Swansea 1st XI, and during June 1906, after making an impressive hundred against Cardiff, the opening batsman was invited to make his Glamorgan debut against Monmouthshire at Swansea.

Despite making his county debut in familiar surroundings, it did not prove to be a fairytale start as batting at number three, he made 8 and 12. But more substantial innings came his way during 1907, plus a maiden wicket against Lancashire 2nd XI at the Arms

Park, but his bourgeoning business meant that Percy could only make fleeting appearances at county level.

He was able to find more time to play county cricket in 1911 – the summer of Percy's elevation to the captaincy of the Swansea club – and he was rewarded with half-centuries against Surrey 2nd XI at The Oval, as well as Wiltshire at the Arms Park. The following summer he made his first-class debut, fittingly at St Helen's, as he appeared for the South Wales side against the 1912 South Africans. Percy though made 0 and 2 batting at number five as the tourists won by the comprehensive margin of 230 runs.

By a strange stroke of coincidence, some of Percy's

Percy Morris, as seen in an image from 1908.

best performances for Glamorgan came against Surrey as he struck another assured fifty against them at The Oval in 1913, followed by a seven-wicket match haul in the fixture at the Arms Park in August 1920. Percy's finest hour however with the ball came three weeks later, fittingly at St Helen's where his, by now, nagging medium-pace bowling saw him take 9/28 in the MCC's first innings of what was Glamorgan's final-ever game as a Minor County. He also struck an assertive 39 before the Welsh county celebrated their elevation by winning the contest by ten wickets.

Percy continued to lead Swansea during 1921, besides making the first of eight Championship appearances, including the Welsh county's inaugural first-class fixture against Sussex when he opened the bowling at the Arms Park. He made further appearance that summer, against Hampshire at Cardiff, but his business commitments allowed him to appear on five occasions during 1922, with two further appearances in games at Swansea, plus the matches in Leicester, Worcester and Bristol.

Three years later, Percy made his final appearance for Glamorgan, against Essex at Swansea where he opened the batting with Norman Riches and made 30 and 3. He continued to play in club cricket for Swansea throughout the 1920s.

161.
BIGGS, Cecil Frederick

Born – Kingston-upon-Thames, 22 May 1881
Died – Southam, Banbury, 5 October 1944
Amateur
RHB, OB
1st XI: 1906
Club: Cardiff

Batting and Fielding Record

M	I	NO	RUNS	AV	100	50	CT	ST
2	2	0	14	7.00	-	-	2	-

Bowling Record

Balls	M	R	W	AV	5wI	10wM
42	3	14	0	-	-	-

Career-bests
9 v Monmouthshire at Rodney Parade, Newport, 1906

Cecil Biggs.

Cecil Biggs was another new face to appear in 1906 with his selection following a series of decent innings for Cardiff CC. He duly followed in the footsteps of his elder brothers Norman and Selwyn, by appearing in the Glamorgan side for their Minor County Championship encounters at Newport with Monmouthshire and Carmarthenshire at Llanelli.

He made 9 at Rodney Parade and 5 at Stradey Park, and met with far more success on the rugby field. Like his brothers, Cecil was a talented rugby player, playing in the centre for Cardiff RFC, whom he captained in 1904/05. He had first played for Cardiff during the 1900/01 season, and for the next three seasons was their leading try scorer. Indeed, Cecil is regarded by rugby historians as the finest player of his generation never to win international honours.

Cecil was an insurance broker by trade, acting as secretary of the Ocean Accident and Guarantee Corporation, besides serving for many years on the committee of Cardiff Athletic Club.

162.
LEWIS, Sydney Albert
Born – Cardiff, January 1873
Amateur
Batsman
1st XI: 1906
Club: Cardiff

Batting and Fielding Record

M	I	NO	RUNS	AV	100	50	CT	ST
1	1	0	4	4.00	-	-	-	-

Career-bests
4 v Carmarthenshire at Stradey Park, Llanelli, 1906

Sydney Lewis appeared in one game for Glamorgan against Carmarthenshire at Llanelli in 1906. He was a tobacconist by trade, having succeeded his father in running the family's business in the prosperous suburb of Roath in Cardiff.

With a decent record as a middle-order batsman with the Cardiff club, Sydney was given an opportunity to display his talents in the match with Carmarthenshire at Stradey Park but it proved to be his sole appearance at county level.

Sydney Lewis.

163.
GABE, Rhys Thomas

Born – Llangennech, 22 June 1880
Died – Cardiff, 15 September 1967
Ed – Llanelli Intermediate School and Borough Road, College
Amateur
1st XI: 1906
Clubs: Cardiff, Llanelli
Rugby for Llangennech, Llanelli, Cardiff, London Welsh, Middlesex and Wales (24 caps)

Batting and Fielding Record

M	I	NO	RUNS	AV	100	50	CT	ST
1	1	0	0	-	-	-	2	-

Rhys Gabe was another multi-talented sportsman and Welsh rugby international who played county cricket for Glamorgan. However, he failed to score on his only appearance for the Welsh county, in the trial game against a Colts XVIII at the Arms Park in 1906. He did however take two catches, and impressed with his speedy fielding, as befitted someone who had scored one of the most extraordinary tries in rugby history.

Rhys Gabe

His audacious efforts came during the Wales-England international in 1908 at Bristol – a game which was played in thick fog – and followed the ball going loose after a maul. After pretending to pick up the ball, Percy Bush ran off in one direction whilst Rhys with ball in hand ran in the opposite direction and headed towards the try-line. Given the poor visibility, the England players were unsure which of the two Welshmen had the ball. When they eventually discovered that Percy was the decoy, they headed to the try-line, only to find the referee standing there with Rhys who duly touched the ball down!

This was undoubtedly the most dramatic of his 24 appearances in a Welsh jersey, having made his debut whilst a player with Llanelli against Ireland in 1901 on the wing before switching to the centre. The change of position followed his move to Cardiff where he formed a devastating partnership with Gwyn Nicholls, scoring in all 51 tries during his 115 appearances between 1902/03 and 1909/10.

After Rhys completed his training to teach mathematics at Borough Road College, he secured a post at Howard Gardens School in the Welsh capital and joined their cricket and rugby clubs. He was also a talented cyclist and billiards player and whilst at the training college, he also represented Borough Road at water polo. In later life Rhys took up golf and became a leading member of the Radyr and Cardiff clubs.

164.
ARDASEER, John Grenville

Born – Richmond, September 1882
Amateur
Batsman
1st XI: 1906
Club – Swansea

Batting and Fielding Record

M	I	NO	RUNS	AV	100	50	CT	ST
1	1	0	12	12.00	-	-	-	-

Career-bests
12 v Colts XVIII at Cardiff Arms Park, 1906

John Ardaseer also made a sole appearance for Glamorgan in the Colts Trial during 1906. An electrical engineer by profession, he worked initially in Lancashire before moving to South Wales where John played the bulk of his club cricket for Swansea and enjoyed a good record as a top-order batsman.

He had also opened the batting for the Gentlemen of Glamorgan against the Gentlemen of Essex at Neath in 1905 before playing against the Colts XVIII at the Arms Park. He never played again for the county as midway through the 1907 season he received a lucrative business offer to work in India, and left South Wales.

165.
GIBSON, John

Born – Cardiff, 1880
Amateur
Batsman
1st XI: 1906
Clubs – Canton Wesleyans, Cardiff

Batting and Fielding Record

M	I	NO	RUNS	AV	100	50	CT	ST
1	1	0	4	4.00	-	-	-	-

Career-bests
4 v Colts XVIII at Cardiff Arms Park, 1906

John Gibson was a building contractor, based in the thriving inner suburb of Canton, with his father, John Farquahar Gibson, having moved to South Wales from his native Scotland during the 1870s to create the family's business.

After success for the Canton Wesleyan team, and a move to the Cardiff club, John appeared for the county during 1906 in the trial match against a Colts team at the Arms Park. Despite not playing again for Glamorgan, John remained a successful batsman in club cricket and was an influential figure behind the scenes with Cardiff Athletic Club.

166.
MOORE-GWYN, Joseph Gwyn

Born – Neath, 15 May 1879
Died – Liss, 17 February 1937
Amateur
Batsman
Ed – Winchester College and Hertford College, Oxford
1st XI: 1906
Clubs: Neath
Son of JE Moore-Gwyn and brother of HG Moore-Gwyn

Batting and Fielding Record

M	I	NO	RUNS	AV	100	50	CT	ST
1	1	0	4	4.00	-	-	1	-

Career-bests
4 v Devon at Devonport, 1906

Joseph Moore was a late selection for Glamorgan's away match with Devon in Plymouth during August 1906. He duly played alongside his younger and more talented brother with his call-up following some decent performances in club cricket for Neath.

Educated at Winchester and Oxford, Joseph enjoyed a successful military career having joined in 1903 the Glamorgan Yeomanry, where he rose to the rank of Major. During the Great War, he also served in Egypt as a Lieutenant-Colonel in the Fifth Battalion of the Worcestershire Regiment.

At the time of his call-up to the Glamorgan side in 1906, Joseph was in his fourth year on the Club's committee, and had planned originally to travel to Devon to watch his brother play and assist with any off-field administration. He continued to serve on the committee until 1909, but never had any other surprise call-ups.

In 1907 he married Olive, the grand-daughter of William Gilbertson, an industrialist and politician who had been one of the promotors of the match between Neath and South Wales and the All England XI in 1855.

1907

1907 saw a change to the format of the two-day Minor County Championship with the teams divided into four regional groups, and the top side in each progressing to the semi-finals, with the two winners meeting in the final. The new system coincided with a marked improvement in Glamorgan's fortunes and rekindled the campaign for elevation into the first-class ranks.

The Welsh county comfortably won six of their eight group matches against Monmouthshire, Cornwall, Devon and Dorset, with Norman Riches scoring 171 away to Devon and an unbeaten 217 in the game with Dorset. The match at Exeter also saw Jack Brain make 117, whilst Rhys Sweet-Escott posted 93 as Glamorgan totaled a mammoth 540 – the highest-ever score by any Minor County team. Useful contributions with the bat also came during the season from the Swansea duo of Billy Bancroft and Percy Morris, whilst Fred Preedy, the well-travelled professional delivered some hostile spells with the ball.

Their combined efforts saw Glamorgan clinch a home semi-final with Surrey 2nd XI. After Jack Nash took 7/68 in the visitors' first innings, and Harry Creber 5/54 in their second, Bancroft led the victory charge with an unbeaten 86 as the Welsh county won by four wickets. Lancashire 2nd XI were their opponents in the final, also staged at the Arms Park where a fortnight earlier South Wales had also met and lost to the South Africans.

Once again, a large crowd watched the game with the northern county, hoping that Glamorgan would fare better than the South Wales side, but after James Heap made 81 in Lancashire's first innings, the Burnley-born all-rounder took six wickets with his left-arm spin as the home side were dismissed for 74. After batting again, Lancashire set Glamorgan a stiff target of 291, and despite a fighting 80 by Jack Brain, Lancashire won by 108 runs and became Minor County champions.

Percy Morris, the captain of Swansea, has a heated discussion with the groundsman at the Arms Park in 1907 ahead of the club's match against Cardiff.

167.
THOMAS, Herbert ('Herbie')

Born – Cowbridge, January 1886
Died – Neath, 7 February 1935
Amateur
Batsman
1st XI: 1907-1911
Clubs: Llantwit Major, Cowbridge, Glamorgan Gypsies

M	I	NO	RUNS	AV	100	50	CT	ST
5	7	0	114	16.29	-	1	7	-

Career-bests
62 v Carmarthenshire at Stradey Park, Llanelli, 1911

Herbie Thomas, as seen in a photograph from 1908.

Herbie Thomas had a fine record as a batsman with various teams in the Vale of the Glamorgan during the years leading up to the Great War. His reward was selection in five matches for Glamorgan.

His first call-up to the county side came in May 1907 after some bludgeoning innings for Llantwit Major CC. The 21 year-old made 14 against Monmouthshire at Rodney Parade, before re-appearing the following year against Carmarthenshire at Neath. Herbie also featured in the Welsh county's tour to Devon and Cornwall, but he failed to produce a substantial innings in the West Country.

As a result, Herbie did not feature again until July 1911 when, after some decent scores for the Glamorgan Gypsies, he made 62 in the game against Carmarthenshire at Llanelli. The match at Stradey Park saw several other fringe players appear in the Glamorgan side, but it proved to be his final appearance at county level.

The son of Alderman David Thomas, he continued to play with some success for several years after the Great War for Cowbridge.

168.
HIRST, Joseph Owen

Born – Wakefield, June 1867
Died – Cardiff, 12 March 1948
Professional
RHB
1st XI: 1907
Durham Colts 1889
Clubs: Ferguslie, Drumpellier, Bishop Auckland, Sedgefield, Burnley, Accrington, Cardiff, Neath, Tondu, Chippenham, Cardiff Alpha

Batting and Fielding Record

M	I	NO	RUNS	AV	100	50	CT	ST
6	9	0	85	9.00	-	-	2	-

Career-bests
43 v Cornwal at Penzance, 1907

The son of a coal miner from Leeds, Joe Hirst was a well-travelled cricket professional in Northern England before moving to Cardiff in 1906, playing for Glamorgan the following summer and spending the rest of his life in the Welsh capital.

Joe had first come to prominence with his older brother Billy in club cricket in County Durham, with Joe's prowess as a free-scoring batsman with Tudhoe and Sedgefield winning him a place in the county's Colts side in 1889. Whereas Billy went on to enjoy a seven-year career with Durham, Joe secured a professional appointment with Bishop Auckland before moving north to Scotland where he played for the Ferguslie club.

He then headed back south and spent time in the Lancashire Leagues with Burnley and Accrington before, in 1906, the hard-hitting batsman joined Cardiff CC. Joe made a promising start with his new club and during early May played for South Wales against Yorkshire at the Arms Park. But batting at number three, he failed to score against the county of his birth.

1907 saw the Yorkshireman play for Neath for whom he struck a high-class and unbeaten 100 against Gorseinon, besides making six successive appearances for Glamorgan. These began with the contest against Monmouthshire at Newport during the final week of May before Joe went on the tour to Cornwall, Devon and Dorset, and struck 43 in the opening match at Penzance. It proved though to be Joe's only innings of substance and, after making a pair in the return match against Dorset at the Arms Park, he was dropped from the side.

Joe Hirst, as seen whilst coaching in 1911 at Cardiff Intermediate School.

Joe was attached to the Tondu club in 1908, before returning to Cardiff in 1909, followed by a year with Chippenham. He was back however in the Welsh capital prior to the Great War, attached to the Cardiff Alpha club in addition to securing a coaching position in football, hockey and cricket at both Monkton House and Cardiff Intermediate School.

After the war, he continued to mix his coaching duties with work as an orderly at Cardiff Mental Hospital. He also became an umpire of repute in local club cricket, as well as a referee of local football games. In 1927 Joe was called upon to officiate in Glamorgan's friendly against HDG Leveson-Gower's XI at Swansea. He was believed to also have been a relative of George Hirst, the famous Yorkshire and England bowler.

169.
PREEDY, Ernest Alfred ('Fred')

Born – Ross-on-Wye, September 1876
Died – Clitheroe, 20 February 1964
Professional
RHB, RFM
1st XI: 1907-1909
Hong Kong 1901/02, Devon 1912-1913
Clubs: Ross, Cardiff, Gloucester, Ribblesdale Wanderers

Batting and Fielding Record

M	I	NO	RUNS	AV	100	50	CT	ST
23	30	7	340	14.78	-	-	11	-

Bowling Record

Balls	M	R	W	AV	5wI	10wM
1537	56	766	52	14.73	5	-

Career-bests
42* v Cornwall at Penzance, 1907
6/17 v Devon at St Helen's, Swansea, 1908

Fred Preedy was another well-travelled professional who appeared for Glamorgan during the late 1900s. In all, he made 23 appearances and during the match with Lancashire 2nd XI at the Arms Park in September 1907 Fred became the first, and so far only, Glamorgan batsman to be dismissed 'obstructing the field'.

The incident occurred during Glamorgan's first innings with Preedy arriving in the middle with his side on 44/7 in reply to Lancashire's decent total of 243. This, however, did not excuse him for his actions after miscuing a drive against James Heap high into the air. As the correspondent of the *Western Mail* wrote, "Blomley the wicket-keeper, got under the ball to take the easiest of catches. But Preedy in getting back into his crease, cannoned against him with his back. Upon an appeal by the Lancashire captain, the umpire gave Preedy out for obstructing the field."

Born and raised in Ross-on-Wye, the right-handed batsman and fast-medium bowler played his cricket initially for his home town as an amateur, before enlisting with the

Royal Welch Fusiliers and serving in India and China. He later joined the Gloucestershire Regiment and fought in the Boer War, before returning to the Far East and playing as a cricket professional for Hong Kong.

Fred returned to play as a professional for Ross in 1904, before moving again to join Cardiff in 1906. His decent performances for the city club saw him play on a regular place in the Glamorgan side during 1907 and 1908. In his debut season, Fred took five-wicket hauls against Devon at Exeter as well as Dorset at the Arms Park, before the following summer claiming 6/47 against Carmarthenshire at Neath and a career best 6/17 against Devon at Swansea. He also played for the South Wales sides against the 1907 South Africans and the following year the Gentlemen of Philadelphia at the Arms Park.

Fred made a single appearance for Glamorgan in 1909 before leaving South Wales and acting as Gloucester's professional in 1910. He was on the move again the following year, perhaps as a result of his outstanding bowling performance in 1908 at St Helen's, as he moved to Devon, whom he represented in

Fred Preedy demonstrates his bowling action at the Arms Park in 1908.

Minor County cricket between 1911 and 1913. He then headed north in 1914 and joined Ribblesdale Wanders in the Lancashire Leagues. At the end of the 1914 season Fred did his bit for King and Country by joining the Seaforth Highlanders, but whilst serving in Mesopotamia he was badly wounded in his left leg and was forced home.

Fortunately the wound healed and in 1920 he helped Ribblesdale Wanderers win their local league. He also married a local girl and remained in Clitheroe for the rest of his life, serving as groundsman for the Ribblesdale club. Their son, Reginald, subsequently played football for Darwin FC as a centre-forward.

1908

1908 saw Glamorgan, once again, reach the final stages of the Minor County competition, as well as the South Wales side lose their showpiece contest against the touring Philadelphians at the Arms Park.

However, Glamorgan's progression to the semi-finals was not without more than a whiff of controversy after they had tied with Monmouthshire on top of the Western Division.

A play-off was held in the last week of August but only one innings was completed because of the weather and it was left to Sir Francis Lacey, the MCC Secretary, to decide in Glamorgan's favour on the rather dubious grounds that they had won the group the year before. His decision did not go down well in Monmouthshire given that they had enjoyed, by far, the better of the group match at Cardiff where Arthur Silverlock scored an unbeaten 187.

With Jack Brain moving into semi-retirement, Arthur Gibson was appointed as the Club's captain, but the veteran returned for the play-off with Monmouthshire. With Gibson unavailable for the semi-final away to Wiltshire, it was Brain who led the Welsh county at Chippenham. Rain washed out the first two days of the contest, and after the home team had elected to bat on the last day, Harry Creber took 8/18 as Wiltshire were dismissed for 41. Glamorgan replied with 172 and although the match was drawn, the Welsh side comfortably progressed to the final by virtue of their higher first innings total.

Their opponents in the final were Staffordshire, and for the journey to Stoke, Jack Brain was replaced by Billy Spiller, the multi-talented sportsman and Cardiff bobby. However, the Welsh rugby international, like the rest of his Glamorgan colleagues, had no answer to the skills of Sydney Barnes. The legendary bowler virtually won the title singlehandedly for Staffordshire, with a match haul of 15/54 as Glamorgan were dismissed by a paltry 60 and 79, before losing by ten wickets.

170.
SYMONDS, Henry George ('Harry')

Born – Cardiff, 24 June 1889
Died – Canton, Cardiff, 1 January 1945
Amateur
LHB, SLA
1st XI: 1908-1925
Club and Ground: 1923
Cap: 1921
South Wales 1912
Club: Cardiff

Batting and Fielding Record

	M	I	NO	RUNS	AV	100	50	CT	ST
Minor	39	55	6	850	17.35	-	2	9	-
F-c	22	40	1	547	14.02	-	2	4	-

Bowling Record

	Balls	M	R	W	AV	5wI	10wM
Minor	211	3	113	3	37.67	-	-
F-c	264	0	201	4	50.25	-	-

Career-bests

Minor –   73* v Staffordshire at Cardiff Arms Park, 1911
            1/24 v Surrey 2nd XI at The Oval, 1920
First-class – 76 v Worcestershire at Cardiff Arms Park, 1922
            2/41 v Surrey at The Oval, 1923

Born a couple of days after Glamorgan's inaugural match against Warwickshire at the Arms Park in 1889, Harry Symonds had an outstanding record in club cricket for Cardiff, besides making over 60 appearances for the Welsh county and, in later life, acting as Racing Manager of the Arms Park Greyhound Racing Company.

The son of a Devon-born shipowner, Harry made his debut for Glamorgan in 1908 aged nineteen, In all, the young left-hander played in eleven games and showed much promise as a batsman and spin bowler as the Welsh county blooded new talent.

Harry worked initially as a coal merchant's clerk in Cardiff Docks, and in 1911 made 55 against Carmarthenshire at Swansea, followed by an unbeaten 73 in the friendly with Staffordshire at the Arms Park. Local journalists were impressed by the crispness of his driving and deft placement, as well as the agility of his ground fielding so it was no surprise that he was chosen that summer in the South Wales side against the 1911 Indians at the Arms Park.

The following summer he made his first-class debut at Swansea playing for the South Wales side against the 1912 South Africans and with some solid performances under his belt, he was viewed as one of the Club's rising stars. However, his promotion within the coal trade at Cardiff Docks prevented the amateur from taking off time to assist

Glamorgan during 1913 and 1914. Neverthless, he continued to be a heavy scorer in club cricket

Soon after the outbreak of War, Harry enlisted as a Second Lieutenant in the Welch Regiment and, given his athleticism, he became a messenger cyclist in the 7th Battalion. He undertook his training in Milford Haven, learning how to swiftly ride the bicycles around the lanes of rural Pembrokeshire before heading off to the more grim surroundings of the Western Front.

Harry Symonds, as seen in 1908.

Harry returned physically unscathed from the Great War, having ferried messages back from the trenches to the Brigade base camp. But he had seen many cricketing friends and colleagues from the Docks become injured or killed, and subsequently spoke little about his experiences on the front line. But according to others, his swift cycling had saved a higher loss of life as he put into practice what he had learnt in West Wales and helped to swiftly garner reinforcements and extra ammunition. His rise to the role of Captain was a reflection of these efforts.

As a member of the next generation of Cardiff cricketers, Harry took over as the club's captain, besides taking part in some of Glamorgan's games during 1920 as they prepared for life in the County Championship. Harry proudly appeared in their inaugural first-class match against Sussex at the Arms Park, and secured enough leave to feature on a fairly regular basis for the next two seasons. His finest hour in Glamorgan's ranks in the Championship came in 1922 against Worcestershire at the Arms Park where he scored a handsome 76 against Worcestershire.

It was fitting that the Cardiff venue should witness his career-best because the Arms Park became an increasingly important part of his life, following the creation later that year of the Cardiff Athletic Club and its subsequent management of sporting activities at the city centre ground. Harry duly became the Racing Manager of the Arms Park Greyhound Racing Company whose track ran around the perimeter of the rugby field and hosted regular races until the 1960s.

His regular involvement with Glamorgan in Championship matches declined as a result, with Harry making a couple of appearances during 1925. He still appeared in Club and Ground matches and, as a good friend of Norman Riches, he also turned out for the Wales side against Ireland in 1926, and against the MCC in 1929. In his youth, Harry had also played football for Cardiff Corinthians, whilst he served in the Home Guard during the Second World War.

171.
BANCROFT, John ('Jack')

Born – Swansea, 18 October, 1879
Died – Swansea, 7 January, 1942
Amateur
RHB, WK
1st XI: 1908 – 1922
Cap: 1922
Club: Swansea

Batting and Fielding Record

	M	I	NO	RUNS	AV	100	50	CT	ST
Minor	20	32	7	189	7.56	-	-	13	8
F-c	9	18	3	36	2.40	-	-	4	3

Career-bests

Minor –   40 v Monmouthshire at Cardiff Arms Park, 1909
First-class –   5* v Sussex at Hove, 1922

Jack Bancroft was the younger brother of Billy Bancroft and also played rugby for Swansea and Wales, besides appearing in Minor County and first-class cricket for Glamorgan. For much of his career, Jack remained in the shadows of his ebullient elder brother, but with his straight-forward and no-nonsense play, Jack enjoyed a more productive international rugby career for Wales, with 88 points compared with Billy's 60: something in later years which Jack revelled in reminding people about!

F. & J. SMITH'S CIGARETTES

SWANSEA, R.F.C.
J. BANCROFT.

The Swansea full-back made his debut against England at the Arms Park in 1909 as a result of an injury to their first choice. Jack's steady play duly won him a further seventeen caps, and in 1910 he posted 19 points against France – at the time a Welsh record. He also captained Wales against Ireland in 1912, with his final international appearance coming in March 1914 against France, fittingly on his home turf at St Helen's, Swansea.

By this time, Jack had a string of Minor County appearances to his name for Glamorgan, having succeeded Dan Thissen to the role of Swansea's first choice wicket-keeper. His agile glovework resulted in an appearance during 1908 for Glamorgan, alongside his illustrious brother against Monmouthshire at Newport. He made seven appearances the following summer, during which the lower-order batsman posted a career-best 40 against Monmouthshire at the Arms Park.

Three further appearances followed during 1910, before Jack concentrated on his work at a copper yard in Swansea, besides handing over the gloves to his Swansea colleague Edgar Billings. Jack remained however one of the best wicket-keepers in club cricket in South Wales and in 1922, at the age of 43, he answered a call from the Glamorgan selectors by appearing in nine County Championship games, largely during May and June when others were unavailable.

His first-class debut came at Old Trafford against Lancashire during which Jack conceded 27 byes. He let through a further 29 byes in the next match against Yorkshire at the Arms Park, but with others unavailable, he remained behind the stumps. Fortunately, Jack upped his game, and although his batting was now on the moderate side, he claimed four catches and three stumpings in the remaining games.

His final Championship appearance came in July 1922 against Lancashire on his home turf at St Helen's. Jack continued to play for Swansea during the 1920s by which time he had switched careers and was now the jovial landlord of the York Hotel.

172.
FREETHY, Albert Edwin
Born – Swansea, 27 April 1885
Died – Cimla, 17 July 1966
Amateur
RHB
Ed – Cwrt Sart School, Neath
1st XI: 1908-1921
Clubs: Neath, Old Melyn

Batting and Fielding Record

	M	I	NO	RUNS	AV	100	50	CT	ST
Minor	11	15	2	158	12.15	-	-	4	-
F-c	3	4	1	79	26.33	-	-	1	=

Bowling Record

	Balls	M	R	W	AV	5wI	10wM
Minor	18	0	16	0	-	-	-

Career-bests
Minor – 30 v Wiltshire at Marlborough, 1920
First-class – 31 v Worcestershire at St Helen's, Swansea, 1921

Albert Freethy, a schoolmaster from Neath played fourteen times for Glamorgan but he won fame and notoriety in the world of rugby, becoming the first referee to send off a player in an international match

The incident occurred on 3rd January 1925 at Twickenham during the match between England and New Zealand when he dismissed Cyril Brownlie after a violent start to the game. During the opening eight minutes, Albert had already issued three warnings to the two teams, so when Brownlie – under the full gaze of the referee – stamped on the leg of an England player lying prostrate face down, Albert gave the burly forward from Hawkes Bay his marching orders.

The son of a railway inspector on the Great Western Railway, Albert was educated in Neath, and shone as a young sportsman, excelling for the town's cricket and rugby clubs. An injury cut short his rugby career but, after qualifying as a schoolmaster, Albert's success for both the Neath and Old Melyn clubs saw his call-up by Glamorgan for their friendly against Wiltshire at the Arms Park in July 1908.

His next appearance came on his home turf at The Gnoll, as Neath hosted Glamorgan's match against Surrey 2nd XI, with the Glamorgan selectors no doubt hoping that the inclusion of the talented local batsman would help to swell the attendance. Another appearance came the following summer at St Helen's against Carmarthenshire, before playing again against Wiltshire at the Arms Park in July 1912. Two years later, he appeared in three home games, against Essex, Monmouthshire and Surrey 2nd XI, before playing in three further matches in 1920, including Glamorgan's West Country tour to meet Wiltshire at Marlborough and Devon at Plymouth.

With a decent batting record for Neath after the Great War, Albert also appeared

in Glamorgan's final inter-county match in 1920 prior to their elevation to first-class status, playing against Carmarthenshire at St Helen's in late August, before accepting invitations in July and August 1921 to play in the Club's County Championship matches against Worcestershire at Swansea, followed by the visits to Weston-super-Mare to play Somerset and Hastings for the match with Sussex. Although past his best, he made a composed 31 opening the batting with Norman Riches in the match at St Helen's and sharing an opening stand of 89 against the Worcestershire attack.

By this time, Albert's stock as a rugby referee had significantly risen, with the schoolmaster from Alderman Davies School also helping to coach the young players in the Neath area during the winter months, besides refereeing club matches in South Wales. In 1923 he officiated in his

Albert Freethy, as seen in rugby refereeing mode during the 1920s.

first international game, between France and England in Paris, before acting as the referee in the final of the 1924 Olympic Games between France and the USA.

In all, Albert was the referee of 18 internationals between 1923 and 1931, besides serving on the committee's of Neath RFC, the Welsh Rugby Union and Glamorgan CCC. He also gave his name to the Freethy Florin, a coin given to him by Hector Grey, a Kiwi supporter from Dunedin, after the two captains and referee had walked out to toss for choice of kick-off prior to the infamous Test between England and New Zealand at Twickenham in January 1925. Realising that they did not have a coin, Hector – who was sitting nearby – helped out by dipping into his pocket, and the coin is now used in the toss between captains at the opening match of every Rugby World Cup.

173.
PENFOLD, William Henry

Born – Acton, 15 February 1884
Professional
RHB, WK
1st XI: 1908
South Wales, London County, Middlesex 2nd XI
Clubs: Hill's Plymouth, Colne

Batting and Fielding Record

M	I	NO	RUNS	AV	100	50	CT	ST
1	2	1	10	10.00	-	-	1	1

Career-bests
9* v Wiltshire at Cardiff Arms Park, 1908

William Penfold was on Middlesex's books as a young wicket-keeper and appeared for their 2nd XI as well as for London County during 1907. The following year he accepted a position with the affluent Hill's Plymouth club in Merthyr with his move to South Wales seeing him make his Glamorgan debut in their friendly against Wiltshire at the Arms Park in July 1908.

The following year, the Londoner also kept wicket for the South Wales side against the Gentlemen of Philadelphia at the Arms Park, whilst in 1909 he was behind the stumps again as South Wales met the Australians.

After the Great War, Penfold moved to Lancashire and appeared for Colne.

174.
STAPLETON, Ernest ('Ernie')

Born – New Basford, 15 January 1869
Died – Nottingham, 14 December 1938
Professional
RHB
1st XI: 1908-1909
Derbyshire 1902
Club: Hill's Plymouth

Batting and Fielding Record

M	I	NO	RUNS	AV	100	50	CT	ST
2	3	-	11	3.67	-	-	3	-

Career-bests
6 v Wiltshire at Cardiff Arms Park, 1908

Ernie Stapleton was a clerk at Pilsley Colliery who played once for Derbyshire against the MCC at Lord's in June 1902 before moving to South Wales to work in steelworks in the Merthyr area. As a result, he appeared twice for Glamorgan.

The brother-in-law of George Gunn, Ernie had married the sister of the Nottinghamshire and England opening batsman, and his first break in big cricket came with the East Midlands side when he played for Nottinghamshire Colts against their counterparts from Yorkshire at Worksop.

Ernie continued to be a heavy scorer in club cricket in the Derbyshire area, and won a place in the county's side for their visit to play the MCC. The right-handed batsman failed to impress and subsequently took a professional appointment in 1907 with the Hill's Plymouth side in Merthyr. In his debut season Ernie made a fine 108 for the Hill's Plymouth side against Penarth, and the following year he hit a superb 151 against Cardiff, besides making half-centuries against Llanelli and Brecon.

His efforts saw him included in Glamorgan's friendly with Wiltshire at the Arms Park in July 1908 but Ernie made just 6 in his only innings. The following year, Ernie deputized for Tom Whittington in the match with Devon at the Arms Park, but was dismissed for 5 and 0 in what proved to be his final appearance in a major match.

175.
HACKER, William Stamford ('Stan')
Born – Chipping Sodbury, 8 December 1876
Died – Bristol, 8 December 1925
Professional
RHB, RM
1st XI: 1908-1923
Cap: 1921
Gloucestershire 1899-1901, Herefordshire 1904
Clubs: Westbury-on-Trym, Flax Bourton, Frenchay, Coalpit Heath, Hill's Plymouth, Briton Ferry Town

Batting and Fielding Record

	M	I	NO	RUNS	AV	100	50	CT	ST
Minor	61	78	20	622	10.72	-	1	33	-
F-c	21	34	10	210	8.75	-	-	6	-

Bowling Record

	Balls	M	R	W	AV	5wI	10wM
Minor	8551	345	3842	303	12.68	32	7
F-c	3617	131	1689	80	21.11	3	1

Career-bests
Minor –   64 v Monmouthshire at Cardiff Arms Park 1909
              9/75 v Wiltshire at Marlborough, 1920
First-class –   27* v Northamptonshire at Northampton, 1921
              7/84 v Northamptonshire at Northampton, 1921

Stan Hacker was one of the leading fast-medium bowlers in club cricket in South Wales during the years prior to World War One. He still retained subtle arts of swing and seam after the War ended, and went on to make 21 first-class appearances for Glamorgan as they began life in the County Championship.

Born in Chipping Sodbury, he had first played for his native Gloucestershire as a tearaway fast bowler in their 2nd XI in 1898, apparently after impressing WG Grace bowling for Westbury-on-Trym in a local club match. His first-class debut came the following year against Kent at Blackheath, followed by a further appearance the following month against Warwickshire at Edgbaston.

Despite his raw pace, Stan did not play again for Gloucestershire until 1901 when he was included in their side for the visit to Leyton to meet Essex. It was almost twenty years though before he played his next Championship match. In the interim, Stan played for a while in Herefordshire before securing a professional appointment with the Hill's Plymouth club in Merthyr. In April 1906 he hit the headlines by taking nine wickets, including the hat-trick, against Moorlands CC of Cardiff, before two years later taking 7/29 for the Merthyr club as they beat a Glamorgan XI by 27 runs, with his impressive haul including the wickets of Jack Brain, Vernon Hill and Billy Bancroft.

Stan Hacker, seen in front of the Arms Park pavilion in 1912.

Jack Brain was suitably impressed by Stan's bowling prowess, so a couple of weeks later the fast bowler was included in the Welsh county's team for the friendly against Wiltshire at the Arms Park. Stan bowled a hostile eleven-over spell and struck 26, courtesy of the long handle, and duly appeared in four county matches that summer.

He was a regular face in the Glamorgan side for the next ten years, taking 7/98 against Wiltshire at the Arms Park in 1909, 7/27 against Surrey 2nd XI in 1910 and 7/35 against Carmarthenshire at Llanelli where the local newspaper correspondent wrote "the West Walian amateurs had rarely faced such a sustained spell of fast-medium bowling with Hacker's pace and swerve proving far too good for them."

Stan also played twice for the South Wales side against touring teams, with his first appearance coming against the 1911 Indians at the Arms Park. His efforts with the ball saw the home team defeat the tourists with Stan taking 6/17 and 6/64, with the Indian batsmen faring no better than the Carmarthenshire batsmen the previous summer with none being able to cope with his lively pace and probing accuracy. In 1912 Stan also claimed five wickets against the South Africans at Swansea, but the more experienced Springboks proved more resilient opponents and defeated the South Wales team by 230 runs.

In all, Stan claimed 7 ten-wicket hauls for Glamorgan with many of his best performances coming against Wiltshire – a county who ironically had courted his services in the early 1900s after his appearances for Gloucestershire. They approached him again in 1909 at a time when the Chippenham club were also seeking a professional bowler for the following season. A lucrative offer was on the table, but they opted instead for Fred Preedy, his Glamorgan colleague; Stan never let the Wiltshire authorities forget about what he believed was the wrong decision, taking 7/69 against them at Trowbridge in 1911, followed by a hostile salvo at the Arms Park in 1912 during which Stan returned match figures of 11/95.

Stan also claimed a ten-wicket haul in the game with Wiltshire at Trowbridge in 1913, but that summer his finest performance came against Surrey 2nd XI at the Arms Park where he claimed 12/104. He repeated the ten-wicket feat against the Londoners in the corresponding match the following summer, by which time Stan was attached to the Briton Ferry Town club, and just for good measure he also overwhelmed the Wiltshire batsmen on their visit to Cardiff, taking 11/70, against Wiltshire at the same ground.

Even after the Great War, Stan continued to wreak havoc in the Wiltshire ranks, and in 1920 took 9/75 and 5/128 against them in their contest at Marlborough. Their batsmen must have heaved a huge sigh of relief when they arrived at the Arms Park for the return game later that summer to find that other seam bowlers were being given a trial as Glamorgan sought fresh talent ahead of their Championship campaign.

By this time, Stan had lost much of his venom and was an accurate medium-pacer. His work commitments in the Neath area restricted him to just six appearance in Glamorgan's inaugural summer of first-class cricket, the first of which came against Lancashire at the Arms Park in June. But in the next, against Northamptonshire in July, he showed he still possesses some subtle skills as he claimed his one and only ten-wicket haul for the Welsh county in Championship cricket.

In August 1922 he played a major hand in Glamorgan's 117-run victory over Somerset at Weston-super-Mare as the home side failed in their final day run chase with Stan claiming 6/39 with a mix of gentle swing and sharp cutters on the worn surface at Clarence Park. It proved to be his swansong in the county game as, after making seven further appearances in 1923, Stan informed the Glamorgan committee that he planned to retire from playing, having secured a post as the groundsman at Bristol Mental Hospital CC.

During his career, Stan had held few pretentions as a batsman, but he did have his moments with the bat in hand, most notably in 1909 when he struck 64 against Monmouthshire at the Arms Park, with a local journalist describing his innings as "including strokes not to be usually found in the finest of coaching manuals! Unconventional they may have been, but they were highly effective, much to the delight of his colleagues who loudly applauded every muscular swipe."

176.
THOMAS, Arthur W.

Amateur
RHB, WK
1st XI: 1908
Clubs: Neath

Batting and Fielding Record

M	I	NO	RUNS	AV	100	50	CT	ST
2	3	1	24	12.00	-	-	2	1

Career-bests
19 v Cornwall at Truro, 1908

Arthur Thomas was a police sergeant in Neath who kept wicket for the Neath club. A good friend of Tom Whittington, he was chosen as Glamorgan's wicket-keeper on their West Country tour in 1908, playing against Devon at Exeter and Cornwall at Truro. Arthur's work commitments though with the South Wales Constabulary prevented further appearances at county level.

After retiring from playing, Arthur became an umpire of note in club cricket, with few batsmen arguing with his decisions in case he arrested them for disorderly conduct!

Sergeant Thomas, as seen in 1908.

177.
WINDSOR-CLIVE, Hon. Archer

Born – Hewell Grange, Redditch, 6 November 1890
Died – Landrecies, France, 25 August 1914
Amateur
LHB, LM
Ed – Eton and Trinity College, Cambridge
1st XI: 1908-1912
Cambridge University 1910-1912
Tennis Blue 1911-1912
Clubs: St Fagans, I Zingari

Batting and Fielding Record

M	I	NO	RUNS	AV	100	50	CT	ST
5	6	-	28	4.67	-	-	1	-

Bowling Record

Balls	M	R	W	AV	5wI	10wM
18	0	7	1	7.00	-	-

Career-bests
16 v Cornwall at St Helen's, Swansea, 1909
1/7 v Surrey 2nd XI at Cardiff Arms Park, 1912

With Jack Brain moving into retirement, Archer Windsor-Clive, the third son of the Earl of Plymouth, was tipped by many as a future Glamorgan captain. Tragically, he was amongst the first British officers and the first prominent cricketer to lose their life in the Great War being killed during the Battle of Mons during August 1914.

With his family based at St Fagans Castle, young Archer and his brothers Other and Ivor appeared for the local team and were coached by the various professionals who the Earl employed to tend the Club's wicket and work as gardeners on his spacious estate to the west of Cardiff. Born at Hewell Grange in Redditch, Worcestershire – the home of Lady Harriet Windsor – Archer attended Eton and made his debut for their XI in 1907, before the following year making a handsome 105 in the annual match against Winchester.

This century, together with some other decent innings for St Fagans led to his inclusion in the Glamorgan side which met Monmouthshire at Cardiff Arms Park in early August 1908. The schoolboy though met with a modest debut at county level making 5 and 0 as Monmouthshire won by an innings. Further promising performances for Eton in 1909 saw Archer win selection again for Glamorgan against Cornwall at Swansea and against Nottinghamshire 2nd XI at the Arms Park.

During the autumn of 1909, Archer went up to Cambridge and the following summer appeared in the Freshman's Match where he took 7/49 with his left-arm medium-pace bowling, besides making 33 and 110 for the Perambulators against the Etceteras. He duly made his first-class debut for the University in early May against Essex, scoring

Archer Windsor-Clive, as seen in 1912, just two years before his death during the opening weeks of World War One.

13 and 15, besides taking three wickets. He kept his place for the following match against Surrey, against whom he made 3 and 11, but as promising as these performances were, Archer failed to win a Blue and only made one further appearance that summer for the Light Blues, against Kent at Fenner's.

In 1911 Archer again impressed in the early season trials, making 45 plus an unbeaten 80 in the Seniors Match, but again failed to win a regular place in the University XI, and instead won the first of two tennis Blues. He met with more success on the cricket field in 1912 appearing, in all, in four further matches for the University, but after bagging a pair against Sussex, the left-hander was overlooked for the Varsity Match and yet again missed out on a Blue.

Lady luck was also not on his side when he appeared again for Glamorgan in August 1912 at the Arms Park against Surrey 2nd XI. His call-up followed a decent series of scores for both St Fagans and I Zingari, but after taking a wicket and making a catch, he did not get the chance to display his batting skills as rain washed out the rest of the contest. The following month Archer commenced his military career with the Coldstream Guards, serving as a Second Lieutenant, and hoping to further develop his latent leadership skills as well as playing a decent standard of Services and club cricket. Indeed, during June

1914 Archer appeared for the Household Brigade against the Band of Brothers in their two-day match at Burton's Court in Chelsea. He opened the batting, making 0 and 34, besides claiming three wickets in what tragically proved to be his last major game.

On 12 August, 1914 Archer was amongst the first wave of British troops to head across to Channel to fight on foreign soil. As a Lieutenant in Number 2 Company of the 3rd Battalion he left Chelsea Barracks and travelled by train to Southampton before crossing with the other Guardsmen on the SS *Cawdor Castle* before proceeding on to Harveng where defensive positions were dug on 23 August.

The following day, other troops in the British Expeditionary Force began their retreat from Mons, so half of Archer's battalion were instructed to head back via Malgami to Landrecies where they were positioned as outposts in a bid to delay the advancing Germans. Around dusk on that evening, a column was seen heading up the Le Quesnoy road, and an officer then appeared in French uniform, and speaking in French he announced that a large body of French troops were approaching, and added that he had come in advance to alert the 600 or so Coldstream Guards so that they did not fire on their allies by mistake.

Sadly, it was a cruel trick as shortly afterwards, the column duly appeared, singing French songs and those at the front wearing French and Belgian uniforms. But at the back were German troops, and they opened heavy fire on the Coldstream Guards, with Archer being struck by a shell as he and his men defended an important bridge. Archer never recovered from the awful wounds he sustained and was one of three Guardsmen to be killed in the initial skirmish. A further eighteen were wounded, whereas around 500 of the French and German troops were killed, and a further 2,000 wounded.

News of the death of the popular and much admired young gentlemen came as a huge shock to the residents of St Fagans, and his many friends in both Cardiff and London. The Earl was mortified by the news of his death Three weeks later, the Earl chaired a packed public meeting held in the Queen's Hall, London, attended mainly by members of the London Welsh as well as by David Lloyd George. No direct reference was initially made to the poignant loss which the Earl had recently sustained, but the death of the Hon. Archer Windsor-Clive, was in everyone's thoughts as the Earl addressed the meeting and spoke of the heavy sacrifices that would have to be endured in the maintenance of the honour of the nation.

"We must learn," he said, "to say the words of Mr Rudyard Kipling, and say it with deep conviction, 'Who dies if England lives?' There was another moving moment towards the close of Lloyd George's speech when he turned to the Earl and said "Some have already given their lives. Some have given more than their own lives – they have given the lives of those who are dear to them. I honour their courage, and may God be their comfort and their strength." Tears came into the eyes of the Earl as the audience spontaneously applauded. It was many weeks before the Earl got over the tragic loss, and contemporaries say that life was never the same either at the cricket club or in the house following Archer's death, with his bedroom left untouched as a tribute to the loss of a favourite and favoured son.

1909

The winter months had seen Tom Whittington appointed as Glamorgan's new captain and Honorary Secretary, with Arthur Gibson as his able lieutenant. Under this new management team for 1909, Glamorgan hosted another match between South Wales and the touring Australians, as well as reaching the final stages of the Minor County for the third successive summer.

Having topped the Western Division, Glamorgan met Nottinghamshire 2nd XI in the semi-final at the Arms Park. It proved to be another rain-affected contest, but 53 by Norman Riches, plus a return of 6/30 by Jack Nash saw Glamorgan progress to the final by virtue of a higher first innings. The final, against Wiltshire, was also staged at Cardiff, and with James Maxwell taking 7/43 to dismiss the visitors for 122, hopes were high in the home camp. But Glamorgan were bundled out for only 96 before the Wiltshire batsmen put the Glamorgan bowling to the sword. Although Stan Hacker claimed seven wickets, the target of 324 was out of Glamorgan's reach as Wiltshire eased to an emphatic 164-run victory.

Earlier in the season, over 10,000 people had been present at the Arms Park for the match between South Wales and the Australians, with hundreds more peering over the wall in Westgate Street to glimpse the action. Those watching before lunch on the first day saw Arthur Silverlock and Rhys Sweet-Escott guide South Wales to 150/3 as it looked as if the Australians were going to be given a good run for their money. But a

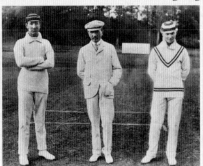

The Earl of Plymouth (centre), flanked by his two cricket-playing sons.

collapse occurred during the afternoon with South Wales dismissed for 228, and although the accurate bowling of Creber and Nash restricted the tourists to a first innings lead of 43, the Australian bowlers yet again made swift inroads into the Welsh batting before successfully chasing a target of 65 for the loss of only two wickets.

Despite this defeat and the loss of the Minor Counties final, there were plenty of smiles on the faces of the Glamorgan officials at the end of the season. The coffers had been swelled by the sizeable attendance at the tourist match, whilst the likes of Riches, Whittington, Creber and Nash were amongst the most productive players in the Minor County competition.

With Worcestershire and Northants having recently made the transition from the Minor County ranks into first-class cricket, the Earl of Plymouth as Club President, plus Jack Brain and the rest of the Glamorgan officials started to plan during the autumn of 1909 a campaign for the Club's elevation into the County Championship.

178.
CLOUGH, Harry
Born – Bacup 1880
Professional
All-rounder
1st XI: 1909
Clubs: Bacup, Accrington, Cardiff, Hill's Plymouth, Penarth, Llanelli

Batting and Fielding Record

M	I	NO	RUNS	AV	100	50	CT	ST
1	1	0	15	15.00	-	-	-	-

Bowling Record

Balls	M	R	W	AV	5wI	10wM
18	0	22	0	-	-	-

Career-bests
15 v Monmouthshire at Rodney Parade, Newport, 1909

Harry Clough was a journeyman professional who initially played, largely as a seam bowler, in the Lancashire Leagues for Bacup and Accrington. In 1904 he moved to South Wales where he secured professional appointments with Cardiff, Hill's Plymouth, Penarth and Llanelli.

During his time in South Wales, Harry made his sole county appearance, playing against Monmouthshire at Newport in the opening match of the 1909 season. He went wicketless in his three overs and as not called up again. Harry was also talented at billiards and played for money in several challenge contests held at the Central Liberal Club in Cardiff.

After the Great War, Harry returned to Bacup where he continued to play until the early 1920s.

179.
MAXWELL, James ('Jimmy')
Born – Taunton, 13 January 1883
Died – Taunton, 27 December 1967
Professional
RHB, RFM
Ed – Taunton School
1st XI: 1909-1914
Somerset 1906-1908
Clubs: New Brighton, Swansea

Batting and Fielding Record

M	I	NO	RUNS	AV	100	50	CT	ST
56	78	11	1616	24.12	3	5	44	-

Bowling Record

Balls	M	R	W	AV	5wI	10wM
4710	151	2516	179	14.06	13	3

Career-bests
113* v Kent at Bromley, 1913
8/57 v Buckinghamshire at The Gnoll, Neath, 1911

Jimmy Maxwell was a hard-hitting middle-order batsman and change bowler who joined Glamorgan after a brief first-class career with Somerset during the early 1900s. He met with decent success for the Welsh county, claiming 179 wickets at just 14 runs apiece and hitting three centuries, besides being a regular in the Swansea side. Sadly, his playing career came to an abrupt end after being badly injured whilst on active service in the Middle East with the Mountain Battery of the Royal Garrison Artillery.

Born and educated in Taunton, the son a local draper made his debut for his native county against Warwickshire in May 1906 playing initially as a tail-end batsman and hostile fast bowler. Despite some promising spells with his fast-medium bowling, Jimmy was not offered professional terms and accepted a short-term professional position with New Brighton. His success with bat and ball in the Lancashire Leagues led to a lucrative offer the next year from Swansea CC and he moved to South Wales.

Jimmy soon made an impact with in local cricket and his success with the St Helen's club saw his inclusion in the Players of Glamorgan side which met the county's Gentlemen at the Arms Park in June 1907. His success also prompted a brief recall by Somerset in 1908, with Jimmy included for their Northern tour, with games against Lancashire at Liverpool and Yorkshire at Dewsbury. He claimed nine wickets in the match at Liverpool but went wicketless at Dewsbury, and failed to secure a contract with Somerset for 1909. Swansea welcomed him back with open arms and with the prospect of also playing for Glamorgan, he set down roots in South Wales and opened a sports outfitters in Swansea.

Jimmy made his Glamorgan debut in June 1909, taking 4/28 against Monmouthshire at Newport and during an impressive season, he also returned the remarkable figures of 6/6 from 5.5 overs in the game against Devon at the Arms Park, as well as 7/43 against Wiltshire at the same ground. These performances also won him a place in the South Wales attack for the game against the 1909 Australians at the Arms Park.

By this time, Jimmy had also developed into a capable batsman and in 1910 saw he made 90 against Carmarthenshire at his adopted home at St Helen's, as well as 108 against Surrey 2nd XI at Neath as he moved up Glamorgan's batting order. 1911 saw Jimmy continue to enjoy much success with the ball with a haul of 6/29 against Monmouthshire, once again at Swansea, as well as match hauls of 13/64 against Carmarthenshire at St Helen's and 13/139 against Buckinghamshire at Neath.

However, Jimmy's greatest all-round performance came during the nine-wicket victory against Kent 2nd XI at Bromley in 1913 where he made an unbeaten 113 and returned match figures of 10/94 as Glamorgan recorded a comprehensive nine-wicket victory. Local reporters described his innings as "containing a range of carefree and well-struck drives to all parts of the ground. The crispness of his hitting, especially off the front foot was a feature of his fine innings". His bowling feats – although covered in less analytical detail – were referred to as "probing and penetrative, with his sharp movement off the pitch being too good for the homesters." Perhaps the best measure of Jimmy's feats at Bromley in 1913 are that only Len Muncer (1951) and Rodney Ontong (1985) have also scored a century and taken ten wickets in a first-class match in Glamorgan's history.

Whilst Jimmy continued to enjoy success with the bat and ball in 1914, it proved to be a difficult season off the field for the all-rounder. Despite taking 6/72 against Monmouthshire and scoring 102 in the game with Essex 2nd XI, it was a summer to forget as his sports outfitters met hard times and he had to close the business. As a result, he returned to Somerset shortly after the declaration of War, before enlisting with the Royal Garrison Artillery.

The burly all-rounder had previously been a member of the West Somerset Yeomanry, so after a brief refresher course he served at a number of positions with the Mountain

Jimmy Maxwell.

Battery, including postings in Cyprus, Salonika, Egypt and Palestine. However, during the latter he was wounded in the arm and leg, forcing Jimmy to return home. His wounds duly recovered but after being discharged in March 1920, Jimmy was unable to resume his cricketing career. However, he returned to Swansea and restarted his drapery business. He met with more success but his premises were destroyed by German bombing in 1943 forcing a return to Taunton where he took over his father's business.

180.
SWEET-ESCOTT, Henry Herbert

Born – Bridgwater, 13 October 1885
Died – Spaxton, 27 December 1954
Amateur
Batsman
Ed – Dulwich College and Merton College, Oxford
1st XI: 1909-1910
Club: Penarth
Hockey for Penarth and Wales (13 caps)

Batting and Fielding Record

M	I	NO	RUNS	AV	100	50	CT	ST
2	3	0	10	3.33	-	-	1	-

Career-bests
7 v Carmarthenshire at Stradey Park, Llanelli, 1909

Henry Sweet-Escott was the son of Rev. Edward Sweet-Escott, the curate of Camberwell and a Housemaster at Dulwich College for over thirty years. Henry attended the school, as well as Merton College Oxford where he showed promise as a young cricketer and hockey player

After coming down he moved to South Wales and lived near his cousins Ralph, Sidney and Rhys in Penarth. He duly joined the town's cricket and hockey club, and in 1907 won the first of thirteen hockey caps for Wales. Henry's athletic prowess, couples with some good scores batting for Penarth led to his inclusion, each time alongside Rhys, in the Glamorgan side in 1909 for their away match with Carmarthenshire, as well as the following year for the game with Somerset at the Arms Park. He only made 10 runs in three innings and was not called up again.

Henry subsequently went into the brewing trade, and acted as Chairman of Brain's Brewery from 1934 until 1955. He was also a talented golfer with the Glamorganshire club.

Henry Sweet-Escott.

181.
WHITE, Michael Edgar
Born – Haverfordwest, July 1876
Amateur
Batsman
1st XI: 1909
Ed – Aberystwyth University
Club: Swansea

Batting and Fielding Record

M	I	NO	RUNS	AV	100	50	CT	ST
1	1	-	17	17.00	-	-	-	-

Career-bests
17 v Carmarthenshire at St Helen's, Swansea, 1909

Born in Pembrokeshire and educated in Ceredigion, Michael White was a chemical engineer based in Swansea. He played for the town club and his one appearance for Glamorgan in 1909 came about when he was called up as a late replacement for the unwell Tom Whittington on the morning of Glamorgan's match against Carmarthenshire at St Helen's. he did not let anyone down and made a steady 17 in what proved to be his only appearance for the county.

Later in life, Michael became HM Inspector of Factories in South Wales.

182.
DAVIS, John Darelan David
Born – St Mellons, Cardiff, March 1879
Died – Neath, 27 November 1950
Amateur
Batsman
1st XI 1909-1911
Clubs: Neath

Batting and Fielding Record

M	I	NO	RUNS	AV	100	50	CT	ST
3	1	0	27	27.00	-	-	2	-

Career-bests
27 v Buckinghamshire at The Gnoll, Neath, 1911

'JDD' Davis was a stalwart member of Neath CC, and his success as a batsman in club cricket during the years prior to the Great War saw the civil engineer make three appearances for Glamorgan – one each in 1909, 1910 and 1911.

The son of a leading iron, steel and timber merchant in Neath, he first played for the Gentlemen of Glamorgan against their counterparts from Carmarthenshire at The Gnoll in 1907. A good friend of Tom Whittington, he followed his pal into the county side in

1909 at Swansea against Carmarthenshire as Glamorgan's selectors gave opportunities to several amateurs in the west of the county to display their talents.

However, the Glamorgan innings was dominated by Norman Riches who struck 141 before the declaration came on 228/7 with 'JDD' still with his pads on awaiting a chance to take strike. The Glamorgan bowlers then enforced the follow-on before clinching an innings victory with Davis having played an anonymous role in the victory.

His next appearance, against Carmarthenshire at Swansea in mid-June at least saw 'JDD' claim a catch but with Whittington and Charles Elers each scoring hundreds, he did not get an opportunity to bat. This finally came the following year when Buckinghamshire visited The Gnoll during mid-August with John making 27 besides taking catch as the Welsh county secured an innings victory.

'JDD' served on the committee of Glamorgan from 1907 until 1926, besides being secretary of Neath CC until after the Second World War, and was delighted to see The Gnoll ground stage county matches. He also acted as secretary of the Welsh Engineers' Association.

An image of The Gnoll in Neath during Glamorgan's match against Carmarthenshire in 1911.

1910

As the enthusiastic Glamorgan officials planned for higher things, there were further changes in 1910 to the format of the Minor County Championship. The teams were now split into two groups not four, and the winners of each meeting in the final. Glamorgan's fixtures in the re-structured competition were augmented by home friendlies against Worcestershire and Somerset, plus a match with Sussex at Hove as Glamorgan tested their strength against a trio of first-class counties.

If Glamorgan were going to join them in the County Championship, their capital reserves would need further strengthening in order to commit to the requirement of eight home and eight away matches. Consequently, the Earl of Plymouth and Tom Whittington issued a circular to all clubs and businesses in South Wales appealing for donations, whilst a three-day fund-raising match was organized at the Arms Park between a side representing the East of England and a side from the West, with the latter including Gloucestershire's Gilbert Jessop, plus Whittington and Billy Bancroft.

With Neath-born Whittington at the helm, it was no surprise that Glamorgan's home games with Monmouthshire and Surrey 2nd XI were staged at The Gnoll. With the likelihood of needing an additional venue for first-class matches, it must have greatly pleased Whittington and others from the Neath area to see a healthy gate, besides Glamorgan winning both games.

But this was the only silver lining during a summer when the ambitions of the Welsh county took a hit, both from a cricketing and financial perspective. Glamorgan finished as runners-up in their group behind Berkshire, and greatly missed the prolific run-scoring of Norman Riches who, having contracted enteric fever, missed the first five games. Although he marked his return to action with 152 against Sussex at Hove, he only passed fifty twice in the remaining games and with others out of form, Glamorgan's batting was not as strong as in previous years. Their low point came against Worcestershire at the Arms Park where they were dismissed within 55 minutes for just 36, with the Australian John Cuffe taking 9/5 with his left-arm spin.

The additional fixtures with Worcestershire and Somerset had also hit the Club's expenditure and with rain affecting several home games, gate receipts fell. At the end of the season, Hugh Ingledew, the Honorary Treasurer reported that the overdraft stood at £574 and, after studying the balance sheet, Whittington and the Earl of Plymouth realized that the situation was so grave it cast doubt over the Club honouring its Minor County fixtures for 1911, never mind seeking first-class status.

183.
ELERS, Captain Charles <u>George</u> Carew

Born – Lyme Regis, 2 January 1867
Died – Torpoint, 11 December 1927
Amateur
RHB, WK
1st XI: 1910-1911
Devon 1896, West of England 1910
Clubs: Seaton, Bridgend, MCC

Batting and Fielding Record

M	I	NO	RUNS	AV	100	50	CT	ST
7	12	5	309	44.14	1	1	10	7

Career-bests
151 v Carmarthenshire at St Helen's, Swansea, 1910

George Elers, a former Captain in the Devonshire Regiment, kept wicket for Glamorgan during 1910 and 1911. In the latter season, he also played for the West of England against their counterparts from the East at the Arms Park having the previous summer struck an impressive 151 for Glamorgan against Carmarthenshire at Swansea.

The son of Charles Elers, who played for Somerset, Dorset and the Channel Islands, George pursued a military career joining the West Somerset Yeomanry at the age of 20 before serving with the Devonshire Regiment between 1889 and 1899. During this time, George also appeared for Devon in the Minor County Championship in 1896, as well as the MCC and Seaton before moving to South Wales.

George duly joined Bridgend and with Sam Brian going into semi-retirement, he had an extended run during 1910 as Glamorgan's wicket-keeper. Besides the 151 against Carmarthenshire, George struck an unbeaten 50 against Monmouthshire at Neath and he played again in the opening match of the 1911 season against Surrey at The Oval. But aged 44, his best years were in the past and with an eye to the future, the Welsh county's selectors opted for younger glovemen. George duly served on the Glamorgan committee between 1912 and 1914.

184.
ROBATHAN, George Lionel

Born – Brighton, 18 July 1878
Died – Lower Bourne, Farnham, 3 August 1951
Amateur
RHB
Ed – Llandaff Cathedral School, Epsom College and Hereford College
1st XI: 1910-1911
Monmouthshire 1897, Gloucestershire 1922
Clubs: Newport, Cardiff

Batting and Fielding Record

M	I	NO	RUNS	AV	100	50	CT	ST
8	13	1	94	7.83	-	-	3	-

Career-bests
30 v Staffordshire at Stoke-on-Trent, 1911

Lionel Robathan was one of five sons born to Dr George Beckett Robathan, a well-known GP in Cardiff. Lionel and his brothers grew up in Radyr, a prosperous suburb to the

Lionel Robathan.

north of the city, before learning the rudiments of cricket at Llandaff Cathedral School. He then completed his education at Epsom College and in Hereford, before trained as a teacher and securing a post in Newport. This led to Lionel playing for the town club, as well as for Monmouthshire, before he moved to a school in Margate.

He only spent a short time in Kent before returning to South Wales and joining Cardiff. A series of fluent innings led to Lionel being included in the Glamorgan side for their friendly against Worcestershire at the Arms Park in early June, 1910. He only made 4 and 0, but was an ever-present during July and August in 1911.

The following year, Lionel was appointed Head of Llandaff Cathedral School and became the first non-clerical head of the famous seat of learning. After skillfully guiding the school through the austerity years of the War, Lionel moved to Newnham in Gloucestershire during 1919 to become the head of a preparatory school.

Three years later, the 43 year-old schoolmaster made three appearances for Gloucestershire, against Middlesex and Derbyshire at Gloucester, as well as the game against Kent at Tonbridge. His son, Douglas, played in domestic cricket in India during 1940/41 as well as appearing for Sussex 2nd XI.

185.
THOMAS, Dr John Leslie _Gwyn_

Born – Neath, 4 March 1891
Died – Neath, 10 April 1932
Amateur
RHB
Ed – Neath GS and Edinburgh University
1st XI: 1910-1922
Gentlemen of Carmarthenshire
Clubs: Neath, Llanelli
Rugby for Neath and Edinburgh University. Reserve for Wales in 1921.

Batting and Fielding Record

	M	I	NO	RUNS	AV	100	50	CT	ST
Minor	20	32	2	387	19.35	-	-	5	-
F-c	1	2	0	27	13.50	-	-	-	-

Career-bests
Minor –   44 v Surrey 2nd XI at The Oval, 1920
First-class –   21 v Leicestershire at Cardiff Arms Park, 1921

Gwyn Thomas, as seen in 1920 when Glamorgan met the MCC.

Gwyn Thomas, was the eldest son of Dr James Thomas, a former mayor of Neath, and he followed in his father's footsteps by becoming a leading personality in the sporting life of the West Glamorgan town, playing twenty times for Glamorgan during their Minor County days, besides making a solitary appearance in their inaugural year in first-class cricket. "Doctor Gwyn" as he was known in local circles, also won the Military Cross in November 1916 for heroic actions during the Battle of the Somme.

Gwyn attended Neath Grammar School before reading medicine at Edinburgh University. Despite his studies, he still found plenty of time to represent Neath at both rugby and cricket. In particular, he was a bold striker of the ball, and was renowned for the way he freely scored against all types of bowling, often almost effortlessly lifting the ball out of The Gnoll ground, and into the gardens of the adjoining houses.

His success in club cricket led to his selection in Glamorgan's Minor County game against Carmarthenshire at Swansea in 1910, but he scored only five out of his side's mammoth total of 531-9 declared en route to a comfortable innings victory. Gwyn was chosen again in 1911 when the match with Buckinghamshire was staged at The Gnoll but the local man again met with little success as he was discussed for a duck.

Despite these failures Gwyn was called up by the Glamorgan selectors on four occasions during 1912, besides appearing for the Gentlemen of Glamorgan against the Players. Yet again, he met with modest success with the bat, but Gwyn's outstanding performances in club cricket led to further games for the Welsh county during 1913 and again in 1914 as the county's selectors kept faith with him, hoping that his good form for Neath would eventually rub off on his county appearances.

Following the outbreak of War, Gwyn's links with Scotland saw him enlist as a medical corporal in the Brigade Field Ambulance section of Scottish Horse. He later transferred to the Northumberland Fusiliers where Gwyn rose to the rank of Second Lieutenant. He was in the First Battalion of the Fusiliers when they were involved in the Battle of the Somme, and was awarded the Military Cross for his gallant actions in a raid on German lines. According to his citation, Gwyn "advanced with a trench gun through a heavy artillery and machine gun barrage, before taking up his position with a company of another battalion, in conjunction with which he captured a battery of hostile trench mortars. Later in the day, he also advanced with the other company."

During March 1918, Gwyn was badly wounded in the groin as a result of shellfire and was taken home to Wandsworth Hospital following the removal of one of his testicles. He duly recovered and during 1919 Gwyn returned to South Wales and resumed his sporting career. He captained Neath RFC during the 1920/21 season, with the full-back also being chosen as a reserve in the Welsh side. As far as his cricketing was concerned, Gwyn continued to be a heavy scorer in club cricket for Neath, and again in 1920 represented the Gentlemen of Glamorgan against the Players, besides appearing in the Welsh county's matches against Surrey 2nd XI, Cheshire, Devon, Wiltshire, Monmouthshire and Carmarthenshire.

Once again, Gwyn played attractive but brief innings for the county and failed to register a half-century. With Glamorgan having been elevated into the County Championship, Gwyn was viewed by some to be a little too loose in his strokeplay to succeed in first-class cricket. But with a number of other amateurs unavailable for the closing match of 1922, against Leicestershire at the Arms Park, he was drafted into the makeshift Glamorgan side. Gwyn made 21 and 6 against the East Midlands attack in what proved to be his one and only first-class appearance.

A diabetic, his experiences during the Great War did not help his condition and he sadly died during April 1932 at his home in Woodside Avenue, Neath because of this illness.

186.
VEAL, Capt. Charles Lewis

Born – Bridgend, 29 August 1876
Died – Kensington, London, 1 June 1929
Amateur
Batsman
Ed – Charterhouse and Repton
1st XI: 1910
Middlesex 2nd XI 1907-1908
Clubs: Bridgend, Folkestone, MCC, Cardiff, Gloucestershire Gypsies.

Batting and Fielding Record

M	I	NO	RUNS	AV	100	50	CT	ST
2	3	0	32	10.67	-	-	1	-

Career-bests
21 v Monmouthshire at Rodney Parade, Newport, 1910

Charles Veal was another man who mixed military service with playing a high standard of cricket with the Bridgend-born amateur appearing twice for Glamorgan during 1910.

He joined the Welsh Regiment after completing his education at Charterhouse and Repton, and served as a Second Lieutenant in the Boer War. However, Charles was badly wounded in his torso during the Battle of Paardeberg in February 1900 and was forced home with his injuries. His gallantry under fire won him the Queens Medal, but thankfully Charles fully recovered after a period in a military hospital and a nursing home.

Charles was based for a while in the Folkestone area before moving to the Home Counties with his fearless batting seeing him selected for both the MCC and Middlesex 2nd XI. During this time, he also made a series of first-class appearances for the MCC, starting with games against Worcestershire and the West Indians in 1906, followed by the match with Oxford University in 1908 and then a trio of games in 1910 against Yorkshire and Leicestershire as well as the Oxford students once again.

1910 also saw Charles – now a captain in the Welsh Regiment – back home in South Wales and attached to Cardiff. His success in club cricket saw him chosen twice by the Glamorgan selectors. His first appearance came against Monmouthshire at Rodney Parade during early July with Charles opening the batting with Tom Whittington, whilst the second saw him occupy the number five slot against Surrey 2nd XI at Neath in the closing game of the summer.

Despite still scoring runs in club cricket, Charles was not called up again by the Glamorgan selectors. He subsequently served as Assistant Provost Marshall in the War Office during the Great War. After hostilities were over, Charles was elevated to the rank of Major and also played cricket for the Gloucestershire Gypsies.

187.
JONES, John <u>Walter</u>

Born – Neath, March 1886
Died – Neath, December 1962
Amateur
RHB, SLA
1st XI: 1910-1920
Clubs: Neath, Briton Ferry Town

Batting and Fielding Record

M	I	NO	RUNS	AV	100	50	CT	ST
17	25	3	401	18.23	1	2	7	-

Bowling Record

Balls	M	R	W	AV	5wI	10wM
450	9	290	11	26.36	-	-

Career-bests
108* v Monmouthshire at Rodney Parade, Newport, 1913
2/7 v Surrey 2nd XI at The Oval, 1912

Walter Jones was another stalwart of Neath CC in the years either side of the Great War and followed his good friends Tom Whittington and Albert Freethy from the Neath side into the Glamorgan team.

Like Freethy, Walter was a schoolmaster in the Neath area, besides being a free-scoring batsman and an accurate left-arm spinner. The pair helped Neath to a series of fine wins in the local league and in early August 1910 Walter made his Glamorgan debut in the closing two games of the season, against Hertfordshire at Swansea, followed by the match with Surrey 2nd XI on his home patch at The Gnoll.

The son of a chandler from Carmarthenshire, Walter re-appeared in six games during 1912, although the presence of Harry Creber in the side meant he only had limited opportunities with his left-arm spin. However, Walter more than made up for this the following summer as he struck his maiden hundred for Glamorgan, against Monmouthshire at Newport and shared a vibrant partnership with Welsh rugby

Walter Jones, a stalwart of Neath CC, as seen in his youth in 1905.

273

international Reggie Gibbs as Glamorgan followed-on. Their stirring efforts though could not prevent a defeat by seven wickets.

The following week at Trowbridge, Walter was in the runs again as he top-scored with 76 against Wiltshire with his runs at number eight in the order giving his side a lead in excess of 200, and one from which they were able to force an innings victory. He added another fifty to his tally as he played for Glamorgan during his break from teaching over the Whitsun Holiday period in 1914, with the right-hander scoring an unbeaten fifty against Durham at Sunderland.

Walter re-appeared in a couple of games during 1920 as the Welsh county assessed their talent ahead of their campaign in first-class cricket. Despite boundless enthusiasm, the schoolmaster was past his best and after a duck against Wiltshire at Marlborough he turned down other invitations to play and, in his typically magnanimous way, recommended to his friend Tom Whittington that other, much younger players, should be given a chance.

A Neath man through and through, Walter continued to play for the town during the 1920s before proudly accepting the offer of serving as the town's Mayor.

1911

The spring of 1911 was a depressing time for the Glamorgan officials as a series of cost-saving measures were introduced and fewer contracts were drawn up with the talented professionals in the region. Another circular was sent to the business and sporting community of South Wales, this time drawing attention to the Club's plight. Rather than outlining the ambitious plans for elevation into first-class cricket, it said:

> "There are many gentlemen in the county who are interested in the well-being of our national game and who would deplore any circumstances which would lead to the winding up of the County Cricket Club owing to want of support. On the other hand, it is manifest that unless some steps can be taken to relieve the Club of their present burden of debt, and at the same time broaden the area of support by largely increasing the members' subscriptions, the county cricket club cannot hope to justify its existence."

The grave financial situation meant that more amateurs made appearances during the summer than before. Ironically, the results improved with Glamorgan winning seven of their dozen games, whilst South Wales also defeated the All-Indian tourists at the Arms Park by seven wickets. Stan Hacker took 6/17 as the Indians were dismissed for 53, before Henry Symonds, one of the new generation of Glamorgan batsmen, made an attractive 56. Although the tourists made 233 batting for a second time, Hacker claimed six wickets again, and with a target of just 81, Norman Riches and Tom Whittington saw their side to victory.

Norman Riches.

1911 was an exceptional year for Riches as he became the first Minor County batsman to score 1,000 runs in a season. His tally of 1,015 runs at an average of 92.27 was one of the reasons why Glamorgan recorded three successive innings victories with the opener making 159 as Monmouthshire were defeated at Swansea, plus 150 as Carmarthenshire were beaten at Llanelli. Just for good measure, Whittington weighed in with 176 as Carmarthenshire lost at St Helen's, before Riches added further to his tally with an unbeaten 167 as Monmouthshire lost by an innings at Newport, before making 194 at The Gnoll as Buckinghamshire subsided to a defeat by an innings and 176 runs.

Many tributes were paid to the Cardiff opener at the end of a run-laden summer with the *Western Mail*'s correspondent writing "when the loose ball comes along, he revels in putting the full face of the bat hard against it. Perfect footwork, perfect timing, an elegant flash of the bat and the scorebox is ringing up another four."

188.
BILLINGS, Edgar Arthur

Born – Swansea, 8 May 1882
Died – Mumbles, 9 September 1952
Amateur
RHB, WK
1st XI: 1911-1914
Club: Swansea

Batting and Fielding Record

M	I	NO	RUNS	AV	100	50	CT	ST
17	23	2	290	13.81	-	1	17	21

Career-bests
62 v Carmarthenshire at St Helen's, Swansea, 1911

Edgar Billings was a talented all-round sportsman playing cricket, rugby and water polo for Swansea, in addition to regularly appearing behind the stumps for Glamorgan from 1911 until the outbreak of the Great War.

Having been coached as a youngster by Billy Bancroft and Dan Thissen, Edgar's county debut came in 1911 after some excellent performances behind the stumps in club cricket for Swansea, plus some good work in conjunction with spinner Harry Creber. Edgar's debut for Glamorgan came during June 1911 as he played against Wiltshire at Trowbridge. He appeared in four further games as well as against Carmarthenshire during mid-July where he was able to display his batting prowess by completing his maiden fifty on his home turf at St Helen's.

Like many of his generation, the War put a premature end to his county career. Having led Swansea in 1914, Ernie resumed the captaincy when cricketing activity resumed at St Helen's. At the age of 39, his best years were behind him but his outstanding record of having more stumpings than catches to his name for Glamorgan bore testament to his abilities behind the stumps, as well as an almost innate understanding with his spin bowling colleagues.

Short and squat in physique, Edgar was a builder and architect by trade, and continued to play for Swansea until the late 1920s. His son Ernie followed in his father's footsteps by playing cricket for the Swansea club, besides serving on the Glamorgan committee.

EDGAR BILLINGS (THE "SKIPPER"),

EDGAR

Edgar Billings keeping wicket at Swansea in 1913.

276

189.
CHANDLESS, John

Born – Cardiff, 21 August 1884
Died – Whitchurch, Cardiff, 1 June 1968
Amateur
RHB, RM
1st XI: 1911-1927
Club and Ground: 1915-1933
Clubs: Cardiff, Cardiff YMCA

Batting and Fielding Record

	M	I	NO	RUNS	AV	100	50	CT	ST
Minor	9	9	2	77	11.00	-	-	3	-
F-c	1	1	0	2	2.00	-	-	-	-

Bowling Record

	Balls	M	R	W	AV	5wI	10wM
Minor	423	20	183	7	26.14	-	-
F-c	198	10	61	3	20.33	-	-

Career-bests

Minor –	20	v Buckinghamshire at Aylesbury, 1911
		v Monmouthshire at St Helen's, Swansea, 1911
	3/41	v Wiltshire at Cardiff Arms Park, 1920
First-class –	2	v Somerset at Cardiff Arms Park, 1927
	3/13	v Somerset at Cardiff Arms Park, 1927

John Chandless was a stalwart figure with Cardiff CC with the wholehearted all-rounder appearing in ten matches for Glamorgan between 1911 and 1927, with his county career spanning their time as a Minor County before the Great War to their difficult days in the County Championship during the late 1920s.

The son of a draper, John worked initially as a solicitor's clerk before securing a position with a building society. His decent all-round performances for the Cardiff club led to a first taste of county cricket in 1911 when Glamorgan visited Trowbridge to meet Wiltshire. It was an inauspicious debut as he made a duck and went wicketless, but he played in five further games that summer with his energetic fielding being a feature of these appearances.

He and his brother Arthur, a commercial traveller, also appeared together in the match between a Glamorgan XI and Barry in 1915, with John getting leave from his military duties with the catering corps. It wasn't until 1920 when John played his next Minor County Championship match for the Welsh

John Chandless.

county, against Surrey 2nd XI at The Oval. He appeared in two further matches that summer, each at the Arms Park, with his duties for the building society prevented him from making regular appearances at county level.

John continued to be a decent performer with Cardiff during the 1920s and in 1926 made his first-class debut as he played for Wales against Ireland at Belfast. He opened the bowling in the Irish first innings and claimed a trio of cheap wicket with his cutters.

The following year, he also answered an SOS from his good friend Norman Riches to play for Glamorgan when other amateurs dropped out ahead of the Championship fixture with Somerset at the Arms Park. Despite being in his forties, he acquitted himself well, especially with the ball. Later that summer, he also played for the Welsh Cygnets against the 1927 New Zealanders at Llandudno.

190.
TAIT, John Robert ('Jock')

Born – Lerwick, Shetland Islands, 20 November 1886
Died – Clifton, Bristol, 13 April 1945
Amateur
RHB, OB
1st XI: 1911-1926
Cap: 1921
Clubs: Swansea, Cardiff, Welsh Cygnets
Rugby for Swansea. Football for Cardiff Corinthians, Newport County, Ireland (1 amateur cap) and Wales (1 amateur cap)

Batting and Fielding Record

	M	I	NO	RUNS	AV	100	50	CT	ST
Minor	30	49	4	1200	26.67	1	7	11	-
F-c	43	81	1	1475	18.43	-	7	20	-

Bowling Record

	Overs	M	R	W	AV	5wI	10wM
Minor	235	6	156	3	52.00	-	-
F-c	132	4	87	1	87.00	-	-

Career-bests

Minor –	100*	v Sir Harry Webb's XI at Cardiff Arms Park, 1913
	1/17	v Surrey 2nd XI at The Oval, 1920
First-class –	96	v Sussex at Cardiff Arms Park, 1921
	1/5	v Sussex at Hove, 1922

'Jock' Tait came within four runs of writing his name in Glamorgan's history by scoring a century in the Club's inaugural first-class contest against Sussex at Cardiff Arms Park in 1921.

The insurance broker had ended the second day's play unbeaten on 96 after a forthright innings during which he played some cavalier strokes, besides riding his luck as three catches were spilled by the Sussex fielders, some of whom may have still been feeling the after-effects having attended a lavish smoking concert and dinner the previous evening in the Grand Hotel, overlooking the Arms Ground ground. But there were plenty of clear heads the next morning as play resumed and the Glamorgan batsman was bowled by his namesake, Maurice Tate, in the day's opening over. Jock returned to the pavilion somewhat crestfallen and told his colleagues "the ball looked as big as a football last night; this morning it seemed as small as a pea!"

Born in the Shetland Islands in November 1886, Jock was a multi-talented sportsman, as he displayed shortly after moving to work in South Wales during the early 1900's. He played playing cricket and rugby for Swansea, as well as football for Cardiff Corinthians and Newport County. His good form for the Corries led to Jock being chosen for Ireland in their amateur international against England in Belfast in 1913. After the game, the Irish selectors realized that they had acted in error with his birthplace having made him eligible for the Scottish team. His period of residence in South Wales also though allowed him to play for the

Jock Tait – the man who so nearly became Glamorgan's first Championship centurion.

Welsh amateur side and later that year Jock was chosen in their team for the match against England at Llandudno.

His first cricket match of note had been during June 1910 when Jock played for the Cardiff and District XI against Sammy Wood's XI in the fund-raising friendly at the Arms Park. Further decent scores for Cardiff saw him make his Glamorgan debut against Monmouthshire at Swansea during late June 1911. Two months later, he confirmed both his promise and prowess as a batsman by making 66 against Staffordshire at Stoke-on-Trent. However, Jock's business commitments during 1912 restricted him to a solitary appearance in Minor County cricket, but he was available on a more frequent basis in 1913 and struck half-centuries against Monmouthshire at the Arms Park and Wiltshire at Trowbridge, before posting his one and only hundred for the Welsh county against Sir Harry Webb's XI at Cardiff.

Having moved up the order to open the batting, Jock made 93 against Durham at Sunderland in June 1914, but just as he seemed to be fulfilling his potential, the Great War broke out. Jock joined the Welch Regiment and served as a Lieutenant in their 1st and 2nd Battalions. However, he was struck by a shell whilst serving on the Western Front and was invalided home. Fortunately, the shrapnel wounds to his torso and right leg healed allowing Jock to secure a posting with the Tees Garrison during 1917 and 1918.

When club cricket resumed in 1919, Jock continued to be a heavy scorer for Cardiff, and the following summer, when the Minor County programme began, Jock opened the batting again with Norman Riches, making 70 against Cheshire at Swansea and 54 against Wiltshire. He was subsequently able to play on a frequent basis for Glamorgan in the County Championship between 1921 and 1923, and in the latter season he deputized as captain when Tom Whittington was unavailable.

Jock also served on the county's committee between 1921 and 1926. His thriving insurance business in the booming docks in Cardiff meant that he had a host of useful contacts, and he was able to draw upon them as the Welsh county looked for financial assistance to assist with rising costs. Through his friendship with Norman Riches he also played for Wales against Scotland at Perth in 1923, thereby becoming the first person to play both football and cricket for Wales.

His final appearance for the Welsh county came in June 1926 against Warwickshire at Edgbaston, but he continued to play club cricket for several years for Cardiff, besides helping Maurice Turnbull by turning out for the Welsh Cygnets – a team of schoolboys and other youths – in their matches against clubs across the region as Glamorgan sought fresh talent.

191.
TURNBULL, Bertrand ('Bertie')

Born – Cardiff, 19 April 1887
Died – Canton, Cardiff, 17 November 1943
Amateur
RHB, occ WK
Ed – Downside
1st XI: 1911-1920
Gloucestershire 1911
Club: Penarth
Hockey for Penarth, Cardiff, Great Britain and Wales (19 caps); Rugby for Penarth

Batting and Fielding Record

M	I	NO	RUNS	AV	100	50	CT	ST
4	4	0	64	16.00	-	-	1	-

Career-bests
45 v Carmarthenshire at St Helen's, Swansea, 1920.

Bertie Turnbull, a member of the well-known ship-owning family at Cardiff Docks, played for Glamorgan during their final years as a Minor County, besides playing once for Gloucestershire, as well as appearing for the Great Britain hockey side during the 1908 Olympics.

However, Bertie's greatest achievement from a Glamorgan perspective was persuading his nephew Maurice Turnbull to take over the captaincy of the Welsh county and transforming the Club from a shamefaced debtor, lurching from one defeat to another into one with a decent profit and a position in the top half of the Championship table. His intervention – in his guise as Glamorgan's Chairman – came about during 1929 after yet another dreadful season, and a summer when the captaincy was shared around amongst a small cabal of amateurs. Maurice had also received a decent offer to work in the City of London and, with his nephew being the mainstay of the Glamorgan batting, his departure was a potential hammer blow for the Club.

Aware of his decent record captaining the Cambridge University XI, Bertie had a quiet word in his nephew's ear to see if the offer of the county captaincy would make him stay in South Wales. Maurice answered in the affirmative, and – not wanting to be accused of nepotism – Bertie arranged for his nephew to have a short trial as captain during the closing games in August 1929. It proved to be a resounding success and neither the Club, or Maurice, looked back.

In his youth, Bertie had been a talented sportsman, playing rugby, cricket and hockey for both Penarth and his school, Downside, the famous Catholic public school run by Benedictine Monks to the south of Bath. Hockey was the sport in which he really excelled and in 1907 Bertie followed his cousin Bernard into the Welsh hockey side, playing in goal against England at Llandudno. Bertie was an outstanding goalkeeper and a fine captain as well, leading Cardiff Hockey Club in 1909/10. Both Bernard and Bertie won

281

selection in the Welsh line-up for the game against Ireland which staged at Shepherd's Bush in London as part of the 1908 Olympic Games. Although they were defeated by 3 goals to 1, they won the bronze medal, and were able to proudly tell their offspring that they had taken part in the Olympic tournament. In all Bertie played nineteen times for the Welsh hockey side and acted as their captain during 1914

Bertie was also a hard-hitting batsman and occasional wicket-keeper for both Penarth and Cardiff, whilst in 1911 he made his debut for Glamorgan against Carmarthenshire at Swansea, as well as keeping wicket for Gloucestershire in their friendly against Cambridge University at Fenner's. But he only made three further appearances for the Welsh county over the course of the next ten years. His work for his father's ship-owning business at

Bertie Turnbull.

Cardiff Docks, including brief spells overseas, was the main reason why he did not appear again for Glamorgan until 1914 when he was chosen for the match against Monmouthshire at the Arms Park. Then the Great War meant Bertie's next games at county level did not occur until August 1920 when he appeared at Swansea against both the MCC and Carmarthenshire.

He continued to play club cricket for Cardiff, besides leading Cardiff Hockey Club, as well as joining the Glamorgan committee in 1922. The previous August, Bertie and his brother Cyril had diversified their business interests by founding Turnbulls (Cardiff) Ltd., a coal merchant's business, based in the Merchant's Exchange at the Bute Docks, before creating Turnbull Coal and Shipping Company, following the purchase of steamships from Norway, France and Canada – three of the destinations to which they had sent coal.

Bertie also served as Director of the British Steamship Owners Association, but the trade slump of the early 1930s hit his company very hard, and with dwindling orders, he and his brother sold their vessels. In April 1937, Turnbull Coal and Shipping Company was wound up. Bertie, who lived with his wife at Southerndown House, continued to serve as Glamorgan Chairman until 1939 before overseeing the formation of an Emergency Committee to oversee the running of the Club during the Second World War. Sadly, four years later he was taken ill and he died in St Winifred's Hospital in Canton, Cardiff during mid-November 1943.

192.
HILL, Ernest Edward

Born – Clifton, Bristol, 23 September 1868
Died – Penylan, Cardiff, 6 December 1931
Amateur
Batsman
Ed – Lewisham House School, Weston-super-Mare
1st XI: 1911
Clubs: Cardiff, Fairwater, Monmouth
Rugby for Cardiff and Somerset

Batting and Fielding Record

M	I	NO	RUNS	AV	100	50	CT	ST
1	1	1	18	-	-	-	1	-

Career-bests
18* v Carmarthenshire at Stradey Park, Llanelli, 1911

Edward Hill, an accountant and auditor, played once for Glamorgan in 1911, appearing in the match at Llanelli against Carmarthenshire. It followed a series of decent batting performances for Cardiff CC, and with fewer professionals turning out for the cash-strapped club, Edward had his chance to impress.

Edward Hill in his rugby kit.

His father was a distant cousin of the Hill family of Rookwood House, and ran a successful business at Bristol Docks importing mahogany. Through his family connections, he also played cricket for Fairwater, as well as playing rugby for Cardiff and Somerset.

Edward initially entered the office of Messrs Clarke and Dovey, rising to the position of head of accountancy, before in 1907 moving to work in partnership with Sidney Clutterbuck, OBE prior to opening his own practice in High Street, close to the office block where Glamorgan had an administrative base.

193.
DUNN, Francis William Morgan

Born – Llanblethian, July 1886
Died – Gallipoli, 16 August 1915
Amateur
Batsman
Ed – Cowbridge GS and University College, Cardiff
1st XI: 1911
Hockey for Cardiff University
Clubs: Cowbridge, Glamorgan Gypsies, Llanblethian

Batting and Fielding Record

M	I	NO	RUNS	AV	100	50	CT	ST
2	2	0	1	0.50	-	-	1	-

Career-bests
1 v Staffordshire at Cardiff Arms Park, 1911

Frank Dunn was a prominent amateur cricketer in the Vale of Glamorgan during the years leading up to the Great War. His outstanding batting record with Cowbridge CC resulted in his selection twice for Glamorgan during 1911. His business commitments prevented him from accepting further offers to play at county level and translate his club form into a decent innings for Glamorgan. Tragically, four years later Frank was one of hundreds killed whilst serving with the Welch Regiment in Gallipoli.

His father Frederick was a mining engineer who, after much business success in the Rhondda Valley, lived at The Cross, a large manor house in the village of Llanblethian. Frank had three brothers, as well as a sister, with all of the Dunn boys attending Cowbridge Grammar School where they shone in the classroom as well as on the sports field. Indeed, much to their father's delight, the Dunns were able to raise their own family XI which played at the Cowbridge ground with Frank's sister acting as scorer.

Frank had been one of the leading schoolboy batsmen in South Wales during the 1900s and, after leaving Cowbridge Grammar, the tall and imposing young man attended Cardiff University whom he also represented with some success before training as an engineer. After some impressive innings for Cowbridge CC and the Glamorgan Gypsies, he was called up by the Glamorgan selectors for the Minor County Championship match against Carmarthenshire at Stradey Park in Llanelli.

It proved to be a fairly anonymous debut for Frank who did not bat or bowl, but did take a catch. A fortnight later, Frank was included again in the Glamorgan side which met Staffordshire in a fund-raising two-day match at the Arms Park. Frank batted at number ten in the first innings and managed a single before being bowled by the legendary Sidney Barnes, but he met with less success in the second innings where batting at number nine he was dismissed for nought. Sadly, the game with Staffordshire was also the last time his proud father saw him play in a major game as, at the end of August, Frederick Dunn died aged 67.

The outbreak of War saw Frank and his elder brother Jack join the Fifth Battalion of the Welch Regiment. They were initially stationed at Pontypridd, before moving during the autumn of 1914 for further training near Tunbridge Wells in Kent. February 1915 saw the Battalion travel to Scotland to form part of the Forth and Tay Defences. After a month or so, they were transferred to Bedford where further training took place ahead of the campaign in the Dardanelles.

Frank and Jack duly departed on 19 July with their Battalion from Devonport Services in Plymouth and were involved in the manoeuvres on Turkish soil at Suvla Bay on 9 August. The day after the landings, Frank – aged 29 – was killed during the heavy crossfire from Turkish positions as the Battalion tried to move inland. Just five days later Jack also lost his life in skirmishes with the Turkish troops as the Welsh Regiment attempted to consolidate their position near some wooded hills overlooking the Bay.

By the time the brigade were evacuated from Gallipoli to Egypt during December 1915, it was estimated that they had lost around 85% of their full strength and, like so

Frank Dunn, in his military uniform.

many others who lost their lives in the abortive campaign, neither Frank or Jack have any known graves and are instead commemorated on the Helles Memorial.

194.
MURRAY, *Walter*

Born – Middlesbrough, 30 January 1878
Died – Malden, Surrey, 6 January 1956
Professional
Batsman
Ed – Bondgate Wesleyan School and Darlington GS
1st XI: 1911
Durham – 1907
Clubs: Darlington, Hill's Plymouth, South Shields, Teeside Wanderers.

Batting and Fielding Record

M	I	NO	RUNS	AV	100	50	CT	ST
1	2	1	101	101.00	-	1	1	-

Career-bests
78* v Staffordshire at Stoke-on-Trent, 1911

Walter Murray was a professional from north-east England, who played for Glamorgan in 1911 against Staffordshire at Stoke whilst attached to the Hill's Plymouth club in Merthyr. He made an impressive half-century during the second innings, and had the Welsh county been in a better financial position, the Middlesbrough-born batsman would have been selected more often.

He grew up in the Darlington area and trained as a civil engineer before working with a local railway company. His performances for the local cricket club saw him win a place in the Durham Colts side in 1901 and 1902, before further decent innings in league cricket saw Walter make five appearances in Minor County matches for Durham in 1907.

Walter subsequently moved south and secured employment in Staffordshire, before in 1911 gaining employment with a railway company in South Wales and being offered terms as a professional by the Hill's Plymouth club in Merthyr. He enjoyed a good summer and during August was selected for the Glamorgan side in their away match with Staffordshire. Batting at number four in the second innings, he made an assured and unbeaten 78 as he helped the Welsh county secure a draw against one of the leading Minor County teams at that time.

He continued to play for the Merthyr club up until the outbreak of the Great War when he served as an Army engineer. Walter returned to the Darlington area during the 1920s where he continued to work as a civil engineer and play in a decent standard of club cricket.

195.
DAVID, Alexander Charles Robert

Born – Cardiff, 5 November 1889
Died – Montgomery, 8 March 1967
Amateur
Batsman and seam bowler
Ed – Arnold House and Keble College, Oxford
1st XI: 1911-1913
Son of EU David
Clubs: Cardiff, St Fagans

Batting and Fielding Record

M	I	NO	RUNS	AV	100	50	CT	ST
3	2	0	19	9.50	-	-	4	-

Bowling Record

Balls	M	R	W	AV	5wI	10wM
60	0	63	1	63.00	-	-

Career-bests
11 v Staffordshire at Cardiff Arms Park, 1911
1/30 v Staffordshire at Cardiff Arms Park, 1911

Being the son of Glamorgan's first-ever captain, Alexander David had much to live up to on the cricketing fields of South Wales. However, he opted to follow a career in Law and played just three times for the Welsh county. He was also decorated for extreme bravery during the closing years of the Great War when, during a skirmish in the Battle of Cambrai, Alexander single-handedly extinguished an ammunition dump which had been set alight.

Alexander was educated at Arnold House as well as Keble College, Oxford, where he showed great prowess as an all-round sportsman, playing cricket, football, hockey,

Alexander David.

athletics and rugby. After graduating in Law, he began his solicitor's training in Cardiff, besides finding time to play rugby for the town's rugby club as well as for the cricket club.

His prowess as a free-scoring batsman and seam bowler for Cardiff, plus a few kind words in the selectors ear from his well-known father, led to Alexander's call-up for Glamorgan in August 1911 as he appeared against Monmouthshire at Rodney Parade. It was though very much a watching brief as he did not bat or bowl in either innings as Glamorgan won by an innings. A couple of weeks later, he also played for Glamorgan against Staffordshire at Stoke-on-Trent and made 11 in his first innings for the Welsh county.

In 1913 Alexander was chosen again for Glamorgan for their Minor County Championship match against Monmouthshire at the Arms Park. Once again, he played a minor role as he made just 8 in Glamorgan's first innings as they went on to record a seven wicket victory. Later in the month he was rather more active in the all-amateur match between Glamorgan and Carmarthenshire at Llanelli, taking three wickets with his seam bowling, but scoring just 3 and 5 as Carmarthenshire completed a victory.

Alexander did not play for Glamorgan in 1914 as his legal training took priority but the outbreak of War brought a change to everything as he joined the Royal Field Artillery and secured a place with the 113th Brigade Ammunition Column. His role as a Second Lieutenant was to help oversee the supply of ammunition to the front line, and from 1915 he saw active service on the Western Front.

By August 1917 Alexander had become an Acting Captain in the 113th Brigade and in early December, he won the Military Cross for his actions in putting out a fire at one of the brigade's ammunition dumps which supplied material for the Battle of Cambrai. With the German counter-attack in full swing, he knew how important it was to prevent the loss of valuable ammunition, and as his citation read "when the ammunition dump had been struck and set alight by hostile shell fire, he ordered all the men except one NCO to take over and at great personal risk left his post and extinguished the fire. His presence of mind and quick decision undoubtedly saved many casualties and prevented the fire from destroying the battery position with all its ammunition."

This was his finest hour on the Western Front, despite being involved in further skirmishes and thankfully less dramatic advances during the Hundred Days Offensive. He duly returned to South Wales in the autumn of 1918, and resumed his duties as a solicitor, working in Cardiff and Cowbridge between 1919 and 1923, before moving to Mid-Wales and working in legal practices in the Newtown and Welshpool area between 1923 and 1944. Indeed, shortly after his move to Mid Wales, he won a place in the Montgomeryshire hockey team and gained a place in the final Welsh trial.

196.
BAINTON, Henry George

Born – Hilperton, Melksham, March 1886
Died – Chippenham, November 1942
Professional
RHB, RM
1st XI: 1911
Worcestershire 2nd XI 1907
Clubs: Trowbridge, Cardiff, Grange

Batting and Fielding Record

M	I	NO	RUNS	AV	100	50	CT	ST
1	2	1	89	89.00	-	1	-	-

Bowling Record

Balls	M	R	W	AV	5wI	10wM
12	0	22	0	-	-	-

Career-bests
72* v Staffordshire at Stone, 1911

With Glamorgan's finances in a wafer-thin state, 1911 saw the Club hire professionals on a match-by-match basis, rather than offering season-long retainers. As a result, Henry Bainton, a journeyman professional was chosen for the away match with Staffordshire. It proved to be his only appearance.

At the time, Henry was attached to the Cardiff club for whom he played for a couple of years before moving to Scotland where he played for the Grange club in Edinburgh. He had first played with success for the Trowbridge club in his native Wiltshire, before having a trial with Worcestershire during 1907. Henry failed to secure terms with the West Midlands club, but his appearance for Glamorgan during 1911 gave him another chance to showcased his abilities with the bat.

He duly made an unbeaten 72 against the powerful Staffordshire attack, having the previous August enjoying a purple patch with the ball, taking 8/16 for Cardiff against Swansea, and 6/23 against Clifton. How the Glamorgan selectors must have wished they could have afforded his services more often.

Henry was also a decent footballer and during September 1910 he played in a trial match for Cardiff City against a local club. Playing at inside-left, he headed a goal in the victory but no terms were offered and after completing his contract with Cardiff the following summer, Henry sought employment elsewhere. He never though fulfilled his ambition of playing League football and regular county cricket.

1912

By 1912 Glamorgan's fund-raising campaign and cost-saving measures had reduced the deficit to £175. With the tri-angular series with Australia and South Africa offering two potentially lucrative home games for a South Wales side against the tourists, there was an opportunity to further chisel away at the debt with the Australian match being allocated to the Arms Park whilst the South African game took place at Swansea.

So much for the best laid plans as the match with the Australians at Cardiff was washed out whilst the match with the South Africans was a very one-sided affair, with the tourists winning by 230 runs despite some stout resistance from Tom Whittington, the Glamorgan captain.

With an emphasis still on amateur talent, Glamorgan only won three of their eight games during the summer and slipped back to tenth place in the table. They had been dealt a blow even before the first ball was bowled as Jack Nash left South Wales after accepting a lucrative position in Lancashire. Harry Creber and Stan Hacker did their best, but Glamorgan's bowling in 1912 was less effective than in previous summers.

On the batting front, none of the Welsh county's players scored hundreds in what proved to be a summer which had promised much but delivered very little, as the plans for mounting a campaign for first-class status remained on the back burner.

The St Helen's ground in Swansea, which staged the match against the 1912 South Africans.

197.
WEBB, Arthur Stuart

Born – Bridge, Kent, 6 August 1868
Died – Briton Ferry, 3 December 1952
Professional
RHB, RM
1st XI: 1912
Club and Ground: 1933
Kent 2nd XI 1885-1895, Hampshire 1895-1904, Players of the South 1904
Clubs: Bridge, Manchester, Hill's Plymouth, Briton Ferry Steel, Llanelli, Panteg

Batting and Fielding Record

M	I	NO	RUNS	AV	100	50	CT	ST
1	2	0	38	19.00	-	-	-	-

Career-bests
29 v Surrey 2nd XI at The Oval, 1912

Arthur Webb enjoyed a ten-year career with Hampshire during which the right-handed batsman scored over 5,000 runs, before embarking on a number of professional engagements in Northern England and South Wales. The latter led to his selection once for Glamorgan during 1912, before embarking on a coaching career which saw him rise to the position of the Welsh county's Assistant Coach during the early 1930s.

Born at the White Horse Hotel near Canterbury, Arthur had a brief Army career as a cadet in the Royal West Kents before joining the groundstaff of his native Kent at the age of seventeen. Although he was a prolific scorer in club cricket, he never progressed beyond 2nd XI and colts matches. His record however drew the attention of Hampshire and in June 1895 Arthur made his first-class debut for them against Essex at Leyton. After two further appearances, he secured a contract with the Southampton-based club and played for them until 1904.

During 1897 Arthur scored his maiden first-class century against Sussex at Portsmouth, whilst in 1901 he passed the thousand mark for the one and only time in his career, ending the summer with 1020 first-class runs to his name. Some in the corridors of power at Hampshire had expected Arthur to have more productive seasons and after just 458 runs in 1902, he made just nine appearances in first-class games in 1903, before being released at the end of the 1904. He was though granted a benefit, probably as a sweetener, and as if to prove his detractors wrong, Arthur made a career-best 162* during his Benefit Match against Surrey at the Northlands Road ground in Southampton during 1904.

In 1905 he accepted a player-coach role in Johannesburg, before playing a similar role with Prince Ranjitsinji at various grounds in Sussex. Arthur subsequently secured a professional appointment with the Manchester club, as well as Hill's Plymouth in Merthyr and his batting for the latter resulted in appearances during 1912 for both Glamorgan against Surrey 2nd XI at The Oval as well as South Wales in their first-class match with the South African tourists at Swansea. By this time, he was attached to the Briton Ferry

Arthur Webb, seen towards the end of his days with Hampshire CCC.

Steel club and spent the winter months coaching in Johannesburg whilst his wife and two sons, Arthur junior and Charles, remained in South Wales. Each completed their training to be engineers and secured posts in Ebbw Vale during 1913 and 1914 respectively before both enlisted with the 1st Battalion of the King's Rifle Corps in Swansea in September 1914. Tragically, neither were to return with Arthur junior being killed aged 20 during a raid on German Trenches at Neuve Chapelle on 10 March 1915. Two months later Charles was killed at Festubert during the Battle of Aubers Ridge

After the Great War, Arthur undertook duties as professional and groundsman with other clubs including Llanelli and Panteg. He also secured a coaching position at Christ College, Brecon before acting as assistant coach with Glamorgan during the early 1930s. Arthur though was very much a traditionalist in his coaching methods and was renowned for a rather haughty and austere manner to these duties. He hated anything which was not in the coaching textbook, and remonstrated with batsman who did not play an orthodox stroke. One can only wonder how he would have fared in the modern era of Twenty20 cricket!

His brother Fred was a well-known jockey and won the 1873 Derby aboard a horse called Doncaster, but only because the intended jockey for the race at Epsom had arrived at the course too drunk to take the ride! Fred Webb later trained racehorses in the UK and Hungary.

198.
COOPER, Edgar

Born – Briton Ferry, 12 November 1891
Died – Kettering, 15 March, 1959
Professional
RHB, RFM
1st XI: 1912-1921
Clubs: Llanelli, Briton Ferry Steel

Batting and Fielding Record

	M	I	NO	RUNS	AV	100	50	CT	ST
Minor	3	4	1	26	8.67	-	-	1	-
F-c	4	8	0	46	5.75	-	-	3	-

Bowling Record

	Balls	M	R	W	AV	5wI	10wM
Minor	368	19	139	7	19.86	1	-
F-c	684	17	406	10	40.60	-	-

Career-bests

Minor –   14 v Monmouthshire at Cardiff Arms Park, 1912
              5/45 v Monmouthshire at Ebbw Vale, 1920
First-class –   14 v Gloucestershire at St Helen's, 1921
              4/61 v Sussex at Cardiff Arms Park, 1921

An image of Edgar Cooper from 1922.

Edgar Cooper was a lively right-arm seam bowler who had a decent record either side of the Great War for Llanelli and Briton Ferry Steel. During this time, Edgar also played, as a professional, for Glamorgan in three Minor County matches plus four County Championship games during 1921.

All of his appearances in Minor County games came against Monmouthshire, and during the game at Ebbw Vale in 1920, Edgar took 5/45 against them in a spell of sustained fast bowling. The Glamorgan selectors called upon his services in 1921, with the seamer taking eight wickets in Glamorgan's inaugural match as a first-class county against Sussex at the Arms Park.

However, he only made three subsequent first-class appearances in 1921, against Leicestershire and Gloucestershire at Swansea, besides travelling to Kidderminster for the match with Worcestershire, claiming in all ten wickets at forty runs apiece. Not surprisingly, the Glamorgan selectors looked elsewhere. Had Edgar been ten or so years younger, it might have been a very different story.

1913

1913 saw Tom Whittington hand over the leadership of Glamorgan to Norman Riches. It saw Glamorgan reach the Minor County final again, but no major improvement took place in the financial position. With debts of £450 plus an overdraft of £323, no additional professionals could be hired for the summer, whilst a fund-raising game was agreed with Sir Harry Webb, the MP who lived at Llwynarthen, the country house to the east of Cardiff.

On the eve of game, it was agreed that the contest could be 12-a-side with Sir Harry's team including George Robey, the well-known comedian and a seminal figure in the history of music hall. The man known as The Prime Minister of Mirth and famed for the song "If you were the only girl in the world" had friends and family in South Wales. He was a passionate player and supporter of cricket and gleefully assisted Glamorgan with their efforts at raising funds, besides making guest appearances for Cardiff and other clubs.

George Robey – comedian, singer and cricket-lover.

Despite their limited number of professionals, Glamorgan won five of their eight group games, defeating Wiltshire by an innings as well as both Kent 2nd XI and Surrey 2nd XI by an innings to finish top of their group. The result was that Glamorgan travelled to Norfolk to decide the destiny of the title. The home side batted first and made 204 before Glamorgan replied with 168 before rain interrupted proceedings. When play began on the final afternoon, Harry Creber exploited the damp conditions, taking 8/38 as Norfolk were bustled out for 61.

This left Glamorgan with a target of 98 and it appeared that after all the disappointments of previous years, the game at Lakenham would see them secure their first Minor County title. But rain fell again and when play was called off, Norfolk were declared the champions on the basis of their higher first innings total. Given the way they had come back into the game, it was a bitter pill for the Glamorgan cricketers to swallow as they made their long way back home.

199.
THOMAS, Arthur Emlyn

Born – Briton Ferry, 7 May 1895
Died – Briton Ferry, 11 February 1953
Amateur
RHB
1st XI: 1913
Club: Briton Ferry Town

Batting and Fielding Record

M	I	NO	RUNS	AV	100	50	CT	ST
1	2	0	27	13.50	-	-	-	-

Career-bests
26 v Surrey 2nd XI at The Oval, 1913

A stalwart of Briton Ferry Town CC, Arthur Thomas was one of the talented amateur batsmen who got a chance to play for Glamorgan during 1913. He duly made a composed 26 against Surrey 2nd XI at The Oval, but curiously was never chosen again, despite a handsome record in club cricket.

Arthur Thomas batting at Briton Ferry.

200.
EDWARDS, *William Armine*

Born – Sketty, Swansea, 3 May 1892
Died – Beersheba, Palestine, 1 November 1917
Amateur
Batsman and wicket-keeper
Ed – Harrow and Trinity Hall, Cambridge
1st XI: 1913
Club and Ground: 1913-1914
Clubs: Neath, Swansea

Batting and Fielding Record

M	I	NO	RUNS	AV	100	50	CT	ST
2	3	0	38	12.67	-	-	1	2

Career-bests
37 v Surrey 2nd XI at The Oval, 1913

William Edwards, a talented cricketer from Swansea, was another young player to get a chance to play Minor County cricket during 1913. Sadly, he never got a chance to add further to his tally as in early November 1917 in Palestine he was amongst a group of Welsh soldiers to be killed whilst assaulting the western flank of Beersheba.

Born in May 1892 in Sketty, he was the son of William Henry Edwards, a local JP who lived at The Hill. His sporting talents were nurtured initially at Harrow where he went on to win a place in the school's rugby XV and appeared against Eton in 1909. The Harrovian was also a talented cricketer, having been coached as a youngster by Billy Bancroft and his father at the St Helen's ground. William failed to win a place in the Harrow XI, but the youngster won a place in the Swansea side before going up to Cambridge. He subsequently represented Trinity Hall at both rugby and cricket, but did not make the University teams besides leaving Cambridge without completing his degree.

After returning to South Wales, William switched his allegiance to Neath, largely because Swansea already had two other talented keepers in Jack Bancroft and Ernie Billings. With greater opportunities at the Neath club, he was able to display his talents with the gloves and in May 1913 when others were unavailable, Edwards was called up by the Glamorgan selectors to keep wicket against Surrey 2nd XI. He didn't let anyone down and in the Glamorgan second innings the youngster top-scored with 37 as Glamorgan hung on for a draw on 93/9.

The following month, he was chosen as the wicket-keeper in the Gentlemen of Glamorgan side which played the Players at Neath – confirmation of his standing as one of the best amateur keepers in South Wales. Later that summer, he was also chosen to play for the Welsh county in the return match with Surrey 2nd XI at the Arms Park, and again he kept very capably.

1914 was a bitter-sweet year for William. On a happy note, it was the year when he married his childhood sweetheart, Miss Aerona Sails, the younger daughter of a JP from Glan-yr-Onen in the Mumbles, a prominent figure in local politics in the Swansea area, and an influential supporter of the Suffragette Movement. In mid-July, William was chosen once again to keep wicket for the Gentlemen of Glamorgan against their counterparts from Carmarthenshire at Swansea. The two teams met the following week at Stradey Park in Llanelli but this time he was chosen solely as a batsman and therefore had an opportunity to display his occasional seam bowling. He duly claimed a couple of wickets but, tragically it proved to be the final major game in which he appeared.

William Edwards, in his military uniform.

Following the outbreak of War, William joined up and became a Second Lieutenant in the Glamorganshire Yeomanry. After completing his basic training as a rifleman, He and his colleagues briefly saw action in August 1915 at Suvla Bay in Gallipoli, before being withdrawn from the Dardanelles. After time back in the UK and briefly in France as part of the Mediterranean Expeditionary Force, he was redeployed again into the Egyptian Expeditionary Force and departed in October 1916 to serve in the Middle East.

He subsequently became a member of the 4th Dismounted Bridge of riflemen in the European Expeditionary Force, combining with comrades from Shropshire, Denbighshire, Cheshire, Pembrokeshire and Montgomeryshire. After a year in Palestine, William and his colleagues were involved on the assault on Beersheba, with Edwards leading a platoon in an attack on the western flank on 31 October. Tragically, William suffered a major shrapnel wound as his platoon approached the outskirts of the town where well-placed Ottoman artillery were positioned. He failed to recover and died in the early hours of the next day.

His brother John Bryn Edwards (later Sir John) was a well-known ironmaster and philanthropist who lived at Hendrefoilan House in Swansea. John also played cricket for Swansea and in 1914 appeared alongside William for the county's Club and Ground side, besides being a Welsh hockey international.

201.
MORGAN, Thomas Rees

Born – Pontypridd, 11 April 1893
Died – Glanrhyd Hospital, Aberkenfig, 6 April 1975
Amateur
RHB, OB
Ed – Monmouth School
1st XI: 1913-1925
Club and Ground: 1915-1924
Cap: 1922
Club: Cardiff

Batting and Fielding Record

	M	I	NO	RUNS	AV	100	50	CT	ST
Minor	18	25	5	316	15.80	-	1	8	-
F-class	39	73	5	1044	15.35	-	4	5	-

Bowling Record

	Balls	M	R	W	AV	5wI	10wM
Minor	121	4	52	2	26.00	-	-
F-class	17	0	10	0	-	-	-

Career-bests

Minor –   59 v Monmouthshire at Ebbw Vale, 1920
             2/35 v Carmarthenshire at St Helen's, Swansea, 1920
First-class – 87* v Leicestershire at Aylestone Road, Leicester, 1923

Educated at Monmouth School, Tom Morgan was an obdurate batsman and occasional off-spinner who played for Glamorgan either side of the Great War.

Having made a duck on his debut against Kent 2nd XI at Bromley during 1913, Tom re-appeared during 1914 and played some promising innings but without going on to post a sizeable score. The grave financial position meant that the amateur had an extended run in the side, and hinted at rich promise with his unflappable character.

After serving with the Welch Regiment during the Great War, Tom began a brief career as an insurance broker in Cardiff. He continued his county career and made 59 against Monmouthshire at Ebbw Vale in 1920 and lived up to his nickname of 'Stonewall' with another

Tom Morgan, as seen in a Cardiff CC team group from 1914.

series of resolute innings. Tom made his first-class debut against Northamptonshire at the Arms Park in June 1921 – his sole appearance during the Welsh county's inaugural summer of Championship cricket – before becoming a regular face during 1922 and 1923.

During 1922 Tom carried his bat against Yorkshire, Nottinghamshire and Lancashire, whilst he repeated the feat in 1923 against Leicestershire with an unbeaten 87 at Aylestone Road, with local correspondents describing his batting as "cautious but effective in quelling the effects of the home bowlers." His family ran the Creigiau Hotel, a popular retreat and temperance house, to the north of Cardiff. It was also used as a travel base by cyclists before being converted during the 1930s into the Creigau Golf Club. Tom retired from cricket at the end of the 1924 season in order to run the hotel, and subsequently the golf club's bar.

202.
HARRIS, Kenrick Henry ('Ken')
Born – St Woolo's, Newport, 15 November 1885
Amateur
All-rounder
1st XI: 1913
Monmouthshire 1920-1931
Clubs: Newport

Batting and Fielding Record

M	I	NO	RUNS	AV	100	50	CT	ST
2	3	0	77	25.67	-	-	2	-

Bowling Record

Balls	M	R	W	AV	5wI	10wM
96	0	87	0	-	-	-

Career-bests
36 v Monmouthshire at Rodney Parade, Newport, 1913

Ken Harris appeared twice for Glamorgan during 1913, with the all-rounder making his debut during early August in the Minor County fixture against Monmouthshire at Newport, before later that month appearing in the county's side which met Sir Harry Webb's XI at the Arms Park.

He played for Newport and after the Great War was a stalwart of the Monmouthshire side. In 1925 Ken also appeared for Wales in their first-class match against the MCC at Lord's.

203.
MARTIN, George Edward

Born – South Petherton, Somerset, 1 May 1880
Died – Cardiff, June 1962
Professional
RHB, RM
1st XI: 1913
Clubs: Penarth

Batting and Fielding Record

M	I	NO	RUNS	AV	100	50	CT	ST
1	2	0	9	4.50	-	-	-	-

Bowling Record

Balls	M	R	W	AV	5wI	10wM
168	4	78	3 (+2)	26.00	-	-

Career-bests
8 v Monmouthshire at Rodney Parade, Newport, 1913
3/78 v Monmouthshire at Rodney Parade, Newport, 1913

A professional with Penarth, the Somerset-born seam bowler played once for Glamorgan against Monmouthshire at Rodney Parade in August 1913. He worked for the Taff Vale Railway as a coal tipper.

204.
DAVID, Arthur Cecil Griffith

Born – Amroth, 29 November 1888
Died – Hove, 8 May 1952
Amateur
RHB, WK
Ed – Repton
1st XI: 1913
Club: Cardiff

Batting and Fielding Record

M	I	NO	RUNS	AV	100	50	CT	ST
1	2	0	3	1.50	-	-	1	1

Career-bests
3 v Monmouthshire at Rodney Parade, Newport, 1913

With Glamorgan relying heavily on amateur talent, 1913 saw Arthur David, a talented wicket-keeper play once for Glamorgan. The son of Rev. Thomas David of Llanddewi Vicarage in Narberth, Arthur was a cousin of Edmund David, the Club's first-ever captain. Educated in Derbyshire at Repton School, Arthur moved to South Wales during the early 1910s and secured a place as wicket-keeper in the Cardiff 1st XI.

Some impressive performances behind the stumps led to his call-up by the Glamorgan selectors in 1913 for the away match with Monmouthshire at Newport. He made three runs, besides taking one catch and completing a smart stumping.

After the Great War, Arthur moved to Sussex and became a master at Cottesmore School, a prep school near Pease Pottage in Crawley, West Sussex. Tragically, it appears that he took his life in May 1952 as his body was found on the beach at Hove.

205.
DAVIES, Charles Bernard ('Charlie')
Born – Cardiff, 5 June 1894
Died – France (in action), 9 June 1916
Amateur
RHB,WK
Ed – Cowbridge School and Llandovery College
1st XI: 1913
Rugby for Swansea and Cardiff
Club: St Fagans
Brother of Ewan Gibson Davies (rugby for Cardiff and Wales)

Batting and Fielding Record

M	I	NO	RUNS	AV	100	50	CT	ST
1	1	0	1	1.00	-	-	1	-

Career-bests
1 v Sir Harry Webb's XI at Cardiff Arms Park, 1913

Charlie Davies, was tipped to become Glamorgan's regular wicket-keeper, but tragically the former pupil of Llandovery College died during the Battle of the Somme during June 1916.

Charlie was the son of Daniel Davies, the owner of the Bear Hotel in Cowbridge, and like his elder brother Ewan – who went on to play rugby for Cardiff and Wales – he was a talented all-round sportsman. Charlie played rugby as a strong running centre for Cardiff, Swansea and Caerphilly, besides representing Glamorgan in their fund-raising friendly in August 1913 against an eleven raised by Sir Harry Webb which included Gilbert Jessop and several other famous cricketers plus George Robey, the cricket-mad music hall entertainer.

At the time, the nineteen year-old was amongst the bright young prospects in cricket in South Wales having kept wicket with great aplomb for both Cowbridge School and Llandovery College. Having secured a place at Brasenose College in Oxford for 1914, there were many who hoped that the young Welshman would press for a cricket Blue and become a mainstay in the Glamorgan side when life returned to normal.

This was not to be as in August 1915 he enlisted with the Royal Dublin Fusiliers and after basic training departed the following late spring for France to prepare for the Battle of the Somme. His battalion subsequently made their base at Mailly Wood, but the weather conditions in June 1916 were atrocious. The battalion's diary duly recorded: "8/6/16:

301

Charlie Davies.

Rain commenced – much work cleaning and draining trenches. 9/6/16: Weather still very bad and work held up in consequence."

Given these grim conditions and adverse weather, the battalion were eager to gain information on the precise whereabouts of enemy lines so on the evening of June 8th, Lieutenant Davies, plus three others, undertook reconnaissance. But only one of the party made it to the Allied trenches, with Davies being badly wounded in the raid and being taken prisoner. Indeed, the surviving member of the party recalled "The last I saw of Charlie was when he was struggling with a big German in one of their trenches. Charlie was a hard case and refused to believe he was going to die, although he had been badly wounded in five places and was heavily bleeding."

Davies is believed to have died in captivity the following day although much mystery surrounds events following his capture, with the German authorities eventually confirming in September 1917 that Davies had died shortly after being taken prisoner.

1914

With Glamorgan's deficit now reduced to £42, the Club were able to hire the services of a greater number of professionals during 1914. Bill Bestwick, the former Derbyshire fast-medium bowler and Eddie Bates, a stocky batsman from Yorkshire, were each recruited, having moved to South Wales following lucrative offers from local clubs.

Their recruitment lifted morale within the Glamorgan camp and, during the spring, Dyson Williams , the Honorary Treasure, also oversaw arrangements for a cricket week at St Helen's, with matches against Northamptonshire, Durham and Essex 2nd XI as the county's officials looked to emulate the likes of Cheltenham and Scarborough by having a lucrative Festival of county cricket in Swansea.

As the bank balance continued its modest incline, a few of the committee started to dream about resurrecting the campaign for County Championship status. But a series of blows on both the local and international stage, starting on Saturday, 27 June with confirmation that Jack Brain, the man who had master minded Glamorgan's rise from a lowly third-class county into an outfit with first-class aspirations, had died of a heart attack following complications after an acute attack of bronchitis. That afternoon Cardiff's players wore black-arm bands and flags flew at half-mast at the Arms Park as the city club met Neath, with news of his death and heartfelt tributes occupying many column inches on the Monday morning.

Norman Riches, seen in his military uniform around 1916.

But events the following day, on 28 June in Sarajevo with the assassination of Archduke Franz Ferdinand, had a far wider impact as events on the European stage escalated with World War One being declared on 3 August and the last two matches of the summer, away to Wiltshire and Essex 2nd XI, being cancelled. The last match of the curtailed season saw Glamorgan, under the leadership of Norman Riches beat Surrey 2nd XI. The Glamorgan captain made 116* before setting the visitors a target of 184 to win. However, there were concerns amongst the visiting team over both how, and when, they might travel back to Paddington as the Great Western Railway had announced it was cancelling several planned excursion trains, and with troop movement now a necessity, a revised timetable was drawn up. It may have been no coincidence that Harry Creber swiftly worked his way through the Surrey line-up as Glamorgan secured a facile victory by 81 runs with the visiting players and officials hurriedly leaving the Arms Park and heading off to catch the next available service back to London.

It must have seemed that the fates had conspired once again to thwart the Welsh county's aspirations, just when the Club were getting back on their feet and clearing their debts. The Club's amateurs, as well as leading figures such as Riches and Dyson Williams, duly signed up and went off to do their duty, ruminating no doubt on what might have been achieved during the past few years and believing that the long-held goal of first-class status might never be secured.

THE SLACKERS.

A cartoon from the Western Mail *for 28 August, 1914 shortly after the cancellation of the remaining cricket fixtures following protests from some quarters after sporting activity had continued beyond the outbreak of war.*

206.
BATES, William Ederick ('Eddie')

Born – Kirkheaton, 5 March 1884
Died – Belfast, 17 January 1957
Professional
RHB, SLA
1st XI: 1914-1931
Cap: 1921
Yorkshire 1907-1913, MCC 1911, Wales 1923-1930, HDG Leveson-Gower's XI 1926,
Cheshire 1932 -1936
Clubs: Harrogate, Barnsley, Dewsbury, Rotherham, Briton Ferry Steel, Boughton Hall,
Neston.

Batting and Fielding Record

	M	I	NO	RUNS	AV	100	50	CT	ST
Minor	6	10	-	202	20.20	-	1	-	-
F-c	283	500	15	12600	25.97	10	66	182	-

Bowling Record

	Balls	M	R	W	AV	5wI	10wM
Minor	493	14	299	15	19.93	1	-
F-c	12526	200	8408	224	37.53	4	-

Career-bests

Minor –   56 v Northamptonshire at St Helen's, Swansea, 1914
          6/119 v Surrey 2nd XI at The Oval, 1920
First-class – 200* v Worcestershire at Kidderminster, 1927
          8/93 v Essex at Leyton, 1928

Eddie Bates was the first Yorkshireman to successfully throw in his lot with Glamorgan, with the right-handed opening batsman moving to South Wales shortly before the Great War after playing 113 times for his native county between 1907 and 1913.

During this time, he played some promising innings, but did not make the large score of which many believed he was capable. Indeed, in his debut season with Yorkshire, he scored 71 against Gloucestershire and 69 against Sussex, in addition to impressing with his swift and agile fielding, but according to contemporary newspaper reports, the right-hander gave his wicket away both times when appearing well-set.

Despite some large scores in club cricket, Eddie failed to reach three figures for the White Rose county, and at the end of 1913 his career average – despite eleven fifties for Yorkshire – stood at just 17.

With his place not certain in the Yorkshire 1st XI, Eddie decided at the end of the season to seek new opportunities and accepted a lucrative offer with Briton Ferry Steel for 1914. His presence was a boost for the Glamorgan selectors who chose the Yorkshireman for their friendly with Northamptonshire at Swansea in early July. Eddie duly marked his debut by top-scoring with 56 in Glamorgan's second innings. Thoughts of playing further

Eddie Bates (left) seen, with two fellow soldiers, during the Great War.

county cricket for Glamorgan however were put on hold with the outbreak of War with Eddie joining the Army.

When the Minor County competition resumed in 1920, Eddie was eligible to play for the Welsh county having qualified through residence, and he made his debut in their match against Surrey 2nd XI at The Oval. The following year, he was an-ever present in the Welsh county's side in their first year in the County Championship, but a first-class century still remained elusive. However, in 1922 – at the ripe old age of 38 – he proved that perseverance pays off, as he recorded his maiden Championship hundred with an unbeaten 117 against Northamptonshire at Swansea.

In 1924 Eddie also made his first-class debut for Wales, as several of the Glamorgan professionals assisted the Welsh

Eddie Bates, as seen during 1927.

Cricket Union by appearing in their newly instigated side against Scotland, Ireland and other touring teams. It proved to be a happy experience as he scored another century against Scotland. Eddie duly added further to his tally of hundreds for Glamorgan by scoring 120 against Surrey at The Oval in 1925, plus an unbeaten 100 against Derbyshire at Chesterfield in 1926.

However, Eddie enjoyed a purple patch of form in 1927 during which he scored four hundreds, including a career-best double century against Worcestershire as aged 43, he fully realized the potential which he had shown as a young colt in Yorkshire. His fine run of form began at Leyton, where he scored centuries in each innings against the Essex attack, making 105 and 11, before scoring a superb 200* against Worcestershire at Kidderminster, and a fine 163 against Nottinghamshire at Swansea in a match when Glamorgan turned the formbook upside down and dramatically defeated the men from Trent Bridge and, in the process, prevented them from becoming county champions.

Eddie ended the 1927 season with what was at the time a record aggregate of 1,645 runs, but the following year he lost form and recorded just one century, with the Essex bowlers on the receiving end once again as the veteran opener made 105 at Swansea. For Eddie, the highlight of the 1928 season were career-best bowling figures, with the left-arm spinner showing that besides his batting skills having got better and better with age, the same could be said about his abilities with the ball with the hapless Essex side once again being on the receiving end as Eddie took 8/93 at Leyton.

He failed to reach three figures in 1929 during Championship matches for Glamorgan, but Eddie did post 102 when playing for Wales against the South African tourists at Rydal School. However, the 1929 season was a landmark one for Eddie who on August 28th during the match against Lancashire at Old Trafford scored his 10,000th first-class run for the Welsh county. He reached this milestone in what was his 393rd innings for his adopted county, and duly became the first Glamorgan

Eddie Bates, as seen at Hove in 1923 ahead of the match against Sussex.

batsman to achieve this feat. But there is no place for sentiment in professional sport and the following month, the cash-strapped Glamorgan officials considered their playing staff for the following summer. With the Club looking to cut costs and prune their playing staff, some suggested that the 45 year-old might be surplus to requirements.

His modest form in 1929 meant that only a limited deal could be offered for 1930. There was a sweetener with the committee agreeing for Eddie to have a Benefit Year, but it was a clear sign that his career with the Welsh county was drawing to a close.

Nevertheless, Eddie responded by springing back to form, besides making two substantial centuries for Glamorgan, as well as taking part in a double-century opening stand with fellow Tyke Arnold Dyson. Indeed, the pair must have taken great pleasure in sharing a stand of 233 for the first wicket against Yorkshire at Sheffield in 1930, as Eddie made a fine 146 against the powerful Yorkshire attack.

His efforts secured a one-year contract extension to his contract, with Eddie scoring 1001 runs in 1931. But with their expenditure still rising, the Welsh county released the veteran at the end of the summer. It had though been a summer when Eddie had become the first captain of an all-professional Glamorgan team, with the Yorkshireman, in the absence of Maurice Turnbull and Johnnie Clay, leading out a team comprising eleven players from the paid ranks against Northamptonshire at Kettering.

His departure from Glamorgan was not though the end of Eddie's playing career, as he joined the Boughton Hall club in Chester, and qualified to play Minor County cricket for Cheshire. He continued to play for them until 1936 and, whilst in the north-west, began coaching younger players. This was the direction of Eddie's career after the Second World War, as he secured a coaching position in Northern Ireland, where he remained until his death in 1957.

In his youth, Eddie had been a useful footballer, playing at right-back for both Bolton and Leeds United, and had it not been for his cricketing career, he could have enjoyed a longer career as a professional footballer. His son Ted inherited his love of football, playing with great success as an inside-forward for Southampton from 1937 until 1953, scoring 63 goals in his 202 appearances. After retiring, Bates then managed the South Coast club from 1955 until 1973, fully deserving the sobriquet 'Mr. Southampton' in recognition of his loyal years of service to the South Coast club, who he had joined as a nineteen year-old in 1937. Ted Bates died, aged 85, in 2003, and the Southampton club erected a statue in honour of one of their greatest servants.

Eddie had himself followed in his father Billy's footsteps by playing county cricket for Yorkshire. During a quite colourful career, Billy Bates proved himself to be a fine all-rounder, playing as a batsman and off-spinner for Yorkshire between 1877 and 1887, and winning fifteen Test caps for England before his career was prematurely ended as he lost the sight in his right eye after being struck whilst practicing in the nets. Before this accident he had scaled the heights in Test cricket, as, at Melbourne in 1882 he became the first Englishman to take a Test hat-trick against Australia, and was presented with a smart hat for his efforts.

Billy really appreciated this gift, as he was renowned for his sartorial elegance, and was nicknamed 'The Duke' because of his dapper appearance. But when it came to dress and smartness, Eddie far surpassed his father, so much so that early in his Yorkshire career he acquired the nickname of 'The Marquis'. He maintained these high standards throughout his Glamorgan career, and was always immaculately turned out after play as the Glamorgan professionals quenched their thirst and socialized during the evening.

207.
BESTWICK, William ('Bill')

Born – Heanor, Derbyshire, 24 February 1875
Died – Nottingham, 2 May 1938
Professional
RHB, RFM
1st XI: 1914-1920
Derbyshire 1898-1925
Clubs: Hill's Plymouth, Neath
Father of RS Bestwick
First-class umpire 1927-1937

Batting and Fielding Record

M	I	NO	RUNS	AV	100	50	CT	ST
3	5	2	6	2.00	-	-	3	-

Bowling Record

Balls	M	R	W	AV	5wI	10wM
720	32	187	21	8.90	2	-

Career-bests
3* v JHP Brain's XI at Cardiff Arms Park, 1920
6/44 v Durham at St Helen's, Swansea, 1914

The career of Bill Bestwick in professional cricket had more ups and downs than a Blackpool rollercoaster. The former miner had a hugely successful career as a fast medium seamer with Derbyshire, and his experience of heavy manual labour and long shifts underground from the age of eleven, gave him great stamina, allowing him to shoulder the burden of their attack. But Bill was not without his little peccadillos, and in particular, an almost insatiable thirst. Indeed, his heavy drinking meant that he spent a few years away from the county in the years leading up to the Great War.

Despite having no formal coaching, the teenage Bill enjoyed great success with bat and ball for the Coppice Colliery team and the Heanor Town club. He subsequently came to the attention of Derbyshire whilst having trials with Warwickshire and Leicestershire, and after impressing Levi Wright, the county's opener, Bill agreed terms with Derbyshire for 1898. Over the next decade, he was the bulwark of their attack, with his strong arms and burly shoulders allowing him to extract pace and lift from even the most docile of wickets.

Bill took over a hundred wickets in 1905, and again in 1906, but the latter was not a happy year for him, as his first wife died. Then during the winter, he was also involved in a scuffle with a man called William Brown. Both had been drinking for many hours, and during their struggle, Brown drew a knife on Bill and left him with a facial wound. Later that night, Brown's body was found with a knife wound and Bill was arrested on a charge of unlawful killing. However, these charges were later dropped, as the inquest jury found that Bill had acted in self-defence as Brown lunged at him again with the knife, and Bill was released from custody.

He continued to drink heavily, and his colleagues were often exasperated to find him in a sorry state and unable to bowl the morning after a heavy session the previous night. Despite being the club's leading wicket-taker, Bill was released by Derbyshire in 1909. He was clearly a troubled man, and someone in need of a fresh start in another area. After a spell in the Lancashire League, he moved to South Wales in 1912, where he initially played and worked in Merthyr Tydfil before joining the Neath club.

It proved in many ways to be a good move for him, as whilst based in South Wales, Bill met and married his second wife, who clearly was something of a calming influence on him. Bill had decided to moved to the valleys because of the plethora of jobs in the coal

mines and ironworks, and also because Glamorgan were poised to be admitted into the County Championship. He knew that the county's officials were looking for bowlers with first-class experience, so he agreed to qualify by residence for the county and in 1914 he made his Glamorgan debut against Durham at Swansea.

Everything changed with the outbreak of War, and soon afterwards, Bill returned to live and as a reserved occupation, work in various mines in the Heanor. After doing his bit for the War Effort, Bill accepted an offer to play for Derbyshire when county cricket resumed in 1919. Even though he was 44, he bowled Derbyshire to three victories in their opening five games and finished the year with 89 Championship wickets at 18 runs apiece. His efforts were rewarded with selection for the Players

A cigarette card of Bill Bestwick taken during the 1920s.

against the Gentlemen at Lord's, but the season ended on a sour note when he failed to agree terms with Derbyshire for the following summer.

Hearing that the economy in South Wales had taken a turn for the better, and that his friends in Neath were masterminding another bid for Glamorgan to enter the County Championship, he returned to the Welsh club for 1920. Bill duly enjoyed another fine season and played several times again for Glamorgan, but unfortunately, they did not have enough cash to make a decent offer for Bill to remain for 1921. Some of the Derbyshire officials had been sad to see the lion-hearted seamer leave in the first place, so they made an improved offer and suggested that Bill combined playing with duties as their assistant coach. Glamorgan could not match Derbyshire's offer, so Bill returned north and resumed his career with his native county in 1921.

Bill duly made Glamorgan's officials regret their modest financial position by recording career best bowling figures in Glamorgan's second innings of their Championship fixture at the Arms Park. However, what made Bill's performance even more remarkable was that the 46 year-old had been drinking heavily on the Sunday evening with some of his friends from Neath. This was not the only time in 1921 that Bill had been drunk after play, and

Bill Bestwick demonstrates his bowling action, in a posed photo taken before the Great War.

there had been occasions when he was in such a state that he could not bowl or field the next day.

In an attempt to curb his drinking, George Buckston, the Derbyshire captain, had tasked one of his colleagues to act as Bill's 'minder' and ensure that he remained in a fit enough state for the next day. But on this occasion in Cardiff (and sometimes elsewhere) Bill gave his 'minder' the slip, and the next morning, the Derbyshire captain attempted to teach Bill a lesson by immediately putting him on with the new ball. Bill responded with figures of 19-2-40-10 .

Bill eventually retired at the end of 1925 with a Derbyshire record of 1,452 wickets to his name. He was keen to remain in the county game so he applied to join the umpires list. A few eyebrows were raised at whether he would be able to control his drinking, and some doubted if Bill would last for many years as an umpire.

But Bestwick proved his detractors wrong by going on to umpire in over 200 first-class matches, as well as standing in three Tests. He still enjoyed a drink after a long day in the field, but his new role meant that he could not indulge as much as in the past, when he could always sweat the beer out with a long spell of bowling. Now he needed a clear head, and his 'reward' for cutting back on his drinking eventually came in 1929 when he stood in the Tests between England and South Africa at Lord's and The Oval, as well as the Headingley Test in the 1930 Ashes series.

208.
BENNETT, Frank

Professional
RHB, RFM
1st XI: 1914
Colts: 1922
Clubs: Llwynypia, Hill's Plymouth, Lewis-Merthyr, Aberamman and Mountain Ash,

Batting and Fielding Record

M	I	NO	RUNS	AV	100	50	CT	ST
2	3	1	21	10.50	-	-	1	-

Bowling Record

Balls	M	R	W	AV	5wI	10wM
24	0	15	0	-	-	-

Career-bests
14* v Wiltshire at Cardiff Arms Park, 1914

Frank Bennett was another professional who made two appearances for Glamorgan during July 1914. Both of his appearances came at the Arms Park, against Wiltshire and Monmouthshire respectively.

The all-rounder was attached to a number of valley clubs, and had it not been for the outbreak of war, he might have played again and secured a regular place in the Glamorgan side. He continued playing in League cricket after the War, although he was not called up again by the Glamorgan selectors for any first-class matches. He did however have a brief re-appearance in a trial match in 1922, appearing for a Glamorgan Colts XI against Swansea.

209.
ARUNDALE, Harry

Born – Oldham, 1883
Died – Neath, March 1942
Professional
LHB, LM / SLA
1st XI: 1914-1920
Club and Ground: 1927
Clubs: Neath, Briton Ferry Steel, Maesteg Town and Briton Ferry Town

Batting and Fielding Record

M	I	NO	RUNS	AV	100	50	CT	ST
2	2	0	8	4.00	-	-	-	-

Bowling Record

Balls	M	R	W	AV	5wI	10wM
222	9	90	1	90.00	-	-

Harry Arundale, as seen in 1920.

Career-bests
7 v Cheshire at Aigburgh 1914
1/39 v Monmouthshire at Rodney Parade, Newport, 1920

Had it not been for the Great War, and Glamorgan's modest financial resources, Harry Arundale might have had a decent career in county cricket. Instead, the Lancashire-born all-rounder only played twice – against Cheshire in 1914 and Monmouthshire in 1920.

Harry played for a variety of clubs either side of the Great War in the Neath area and, after retiring from playing cricket, he ran several pubs in the town including the Briton Ferry Workingmen's Club and Institute

314

210.
GIBSON, *William Stephen*

Born – South Shields, 28 December 1882
Died – Cardiff, December 1955
Amateur
Bowler
1st XI: 1914
Club: Cardiff Alpha
Nephew of A Gibson

Batting and Fielding Record

M	I	NO	RUNS	AV	100	50	CT	ST
1	-	-	-	-	-	-	-	-

Bowling Record

Balls	M	R	W	AV	5wI	10wM
51	0	37	2	-	-	-

Career-bests
2/37 v Monmouthshire at Rodney Parade, Newport, 1914

William Gibson, the nephew of Arthur Gibson, followed his uncle from the north-east of England to live and work in Cardiff, besides playing – albeit briefly – county cricket for Glamorgan during 1914.

As a young man, he had secured a post as a conductor on the Cardiff Corporation Tram network and duly rose to the position of Superintendent. His cricket was mainly for the Cardiff Alpha club, who played at the Harlequins Sports Ground off Newport Road, and one of the depots where William was based.

In 1907 he played alongside his uncle in the Gentlemen of Glamorgan's one-day match at the Arms Park against an all-professional eleven. Similarly, he appeared in a fund-raising one-day match in June 1910 at the Arms Park for a Cardiff and District XI, captained by Gilbert Jessop against an eleven raised by Somerset's Sammy Woods.

William's sole appearance for Glamorgan came at the end of July 1914 in the away match against Monmouthshire and

William Gibson, seen in a Cardiff CC team line-up for 1914.

at a time when the Club's modest finances meant the selectors opted for amateurs over professionals. Due to the worsening situation in Europe and the looming War, several other amateurs were unavailable for the game, which proved to be Glamorgan's last away fixture before the War. One can surmise that his call-up was largely through the influence of his uncle. Fortunately, he did not let him down in what proved to be a rain-ravaged contest, with William claiming a couple of wickets during his brief taste of county action.

211.
REASON, Dr Thomas Francis

Born – Cadoxton, Neath, 4 July 1890
Died – Skewen, 15 February 1935
Amateur
RHB, RM
Ed – Neath GS, Queen's College, Taunton, Edinburgh University, Guy's Hospital,
London and St Mary's Hospital, Paddington.
1st XI: 1914-1923
Clubs: Neath, Skewen
Brother of DJ and ELJ Reason

Batting and Fielding Record

	M	I	NO	RUNS	AV	100	50	CT	ST
Minor	9	13	2	207	18.82	-	1	5	-
F-c	1	2	0	13	6.50	-	-	-	-

Bowling Record

	Balls	M	R	W	AV	5wI	10wM
Minor	79	1	45	1	45.00	-	-
F-c	42	1	34	0	-	-	-

Career-bests
Minor –   40* v Devon at Plymouth, 1920
            1/16 v Cheshire at Aigburgh, 1920
First-class – 10 v Somerset at Taunton, 1923

Tom Reason

Tom Reason played in nine Minor County matches for Glamorgan either side of the Great War, besides being selected during 1923 for their County Championship match against Somerset at Taunton.

The medic was the eldest son of Henry Reason, an industrialist associated with the Cape Copper Works in Jersey Marine in Swansea, Educated at Neath Grammar School and Queen's College, Taunton, Tom commended his medical studies at Edinburgh University, before making his debut in the closing games of the 1914 season, against Monmouthshire at Newport and Surrey 2nd XI at the Arms Park, with the promising batsman from Neath making a duck in his only innings in the match at Cardiff.

Contemporaries at Neath CC, for whom he

had first played as a schoolboy at the local Grammar School, believe that he would have been a regular in the Glamorgan side had it not been for the War. Tom duly completed his studies in London at Guy's Hospital and St Mary's Hospital in 1917, before returning to a practice the Skewen area. He joined the local cricket club and duly captained them for several seasons. Following some decent innings in club cricket during 1923 Tom was selected for the away match against Somerset, thereby following in the footsteps of his more talented younger brother David

He was also a leading member of Swansea Bay Golf Club, whom he represented in the Glamorgan Amateur Championships. However, he was taken ill during 1934 and died the following February at his home, Sea View in Skewen, at the age of 44.

1915–1919:
The Wartime Years

Some cricketing activity took place during the Great War involving Glamorgan teams, albeit against club and scratch elevens rather than against other counties. All of these games had the stamp of approval from the Club's temporary committee, which had been formed in the autumn of 1914 to oversee the Club's interests and especially protect their finances and assets during the course of the War.

Norman Riches, the Club's leading batsman in the pre-War era had been appointed Chairman and during 1915 he was approached by officials from Barry Athletic CC – one of the few cricket clubs in South Wales who continued playing fixtures throughout the War – about a fund-raising match at Barry Island.

Barry had a thriving Athletic Club, and several of the members of the cricket section, especially Arthur Osborne, who had played with distinction for the Glamorgan side in Minor County cricket between 1901 and 1911. In his first season of county cricket he had scored 110 against Monmouthshire at Cardiff Arms Park, whilst two years later he took 6/40 against the touring Philadelphians, again at the Arms Park.

Osborne was still captaining Barry in 1914 – a summer which began full of optimism, but ended abruptly in late August with news of the awful death in France with the British Expeditionary Force of Archer Windsor-Clive, the cricket-loving son of Lord Plymouth, who was the Patron of both the Barry Club and the Glamorgan CCC, besides owning the land on Barry Island where the Athletic club was based.

By the time the members of the Athletic Club gathered to mourn the loss of the gifted young batsman, Barry had become a hive of activity. As one of the country's major coal-exporting ports, it was likely to be attacked if a German invasion were to take place and, by September 1914, Barry bore the hallmarks of a garrison town with artillery personnel travelling from Portsmouth to supplement the gunners protecting the docks.

The Athletic Club's members were also very prominent in the recruitment drives which took place in the early autumn with an estimate of 600 men attending the Drill Hall to answer Lord Kitchener's call to arms. The rallying cries and talk of it being all be over by Christmas each proved to be hollow and unfounded as lists of the fatalities of men with local links were published in the weekly newspaper, the *Barry Dock News*, whilst wounded soldiers started to arrive almost on a daily basis by train or boat, prior to transfer to local convalescent homes.

The horrors of war were also literally on the doorstep of Barry when passengers were landed at the town's docks from a vessel attacked by a German submarine, lurking in the waters off Ilfracombe in North Devon. With talk of further attacks, and a possible invasion by German troops, the local authorities could ill afford any panic or mass hysteria. There had already been an element of civil unrest when, shortly after the announcement of war, German seamen on visiting vessels in the Docks were attacked, and others in the local area were rounded up and accused of being spies. It was as much for their own protection that groups of German nationals were transferred to Flat Holm, prior to transfer to internment camps in Hampshire.

Anti-Kaiser feelings were still high the following year and, in May 1915, around 150 tippers and coal trimmers at the Docks went on strike as a protest against the employment of naturalised Germans. It was against this background of a need to preserve an air of normality that Barry Athletic Club held their AGM on 16 April, 1915. Other cricket clubs and sporting organisations had decided not to continue their activities or, like Glamorgan CCC, had appointed a temporary committee to oversee the financial administration until, at least, the end of hostilities.

But Barry Athletic Club was different to many other organisations, especially those inland, as the port was full of military personnel and others who were looking for something to take their minds off the horrors of war. It was because of these reasons that, at the Club's annual meeting, a motion was unanimously passed that the cricket, bowls and tennis sections would all continue their activities in 1915.

Consequently, matches took place in 1915 at the Club's ground on Barry Island against the University Settlement XI from Splott in Cardiff, a Royal Garrison Artillery

XI, a team representing the Royal Engineers, the side from St Andrew's church in Dinas Powys, plus a scratch eleven raised by Cardiff schoolmaster George Cording.

With members serving abroad or elsewhere on active service, it was difficult to raise funds to allow the arrangement of these matches, to cover the expenses and to ensure the upkeep of the playing facilities. An attractive fund-raising match was therefore suggested and, in August 1915, an approach was successfully made to Norman Riches, the Cardiff-based dentist who was chairing Glamorgan's emergency committee, about the possibility of a fund-raising game against a side representing the county club. The outcome of the discussions was a game at the Barry Island ground on Saturday, 28 August, starting at 2 p.m., with admission, by ticket only at sixpence with tea in the Pavilion for an additional ninepence.

A decent-sized crowd duly watched the game with the Barry side, which included Arthur Osborne in its ranks, winning the contest. The Glamorgan side was led by George Cording, who subsequently kept wicket in Glamorgan's inaugural County Championship match against Sussex at the Arms Park in 1921, and also included Tom Morgan, who had made his Glamorgan debut in 1913, and appeared for the Club after the Great War. Trevor Preece, a forceful batsman with Cardiff CC and St Fagans CC, was also in the county side, which he had first represented in 1902, and went on to make a solitary Championship appearance in 1923.

John Chandless, another stalwart of Cardiff CC, plus his brother Arthur, were in the Glamorgan side, together with Warren Ferrier, a fellow insurance agent and another regular in the Cardiff side. The county eleven also included the Dunn brothers from Cowbridge CC, who each had outstanding records with the club from the Vale of Glamorgan. Augustin Ivor (or Guy) Dunn was an Oxford-educated gentleman who was serving locally with the Royal Engineers, whilst Hugh Aubrey Fairfield (or Tom) Dunn was also a second lieutenant in the Royal Engineers.

Tragically, their brothers Frank and Jack, who had also played for Cowbridge CC, had died only a few weeks before at Gallipoli following the landings on Turkish soil at Suvla Bay on 9 August. The day afterwards, Frank had been killed in the heavy crossfire as his Battalion tried to move inland, whilst five days later Jack also lost his life in skirmishes with the Turkish troops as the Welsh Regiment attempted to consolidate their position near some wooded hills overlooking the Bay. To play in this county game must have been a source of comfort for Tom and Guy Dunn, especially the latter who had been tipped as a future batsman with Glamorgan, thereby following in the footsteps of his late brother Frank who had made his Glamorgan debut in 1911. But a few months after playing in this match at Barry, Tom was also badly injured whilst serving with the Royal Engineers and, in May 1916, he died near Monmouth in a drowning accident whilst he was recuperating from the physical and mental scars of warfare.

William Hardman, a teenager from Lancashire was also in the Glamorgan side. Born in Bootle in 1897, he was serving with the 7th North Lancashire Regiment and was stationed in the area. After some decent performances in games between the various service teams, George Cording decided to include the youngster in the Glamorgan line-up in the hope that he might later opt to throw in his lot with the Welsh county. Tragically, it proved to be his only game of note as, later in the year, the youngster departed for Northern France where he was killed in action on 25 October, 1916.

Other emerging cricketing talent also gave their lives for King and Country during the Great War, including Tom David, a young opening batsman who had played for the Gentlemen of Glamorgan against their counterparts from Carmarthenshire in July 1913 was fatally struck by a shell at Ypres on 27 July 1917 during the Battle of Passchendaele whilst serving with the 15th Battalion, the Welsh Regiment. In 1914, the young solicitor had opened the batting for Cardiff CC with Norman Riches and had impressed facing some of the best bowlers on the club cricket circuit.

Alan Boswell, who had won three amateur soccer caps for Wales and had played in August 1914 for the Gentlemen of Glamorgan against a Weston-super-Mare and District XI was killed after being shot down over Belgium on 2 October 1918 whilst undertaking a sortie with 108 Squadron of The Royal Flying Corps. The chemistry graduate from University College, Cardiff had impressed with bat and ball for the Cardiff Alpha Club, and looked set to mix teaching science at Canton High School with playing county cricket and international football.

David Cuthbert Thomas, a promising batsman and outstanding fielder from Christ College, Brecon also died, aged just 20, at Freicourt on 3 March 1916 of wounds after being hit by a sniper whilst undertaking reconnaissance during the Battle of the Somme with 1st Battalion, Royal Welch Fusiliers. He had also represented the all-amateur Glamorgan side against the Gentlemen of Carmarthenshire at Llanelli at the end of July 1914, and like the others, one can only imagine what he and the others might have achieved on and off the cricket field.

As life slowly got back to normal, 1919 saw club and school cricket resume whilst there were some games involving a Glamorgan XI, including one at Ebbw Vale in early June against the local club, whilst during mid-September Dr Gwyn Thomas, a stalwart from the pre-war days, raised his own side containing a number of Glamorgan players which played Briton Ferry Steel CC in a match, largely to raise funds for clubs in the Neath area who were looking to resume their activities after four long years without any cricket.

The Glamorgan officials did consider arranging some proper friendlies but with the military authorities having taken over St Helen's as a parade ground and training camp, there were concerns about the state of the surface at Swansea. In Cardiff, the Arms Park and its spacious pavilion had been used as a military hospital, whilst in Llanelli there were other issues, as reported by the *Llanelli Star:* "owing to the extension of the rugby football season until May, there has been practically no interval between the great winter sport and the commencement of King Cricket. Unfortunately, the state of the turf at Stradey Park at present is not as good as it might be, but the new groundsman hopes to improve its condition by giving it his constant attention." Given these factors, Glamorgan's hierarchy agreed to hold fire during 1919 and to resume fixtures in 1920, besides making another bid for first-class status.

David Cuthbert Thomas

1920

As cricketing activity resumed, albeit on a limited scale during 1919, Glamorgan officials were determined that the dream of achieving first-class status would not fall by the wayside. The torchbearers of the post-war campaign were Norman Riches and Tom Whittington – two men who had played with distinction before the War and were still potent forces with the bat in 1920 as Glamorgan resumed their Minor County campaign

Whittington, combined his duties as a solicitor in Neath by acting as Glamorgan's Honorary Secretary, and together with Riches used his large number of contacts within the business world to garner financial support. To their delight, a substantive offer came from Sir Sidney Byass, the owner of Margam Steelworks agreeing to loan Glamorgan £1,000 over a ten-year period. His 25 year-old son was also a decent club cricketer and some speculated if his father's generosity would result in Geoffrey leading Glamorgan, but after a modest appearance against Carmarthenshire in 1920, as well as a game of little substance for the MCC against the Welsh county, it was apparent that the former pupil of Winchester College, was cut out more for a career in the military rather than cricket.

Fortunately, there were no strings attached to Sir Sidney's benevolence, so with his generous nest egg safely stowed away in the Club's coffers, the Glamorgan committee instructed Whittington during 1920 to make contact with at least eight existing first-class counties for home and away fixtures for 1921. As answers in the affirmative came in,

Glamorgan's team which met the MCC at Lord's in 1920 – their final summer as a Minor County.

the Welsh county took the opportunity of blooding a number of new faces during 1920 as opportunities were given to a number of amateurs and professionals who the selectors believed might assist the Club in their endeavors as a first-class county

The 1920 season began with a four-wicket victory over Surrey 2nd XI at The Oval, before the Welsh county completed the double over the South London club in early August with an innings victory at the Arms Park. An eight-wicket defeat then followed away to Devon but the 1920 season ended in emphatic style with ten-wicket victories at Swansea over both Carmarthenshire and the MCC.

By this time, the mood was buoyant in the Glamorgan camp as Somerset, Gloucestershire, Worcestershire, Derbyshire, Leicestershire, Northamptonshire and Sussex had all agreed to games the following summer. During the autumn, Lancashire and Hampshire also accepted Glamorgan's offer, allowing Whittington to finish the paperwork required by the MCC well ahead of the meeting at Lord's on Friday, 18 February 1921 of their Advisory County Cricket group at which the Welsh county's application for first-class status would be successfully heard.

News that Glamorgan were first-class, at last!

212.
REASON, David Jordan

Born – Cadoxton, Neath, 14 April 1897
Died – Blackheath, 17 February 1955
RHB, WK, occ OB
Ed – Neath GS, Queen's College, Taunton and London University
1st XI: 1920-1922
Colts: 1920-1923
Club and Ground: 1920
Clubs: Neath, MCC, Gentlemen of Essex
Brother of TF and ELJ Reason

Batting and Fielding Record

	M	I	NO	RUNS	AV	100	50	CT	ST
Minor	8	12	3	119	13.22	-	-	2	4
F-c	2	3	0	3	1.00	-	-	5	5

Bowling Record

	Balls	M	R	W	AV	5wI	10wM
Minor	30	0	30	1	30.00	-	-

Career-bests
Minor –   32* v Surrey 2nd XI at The Oval, 1920
             1/30 v Monmouthshire at Ebbw Vale, 1920
First-class –   2 v Northamptonshire at Northampton, 1922

David Reason was another member of the well-known sporting family from Neath with the solicitor keeping wicket for Glamorgan in several of their matches during 1920 besides making a pair of first-class appearances for the Welsh county against Worcestershire at Swansea in July 1921 and in the away match with Northamptonshire during August 1922.

The son of Henry Reason, the owner of the Cape Copper Works in Jersey Marine, Swansea, David was educated at Neath Grammar School and Queen's College Taunton before reading Law and training to be a solicitor. His neat glovework in club and university cricket saw his

David Reason, as seen in a photograph taken during 1920.

elevation into the Glamorgan side with David played alongside his elder brother Tom in five of Glamorgan's matches in 1920.

The young wicket-keeper, who had made his county debut against Surrey 2nd XI at The Oval, was a good friend of Tom Whittington with whom he had first played cricket for the Neath club. Tom hoped that his young pal might be available to keep wicket on a frequent basis for Glamorgan following their entry into the County Championship, but his legal duties meant that he was only able to play in a couple of Championship matches. However, he confirmed his prowess behind the stumps with five catches and as many stumping in these games.

David subsequently moved to the eastern suburbs of London where he became Town Clerk for Ilford and Greenwich. He also played for the MCC and the Gentlemen of Essex. In his youth David had been a talented rugby player, appearing for Neath and London Welsh.

213.
HINWOOD, John William James

Born – Wilton, Wiltshire, 8 April 1894
Died – Swansea, 14 May 1971
RHB, RFM
1st XI: 1920-1923
Colts: 1920
Other: 1924
Clubs: Swansea, Llanelli and Clydach

Batting and Fielding Record

	M	I	NO	RUNS	AV	100	50	CT	ST
Minor	3	5	0	18	3.60	-	-	-	-
F-c	1	2	0	0	-	-	-	-	-

Bowling Record

	Balls	M	R	W	AV	5wI	10wM
Minor	367	11	255	6	42.50	-	-
F-c	48	1	25	0	-	-	-

Career-bests
10 v MCC at St Helen's, Swansea, 1920
3/99 v Cheshire at Aigburgh, 1920

John Hinwood had the misfortune to bag a pair on his debut in both Minor County and first-class cricket for Glamorgan.

The young batsman from Swansea made his first appearance for Glamorgan against Cheshire at Aigburgh in June 1920 and, despite claiming three wickets with his seam bowling, John failed to score in either innings. He got off the mark with 8 runs in his next appearance against Monmouthshire at Ebbw Vale, before making 10 against the MCC in their match during August at Swansea.

During July 1923, John was called into Glamorgan's side for their County Championship match against Northamptonshire at Kettering, but like his Minor County debut in 1920, he bagged a pair.

Nevertheless, John had a prolific record as a batsman in club cricket for Swansea during the 1920s and 1930s. He also captained the St Helen's club in 1925, 1930 and 1934, before playing for Clydach and Llanelli.

John had enlisted as a gunner with the Royal Field Artillery in June 1915. After being demobilized in 1919 he joined an insurance brokerage in Swansea and rose to become manager of the business.

John Hinwood.

214.
EVANS, Herbert Price ('Herbie')

Born – Llandaff, 30 August 1894
Died – Llandough, 19 November 1982
RHB
1st XI: 1920-1922
Colts: 1920
Clubs: Cardiff, St Fagans
Football for Cardiff City, Cardiff Corinthians, Tranmere Rovers and Wales (6 caps)

Batting and Fielding Record

	M	I	NO	RUNS	AV	100	50	CT	ST
Minor	3	6	1	76	15.20	-	-	-	-
F-c	1	2	0	9	4.50	-	-	-	-

Career-bests
Minor –   49 v Monmouthshire at Ebbw Vale, 1920
First-class –   9 v Worcestershire at Cardiff Arms Park, 1922

Herbie Evans was the first person to play both county cricket for Glamorgan and League football for Cardiff City. His footballing career though was blighted by injury as in March 1924 Herbie broke his left leg and spent several months out of the Cardiff City team. Having lost his place the wing-half joined Tranmere Rovers in 1926 only to break his right leg in August 1927. This second injury duly ended his professional career.

Herbie had first hit the sporting headlines in the years immediately after the Great War with the youngster playing cricket for St Fagans and Cardiff, besides winning Welsh schoolboy caps and playing amateur football for Cardiff Corinthians. His prowess with the leather ball brought him a Welsh amateur cap in 1922/23, whilst his prowess with the bat saw him called up three times by Glamorgan during 1920. His first appearance came at Ebbw Vale where he made scores of 11 and 49 in the match against Monmouthshire.

Later that summer, he also played in the friendly against JHP Brain's XI before making his Minor County Championship debut against Wiltshire at the Arms Park in late July 1920. Two years later he answered an SOS from the county's selectors when they were short for the game against Worcestershire at the Arms Park over the Whitsun Bank Holiday, with his call-up following some solid innings in club cricket.

In all, Herbie made 93 Football League appearances for Cardiff City, initially as an amateur, before turning professional in 1923/24. He scored two goals before making 44 League appearances with Tranmere Rovers. An match report from an early appearance for Cardiff described Herbie as "sturdily built and determined to succeed." A later one commented how he was "more

Herbie Evans.

a than a spoiler, he is a constructive half-back capable of initiating and joining in attacking movements."

He also won two Welsh Cup medals with Cardiff City as they beat Ton Pentre in 1921/22 and Aberdare in 1922/23. Herbie was also a talented golfer and had shone at boxing whilst undergoing both his military training and service during the Great War. After retiring from professional football, Herbie worked for the Post office as a sorting clerk and telegraphist.

215.
O'BREE, Colonel Arthur Edwin

(Birth registered as Arthur Edwin O'Bree Oppenheim)
Born: Poona, India, 31 May 1886
Died: Baragwanath, South Africa, 27 December 1943
Amateur
RHB, RM
Ed – Royal Naval School, Mottingham
1st XI: 1920-1923
Club and ground: 1922-1930
Other: 1914-1920
Cap: 1921
Clubs: Cardiff, Port Talbot, Welsh Cygnets, Incogniti

Batting and Fielding Record

	M	I	NO	RUNS	AV	100	50	CT	ST
Minor	9	14	2	370	30.83	1	1	5	-
F-c	18	34	1	431	13.06	-	-	9	-

Career-bests
Minor – 116 v Monmouthshire at Ynysmaerdy Ground, Briton Ferry, 1920
First-class – 42* v Worcestershire at Cardiff Arms Park, 1922

Born into a military family in India, Arthur O'Bree attended the Royal Naval School in Mottingham in Kent before joining the Metropolitan Police. He also played in club cricket in the London area (then as Lieutenant Oppenheim) before securing a new position with the South Wales Constabulary. He joined Cardiff CC and appeared for the Cardiff and District XI against Sammy Woods XI at the Arms Park in June 1910.

He subsequently played for Briton Ferry Town as well as the Gentlemen of Glamorgan, before joining the Welsh Regiment in 1914 and rising to the rank of Colonel. After the Great War, he returned to Cardiff following a posting to Maindy Barracks. He

Arthur O'Bree, as seen in a photograph at the arms Park from 1920.

rejoined the Cardiff club and from mid-June onwards was a regular face in the Glamorgan XI during their final summer as a Minor County. The highlight for the Colonel that summer was 116 against Monmouthshire at Briton Ferry with newspaper reports describing his "free range of hitting besides a series of powerful drives through the covers and mid-off."

Much was therefore expected of Arthur as a middle-order batsman when he secured leave from the Welsh Regiment to appear for Glamorgan in their first batch of Championship fixtures during 1921. But his best years were behind him, and the 36 year-old found the step up into first-class cricket quite a challenge and despite plenty of opportunities he failed to register a half-century in 34 innings .

He retired from county cricket at the end of the 1923 season, but maintained his involvement with Glamorgan by appearing in Club and Ground matches until 1930, besides serving on the county committee.

216.
BEVAN, John Maybery ('Jack')
Born – Llanelli, 12 September 1886
Died – Swansea, 24 June 1970
Ed – Clifton College, Gonville and Caius College, Cambridge
Amateur
1st XI: 1920
Carmarthenshire 1909-1919
Chairman 1940-1948.
Clubs: Neath, Llanelli, Briton Ferry Steel

Batting and Fielding Record

M	I	NO	RUNS	AV	100	50	CT	ST
1	1	0	3	3.00	-	-	1	-

Career-bests
3 v Monmouthshire at Ebbw Vale, 1920

John Bevan, the son of an industrialist from Llanelli, played in one match for Glamorgan in 1920, besides making several appearances for his native Carmarthenshire before the Great War.

Educated at Clifton College and Cambridge University, John inherited his father Isaiah's love of ball-games. Isaiah had been a popular captain of Llanelli CC in the 1880s, besides being a founding member of the town's rugby club. Tragically, in January 1893, Isaiah was crushed, and instantly killed by falling dockside machinery at Briton Ferry.

After completing his education, John Bevan stepped into his late father's shoes and oversaw the management of the family's steelworks at Briton Ferry and Llanelli. He still found plenty of time to play in club cricket for Neath and Llanelli, as well as for Carmarthenshire from 1909 onwards. He made his Minor County debut aged 22 for the West Wales side against Glamorgan at Stradey Park and the young all-rounder batted at number 11 in the order on his first county appearance, besides going wicketless. His maiden wicket for Carmarthenshire came in the match a few weeks later against Cornwall at Camborne. In July 1911 John appeared again for Carmarthenshire in their Minor County Championship match with Glamorgan at Swansea, and his haul of 4/51 included the wicket of Tom Whittington, the opposition captain, who posted a fine 176.

His finest hour in Carmarthenshire ranks came at Stradey Park in July 1914 when he struck an unbeaten 108 against an all-amateur Glamorgan side, before taking 5/59 and then leading his team off the Llanelli ground after they had recorded a thrilling victory by five runs, By this time, other things were on John's mind, especially ensuring the output of steel from his factories would be sufficient to meet the military demands and after ensuring that all was well at his family's works, he joined the Royal Field Artillery and went off to serve King and Country.

He soon rose to the rank of Colonel with the Royal Field Artillery whose units were responsible for the medium caliber guns, larger howitzers and trench mortars which were deployed close to the front line. In September 1918

Colonel Jack Bevan.

during the advance on the Hindenburg, Colonel Bevan was awarded the Military Cross as Allied plus Australian troops crossed the Somme River and broke German lines near the town of Mont Saint-Quentin. His citation duly said that it was for "conspicuous gallantry and devotion to duty throughout sixteen days operations. On one occasion he voluntarily carried a message under heavy, hostile machine-gun fire at about 300 yards range."

Once hostilities ceased, John returned to South Wales and returned to the world of cricket and business as he continued to manage the family's steelworks in Llanelli. His high standing in cricketing circles in South Wales is evidenced by the fact that in June 1920 he was chosen in the Gentlemen of Glamorgan team which met the Players of Glamorgan in a two-day contest at The Gnoll in Neath. A couple of weeks later he made his one and only appearance for Glamorgan against Monmouthshire at Ebbw Vale.

After the Great War, John was largely a specialist batsman and went in to bat at number five for Glamorgan against Monmouthshire. It was a role he fulfilled as well for Carmarthenshire in their all-amateur games with Glamorgan at Llanelli and Swansea in 1920, although in the match at Stradey Park he did service for a while as wicket-keeper following an injury to the regular gloveman and also opened the bowling when Glamorgan batted for a second time.

The 1920s also saw John commence various roles off the field with Glamorgan CCC, as he joined the Club's committee in 1923 and oversaw the introduction of various Carmarthenshire players into the Glamorgan side including Dai and Emrys Davies. Indeed, John's devotion to the west Wales county as well as recognition of his high social standing can be gauged from the fact that in 1929 he was appointed High Sheriff of Carmarthenshire.

In the 1930s he was overjoyed when Glamorgan staged County Championship matches at the Stradey Park ground, with the inaugural game against Worcestershire in 1934 drawing a bumper crowd. When the Second World War broke out, he agreed to act as Chairman of the Emergency committee which oversaw the Club's affairs during the wartime years, and when hostilities were over, he remained in the position of Chairman. Indeed, after his lifetime of service to cricket and the sporting community in West Wales, there was no more delighted person than John Bevan who, as the Glamorgan Chairman in 1948, could celebrate when the Welsh county won the County Championship title for the first-ever time.

217.
STORRIE, John Hubert

Born – Cardiff, 27 July 1903
Died – Malvern, July, 1991
RHB, RM
Professional
Ed – Cardiff HS
1st XI: 1920
Colts: 1920
Clubs: Cardiff, Briton Ferry Town, Hawick

M	I	NO	RUNS	AV	100	50	CT	ST
1	1	0	9	9.00	-	-	1	-

Bowling Record

Balls	M	R	W	AV	5wI	10wM
81	1	65	4	16.25	-	-

Career-bests
9 v Monmouthshire at Ebbw Vale, 1920
3/27 v Monmouthshire at Ebbw Vale, 1920

Born and raised in Cardiff, John Storrie secured a professional position with the town club and as a result, appeared for Glamorgan in their friendly with Monmoutshire at Ebbw Vale in June 1920. He claimed four wickets with his medium-pace bowling but was not called up again.

John subsequently played for Briton Ferry Town before moving to Scotland where he secured an appointment with the Hawick club.

His father was a schoolmaster in Cardiff for many years, and after retiring from playing cricket, John secured employment working as a labourer on various farms in the Cowbridge area.

John Storrie.

218.
TENNICK, Leslie

Born – St Fagans, 18 January 1899
Died – Fairwater, Cardiff, 9 August 1969
Amateur
All-rounder
1st XI: 1920
Colts: 1921-1922
Club: St Fagans
Brother of Cyril Tennick

M	I	NO	RUNS	AV	100	50	CT	ST
1	1	0	26	26.00	-	-	2	-

Bowling Record

Balls	M	R	W	AV	5wI	10wM
24	0	24	0	-	-	-

Career-bests
26 v Monmouthshire at Ebbw Vale, 1920

Leslie Tennick, seen with his colleagues in a hockey team group.

Leslie Tennick played in one Minor County match for Glamorgan in 1920, besides appearing for the Club's Colts team during 1921 and 1922. However, he was more able at hockey and after starring on the left-wing for the St Fagans hockey team he one a Welsh hockey, playing against Monmouthshire on 22nd January 1925.

His sole appearance for Glamorgan came against Monmouthshire at Ebbw Vale during June 1920 as the Club were looking for new talent ahead of their campaign in the County Championship. After some useful performances for the St Fagan's club, the all-rounder made 28 batting at number ten in in the Glamorgan first innings, but he went wicketless and was not called up again.

He and his brother Cyril, who also played for the Glamorgan Colts, continued to meet with success with bat and bat for the St Fagans club during the 1920s. Their father Arthur was the landlord of the Plymouth Arms in the pretty village on the western outskirts of Cardiff, besides acting as Secretary of the St Fagans hockey club. Leslie followed his father into the brewing business and worked for many years as a stocktaker for Hancock's.

219.
GEMMILL, *William Neilson*

Born – Thio, New Caledonia, 14 June 1900
Died – Canterbury, 18 September 1987
RHB, RM
Amateur
Ed – King's, Taunton
1st XI: 1920-1926
Colts: 1920
Club and Ground: 1920
Cap: 1921
Club: Swansea

Batting and Fielding Record

	M	I	NO	RUNS	AV	100	50	CT	ST
Minor	4	6	2	44	11.00	-	-	7	-
F-c	47	88	2	1169	13.59	-	4	31	-

Bowling Record

	Balls	M	R	W	AV	5wI	10wM
Minor	72	2	34	2	17.00	-	-
F-c	132	4	104	0	-	-	-

Career-bests

Minor –   15 v Devon at The Gnoll, Neath, 1920
           2/18 v Carmarthenshire at St Helen's, Swansea, 1920
First-class –   77 v Sussex at Hove, 1922

Willie Gemmill can claim to have had, so far, one of the most exotic birthplaces of any Glamorgan cricketer having been born in 1900 at Thio on the island of New Caledonia in the Pacific Ocean. His father, Arthur William Gemmill, was based on the French-owned island as part of his work for the Anglo-French Nickel Company.

In the year of Willie's birth, the Company acquired the nickel and cobalt smelting works at Hafod which had been created in 1870 by Henry Hussey Vivian, the Swansea-based industrialist and philanthropist. Shortly afterwards, Arthur Gemmill was appointed the deputy manager of the Hafod works on the eastern outskirts of Swansea. He later rose to the position of works manager, and duly became a major figure in the sporting and public life of the town. The Scotsman became a leading member of the Swansea Bay Golf Club, besides taking part in the motor cycle races held on Pendine Sands, and acting as the Chairman of the Swansea and District Boy Scouts Association.

Willie inherited his father's love of recreational activities and whilst a pupil at King's Taunton he developed his skills as a cricketer and hockey player. They stood him in good stead as he went on to win 8 hockey caps for Wales, besides playing over 50 times for Glamorgan during their formative years as a first-class county. Indeed, in 1920 he appeared in the Colts trial match which the county's selectors had arranged to assess the young talent who might be called upon when the Club were elevated into the County Championship. In fact, Willie did not have to wait too long for his call-up because having played a fluent innings in the trial match, besides impressing with his swift fielding, Willie fittingly played in four of Glamorgan's matches during 1920 – three were on his home turf at St Helen's, including his debut against Cheshire in late June.

The first three of Willie's Championship appearances also came at Swansea, with his first-class debut taking place at the ground during late May 1921 as he was chosen to play against Leicestershire. He subsequently struck four half-centuries in Championship cricket, twice posting fifties against Surrey, as well as making 54 against Derbyshire. His finest innings though came during 1922 in the away match at Hove where Willie made an assertive 77 against a full-strength Sussex attack which included England's Maurice Tate. Indeed, newspaper reports noted the "bold and carefree strokeplay of the Swansea amateur."

However, his career-best first-class score came for Wales in their match at Perth against Scotland in July 1923. Given his father's links with the Lanark area, it was fitting that Willie's most productive innings should come on Scottish soil, with the tall and hard-hitting batsman opening the batting with Norman Riches and top-scoring with 74 as Wales won by an innings.

Willie Gemmill, walking out to bat at the Arms Park during 1921.

August 1926 saw Willie play his final game for Glamorgan, against Gloucestershire at Swansea, before moving to work in London. He subsequently stayed in the south-east of England, and died in September 1987 at the Kenfield Hall Nursing Home at Petham, near Canterbury. His grandson Tristan, is an actor who has appeared in roles in the primetime TV programmes of *Casualty* and *Coronation Street*.

220.
JAMES, Edward Hugh ('Tuan')

Born – Briton Ferry, 14 April 1896
Died – Briton Ferry, 15 March 1975
LHB, SLA
1st XI: 1920-1922
Colts: 1920
Club and Ground: 1920
Clubs: Briton Ferry Steel, Gowerton, Maesteg Town..
Father of DH James and brother-in-law of H Tomlinson

Batting and Fielding Record

	M	I	NO	RUNS	AV	100	50	CT	ST
Minor	4	6	1	78	15.60	-	-	1	-
F-c	3	6	0	13	2.16	-	-	-	-

Bowling Record

	Balls	M	R	W	AV	5wI	10wM
Minor	494	12	210	24	8.75	3	1
F-c	353	5	209	7	29.85	-	-

Career-bests

Minor –   41   v JHP Brain's XI at Cardiff Arms Park, 1920
                7/44 v Devon at The Gnoll, Neath, 1920
First-class –   4   v Lancashire at Old Trafford, 1922
                     v Yorkshire at Cardiff Arms Park, 1922
                4/79 v Lancashire at Old Trafford, 1922

Tuan James was one of the leading club cricketers in the South Wales during the 1920s, with the left-handed batsman and spin bowler creating many records with Briton Ferry Steel besides also playing for Gowerton and Maesteg Town.

He was also regarded by contemporaries as the most complete left-arm spinner to play in club cricket in South Wales – one writer said "his armoury and his artistry were complete. He was a master of flight and dip, and could spin the ball two inches or two feet. He employed changes of pace that occasionally rose above medium pace as he used every allowed inch of the crease to disguise the direction of his attack."

Tuan was discovered during 1909 by Arthur Webb playing as a schoolboy with friends on a patch of rough grass close to the nets at the Steelworks ground. "At first I thought the ball was bouncing and turning off the uneven ground," remembered Webb, "then I thought perhaps the ball was out of shape. I called him over, gave him a good ball and went into bat in the nets. Damn me, he could it all!" A week later, the thirteen year-old made his debut for the Briton Ferry Steelworks 2nd XI and by the end of the season had also played for the 1st XI.

He had a short career with Glamorgan playing in four Minor County games during 1920, with his accurate left-arm spin bringing him returned of 4/54 and 5/34 against

Monmouthshire at Briton Ferry, 5/24 against JHP Brain's XI at the Arms Park, plus a ten-wicket match haul in the contest against Neath at The Gnoll.

Tuan also impressed in the Colts matches which the county officials had organized to assess the emerging talent. His career though coincided with that of Harry Creber, and the Glamorgan selectors, whilst highly impressed by Tuan's abilities, opted for the tried and trusted left-arm spin of the Swansea professional when Glamorgan entered the County Championship in 1921.

However, when Creber was injured and unavailable for the first fortnight of May 1922, Tuan was called up by the Glamorgan selectors for the matches against Lancashire at Old Trafford, Yorkshire at the Arms Park and Nottinghamshire at Trent Bridge. All three ended in heavy innings defeats for the Welsh county, but in the game at Old Trafford, Tuan impressed with four wickets. With Glamorgan subsequently hiring the services of Frank Ryan, the former Hampshire left-arm spinner, Tuan never appeared in first-class cricket again for Glamorgan, but he remained a prolific wicket-taker in the Leagues.

He was also very proud to see his son David progress from being in the Briton Ferry side to winning a place in the Glamorgan line-up during their Championship-winning summer of 1948.

221.
TOMLINSON, Harry

Born – Barwell, Leicestershire, March 1886
Died – Briton Ferry, 29 November 1944
Professional
LHB, OB
1st XI: 1920-1923
Other: 1913
Cap: 1922
Clubs: Briton Ferry Steel, Briton Ferry Town
Brother-inlaw of EH James

Batting and Fielding Record

	M	I	NO	RUNS	AV	100	50	CT	ST
Minor	2	3	0	143	28.00	-	2	-	-
F-c	8	16	0	244	15.25	-	-	2	-

Bowling Record

	Balls	M	R	W	AV	5wI	10wM
Minor	54	0	118	0	-	-	-
F-c	288	10	163	1	163	-	-

Career-bests

Minor –   473 v Carmarthenshire at Stradey Park, Llanelli, 1920
First-class –   36 v Somerset at St Helen's, Swansea, 1921
                 v Northamptonshire at St Helen's, Swansea, 1921
            1/30 v Northamptonshire at St Helen's, Swansea, 1921

Harry Tomlinson was another stalwart of club cricket in Briton Ferry, playing with success as a batsman and off-spin bowler for both the Town and Steelworks club. He had first enjoyed success with the Barwell club in his native Leicestershire and had been invited to trials by the county club.

He subsequently played as a professional in the Midlands before moving to South Wales in 1911 and joining the Briton Ferry Steel club. He also secured work at the Gwalia Tinplate Works and having married

Harry Tomlinson, seen at Brecon Ferry during 1922.

the sister of Tuan James, he subsequently spent the rest of his life in the town.

Harry's skills as a batsman were given a go by Glamorgan during 1920 as the selectors ran their eye over the professional and amateur talent in the area ahead of the commencement of first-class cricket. He duly scored half-centuries in his first two innings, making 50 against Monmouthshire at Briton Ferry and 73 against Carmarthenshire at Llaneli, and went down in the selectors notebooks as someone worthy of playing in the County Championship.

222.
MORRIS, Vernon Leslie
Born – Briton Ferry, 13 June 1894
Died – Exmouth, 11 January 1973
RHB, RM
Amateur
1st XI: 1920-1929
Cap: 1925
Clubs: Swansea, Briton Ferry Town
Father of R J Morris

Batting and Fielding Record

	M	I	NO	RUNS	AV	100	50	CT	ST
Minor	2	2	0	56	28.00	-	-	1	-
F-c	18	33	1	407	12.72	-	-	9	-

Career-bests
Minor –   46 v Wiltshire at Marlborough, 1920
First-class – 42 v Hampshire at Southampton 1922

Vernon Morris enjoyed a decent career in club cricket either side of the Great War for both Briton Ferry Town and Swansea, besides playing sporadically for Glamorgan during the 1920s.

The son of Thomas Morris, the Headmaster of a school in Neath, Vernon first enjoyed success as a batsman with the Briton Ferry Town club before serving as a Second Lieutenant in the Sherwood foresters (Nottinghamshire and Derbyshire Regiment). Despite being involved in several skirmishes on the Western Front, he safely returned to South Wales and continued his playing career with Swansea.

He made his Glamorgan debut in July 1920 at Briton Ferry in the match against Monmouthshire before the following year making his first-class debut against Worcestershire at Kidderminster. It was his only appearance that summer, before playing in four further matches in

Vernon Morris – as seen during 1922.

1922. His business commitments meant that he did not appear again for three years, before helping out in 1927 and 1928 when other amateurs were unavailable.

Vernon was only too delighted to travel from his home at Penllergaer to help out the Welsh county, although a first-class fifty remained elusive for the middle-order batsman. His final appearance for Glamorgan came in 1929 when he made his one and only appearance that summer for the Welsh county in their match at Ynysangharad Park against the South Africans. With his best years well and truly behind him, he made 0 and 9. His son Robert won a cricket Blue at Cambridge in 1949 and played for Kent during 1950.

223.
JOHNS, John ('Jack')

Born – Briton Ferry, 15 October 1885
Died – Neath, 10 January 1956
Professional
RHB, RM/OB
1st XI: 1920-1922
Clubs: Briton Ferry Town
Brother of TS Johns

Batting and Fielding Record

	M	I	NO	RUNS	AV	100	50	CT	ST
Minor	2	3	0	0	-	-	-	-	-
F-c	1	2	1	4	4.00	-	-	-	-

Bowling Record

	Balls	M	R	W	AV	5wI	10wM
Minor	193	2	118	11	10.73	1	1
F-c	108	3	62	2	31.00	-	-

Career-bests

Minor –   6/44 v Monmouthshire at Ynysmaerdy Ground, Briton Ferry, 1920
First-class –   3 v Somerset at Cardiff Arms Park, 1922
                2/29 v Somerset at Cardiff Arms Park, 1922

Jack Johns – a bowler who took a hat-trick on his Championship debut for Glamorgan.

To take a wicket with your first ball in county cricket is something which every bowler aspires to, and for Jack Johns in 1922, a builder from Briton Ferry, his dream came true as he claimed a wicket on his Championship debut against Somerset at Cardiff Arms Park. It was an even more remarkable debut as the 36 year-old achieved the feat in what proved to be his one and only first-class match for Glamorgan.

Either side of the Great War, the seamer and off-cutter from Briton Ferry had an outstanding record in club cricket, and in 1920 he played twice for Glamorgan in their Minor County matches, against Monmouthshire and Devon, returning figures of 6/44 and 5/58 in the former match at Briton Ferry. Two years later, he was called up for the match in mid-July against Somerset when regular off-spinner Jack Nash was struggling with a leg injury.

It proved to be an eventful first day for Jack as Glamorgan, after winning the toss, were bundled out for 99 by the visitor's in between a series of showers. Somerset had an hour and a quarter to bat before the close on the rain-affected first day, and in this time they slipped to 64/7. Jack opened the bowling and with the first ball of the innings he had Sydney Rippon deftly stumped by wicket-keeper Norman Riches who was standing up to the off-cutter. In his fourth over Jack added a second scalp as Jack MacBryan was clean bowled, leaving Somerset on 3/2. They subsequently recovered, but the *Western Mail's* correspondent wrote how "Johns bowled admirably for an hour."

Somerset were eventually dismissed for 77, with Jack returning figures of 2/29 from his eleven overs before Glamorgan replied with 139 in their second innings to leave the West Country side a target of 161 on the surface which had now dried out. Jack opened the bowling again, delivering seven overs without any wickets as Rippon enjoyed better fortune making an unbeaten century as Somerset romped to a nine-wicket victory and all with a day to spare.

Nash duly returned for Glamorgan's next match, against Lancashire at Swansea and Jack returned to club cricket where he continued to bowl with great success for Briton Ferry Town, often in tandem with his brother Tom, a more classical off-spinner, but equally effective.

224.
BESTWICK, *Robert James Saxton* ('*Bob*')
Born – Heanor, 29 September 1899
Died – St Ouen, Jersey, 3 July 1980
RHB, RFM
Professional
1st XI: 1920
Derbyshire 1920-1922
Club: Neath
Son of Bill Bestwick

Batting and Fielding Record

M	I	NO	RUNS	AV	100	50	CT	ST
1	1	1	0	-	-	-	2	-

Bowling Record

Balls	M	R	W	AV	5wI	10wM
72	0	46	0	-	-	-

Career-bests
0* v Monmouthshire at Ynysmaerdy Ground, Briton Ferry

Bob Bestwick was the son of Bill Bestwick and inherited his father's skills as a bowler, but thankfully not his legendary thirst. After success in the Derbyshire Leagues, he followed his illustrious father to South Wales and played briefly as a professional at Neath.

His time in South Wales followed a spell from September 1917 as a pilot with the Royal Flying Corps before securing a place on Derbyshire's junior staff. He made his first-class debut for Derbyshire against Warwickshire in late May 1920 but went wicketless and no doubt, on the recommendation of his father, accepted an invitation to play for

Glamorgan in early July in their friendly against Monmouthshire at Briton Ferry. The young paceman failed to take a wicket again, before returning north and in early August playing again for Derbyshire, this time at Chesterfield against Sussex. Once again he went wicketless, but a place on Derbyshire's permanent staff was offered.

Bob subsequently three further Championship matches for Derbyshire during 1922, the first of which – against Warwickshire at Derby – saw him open the bowling with his father, who had also returned to the Peakites. Bob claimed 2/47 in the first innings but these proved to be the only first-class wickets of his brief career in county cricket.

He returned to club cricket in Derbyshire and South Yorkshire, and played for several years for Colne, where he also worked during the winter months in the local textile industry. He also served as an Air Raid Warden during the Second World War.

225.
HANSFORD, Gordon

Born – Isle of Portland, 24 August 1887
Died – Canton, Cardiff, 23 January 1957
Batsman
Amateur
1st XI: 1920
Clubs: Cardiff Alpha, St Fagans, Glamorgan Nomads
Father of Gabriel Hansford

Batting and Fielding Record

M	I	NO	RUNS	AV	100	50	CT	ST
2	3	0	24	8.00	-	-	1	-

Career-bests
12 v JHP Brain's XI at Cardiff Arms Park, 1920

Gordon Hansford, who played twice for Glamorgan during 1920 enjoyed a good career as a batsman in club cricket, playing for Cardiff Alpha, St Fagans and Glamorgan Nomads.

The Dorset-born batsman was also one of the players whom the Glamorgan selectors ran their eyes over during 1920, with Gordon playing against JHP Brain's XI in the friendly match at the Arms Park in mid-July, as well as the Minor County contest against Wiltshire at the same ground a fortnight later. Having made 12 and 10 in the friendly against Captain Brain's scratch side, Gordon only made 2 in the game against Wiltshire and was not chosen again.

His son Gabriel followed in his father's footsteps by also playing for St Fagans as well as the county Colts later in the

Gordon Hansford.

1920s. Gordon was an accountant by profession and served as a gunner with the Royal Garrison Artllery during the Great War.

341

226.
TAYLER, Herbert William ('Bert')

Born – Aldsworth, Gloucestershire, 6 December 1887
Died – Dawlish, 17 April 1984
RHB, RM
Ed – Burford School, Wellingborough School
Amateur
1st XI: 1920-1927
Club and Ground: 1923-1929
Cap: 1924
Gloucestershire 1914
Club: Cardiff
Brother of FE Tayler (Warwickshire and Gloucestershire)

Batting and Fielding Record

	M	I	NO	RUNS	AV	100	50	CT	ST
Minor	1	2	0	19	9.50	-	-	-	-
F-c	10	19	3	260	16.25	-	-	3	-

Career-bests
Minor –   10 v JHP Brain's XI at Cardiff Arms Park, 1920
First-class –   44 v Nottinghamshire at St Helen's, Swansea, 1926

Bert Taylor played county cricket for Gloucestershire and Glamorgan, with his playing career interspersed by service with the Royal Artillery during the Great War, with the batsman being decorated for his brave actions.

Born in Aldsworth, Gloucestershire, Bert hailed from a farming family who also dabbled in brewing. He was educated, along with his cousin Fred Tayler (who played county cricket for Warwickshire & Gloucestershire) at Burford School and then subsequently Wellingborough School, where both won a place and played in the cricket XI.

After leaving school, he worked in the family's brewery at Northleach, and in August 1914, after some outstanding batting performances for the local club, he was called up by Gloucestershire to play against Sussex and Surrey in the Championship matches which were part of the historic Festival at the Cheltenham College ground. Bert marked his first-class debut by making 13 and 43* batting at number seven in the draw against Sussex, before making 23 and 5 against Surrey, but the latter match ended in an innings defeat and a loss inside two days for the West Country side, and Bert was not called up for Gloucestershire's remaining two fixtures of the season at Bristol and The Oval.

Shortly afterwards, Bert enlisted with the Royal Artillery and subsequently undertook training with the Tank Corps where he duly rose to the rank of Sergeant as his unit undertook several successful missions on the Western Front. However, his finest hour came in mid-July when his unit was summoned to the Amiens area as part of the manoeuvres to regain Moreuil Wood and to further quell the German Spring Offensive. On 23 July he took part in an assault on German positions, and after losing his commander, Bert seized the initiative himself and led his tank in a successful raid on a machine-gun nest, before

342

moving into a position where he was able to protect the advancing Allied troops and help them regain an important section of the Wood.

His fearless actions won Bert both the DCM and the French Medaille Militaire, with his citation reading: - "in the absence of the tank commander, Sergeant Tayler commanded the tank throughout the action with conspicuous success, and showed great skill and gallantry in destroying upwards of a dozen machine-gun nests, as well as bringing in several guns complete with spare parts. On his own initiative, Sergeant Tayler advanced through our protective barrage and patrolled far in advance of the infantry, thereby rendering great assistance. By his cheerfulness, personal control and gallantry, Sergeant Tayler set a splendid example to his crew."

Bert Tayler.

After being demobilised, Bert moved to South Wales where he joined his maternal uncle, Percy Cadle who ran a tobacco manufacturing and retail business in Cardiff. His decision to settle in South Wales was also influenced by the prospect of playing further county cricket and qualifying as an amateur for Glamorgan. Bert duly played for the Cardiff club and made his Glamorgan debut in 1920 in their friendly against JHP Brain's XI at the Arms Park. In June 1921 Bert made his Championship debut for the Welsh county at the Arms Park against Northamptonshire, but it proved to be an inauspicious first appearance as he was dismissed for a duck.

Bert re-appeared in four matches for Glamorgan during 1923, and struck 31 in their match against his former colleagues from Gloucestershire. The amateur, who continued to enjoy much success in club cricket, also played against Yorkshire in May 1924, plus three matches in June and July 1926, during which he made an assertive 44 against the powerful Nottinghamshire side. After his bravery on the Western Front, the fiery bowling of the visiting attack certainly did not ruffle his feathers, but his business commitments prevented him from playing for Glamorgan on a regular basis and he made only one further Championship appearance, in June 1927 when he scored 42 against Derbyshire.

227.
SNELL, Henry S

1st XI: 1920
Batsman
Clubs: Swansea

Batting and Fielding Record

M	I	NO	RUNS	AV	100	50	CT	ST
1	2	0	1	0.50	-	-	-	-

Career-bests
1 v Carmarthenshire at Stradey Park, Llanelli, 1920

Henry Snell played cricket for Swansea and was called up as a late replacement in July 1920 to play for Glamorgan in their friendly against Carmarthenshire at Llanelli. He scored 0 and 1.

The businessman lived at Vine Villa in the Mount Pleasant district of Swansea.

228.
BAXTER, Herbert Wood

Born – Brinnington, Stockport, 2 April 1883,
Died – Shaw Heath, Stockport, 25 April 1962,
RHB
Amateur
Ed – Highfields School, Stockport
1st XI: 1920-1921
Club and Ground: 1920
Clubs: Sketty, Swansea

Batting and Fielding Record

	M	I	NO	RUNS	AV	100	50	CT	ST
Minor	1	2	1	61	30.50	-	1		
F-c	1	2	-	11	5.50	-	-	4	-

Career-bests
Minor –   56* v Carmarthenshire at Stradey Park, Llanelli, 1920
First-class –   10 v Northamptonshire at Cardiff Arms Park, 1921

Cheshire-born Herbie Baxter was a steady batsman with a decent record in club cricket with Swansea either side of the First World War, though his best years were lost to the hostilities.

Born in Brinnington and raised in Altrincham, his father rose from being a tin and copper smith to becoming the Inspector of Weights and Measures for Cheshire. Despite many opportunities on following in his father's footsteps, Herbie started to train as a plumber on leaving school and in the mid-1900s he moved to the Swansea area.

He played initially for the Sketty club before his run-scoring in local cricket, saw him join during the early 1910s. By 1914 he had secured a regular place in the Swansea top order, but the Great War interrupted his playing career and deprived him of a chance of breaking into Glamorgan's Minor County side. His opportunity eventually came in 1920 when, aged 37, he played in the friendly fixture with Carmarthenshire at Llanelli. Herbie showed his talents by making an assured 56 on his county debut, but his business commitments prevented him from accepting invitations to play on a regular basis for Glamorgan at other times that summer. He did though accept an offer to join the county committee for 1921 and helped to organize the county's matches at St Helen's.

June 1921 also saw Herbie play against Northamptonshire at Cardiff Arms Park – a game that proved to be his sole appearance at first-class level. The step up to Championship cricket was perhaps too great for the right-handed batsman who failed to stamp his authority on the Northants bowling and was not chosen again.

He had been appointed as captain of Swansea CC in 1920, with his knowledge of playing talent in the local leagues being invaluable to the Club's selection committee as they looked to recruit new faces. Herbie's pool of business contacts in the Swansea area were also useful to the Welsh county's officials as they sought financial assistance in staging of matches at the St Helen's ground. He continued to play for Swansea 1st XI until 1929 and remained a valued advisor to the Glamorgan committee during this period.

229.
RICHARDS, John Harold Brynmor

Born – Neath, April 1895
Died – Pontypridd, March 1922
Batsman
Amateur
1st XI: 1920
Clubs: Briton Ferry Town, Briton Ferry Steelworks

Batting and Fielding Record

M	I	NO	RUNS	AV	100	50	CT	ST
1	2	0	22	11.00	-	-	1	-

Career-bests
19 v Carmarthenshire at Stradey Park, Llanelli, 1920

"Johnny" Richards was one of a group of promising young batsmen who were given a chance to display their talents by Glamorgan's selectors in friendly fixtures during 1920 as the Welsh county's administrators assessed local talent ahead.

He had a decent record with both Briton Ferry Town and Briton Ferry Steel and was called up for the match against Carmarthenshire at Llanelli. Johnny duly made 19 and 3, but others took the opportunity to catch the selectors eye and he was never called up again. Tragically, he died two years later, with the young carpenter passing away at the age of 27.

He had served as a Corporal in the Royal Welch Fusiliers and had it not been for the outbreak of war, he might have had earlier, and further, opportunities to play county cricket.

230.
JACOB, Norman Ernest
Born – Neath, 9 July 1901
Died – Grimsby, 12 March 1970
Amateur
RHB, RM
Ed – Tonbridge School
1st XI: 1920-1922
Colts: 1920
Club and Ground: 1922
Cap: 1922
Clubs: Neath, Port Talbot and Penarth

Batting and Fielding Record

	M	I	NO	RUNS	AV	100	50	CT	ST
Minor	1	2	0	8	4.00	-	-	-	-
F-c	7	13	0	79	6.07	-	-	2	-

Bowling Record

	Balls	M	R	W	AV	5wI	10wM
Minor	120	6	45	3	15.00	-	-
F-c	42	0	42	0	-	-	-

Career-bests
Minor –   4 v Carmarthenshire at Stradey Park, Llanelli, 1920
              3/39 v Carmarthenshire at Stradey Park, Llanelli, 1920
First-class –   19 v Lancashire at Old Trafford, 1922

Norman Jacob was a well-known golfer, and later a leading administrator, who played a handful of games for Glamorgan during their early years as first-class county.

The Neath-born all-rounder impressed with his seam bowling in the friendly fixture against Carmarthenshire at Llanelli during 1920, as well as in the various Colts matches which were organized that summer as the Glamorgan selectors assessed the emerging talent. Bolstered by a decent record as a cricketer at Tonbridge School, Norman was drafted into the Glamorgan side during May 1922, making his Championship debut against Lancashire at Old Trafford. He played in a further six games that summer but had little impact with either bat or ball

He went on, though, to greater fame in the world of golf, winning the Glamorgan and West Wales Championship during the 1930s and representing Wales in their Home Internationals between 1932 and 1936. He subsequently served as Secretary of Dinas Powis Golf Club and also the Glamorgan County Golf Union. He had also played rugby for Penarth during the early 1920s.

Norman Jacob.

231.
WILLIAMS, *Frederick Luther*
Born – Llanelli, 22 January 1888
Died – Stafford, September 1969
1st XI: 1920
Amateur
Club: Llanelli

Batting Record

M	I	NO	RUNS	AV	100	50	CT	ST
1	2	-	24	12.00	-	-	-	-

Career-bests
24 v Carmarthenshire at Stradey Park, Llanelli, 1920

Freddie Williams, a carpenter in Llanelli, was a late replacement in the Glamorgan side for the friendly against Carmarthenshire at Stradey Park in 1920. He made 0 in his first innings but met with better success in the second innings, against several of his Llanelli team-mates by making 24.

He had served as a pilot with the Royal Flying Corps during the Great War.

232.
JONES, *Hopkin Bevan Thomas*
Born – Pyle, October 1883
Died – Port Talbot, 2 August 1956
Ed – Queen's College, Taunton
Batsman
Amateur
1st XI: 1920
Clubs: Taibach, Margam, Neath, Port Talbot

Batting and Fielding Record

M	I	NO	RUNS	AV	100	50	CT	ST
1	2	-	3	1.50	-	-	1	-

Career-bests
2 v Carmarthenshire at Stradey Park, Llanelli, 1920

Hopkin Jones, who played for the Welsh county against Carmarthenshire at Llanelli in 1920, was a leading figure in the sporting and public life of Aberavon, playing cricket and rugby for various teams in the town, before serving as mayor of Aberavon and Port Talbot during 1925/26.

He had a decent record as a batsman either side of the Great War, playing for Taibach (Aberavon), Margam, Neath and Port Talbot, as well as in schools cricket for Queen's College, Taunton. Like many of his generation his best years were lost to the War, but given his decent record, he was given a chance to display his talents in the friendly against Carmarthenshire at Llanelli in 1920. He made just 1 and 2, and never appeared again.

His family owned Higher Tythegson Farm, situated between Bridgend and Aberavon, with Hopkin subsequently running the farm after the death of his father in addition to a business in Aberavon. He also played rugby for Aberavon. In later life, he was a leading member of the Royal Porthcawl Golf Club.

233.
JOHNS, Thomas Samuel

Born – Briton Ferry, December 1883
Died – Neath, 2 January 1964
RHB, OB
Professional
1st XI: 1920
Club: Briton Ferry Town
Brother of J Johns

Batting and Fielding Record

M	I	NO	RUNS	AV	100	50	CT	ST
1	2	2	14	-	-	-	1	-

Bowling Record

Balls	M	R	W	AV	5wI	10wM
240	11	93	9	10.33	1	-

Career-bests
8* v Carmarthenshire at Stradey Park, Llanelli, 1920
6/47 v Carmarthenshire at Stradey Park, Llanelli, 1920

Tom Johns was the elder brother of Jack Johns, and after the Great War was a leading figure in the affairs of Briton Ferry Town who he captained in 1920, as well as from 1922 until 1929.

Like his brother, he was a talented spinner, with a high classical action, and first played for the club before the outbreak of war. When Glamorgan regrouped in 1920, Tom was one of the players to get a chance to display his talents at county level, and he responded with a nine-wicket haul against Carmarthenshire at Llanelli. With Jack Nash as the regular off-spinner in the Glamorgan side, Tom did not get another chance with Glamorgan, but continued to be a prolific wicket-taker in the Leagues.

Tom Johns demonstrates his bowling action at Briton Ferry during the 1920s.

A builder by trade, Tom's family undertook work at the Briton Ferry ground to improve facilities.

234.
PRITCHARD, Archibrook Jefferies ('Archie')

Born – Swansea, 12 April 1877
Died – Tycoch, Swansea, 2 February 1953
RHB, RFM
Professional (1902-1912) / Amateur (1913-1925)
1st XI: 1920
Clubs: Swansea

Batting and Fielding Record

M	I	NO	RUNS	AV	100	50	CT	ST
1	1	0	2	2.00	-	-	-	-

Bowling Record

Balls	M	R	W	AV	5wI	10wM
138	7	55	3	18.33	-	-

Career-bests
2 v Carmarthenshire at Stradey Park, Llanelli, 1920
3/44 v Carmarthenshire at Stradey Park, Llanelli, 1920

Archie Pritchard was a fast bowler with Swansea CC either side of the Great War, playing as the club's professional from 1902 until 1912 when he badly fractured his bowling hand. It meant he was unable to bowl again at express pace, and played after this unfortunate accident as an amateur. It was in this capacity that he played for Glamorgan in 1920 against Carmarthenshire at Llanelli, at the age of 43. It was no surprise that he only claimed three wickets and was not called up again by the county's selectors. After retiring in 1925, Archie became an umpire and latterly a coach. He lived in Sketty and supplemented his earnings from cricket by acting as a hay merchant.

During the 1940s, Archie also secured a coaching post at Christ College, Brecon.

235.
PINCH, Francis Brewster

Born – Bodmin, 24 February 1891
Died – Ashford, 8 October 1961
Amateur
RHB, RM
Ed – Ashford GS
1st XI: 1920-1926
Club and Ground: 1923-1924
Other 1922-1924
Cap: 1921
Sir Julian Cahn's XI 1928
Clubs: Barry, Cardiff, Ashford, Incogniti.
Schoolmaster

Batting and Fielding Record

	M	I	NO	RUNS	AV	100	50	CT	ST
Minor	6	7	0	184	26.29	1	-	3	-
F-c	41	72	5	1068	15.94	1	2	24	-

Bowling Record

	Overs	M	R	W	AV	5wI	10wM
Minor	866	47	360	30	12.00	2	1
F-c	2412	84	1233	37	33.32	-	-

Career-bests

Minor –   109 v Wiltshire at Marlborough, 1920
                9/25 v Carmarthenshire at St Helen's, Swansea, 1920
First-class –   138* v Worcestershire at St Helen's, Swansea, 1921
                4/48 v Sussex at Cardiff Arms Park, 1923

In 1921 Frank Pinch etched his name into the Glamorgan record books by scoring a century on his first-class debut for the Welsh county. The Cornish-born batsman struck an unbeaten 138* against Worcestershire at St Helen's, Swansea in his maiden County Championship innings during Glamorgan's inaugural season as a first-class county, with newspaper reports noting how "the tall batsman fully used his reach, with some fierce cuts and pulls to make the most of some short and wayward bowling from the visitors."

This was not though his first innings for Glamorgan as Frank had played in six games during 1920 for the Welsh county's during their final season as a Minor County. The schoolmaster was a regular in the Glamorgan side during July and August, with Frank, after scores of 0 against Wiltshire and 3 against Surrey 2nd XI, making 109 against Wiltshire in the return match at Marlborough. His medium-pace bowling also saw him claim nine wickets in the friendly with Carmarthenshire at Swansea in 1920.

The son of a Cornish farmer, Frank had first come to the attention of their selectors before the Great War as a free-scoring batsman and useful right-arm seam bowler for Barry Cricket and Athletic Club, and he played in various Club and Ground matches during

350

Frank Pinch, as seen with Barry CC during 1913.

1914. After the War, he completed a teaching diploma and moved to the Home Counties. Despite teaching in Kent, Frank retained his links with the Glamorgan officials and continued to appear during his school holidays between 1921 and 1926.

The stylish amateur failed to score another hundred in 41 appearances for Glamorgan in first-class cricket, although he did play a crucial role in 1923 in the victory over the West Indies at the Arms Park – Glamorgan's first-ever against a touring team. During the Welsh county's second innings, Frank shared a vibrant stand of 137 with Jimmy Stone for the fifth wicket which helped Glamorgan build what proved to be a match-winning total. His contribution was an assertive 55 whilst his partner went on to complete a century before the home bowlers worked their way through the tourists batting to complete a 43-run victory.

As far as County Championship matches were concerned, Frank's best score after 1921 was 64 against Warwickshire at Edgbaston in 1924. He continued to be a heavy scorer in club cricket on his summer sojourns to South Wales. Besides playing for Glamorgan, Frank also played for Wales in 1923 against Ireland and in 1924 against Scotland, besides appearing for Sir Julian Cahn's XI against the 1928 West Indies at West Bridgford.

He continued to play in Kent for the Ashford club until after the Second World War. On retirement for teaching, Frank was the Head of Ashford Technical Institute, and in his later years he helped out at Ashford CC by coaching the young players.

236.
BRAIN, John Henry Patrick ('Pat')

Born – Caerau, Cardiff, 17 March 1896
Died – Dinas Powis, 11 December 1945
RHB, WK
Amateur
Ed – Winchester
1st XI: 1920-1928
Cap: 1922
Oxford and Cambridge Universities 1922
Clubs: Cardiff, South Wales Hunts, Cryptics
Son of WH Brain and brother of MB Brain

Batting and Fielding Record

	M	I	NO	RUNS	AV	100	50	CT	ST
Minor	4	6	0	67	11.17	-	-	1	2
F-c	6	11	2	86	9.55	-	-	4	1

Career-bests
Minor –   42 v Carmarthenshire at Stradey Park, Llanelli, 1920
First-class – 19* v Derbyshire at Queen's Park, Chesterfield, 1921

Pat Brain maintained the link between the county club and the Cardiff brewing dynasty after the Welsh county had secured first-class status in 1921. Up until his premature death at the end of the Second World War, Pat was a fervent supporter of Glamorgan Cricket as well as other country pursuits and organized his own eleven on many occasions to play the county side.

He also emulated the achievements of his father Sam Brain by keeping wicket for Glamorgan during four Minor County matches in 1920. He also showed himself to be a capable lower order batsman, making 42 against Carmarthenshire at Llanelli, besides being a neat and efficient wicket-keeper.

These skills behind the stumps led to Pat playing again for Glamorgan in Championship cricket during 1921 after the Club, much to the delight of his father, were elevated into first-class cricket. All four of his appearances that summer were in away games – at Chesterfield, Bristol, Leicester and Manchester – when others entrusted with the wicket-keeping gauntlets were unable to get time off work to travel.

However, his military duties with the Welsh Regiment and later the Territorial Army, and subsequently his flourishing business interests, meant that he was unable to play regularly for the Club. However, he was always ready to help out when others were injured or unavailable, as in 1922 when he played a further Championship match and a friendly, before re-appearing six years later when Glamorgan visited The Parks in 1928 to play Oxford University.

Pat served on the Glamorgan committee from 1922 until 1925, during which his presence helped to foster important links with the local business community as the club desperately sought to garner enough financial support as possible in order to maintain their status as a first-class county. He was also something on a talent scout, and by playing regularly for the Cardiff club, as well as the South Wales Hunts, he was able to keep a look-out for promising talent.

Pat Brain, seen in action as a substitute at a pre-season game at the Arms Park during 1991.

Indeed, Pat was something of an archetypal country gentleman, playing cricket in the summer whilst hunting in the winter. Indeed, he owned several successful racehorses and greyhounds, and he was a well-known face at point-to-points across South Wales. In the late 1920s Pat also raised his own eleven which played in friendly matches against other Welsh clubs and wandering elevens. Until the outbreak of the Second World War, he also assisted the county by arranging a scratch eleven to meet the Club in a one-day game as part of the county's pre-season preparations.

237.
RICKERS, George Herbert Ivor, MBE
Born – Roath, Cardiff, 30 October 1885
Died – Rochester, 15 November 1953
Amateur
1st XI: 1920
Club: Cardiff

Batting and Fielding Record

M	I	NO	RUNS	AV	100	50	CT	ST
1	1	0	0	-	-	-	-	-

George Rickers, an enthusiastic member of Cardiff CC and a good friend of Norman Riches, travelled with the Glamorgan squad to primarily act as 12th man and scorer for their back-to-back away matches against Wiltshire at Marlborough and Devon at Plymouth during August 1920. However, an injury to his friend on the morning of the game at Plymouth saw George make a surprise debut for the county against Devon. He failed to score in his only innings.

The son of a cobbler in Cardiff, George had attended Monkton House with Norman and their friendship latest for many years after school. During World War One, George served as a schoolmaster on various naval vessels, including HMS *Impregnable*, and when hostilities were over he continued in his naval role, rising to the rank of Lieutenant-Commander. He was awarded the MBE for his services to naval education in 1936.

238.
EVANS-BEVAN, Sir David Martyn
Born – Neath, 4 March 1902
Died – St Peter Port, Jersey 9 December 1973
Batsman
Amateur
Ed – Uppingham
1st XI: 1920
Club: Neath

Batting and Fielding Record

M	I	NO	RUNS	AV	100	50	CT	ST
1	1	0	4	4.00	-	-	1	-

Career-bests
4 v Carmarthenshire at St Helen's, Swansea 1920

David Evans-Bevan, whose family owned the Vale of Neath and Swansea Valley Breweries, appeared for Glamorgan during their final match as a Minor County against Carmarthenshire at Swansea in 1920. He had a decent record as a batsman for Uppingham and Neath in school and club cricket, but only made four in what proved to be his one and only appearance for Glamorgan.

David subsequently enjoyed an illustrious business career, serving as a director of the Phoenix Assurance Company and Barclays Bank from 1938 until 1972. During this time, he also acted as a patron of Glamorgan CCC from 1951, besides serving as a borough councillor and President of Neath RFC.

He also served as High Sherrif of Breconshire in 1929/30 as well as for Glamorgan in 1951/52, before being created the First Baronet of Cadoxton-juxta-Neath in 1958.

239.
BYASS, Geoffrey Robert Sidney

Born – Port Talbot, 30 September 1895
Died – Tilford, Surrey, 4 November 1976
RHB
Amateur
Ed – Winchester
1st XI: 1920
Clubs: Bridgend, South Wales Hunts

Batting and Fielding Record

M	I	NO	RUNS	AV	100	50	CT	ST
1	1	0	21	2.00	-	-	-	-

Bowling Record

Balls	M	R	W	AV	5wI	10wM
108	5	38	1	38.00	-	-

Career-bests
21 v Carmarthenshire at St Helen's, Swansea, 1920
1/25 v Carmarthenshir at St Helen's, Swansea, 1920

Geoffrey Byass was the son of steel magnate Sir Sidney Byass, and served with the 24th Battalion Welsh Regiment during the Great War before making one appearance for Glamorgan in their friendly with Carmarthenshire at Swansea during 1920.

Born at Craigafon, Port Talbot in September 1895, Geoffrey had been educated at Winchester where he showed great promise as a sportsman. After attending Sandhurst he joined the Glamorgan Yeomanry and swiftly rose to the rank of Lieutenant in April 1915 before being promoted to the rank of Captain in February 1917. This followed a successful campaign with the Yeomanry in Palestine, before the regiment was redeployed to France for the Hundred Days Offensive.

Geoffrey and his colleagues arrived at Marseilles in May 1918 before heading north and taking part in the Second Battle of the Somme as well as the advance on the Hindenburg Line. Captain Byass subsequently took part in a final advance into Flanders and was at the small town of Ath in Belgium when hostilities finally ceased on 11 November, 1918.

He subsequently returned to South Wales and to his family's new home at Llandough Castle – a rebuilt and fortified manor house, dating back to the fourteenth century which in the early 1800s had several castellated effects added to the main building. The house had a great cricketing pedigree as during the second half of the nineteenth century it was the home of the Stacey family who were highly influential in cricket in South Wales, whilst from the 1890s onwards it had been the home of Harry Ebsworth, a wealthy businessman and cricket fanatic who oversaw the creation of a ground for Cowbridge and personally financed the acquisition of a professional.

Given the Byass family's social standing and great cricketing interest, Llandough Castle was a fitting new home. In September 1919 Geoffrey married Marian Bruce, the daughter of Sir Gerald Trevor Bruce of St Hilary and sister of Clarence Bruce, the Middlesex and Wales cricketer.

Geoffrey Byass.

Indeed, it may well have been at a match staged by the MCC, of which both gentlemen were playing members, that Geoffrey first met Marian. Geoffrey was a very talented all-rounder, playing with distinction for Bridgend Town CC, as well as for the South Wales Hunts and for Glamorgan in 1920 against Carmarthenshire at Swansea.

Had the Great War not taken place, Geoffrey might well have played for Glamorgan on a regular basis. As it was, the match at the St Helen's ground was his sole game in the county's colours, with Geoffrey opening the bowling. He went wicketless in the first innings, but did claim one wicket a second time around, whilst at the other end Frank Pinch took nine wickets. 1920 also saw Geoffrey play for the MCC against Glamorgan, again at Swansea, where he made 0 and 15 against the county professionals.

Geoffrey's cricketing credentials as well as his social contacts saw him subsequently play against Glamorgan during the mid-1920s for JHP Brain's XI in their annual pre-season matches at Cardiff Arms Park as the county players prepared for the new season. Several other members of the South Wales Hunts also played for Captain Brain's side and in 1926 his younger brother Rupert also appeared in the side which met Glamorgan. His father Sidney was also a fervent supporter of Glamorgan CCC and for a short while acted as the Club's Chairman besides providing them with a £1,000 loan in 1921 to assist with their arrangements as they made their bow as a first-class county.

Geoffrey maintained his military links by serving with the Territorial Army during the 1920s and commended the 323 Battery. In 1924 Geoffrey also went into local politics, serving on the local council in Port Talbot as well as learning about the management of his father's business. Sidney died in February 1929 and Geoffrey, as the eldest son, duly became sthe econd baronet Byass and inherited his late father's steel and tinplate business. During the 1930s he oversaw the operation of the Margam and Port Talbot works, besides serving as Mayor of Port Talbot in 1937/38. The following year however, he sold the Margam complex to Richard Thomas and Baldwins.

Geoffrey had five children, and in 1949, on the marriage of his daughter Daphne, he became father-in-law of Guy Mathews, an Army Captain who like Geoffrey was a talented cricketer and member of the South Wales Hunts, who played for Glamorgan in friendly matches during their Championship-winning summer of 1948. Geoffrey Byass died in Surrey in November 1976 after a busy life in the military, business and cricketing world.

240.
REASON, Dr Edgar Lewis Jones ('Lew')

Born – Neath, 24 December 1894
Died – Canton, Cardiff, 17 March 1953
Ed – Neath GS, Queen's College, Taunton and St Mary's Hospital
1st XI: 1920
Clubs: Neath
Brother of DJ and TF Reason

Batting and Fielding Record

M	I	NO	RUNS	AV	100	50	CT	ST
1	1	0	0	-	-	-	-	-

Bowling Record

Balls	M	R	W	AV	5wI	10wM
12	1	7	1	7.00	-	-

Career-bests
1/7 v Carmarthenshire at St Helen's, Swansea, 1920

Lew Reason was the youngest son of Henry Reason, the owner of the Cape Copper Works in Jersey Marine in Swansea, who qualified as a medic in 1914.

During 1920 he followed his brothers Tom and David into the county's side for the match against Carmarthenshire at Swansea. He had produced some decent performances with bat and ball for Neath, but he failed to score and picked up just one wicket in what proved to be his only game for the Welsh county.

His father was the manager at a copperworks in Neath and, whilst studying at St Mary's Hospital in London, Lew also played rugby for London Welsh.

Lew Reason – another 1920 debutant.

Acknowledgements

This book would not have been possible without the kind assistance of a number of people, cricket clubs and other organizations. In particular, the author would like to thank following for their assistance with research queries and/or photographs – Anthony Alexander; Philip Bailey; Martyn Bevan; the late John Billot; Jeff Bird; Chris Brain; Judith Chandless; Jeff Childs; Guy Clarke; Katrina Coopey; Tony Davies; Bob Edwards; Dafydd Edwards; Susan Edwards; Gerald Gabb; the late Bob Harragan; the late David Herbert (senior); Lawrence Hourahane; Brian Hunt; the late David James; Jane James; John Jenkins; Bryn Jones; Mike and David Knight; Julian Lawton Smith; Brian Lile; Tim Mathias; Bob Mole; Tiffany Noble; Tony Peters; Duncan Pierce, Ceri Preece; Gwyn Prescott; Edwina Smart; the late Mike Spurrier; the late Hugh Thomas; Ryland Wallace; Gareth Watkins; Tony Webb; Prof. Gareth Williams; Sian Williams and Anthony Woolford, as well as the Archivists at Llandaff Cathedral School, Monmouth School, Christ College Brecon, Llandovery College, Glamorgan Archives, Dyfed Record Office, West Glamorgan Archives, The Cardiff Story, The South Wales Miners Institute, Cardiff Local History Library and the National Library of Wales.

Alphabetical Index of Glamorgan Players: 1889-1920